THE PEACE SHIP

The
PEACE SHIP
Henry Ford's Pacifist Adventure
in the First World War

BARBARA S. KRAFT

Macmillan Publishing Co., Inc.
NEW YORK

Collier Macmillan Publishers
LONDON

Macmillan Publishing Co., Inc.
866 Third Avenue, New York, N.Y. 10022
Collier Macmillan Canada, Ltd.

Library of Congress Cataloging in Publication Data
Kraft, Barbara S.
   The peace ship.
   Bibliography: p.
   Includes index.
   1. Henry Ford Peace Expedition, 1915–1916.
2. European War, 1914–1918—Peace. 3. Ford, Henry, 1863–1947. 4. Oscar II (Ship) I. Title.
D613.5.K7   940.3'12   77–25872
ISBN 0–02–566570–7

FIRST PRINTING 1978

Printed in the United States of America

FOR
my father, Louis Kraft
(1891–1975)
AND
my mother, Isabelle Jacobsohn Kraft
(1895–1972)

but mostly for
my brother, Arthur Jonathan Kraft
(1925–1958)

"Some people must dream broadly and guilelessly, if only to balance those who never dream at all."

—Arthur M. Schlesinger, Jr.,
The Age of Jackson

"Whether your pilgrimage will realize its aim or not, it will remain in the memory of mankind as an example of the dauntless faith which has achieved the truly great deeds in this world."

—Ellen Key to the members of the
Ford Peace Expedition, quoted in
Louis P. Lochner, *America's Don Quixote:
Henry Ford's Attempt to Save Europe*

Contents

List of Illustrations

Acknowledgments

MANY MEMBERS OF the Ford Peace Expedition hoped that in a more objective time than their own, historians would tell their story. In my attempt to fulfill this expectation I have studied the great volume of papers they left behind and read many diaries, letters and other personal accounts, and for access to this material I am deeply obliged to a great many people.

First, I wish to thank the following participants of the peace mission and members of their families who loaned me the memorabilia they had saved for more than fifty years and generously answered my queries: Mark M. Abbott, C. Bakker van Bosse, George Bowman, Irving Caesar, Frieda Mylecraine Cornick, Burnet Hershey, Albert J. Hettinger, Elinor R. Hixenbaugh, Walter A. Hixenbaugh, Elli Eriksson Hyyrylaeinen, Donald R. Jones, Helen Karsten, Donald M. Love, Luc C. Lozier, Lewis Maverick, Lockton Park, Kenneth Pringle, Sophie Ramondt, Christine Ragaz, Nell M. Reeder, Rebecca Shelley, Helen Heberling Smith, Lamar Tooze, Earl W. Tucker, Van Arsdale Turner, A. Letitia Wales, John Weatherly, Ora Guessford Weir, Mrs. Francis Stirling Wilson and George Wythe. Two members, Paul Fussell and Louis P. Lochner, were especially encouraging and helpful. Herbert Coggins, Laurence Gomme, Richard A. Picard, Sara Bard Field Wood and Kate Hall Zimmerman also shared their recollections of the participants and events, and Robert W. Harvey and Alison Wilson helped me find some members.

For sharing their research materials I am obliged to David S. Patterson and Blanche W. Cook, and for reading early drafts of the manuscript to Charles Chatfield, Frederick Voss, Arthur E. Ekirch, Jr., Robert Beisner and Dorothy Gondos. The work of Gordon W. Davidson and Peter G. Tuttle was also helpful in the first stages of my research.

Of the many archivists in the United States and Europe who aided my research, I am especially indebted to Henry Edmunds, Win Sears and David Crippen of the Henry Ford Museum; Ardith Emmons and Bernice Nichols of the Swarthmore College Peace Collection; Josephine Harper of the State Historical Society of Wisconsin; Arline Paul of the Hoover Institution on War, Revolution, and Peace; John Broderick, Carolyn Sung, Eileen Donahue and the Manuscript Division staff of the Library of Congress; and Albert Blair, William Lind and the Research Branch of the National Archives.

I was surprised repeatedly by the kindness of strangers in my search for information, and am particularly obliged to Frank Braynard, Gail Cleland, Charles Stephen, Jr., Richard B. Talcott and Gerda Thorsen.

A number of friends and members of my family provided much appreciated assistance and encouragement: my father, Louis Kraft, who translated many documents and read a painfully long version of the manuscript and showed unfailing interest and concern, but never impatience; Juanita D. Fletcher, who not only read the manuscript and offered thoughtful comments but gave me work space in her home; my brother Stephen Kraft, whose sensitive understanding of the English language improved the manuscript; my nieces Judith and Miriam Kraft, who aided in the research; Rolf Jacoby, Inga Floto and John Reinertson, who translated documents; and Arnold Barach, Eugene and Rosemary Becker, Rita and Arnold Faudman, Barbara and Donald Kaiser, George and Lee Ann Eustis, Lou and Di Stovall, Maureen Jacoby and Carolyn Trager, all of whom made contributions to this study.

Finally, I thank my publishers for their patience, Michael Denneny for his creative editorial suggestions and Henry William Griffin, Ted Johnson, Ilka Shore Cooper, Beth Rashbaum and Joan Fernandes for their competence and concern.

—BARBARA SARINA KRAFT

July 1977
Washington, D.C.

THE PEACE SHIP

CHAPTER 1

"The best people"

O N A BRIGHT, bitterly cold Saturday afternoon early in December 1915 a great and joyful crowd stood on a Hoboken pier cheering, singing and waving handkerchiefs as passengers pushed their way through the throng, past hustling stevedores and brass bands and up the gangplank to Henry Ford's festively decorated peace ship, eager to embark upon their crusade to end the World War. Former Secretary of State William Jennings Bryan waved his umbrella at the departing pacifists, and Thomas Edison and John Burroughs attended their good friend Henry Ford, who stood at the ship's rail throwing roses to his wife on the pier below.*

The automobile manufacturer had taken over the first- and second-class accommodations on the *Oscar II* for his guests, and brashly promised the world he would get "the boys out of the trenches by Christmas!"—a pledge he hastily converted to a well-intentioned slogan. After a series of meetings in the neutral European capitals the peace pilgrims planned to join with like-minded Europeans in establishing a Neutral Conference for Continuous Mediation through whose offices the belligerents could reconcile their war aims. The conference would act as a clearing house

* Sources for quotations and other references are cited by page numbers under "Notes," beginning on page 311.

transmitting peace proposals from both sides until negotiable terms had been developed and the warring powers were ready to meet at the peace table.

The *Oscar II* leaving the Hoboken pier (Courtesy of Henry Ford Museum).

An antagonistic and mocking press characterized the peace pilgrims as cranks and crackpots and lampooned Henry Ford, the peace expedition's benefactor and nominal leader, as a Don Quixote accompanied by an assemblage of Sancho Panzas. Public figures angrily called the endeavor a reckless exercise in personal diplomacy by free-loading nonentities that was bound to alienate the belligerents and prevent responsible statesmen from ever arranging a negotiated peace.

In fact the peacemakers' action was a logical expression of the confident Progressive Era spirit that inspired private citizens to accomplish ends which statesmen and government officials often failed either to attempt or to achieve. In those good days men and women, believing progress to be inevitable, thought that societies' evils—even war—could be more speedily eliminated through knowledge, good will and moral persuasion. It was a time of purpose, of belief that truth shone by its own light and of expectation that ideals could be realized through exhorting people to sign petitions, read pamphlets, attend mass meetings and march in parades. As every aspect of American life reached out to reform itself, even "conservative lawyers, bankers and men of affairs stepped out from their offices and lent their names to radical movements."

In retrospect, the word "twilight" is often used to characterize the years before the First World War, referring to the dusk before the darkness that ended the good years. But for the leaders of the peace movement it was the dawn, the first hours of light that promised a golden day of progress.

In the 1890s religious pacifists and humanitarians were suddenly joined by scholars, statesmen, businessmen and lawyers who endowed the peace movement with the stature and sanction—and conservatism—that men of such influence give to any ideal, bringing it the blessing of the diplomatic establishment and beneficence of millionaires. And in those years college-educated women who had been prevented by custom from pursuing careers found outlets for their energies and abilities in reform organizations, which often included a committee devoted to the preservation of world peace. As the mothers of mankind these women considered themselves morally obliged to prevent wars and uniquely capable of doing so, an accomplishment they noticed men throughout American history had failed to achieve.

For the first time in world history, nations met in The Hague in 1899 to discuss the problems of war and the preservation of peace when the possibility of war was not an impending issue. The delegates accomplished little except to approve procedures for the arbitration, conciliation and mediation of international disputes. A similar peace conference met again eight years later, with similar minimal effect.

During this time two millionaires, textbook publisher Edwin Ginn and retired industrialist Andrew Carnegie, who had for many years generously supported peace societies, national and international conferences and the publication of popular educative peace tracts, handsomely endowed peace foundations.

When they took office in 1913, President Woodrow Wilson and his secretary of state, William Jennings Bryan, both men of fervent religious commitment and both former vice presidents of the American Peace Society, were eager for the United States, the world's missionary, to give mankind the gift of permanent peace. During Secretary Bryan's tenure the United States negotiated almost thirty "cooling-off" arbitration treaties in which the signatories agreed to refrain from fighting for a year while their quarrel was impartially investigated. The international peace movement praised these legal instruments as another sign of the inevitability of peace through reason, and Bryan thought them his greatest achievement. Each time a treaty was concluded he sent the participating ambassador a plowshare paperweight that had been "beaten" from an obsolete sword supplied by the War Department.

Although the American peace movement grew at a tremendous rate in the last years before the war, its leaders were not unmindful of the long and difficult road yet to be traveled. They knew the arms race continued abroad. They knew that half the delegates to the Hague peace conferences wanted to retain war as an instrument of national policy and cared only that it be conducted with a modicum of politesse. They heard Secretary of State Elihu Root praise their power of positive speaking that had resulted in "the enormous impetus given to the principles of arbitration of international controversies in lieu of war" and heard his warning that neither intellect nor reason but the character of mankind was the determinant of permanent peace.

The peaceworkers knew also that as their movement gained the support and involvement of some men of affairs, others, of equal propriety and prestige, also claiming their love of peace, decried the nation's negligible military defenses and demanded that Congress and the president provide sufficient weapons to intimidate any would-be antagonists. Obstacles and opposition, however, provided the stimulus for the pacifists' propaganda campaigns. War as the means of resolving national political rivalries and economic tensions, they argued, was anachronistic; self-preservation and the demand for profit would keep the peace. David Starr Jordan, a former college president, wrote in 1913 that "The Impossible War," the "great war of Europe, ever threatening, ever impending," would never occur because bankers would not finance the arms race indefinitely. Nor would businessmen, laborers and farmers, Congressman Richard Bartholdt argued, tolerate war knowing it would destroy their livelihood.

Like so many generations before and since, the Progressive Era pacifists also believed that the increased effectiveness of weapons developed since the last war would ensure nations against willful self-annihilation. And, all other reasons notwithstanding, the peaceworkers believed that diplomats, being men of reason and good will, would in the event of disagreement between nations give substance to the prospering international peace movement and arbitrate all disputes.

But the pacifists placed too much faith in what was only lip service by the government and the press, the pulpit and the podium. Nor did they appreciate the dichotomy within their own ranks. "The peace movement in the United States was fairly homogeneous and was supported by the best people in the country," a director of the American Peace Society wrote. Homogeneous it was—even to the extent that the term "pacifist" included everyone in the peace movement—but it was not monolithic. All members had the same goal of permanent peace, the pacifists of the tradition hoping to achieve it through faith and moral suasion, the legalists through a system of international law and adjudication. They were able to work together because of their willingness to meet upon the great area of mutuality that lay between their extreme positions. None realized that when war broke out in Europe these disparate views would shatter the peaceworkers' fragile union.

In August 1914 the war the major European powers had long prepared for and expected, but did not want, erupted. The arms race, the secret diplomatic commitments made to preserve the balance of power and the inflexible war plans that the generals insisted could not be altered provided the kindling; the assassination of the heir to the Austro-Hungarian empire by a Serbian nationalist was the match. Instead of offers of mediation and conciliation that might have limited the conflagration, governments sent each other inflammatory ultimatums. Within two weeks seven nations were at the battlefronts.

Americans were stunned by the outbreak of war. Astounded "that such an archaic institution should be revived in modern Europe," the peaceworkers blamed its occurrence on the munitions manufacturers and secret diplomatic machinations. In early August President Wilson, with the nation behind him, offered to mediate in accordance with the Hague peace conference provisions. When each belligerent replied that it had not started the war but was fighting in self-defense and that its national honor required that it fight to the finish, most Americans contented themselves with waiting until barbaric Europe had settled its own problems. In late August fifteen hundred women, dressed in black or wearing mourning bands, marched in silence down New York's Fifth Avenue to the sound of muffled drums as a mark of sympathy with their embattled sisters and as a protest against the inhumanity of war. The president proclaimed the nation's neutrality and announced he would pursue a policy of watchful waiting until a mediation offer was welcome.

In keeping with the accepted tradition that silenced pacifists in time of war, most peaceworkers took a back seat—a collapsed back seat—in the drive for peace. The conservative legalists looked to the postwar world, and the American Peace Society directorate continued to sponsor essay contests and lecture tours. Only the radical pacifists acted; for them the war was a defeat of the intellect and a reproach to civilization.

The war dragged on month after month, absorbing more and more of each nation's resources and citizenry and increasingly distorting its civic institutions. The great European powers were engulfed in a total war of attrition that foretold annihilation in the pursuit of final victory. And no belligerent or neutral government raised its hand to end the deadlocked battle.

The Ford expedition pacifists were confident that as man alone had begun the war so could he end it, and end it through reason not arms. As crusaders who knew the triumphs of practical idealism, those who sailed on the *Oscar II* in December 1915 undertook an unofficial peace initiative as a pragmatic necessity to preserve their perfecting world. As Americans they unquestioningly believed that "the greatest neutral nation owed it to humanity to put a stop to the slaughter at the earliest possible moment." The months between the onset of the war and the pacifists' voyage to Europe had been filled with activity directed toward keeping alive their dream of a mediated peace.

CHAPTER 2

The Idea: "A stroke of genius"

BEFORE BREAKFAST ONE morning in July
1914, Rosika Schwimmer, a short, stocky Hungarian journalist, built
rather like a tree trunk, with heavy, dark brows on a plain round face,
rang the bell of Number Eleven Downing Street, the residence of the
British Chancellor of the Exchequer, David Lloyd George. During the
interview that followed, Lloyd George recalled that the "alarmist,"
whose name he had forgotten, said "that we were taking the assassination
of the Archduke much too quietly; that it had provoked such a storm
throughout the Austrian Empire as she had never witnessed, and that
unless something were done immediately to satisfy and appease resentment, it would certainly result in war with Serbia, with the incalculable
consequence which such an operation might precipitate in Europe."

Twice in the last days before Great Britain entered the war on August
4, Mme Schwimmer and her associates of the International Woman
Suffrage Alliance futilely pleaded for arbitration, once in an appeal which
they delivered personally to the British government and foreign embassies
of the already embattled nations and again at a women's peace rally.

Undaunted, Mme Schwimmer published her own mediation plan, "To
All Men, Women, and Organisations Who Want to Stop the International Massacre at the Earliest Possible Moment," which she distributed as

[7]

widely as she could. In it she asked President Wilson not to trust to traditional diplomacy and not to await an invitation at "the right moment" before he intervened. Instead he, Secretary of State Bryan or former President William Howard Taft should come to Europe and form an "International Watching Committee" with other representatives of neutral countries that would send a mediation offer to the belligerent governments every day. "The Committee must not be offended if the combatant Governments refuse their offer in a rude or purposely offensive tone, or if they don't answer at all. The incessant renewal of this offer is the only means of hastening 'the right moment' for mediation [making] it possible *to accept, instead of to ask for* mediation. This would take away the stigma of humiliation which is dreaded more than anything else by the nations. They prefer to sacrifice any further number of their people because of false pride." Mme Schwimmer also suggested that delegates from unofficial organizations form committees to sit with the commission and plan a postwar international peacekeeping association. The very existence of these committees, she believed, would force their recognition by the belligerent press, which, by printing reports of their peace endeavors, would save the people "from the hopelessness which is ruining their lives."

Though others anxiously appealed to the neutral nations to stop the war, none did so with the inexhaustible determination of Mme Schwimmer. For several weeks she knocked on doors, wrote letters and sent cables to peace organizations and peaceworkers asking them to endorse her plan. Those passive pacifists who disagreed or disapproved, such as Andrew Carnegie, she called "Idiots!" and those who doubted, as did a good friend, she patronized: "I am quite sure that as all far-seeing and broadminded people, you also will agree with it." When her colleagues at the International Woman Suffrage Alliance headquarters would not convert their organization to a pacifist propaganda machine, as she demanded, she angrily resigned as press secretary, a job she had held only a few days. She did not, however, forfeit the power and influence which affiliation with a worldwide organization afforded. (Knowing well that position was nearly everything in life when seeking the support of both the masses and the mighty, she continued to use her title of International Secretary of the Alliance just as she falsely called herself president of the Hungarian Woman Suffrage Society when trying to persuade foreign women in London to organize for peace.)

In mid-August, Great Britain declared war on Austria-Hungary and Mme Schwimmer became an enemy alien. She would not return to her homeland, where the women's rights movement was dormant, nor would she remain in England where her activities would be severely restricted. Only in America, at the White House, could she continue her "mission of urging mediation." To procure passage money she offered her jewelry,

Rosika Schwimmer, Henry Ford and Louis Lochner (Courtesy of Henry Ford Museum).

typewriter and insurance policy to her former employers at the Alliance. Instead, the suffragists asked their president, the American Carrie Chapman Catt, to arrange a paid lecture tour for their colleague, and in late August, Rosika Schwimmer embarked for America.

Rosika Schwimmer was born in Budapest in 1877 to a socially conscious, middle-class Jewish family. After failing the qualifying examination for teaching she determined on a career in social reform, but when she applied for a factory job—that she might learn firsthand of the conditions she hoped to alter—she was refused because she wore a pince-nez, the symbol of the well-to-do. Instead she became a forceful and imaginative organizer of women agricultural laborers and office workers and extended her activities to any aspect of life that had to do with the inequitable status of women. In 1904 she helped found the Hungarian Feminists Association and was president of its political committee and editor of its magazine. She skillfully combined the resourceful techniques of a press agent with her knowledge of European politics, and every organization she touched felt the impact of her intelligence, passion and powerful ambition.

In Budapest in 1913 she had arranged the most extravagant and worthwhile congress the International Woman Suffrage Alliance had ever had. (During the two years Mme Schwimmer spent organizing the affair she was married to and divorced from Paul Bédy, a journalist.) She was at that time, she said, "the best paid woman speaker in Europe," with a full-time career as a writer and lecturer on the continent. In the spring of 1914 she moved to London searching for greener and more lucrative pastures than her native land provided a woman and was just beginning to realize the success of her gamble when the war brought her career to a dead halt.

Among the women's groups that sponsored her, Rosika Schwimmer had acquired a reputation as an artful and articulate orator of "magnetic personality, energy of thought and manner, with a winning sense of humor" who frequently provoked "shouts of laughter amongst the women by her pungent attacks on male mankind." She had also acquired a reputation as a tyrant.

Some of her associates, themselves seeking an omniscient keeper of the flame, served Mme Schwimmer as adoring acolytes. Others admired her talents as "a great leader and a power" and overlooked her resemblance to the stormy petrel. "I have always championed our friend . . . and her doings," an English suffragist wrote her associate Jane Addams, "not because I think everything is best and wisest that she does but because she gets the front page of newspapers for Peace and we can do the rest, including the rectification of her errors." Only a few American suffragists knew Rosika Schwimmer personally, though many who were involved in the international movement knew her work. None, however, had worked with her directly until she came to the States in early September 1914.

Rosika Schwimmer stayed at Mrs. Catt's house in New York for two weeks until her hostess arranged an interview with the president. In the meantime, the publicity-wise pacifist was interviewed by the press. One million women in thirteen countries, she claimed, had commissioned her to ask President Wilson to call a neutral mediation conference, a claim that was so egregious a stretching of the truth that several of the misrepresented European groups, sensitive to their government's positions, angrily complained.

Mme Schwimmer talked alone with the president—her escort, Mrs. Catt, who was more suffragist than pacifist, having been suddenly recalled to New York for a conveniently urgent meeting. Without the cautious Mrs. Catt to hinder her, Mme Schwimmer spoke at some length of her own mediation plan, which, she later reported, the president assured her would "carry great weight." Immediately after the interview Mme Schwimmer committed the faux pas of telling newspaper reporters what the president had just said and embellished her remarks so lavishly— he "would lose no opportunity of taking practical steps to end the war"—that Wilson denied the statement and closed the White House appointment books to future pacifist delegations for many months, fearing that such indiscreet publicity would raise false hopes and damage future peace efforts. The president had in mind not the offers of open mediation advocated by Mme Schwimmer and some American peaceworkers, most ardently by Secretary of State William Jennings Bryan— offers which had just been gently but firmly declined for the second time by the belligerents—but the secret machinations favored by his special agent, Edward Mandell House.

An honorary Texas colonel and state politico, House had ridden out of the West four years earlier looking for the next president of the United States that he might pledge him his fealty, devotion and considerable political skills. In return he asked for the position of power closest to the throne and the privileges of a silent partner. In "the little gray man," Wilson found the confidant he could trust unquestioningly and the source of wisdom and love that he always needed beside him. Taciturn, astute, discreet, persuasive, willing to agree and careful not to contradict, confining his private thoughts to his diary, House suited Wilson precisely.

In the spring of 1914, "enjoying all the optimism of ignorance," House had gone abroad to persuade the kaiser and the king of England's men to adopt his formula for reducing Anglo-German tensions by limiting armaments and granting Germany concessions in South America and Persia. For almost three months European statesmen wined him, dined him and told him what he wanted to hear in order to win his—and Wilson's—favor, a policy which House, an adept sycophant himself, did not perceive then or at several critical times in the future.

House returned to Washington in early summer convinced that if the war broke out neither side would welcome open American intervention. Immediately he began his ultimately successful strategem of displacing the pacifistic Bryan ("I hate to harp on Mr. Bryan, but you cannot know as I do how he is thought of [in Europe]. You and I understand better and know that the grossest sort of injustice is done him.") and installing himself as the president's sole peace intermediary. Whereas Bryan, most anxious to save lives and substance, wanted the war to end at once with peace terms to be settled by compromise regardless of military position, House wanted an Allied victory with fair terms for the Central Powers. Bryan argued that by supplying war materiel the United States was responsible for and affected by the continuance of the war and therefore could properly insist that it must end and should do so in the company of interested European and South American neutrals; House and Wilson thought the United States should act alone and only at the right moment, which was to say, when asked. However, the alarming state of the war at the end of 1914 prompted the president to disregard his earlier rebuffs and try once more.

In Europe during the first days of the war eager recruits had marched to the front to the sound of their cheering, flag-waving countrymen and their leaders' promises of victory within six weeks, a few months at the most. On both fronts, however, the guns of August were still being heard in December, and on the western front soldiers of both sides lined rat-filled, muddy trenches from the North Sea to Switzerland, at times facing each other across a no-man's-land of only twenty yards. They died by the tens of thousands in deadlocked battles that gained or lost only a few yards; by December 1914, after five months of fighting, each side had one million casualties. Then, and for nearly four more years, the war remained at stalemate on French and Belgian soil, both sides too weak to win decisive victories yet strong enough to defend their positions. Nonetheless the opposing powers' military and civilian leaders determined on military victory rather than a negotiated peace. Flagrantly sacrificing soldiers and civilians, the belligerent officials distorted their war aims and inculcated their people with perfervid hatred of the enemy in order to win popular support.

The final days of 1914 were critical. Thereafter, wrote Winston Churchill, then a member of the government, "the rhythm of the tragedy" had been set; the conduct of the war was beyond the realm of conscious choice. Until then, he thought, "the terrific affair was still not unmanageable. It could have been grasped in human hands and brought to rest in righteous and fruitful victory before the world was exhausted, before the nations were broken, before the empires were shattered to pieces, before Europe was ruined." To avoid that catastrophe, but still fearful of offending "the sensibilities of either side by making a proposal before the time is opportune," Wilson sent House to Europe in January 1915 to secretly ask the heads of the warring nations when the president's good offices would be welcome.

The American public knew nothing of Wilson's peace maneuvers; only that he was still waiting for the proper time to intervene. The peace movement itself was nearly dormant. The conservative legalists founded the League to Enforce Peace and began defining the structure of a postwar international government. An informal group of well-known social reformers, more contemplative than active, met at the Henry Street Settlement in New York City to consider what action they could take for permanent peace. Two other organizations, the Woman's Peace Party and the Emergency Peace Federation, were founded in early 1915, the result of the inspiring activity of Rosika Schwimmer and Emmeline Pethick-Lawrence, an English suffragist and lecturer, who had also come to America to organize women for peace.

After Mme Schwimmer fulfilled her lecture obligations in the suffrage campaigns she engaged Katherine Leckie, a former newspaper reporter who ran a feminist lecture bureau and literary agency in New York, as her booking agent. For the next few months the Hungarian pacifist lectured in a number of states to predominantly female audiences that she knew were susceptible to her passionate and lurid descriptions, taken from smuggled letters, of thousands of suicides, the rape of five-year-old children and eighty-year-old women, and "Belgian women made pregnant by Germans and Hindus." In every speech she begged her listeners to heed their "motherhood instinct" and send the resolutions—a copy of which was on each seat—to Wilson insisting that he "demand immediate cessation of hostilities with a force that will make Europe's monarchs bow." She publicly rebuked American peaceworkers for dealing only in "petty theories," in talk instead of action. "Women cannot cry out," she contended while continuing her tirade, "our voices are choked in our throat." Men sympathetic to her ideals thought she was "unstrung and nothing short of hysterical" and that she overstated "what a competent American delegation could do." When they told her that neither her plan nor her resolution was sufficiently specific, she filed their criticisms in a figurative wastebasket and her speeches continued to make great numbers of converts. At a single meeting in Chicago addressed by Mme Schwimmer and

Mrs. Pethick-Lawrence, one thousand people signed the petitions to the president.

The Woman's Peace Party, founded in January 1915 in Washington, D.C., was born of the desire of many women suffragist leaders, among them Jane Addams, that women should help write the peace treaty to be certain that it provided for what Mrs. Pethick-Lawrence and the British Union of Democratic Control, which she represented, termed a "constructive peace." The party's platform was also derived from other previously formulated European and South American plans and was the first publicized, detailed American expression of the pacifists' "foundation for a new Europe." It called for no war indemnities, self-determination of peoples, open diplomacy, freedom of the seas, nationalization of armament manufacture and woman suffrage. As further guarantees of peace the party endorsed Bryan's arbitration treaties and an international organization composed of courts, congress and a police force. There was one plank unique to this program—a call for an *unofficial* mediation conference of neutral nations if the president continued to decline calling an official one. The January meeting won little notice; only the local Washington newspapers and sympathetic national publications gave it coverage. (In mid-February two senators introduced resolutions asking the president to call a neutral mediation conference, but both resolutions were shelved.)

At first, Jane Addams, the Woman's Peace Party's president, had not wanted to come to the meeting, suspecting it would be no more than an emotional evocation, but in the end she had decided that any move toward peace no matter how unconventional was worth trying. It was a decision she found herself making again and again in the following months.

In her characterization of the new breed of middle-class women— "their usefulness hangs about them heavily"—Miss Addams described herself during her early post-college years. Not until she was twenty-nine did she end the purposelessness that distressed her. Then, in 1889, she and a friend founded the Hull House social settlement, which soon became the most vital reform center in Chicago. In time, her fame as a lecturer and writer spread throughout the world, and she was respected and widely loved, not only for her accomplishments and abilities, but for her wisdom and patience, her effectiveness and compassion. The imperialism that followed the Spanish-American War had turned her toward pacifism, and the future Nobel peace laureate had been active ever since, advocating international cooperation.

Returning to Chicago from the Woman's Peace Party founding meeting, Jane Addams set up headquarters for the new organization and then joined with two other activist members of the Chicago Peace Society, Jenkin Lloyd Jones and Louis Lochner, in their preparations for a forthcoming national peace gathering.

The Reverend Jenkin Lloyd Jones, with his full head of white hair, luxuriant beard and shaggy brows above deep-set eyes, resembled an Old Testament prophet in the guise of Santa Claus. He was, in fact, a bit of both as he preached social gospel in his Unitarian church and practiced it in the Abraham Lincoln Centre, his settlement house next door. Each spring he followed the lecture trail and each summer he presided over his own "Chautauqua" a few miles from his family's farm near Madison, Wisconsin.* There "tired ministers, teachers and other city-bound people" communed with nature and spoke of Emerson, Whitman and Browning or listened to Senator La Follette and Susan B. Anthony, as they sat in the assembly hall before a fireplace upon whose lintel was carved the single word EVOLUTION.

Forceful and outspoken, Jones, one of the most popular preachers in the Midwest, worked like a dynamo, spreading his creed of applied universal religion. He used his weekly "unsectarian" journal, *Unity*, to rebel against all conventions that thwarted social change and to persuade the liberals in his "larger parish" to action in the name of peace and progress. With his longtime friend Jane Addams, whom he affectionately called "Chicago's maid-of-all-work," the seventy-year-old patriarch fought for social and civic betterment. Together they revitalized the Chicago Peace Society, and both held high office in the American Peace Society.

The third member of "the enlightened few" on the Chicago Peace Society board was Louis Paul Lochner, a gentle, but aggressive, twenty-eight-year-old pacifist who had gratefully adopted Miss Addams and Dr. Jones as his "spiritual" parents.

The summer before Lochner entered the University of Wisconsin he traveled in Europe, where he became excited by the possibilities that international friendship among college students provided for strengthening the will for world peace. Within a year he arranged the first convention of the collegiate International Cosmopolitan Clubs and later served as the association's president and representative at European conferences.

In the spring of 1914, Lochner was hired as the secretary of the Chi-

---

* The summer encampment is now Tower Hill State Park; the farm is Taliesin East, the architectural school founded by Jones's nephew, Frank Lloyd Wright.

cago Peace Society and director of the Central West Department of the American Peace Society. His new associates remarked upon his frequent participation in peace congresses, his many peace publications and his "ardent" internationalism, and praised him as "an effective public speaker, an indefatigable, systematic and efficient worker . . . personally acquainted with the leading peace workers throughout the world." Lochner was amiable and optimistic and a superb administrator as well, but he had one significant failing: he needed to serve as unquestioning amanuensis to an experienced elder.

At the end of February 1915, summoned by Dr. Jones, Miss Addams and Lochner, three hundred representatives from every organized aspect of American life met in Chicago as the Emergency Peace Federation to consider the long-term goal of educating people to the need for a durable peace settlement and to act on the more urgent need of persuading Wilson to mediate. The resolutions which the federation sent to the president were similar to the Woman's Peace Party plan except that they made no mention of an unofficial neutral action. Instead their petition included a thoughtful plan of action to implement the idea of a neutral conference called "Mediation Without Armistice: The Wisconsin Plan," which had been introduced by John Aylward, district attorney of Wisconsin and chairman of the Wisconsin Peace Party. In fact it was conceived in December 1914 by Julia Grace Wales, a thirty-three-year-old university instructor, who had insisted on anonymity, fearing her idea would not be credited if it was known to be the work of a young woman.

Miss Wales, a Canadian graduate of McGill University and Radcliffe College, taught students who had entered the University of Wisconsin without sufficient preparation in English. She was small, slender, unassuming, graced with "an excellent, logical brain" and a sweet, open face that even a pince-nez could not make stern. When the war began she determined to find a way that would persuade mankind it could solve its conflicts through reason.

Julia Grace Wales had never heard of Rosika Schwimmer, but the general idea they both suggested of a neutral conference was not novel at the time except for the critical element of proposing mediation without invitation from the belligerents. Whereas Mme Schwimmer offered only an emotionally charged idea, Miss Wales had carefully worked out her arguments for "continuous mediation" and her answers to probable challenges. She assumed that both sides really wanted peace as they repeatedly declared and she hoped that a neutral conference would at least define the goals each side was fighting for, thus allowing the discussions and exchanges requisite to settlement. This process would avoid the terms a victor would impose on the defeated, terms that would only provide an interlude to another war. It seemed to her that "a scientific commission" of experts from the neutral countries appointed by their governments to

Julia Grace Wales (State Historical Society of Wisconsin).

act as "a perpetual court of mediation," though having no diplomatic authority, and meeting with or without the belligerents' sanction and with or without an armistice, could, by continuously offering revised "standing proposals" simultaneously to all the belligerents, ultimately arrive at a settlement suitable to both sides without assigning war guilt and without endangering the sometimes precarious position of the neutrals. Further, all peace proposals would be reported in the press, thus giving hope of peace to all Europeans. Her ultimate hope was that from these negotiations and the settlement that followed a supranational organization would be founded. Because she was so seized by the inability of the warring countries to end the war themselves, Miss Wales besought the neutrals to mediate immediately without waiting "until these blind and futile forces have spent themselves."

Miss Wales's scheme was enthusiastically praised by everyone who read it. Some thought her persistence and conviction so sincere and inspiring they called the slight little spinster "a sort of Joan of Arc."

After the Wisconsin Plan was approved in Chicago a delegation was appointed by the conference to present it in person to the president as an act of "kindly helpfulness, not of interference or criticism." But Wilson still was not receiving pacifist pilgrimages, despite a letter from his friend David Starr Jordan calling the plan "a stroke of genius . . . the best scheme which has yet been presented for a settlement of the war." Instead, the president replied he would welcome a memorandum "with all my heart"; when he received it he marked it with his shorthand squiggle for filing in his private office, but took no action. The plan, however, prospered. Within a few weeks it was endorsed by the Wisconsin state legislature, which commended it to the national Congress, and at the end of April it was presented by the American delegation to a remarkable international gathering of women in The Hague.

The International Congress of Women was called by Dutch suffragists to show all women's solidarity against war and to propose a peace settlement that would prevent its recurrence. Jane Addams and the Woman's Peace Party were invited to serve as the American delegation, and Rosika Schwimmer was expected to play a principal part.

The conference was a godsend to Mme Schwimmer. Regaling her audiences in twenty-two states with atrocity stories had been financially rewarding and had increased the number of Woman's Peace Party branches, but her strenuous efforts had not resulted in Americans' acting to end the war. Because the party's executive council, for whom she was working as international secretary, asked to be informed of the policies she was pledging them to and for itemized expense accounts, she thought they distrusted her and fancied them her enemies. Instead of cooperating she followed her customary procedure and resigned a few days before she sailed for Scandinavia in early April. In Norway, Sweden and Denmark she counted on forming large delegations who would follow her lead and disregard the International Congress of Women's policy, a concession to the belligerent nationals, that no action against the present war would be advocated. To further ensure that her plan would be adopted, Mme Schwimmer asked her Dutch friends to give significant committee assignments to two members of the American delegation, Lola Maverick Lloyd and Florence Holbrook, her newly found disciples who sailed with her to Europe.

By blood and marriage, Lola Lloyd was a Maury of Virginia, a Maverick of Texas and the daughter-in-law of Henry Demarest Lloyd, the wealthy socialist reformer; by conviction she was a civic reformer, a Socialist and a suffragist; and by disposition she was "a sort of saint." She was also the mother of four young children and a partner in an unhappy marriage on its way to dissolution when she first heard Rosika Schwimmer speak in Chicago in December. From that moment she hitched her wagon and her pocketbook to the Hungarian pacifist's erratic star and steadfastly supported it on its course for over thirty years. Mme Schwimmer's magnetism and message had the same effect on Florence Holbrook, an elementary-school principal and a diligent member of the Chicago Peace Society.

The rest of the forty-member American delegation to the Hague congress sailed with Jane Addams in mid-April and during their sunny crossing enjoyed twice-daily meetings which consisted of a series of lectures by Louis Lochner (whom Miss Addams had engaged to ghostwrite her newspaper articles), Miss Wales's presentation of her mediation plan and fruitful discussions on the issues listed in the preliminary program. The continuous process of edification united the delegation and tempered the hesitancy of its most cautious members, most notably Jane Addams.

"The whole enterprise has about it a certain aspect of moral adventure but it seems to be genuine," she had written before she left. Believing, however, that "a certain obligation" devolved upon women of independent means who had the "advantage of study and training to take this possible chance to help out," she had decided to go and persuaded several of her Hull House associates and her good friend Emily Greene Balch to join her.

Of those aboard, Miss Balch, a professor of economics and sociology at Wellesley College who had done most of her graduate study in Germany and France and had lived a year with Slavic immigrants in mining camps and city tenements, was undoubtedly the best informed on the problems that caused the war and how they might be resolved. Brilliant, courageous, and of balanced judgment, she was a woman of generous spirit and so modest that after a lifetime of achievement, including the winning of the Nobel peace prize, she described herself as "only the plainest of New England spinsters." She was as hesitant as Miss Addams had been to join so apparently impractical an endeavor, but she could not decline. "We know we are ridiculous," the forty-eight-year-old pedagogue wrote in her ship-

Jane Addams, William Jennings Bryan, Emily G. Balch (State Historical Society of Wisconsin).

board journal, "but even being ridiculous is useful sometimes and so too are *enfants terribles* that say out what needs to be said but what it is not discreet or 'the thing' to say and which important people will not say in consequence."

During the meetings in The Hague, Miss Balch saw the horror of the war imprinted on the belligerent nationals' faces and observed the neutrals' fear of being "dragged into the pit." The battlefront was only 120 miles distant, and in their homes the Dutch women often heard the sound of bursting shells. Since the congress's organizing committee had first met in mid-February the French armies had gained a few yards in a month-long battle near Rheims that had cost both sides thousands of men, and in a three-hour assault at Neuve Chapelle the English had only gained one thousand yards at the rate of 3,266 casualties an hour. Six days before the congress convened, at sunset on April 22, a yellowish-green mist of chlorine gas blew over the French trenches at Ypres, the beginning of another month-long battle that would end, as others would end all spring and summer, in grievous losses and stalemate. Germany's recent announcement that all enemy shipping in the waters surrounding the British Isles would be sunk without warning to passengers and crew and the Allies' retaliatory blockade of German ports greatly increased the tensions in the nearby neutral nations and brought from President Wilson the warning that he would hold Germany to "strict accountability" for the loss of American lives.

The grim war situation increased the women's caution but also contributed to the justifiable exultation at their accomplishment. Over eleven hundred women from eleven countries, not including France and Russia among the belligerents, met in perfect unanimity and in four days passed the best synthesis thus far formulated of an enlightened postwar program, including Miss Wales's plan for a neutral conference for continuous mediation. The resolutions had been worked out in committee; their presentation on the floor produced amendments, but never dissension. Jane Addams chaired the congress, and her patient weaving through the tangled multilingual parliamentary web did much to preserve the delegates' willingness to agree.

On the last day Mme Schwimmer presented the Americans' resolution asking the neutral countries to call a conference for continuous mediation that would "invite suggestions for settlement from each of the belligerent nations and in any case shall submit to all of them simultaneously, reasonable proposals as a basis for peace." It was seconded by Miss Wales and passed unanimously.

The Resolutions Committee had decided to submit the congress's program to the belligerent and neutral diplomatic representatives in The Hague. But Mme Schwimmer, having had enough of trying to get peace through the postal service or by leaving petitions with doormen at foreign embassies, tried to persuade the committee to hand-carry the resolutions to the government leaders in their capitals. She lost, the committee reminding her that the Congress had not been called to end the war. Mme Schwimmer then lined up her support in the Scandinavian delegations she had helped recruit, and when Miss Addams called for new resolutions as the last business of the conference, she took the floor. In virtually the last four minutes, midst a plethora of points of order and personal privilege that nearly split the meeting, she appealed to her audience's hearts while her angered opposition—principally the delegates from Great Britain and Germany—appealed to their heads. "Only Madame Schwimmer could sweep the Congress off its feet and she did it several times," wrote Jane

Addams's traveling companion, Dr. Alice Hamilton, "notably at the end when she succeeded in having them pass the resolutions [providing for hand delivery to the government leaders] which filled most of us with dismay."

At adjournment the congress provided for its continuity as the International Committee of Women for Permanent Peace and elected Jane Addams president and Dr. Aletta Jacobs, the congress's chief organizer, vice president; the officers appointed the remaining board members, including Rosika Schwimmer as second vice president, and selected the envoys to the capitals.

Miss Addams's and Miss Balch's hesitancy in attending the conference had vanished in the face of its evident accomplishment, but it reappeared with far greater intensity at the melodramatic prospect of parading through Europe thrusting their resolutions into the reluctant hands of ministers of state. In tribute to their European sisters' collective judgment, however, they suppressed their mortification and skepticism and set forth. After interviewing the Dutch prime minister, Jane Addams and Aletta Jacobs (and an Italian who left the delegation when her country entered the war) visited the belligerent countries and Switzerland. Rosika Schwimmer, Emily Balch and two others toured Scandinavia, and later Miss Balch visited Russia. In addition, at Miss Addams's suggestion, Louis Lochner acted as her advance man in Berlin and Miss Wales, the secretary of the neutral-nations delegation, went at once to Scandinavia to publicize her plan.

During their interviews, Miss Addams's delegation told each minister that the congress thought it was time to resolve the injustices that had caused the war on merit, not military might, and handing them the resolutions, asked if they would continue sacrificing their young men if a "feasible proposition" for obtaining their war aims was offered. To Miss Addams's amazement, instead of indignation or scorn at their presumption, they were warmly welcomed.

The British foreign secretary, Sir Edward Grey, who was interviewed after the *Lusitania* was torpedoed in early May, said no belligerent could offer mediation without admitting defeat and that the neutrals must act instead. When a member of the delegation remarked that the neutrals were waiting for the right moment, he merely asked them when they thought that moment might come. In Germany, one week later, Secretary of State for Foreign Affairs von Jagow also said the belligerents could not ask for mediation and that the neutrals together should immediately establish a conference as the women suggested. Chancellor Bethmann Hollweg, who had just lost a son in battle, received Miss Addams in his garden with great cordiality, glad, she thought, that "some one had begun to talk negotiations." A few days later, in Vienna, the prime minister, "a large, grizzled, formidable man," banged his fist on the table when Miss Addams suggested he might think it "foolish that women should go about in this way," and told her her remarks were "the first sensible words that have been uttered in this room for ten months." The Austrian foreign minister discounted Wilson's method of *offering* mediation and supported continuous mediation led by European neutrals, and the Hungarian prime minister, intimating his disgust with the course of the war, expressed interest in negotiations.

Switzerland, completely surrounded by warring countries, was fearful of offending its neighbors, and Italy, which had just declared war, showed no interest in peace. The pope and the papal secretary of state, however, were approving. In France, which had forbidden delegates to attend the Hague congress, the women encountered adamant objection to their mission. Prime Minister Delcassé was vehemently jingoistic, and the foreign minister barely conceded that France would "not resent" the founding of a neutral conference. The delegation's last interview, on June 16 in Le Havre, was the most poignant: the exiled Belgian foreign minister, "a sad, gentle person," whose country was a battleground, spoke longingly of a negotiated peace. Soon after, Miss Addams left for home.

The delegation to the neutral European capitals was headed by Rosika Schwimmer, who organized its activities so efficiently and imaginatively and was so considerate of her attentive associates that Miss Balch reassuringly wrote Miss Addams, "I have grown to both admire and love her." The night before each interview Mme Schwimmer rehearsed the envoys in their parts, with Miss Wales standing in for the government ministers, and after each meeting the women hastened back to their hotel to write down what had been said.

Because the Americans were selling munitions to the Allies and not trying to run the blockade, the envoys realized that Germany would not regard unilateral United States mediation as unbiased. Therefore, they asked the Scandinavian ministers if their governments would, with Holland and Switzerland, call the conference, with the assurance that the United States would also participate.

In Denmark and Norway the interviews were "formal though friendly." Geopolitical considerations, Miss Balch observed, made the Danes extremely cautious. (And wisely so; on a subsequent occasion Mme Schwimmer reported her conversation with the Danish foreign min-

ister to the German minister to Copenhagen, who promptly sent a full
report to his foreign office.) The Norwegians, on the other hand, though
making no commitment, warmly welcomed the mediationists. The prime
minister, a pacifist, listened sympathetically and promised to present their
proposal to the cabinet, and the women were also received by the four
parliament presidents, a signal honor. Most unexpectedly, the king
chatted with them for almost two hours, "to no great purpose," Miss
Balch acknowledged, though his interest was encouraging and the cachet
of a royal hearing was rather stimulating. In Stockholm the women were
received only by the foreign minister, but that encounter, Miss Balch enthusiastically reported, "was worth all the others put together." At the
first sign of Wallenberg's evident interest, the envoys persevered until he
said he would call the conference when he had evidence in the form of
"a little billet" from the chief opponents that it would be "not unaccept-
able." Mme Schwimmer went home to Hungary for a brief visit and Miss
Balch and the rest of the delegation left at once for Russia.

In Petrograd, Foreign Minister Sazenov insisted the war would end
only in battle. When the envoys inquired if he would consider the calling
of a neutral conference an unfriendly act, he smiled and asked how could
it be? Without any prompting, the women observed, he even used Wallenberg's phrase. Sazenov approved their notes of his remarks, with the
addition that he did not think the conference would be useful at that time
and the proviso that his comments not be made public. In Stockholm
again, Wallenberg told the envoys their Russian information was valueless
if the gathering was thought useless and asked them to return when they
had something more positive to report.

Confident the Scandinavian countries would participate in a neutral conference if it were called, the delegation returned to Holland in late June to
compare notes with the emissaries to the belligerents. There they found the
Dutch prime minister in "an oncoming mood," and a veiled rivalry developing between Dr. Jacobs and other Dutch moderates, who wanted Holland to be the seat of neutral mediation, and Mme Schwimmer, who
wanted a Scandinavian capital, which would be more receptive to active
mediation and to her personally, to host the gathering. Miss Balch saw no
reason to put their few eggs in only one basket when nothing was yet
certain, and with Chrystal Macmillan, "an unsentimental, right-thinking,
right-feeling" Scottish lawyer and member of her delegation, went to
London to get the approval Wallenberg wanted while Mme Schwimmer
went to Berlin on the same errand.

Von Jagow told Mme Schwimmer that "Germany would find nothing unfriendly in the calling of a conference of neutrals," though he doubted it would be of practical value, and the acting foreign secretary in London directed a letter to his visitors saying only that the "British government would not place any obstacles" in the path of neutral mediation nor "make any protest against its existence." The noncommittal responses did not suffice. Mme Schwimmer returned to Scandinavia for another try, and Miss Balch, pleased with her three-month sojourn in Europe, sailed for home toward the end of July eager to learn how Miss Addams had fared with President Wilson.

In every case the women had been received "gravely, kindly, perhaps gladly," Miss Balch thought, by twenty-one ministers of state, a king, a president and the pope. The leaders had listened attentively, discussed their program and acknowledged women's right to speak for peace. At large peace meetings and small gatherings in the neutral countries the congress's plea for mediation was heartily endorsed. In conversations with second-echelon officials and community leaders in the warring countries, in the Dutch camps for Belgian refugees, in the German fields tilled by prisoners of war and in the farewells of soldiers' families at railroad stations, the envoys saw the saddening results of war.

The women wrote movingly of the wounded men they met, returned from the trenches, and Miss Addams concluded that a significant number of soldiers, not susceptible to the jingoistic slogans of their Victorian elders, had "revolted against war" and did not know why they were fighting. "In our name, and for our sakes, as they pathetically imagine," an English soldier at the front wrote, his elders at home were perpetuating the war "by their appeals to hate, intolerance, and revenge, those very follies which have produced the present conflagration," a sentiment echoed by a German soldier inflamed by those at home who "deceived themselves into finding a justification for all this murdering; and who further believe—Heaven knows why—that there will be great moral effects from this wholesale slaughter."

The women heard of villages taken and retaken and "smashed to dust" and of the dehumanizing horrors of trench warfare which they knew had not been experienced by the policy-making statesmen nor the decision-making generals. An English war correspondent, walking through the lines that summer of 1915, sent self-censored dispatches home, but in a postwar memoir he wrote a description of trench life that no censor would have permitted past his pen: "Bodies, and bits of bodies, and clots of blood, and green, metallic-looking slime, made by explosive gases, were floating on the surface of that water below the [mine] crater banks, when

I first passed that way, and so it was always. Our men lived there and died there within a few yards of the enemy, crouched below the sandbags and burrowed in the sides of the crater. Lice crawled over them in legions. Human flesh, rotting and stinking, mere pulp, was pasted into the mudbanks. If they dug to get deeper cover, their shovels went into the softness of dead bodies who had been their comrades."*

The rigid censorship exercised under martial law particularly distressed Miss Addams, especially "the unscrupulous power of the press" which fomented national hatreds and distorted facts. The neutral conference, she hoped, would provide at the least a desperately needed communications channel between the enemy peoples.

The envoys understood from their conversation with the belligerent government leaders that a properly organized neutral mediation commission might be the instrument used at some future time to begin negotiations. And the neutral governments, they inferred, would convene such a gathering once assured the United States, the strongest power among them, would participate. "We do not wish to overestimate a very slight achievement nor to take too seriously the kindness with which the delegation was received," Miss Addams reported, but neither did she or other concerned Americans intend to forget that Europe had admired their courage and action. It was something of a shock, therefore, to be greeted at home by "irrational and virulent" newspaper attacks, a stream of abusive mail and a somewhat less than hearty welcome from the president.

In July the nation was still recovering from its outrage at the sinking of the *Lusitania* and the consequent loss of American lives. Beyond that, the British government had exclusive control of the cables that carried the news fastest from the battlefront and their dispatches often referred to "our fight," claiming a common heritage between the British Empire and her former colonies. Britain's neutrality violations scarcely had the adverse emotional impact of Germany's invasion of Belgium, unrestricted

* In neutral America, far from the sight and sound of the war, the humor magazine *Life* reduced the war to sardonic doggerel:

Victory!

Five hundred miles of Germans,
Five hundred miles of French,
And English, Scotch and Irish men
All fighting for a trench;
And when the trench is taken
And many thousands slain,
The losers, with more slaughter,
Retake the trench again.

submarine warfare and clumsy propaganda apparatus. In addition, the Eastern establishment press favored the Allies, and America's economic health appeared to be tied to the Allies' cause.

With loyalties so defined and fears nourished, advocates of increased military strength had persuaded Wilson to sponsor a program of "reasonable preparedness." And the pacifists' highest-placed friend at court, Secretary of State Bryan, who tried to practice the neutrality the president preached, had resigned in June in opposition to the harshness of the *Lusitania* note to Germany. In his stead Wilson appointed the legalistic Robert Lansing, who believed the United States would sooner or later drift into war on the Allies' side. His opinions were shared by Colonel House, just returned from his latest peace mission, without the olive branch he had hoped to find on European soil. Mediation at that time, he told the president, would alienate the Allies; to his diary he conceded that Wilson should have forced the Allies to the peace table the previous November before the war "had fastened on the vitals of Europe."

The president never wanted to see the mediationists because he disliked interference and the resultant publicity, yet he needed their political favor and he appeared to derive comfort from their common hope for peace. Warned by House that the foreign ministers had been "not quite candid" with Miss Addams—a fact she knew very well herself—Wilson was gracious and evasive when his guest gave him the Hague congress's resolutions and an account of her interviews. A few weeks later, when Miss Balch reported the neutral officials' remarks to the president, she confided that instead of a large conference Miss Addams and other members of the Henry Street group had come to prefer a small, quasi-official mediation commission staffed by international experts. (Both Miss Addams and Miss Wales had come to believe such a body had a better chance of being established than a large-scale official convocation, which they hoped would later materialize.) Later in August, Miss Balch and Dr. Aletta Jacobs, who had been sent by the Dutch prime minister to inquire unofficially whether Wilson would participate in neutral mediation, were received by Secretary Lansing, who conducted himself, Miss Balch thought, on a moral level considerably lower than the European statesmen. (He, in turn, told Wilson the women were boring, naive and quite vague about what "continuous mediation" meant.)

The pacifists concluded from their talks with the president that he would mediate, but only when certain of success, which was to say, only when he was asked, and he would act alone. Wilson's highly moralistic attitude, evident in his conversations with the mediators, bespoke an exalted standard of behavior few people, let alone nations, could attain. In his messianic vision of America he was the savior of the world, and though he wanted desperately to lead, he would not be precipitate. Messiahs do not make mistakes.

Summer faded into fall, and the peaceworkers grew fearful that the militarists' influence would increase at home as the war dragged on, and with some urgency they met at the Henry Street Settlement again in late September. The most assertive, forceful speaker at the gathering was Rosika Schwimmer, who had returned to America to see Wilson once more. She had finagled an appointment for herself and Chrystal Macmillan as envoys to the president against the wishes of the International Committee of Women for Permanent Peace with the usual outcome for herself—impetuous resignation from office and loss of friends in the suffrage hierarchy. However, the peaceworkers doubted Wilson would see her and in any case knew what he would say if he did, and would not arrange an interview. When Mme Schwimmer learned Jane Addams was advocating unofficial mediation, she bluntly reminded her that as president of the International Committee of Women she was obliged to support their resolution for official action, and as penance Miss Addams asked Mme Schwimmer and Miss Macmillan to explain their position to the Henry Street meeting. Europe would heed only an official convocation involving the United States, Mme Schwimmer emphatically informed her listeners, an opinion she hastened to forget a few weeks later.

The pacifists' principal problem was neither the size nor the status of the peace intervention but how they could goad the president to act, and the means they chose was a publicity campaign they hoped would generate an irresistible national demand for mediation. "We so wholeheartedly believed in those days," Miss Addams recalled, "that if we could only get our position properly before the public, we would find an overwhelming response." The Woman's Peace Party, which had already distributed over 20,000 copies of Miss Wales's pamphlet in the United States and Europe, immediately called a meeting in Chicago, attended by fifteen hundred women who heard Mme Schwimmer, Dr. Jacobs and Miss Macmillan, and then petitioned the president. Next, the congress envoys released their report, which said that after thirty-five visits in fourteen capitals the envoys were convinced that the belligerents "would not be hostile" to the creation of a neutral mediation conference, that five European governments were willing to participate and that the gathering had to be convened at once so that it might function at the next break in the fighting. The neutral countries, the report continued, bore a responsibility for the continuance of the war which they could not escape; the inference was clear that the United States thus far had been dilatory and derelict. When the statement appeared in American newspapers in mid-October, Rosika Schwimmer and Chrystal Macmillan were in California about to address the Fifth American Peace Congress at the urgent invitation of Louis Lochner.

His constitutional optimism notwithstanding, Lochner's spirits had been at their nadir all summer. He was in San Francisco running a conference for the American Peace Society, the program of which had made not even a passing allusion to the war in Europe. His friend's speeches, however, turned the conference around, and the delegates not only passed the mediation resolution but appointed Dr. David Starr Jordan, the pacifist educator, to deliver it to Wilson.

Lochner returned at once to Chicago, where he and other peace-workers arranged a series of spontaneous peace rallies all over the country, timed so that the White House tally of the people's petitions demanding mediation would be completed just before Dr. Jordan stepped over the threshold to the president's office. The superbly co-ordinated action was successful beyond the pacifists' dreams, resulting in over eight thousand meetings and nearly ten thousand telegrams to the White House.

Mme Schwimmer also helped coordinate the campaign between the few lectures she had been asked to give. After a year and a half of war her audiences were smaller and her engagements less frequent than the previous winter, and though she had tried repeatedly she could not find a millionaire to finance her peace ambitions. She had booked passage for Europe in late November.

Dr. Jordan, meanwhile, doubtful of the propriety of telling the president when to act, had consulted Colonel House and been told that "nothing can be done save on the President's initiative," which would not be exercised then because it would not succeed. At the moment of their conversation, however, House was anxiously awaiting Sir Edward Grey's response to a presidential peace proposal. The scheme, conceived by House, was deceitful, conniving and coercive, and bore little resemblance to a neutral mediation.

In secret, House was to ask the Allies if they did not think it was time to end the war, provided the Central Powers agreed to evacuate all occupied territory, which the Germans were hardly likely to do. If the Allies said yes, then Wilson would call a peace conference. If the Germans refused to attend, the United States would sever relations and, if necessary,

join the battle. Wilson only added the critical word "probably" before
the phrase that committed the country to war, and House sent the message.
Astounded at such transparent skulduggery, the British foreign secretary
evaded a direct reply by asking for the answer to an earlier question of his
own: Would the United States join a postwar league of nations designed
to guarantee the peace treaty and prevent future wars? As it happened,
both Wilson and House believed in the principle of a supranational governmental organization, but for the president to make a diplomatic commitment to that effect, even in secret, was quite another matter. The
fawning colonel knew exactly how to overcome the president's hesitancy.
"This is the part you are destined to play in this world tragedy," he wrote
him, "and it is the noblest part that has ever come to a son of man." Not
one to quarrel with destiny and fearful that the United States would soon
be dragged into the war, Wilson approved an affirmative reply to Grey. It
was sent the day before the president received David Starr Jordan, but
during their conversation he kept his own confidence.

By the time Dr. Jordan walked beneath the White House portico on
November 12, he had been reinforced in his initial resolve by his peace
associates. With Lochner at his side he entered the executive office ready
to talk with his old friend as one former college president to another.

Accepting the San Francisco conference resolution, Wilson assured his
visitors he had thought often of the neutral-mediation proposal and had
read the confidential statements obtained by the Hague congress envoys,
but could see no way to act on them. For an hour the president listened
attentively and apparently sympathetically to his guests' arguments and
spoke his objections, namely that the United States could not participate
in a multinational conference where it might be outvoted and that the
Allies would consider an uninvited mediation at that time as unfavorably
partisan. In reply Jordan went at once to the heart of the matter. He was
aware, of course, that Wilson had his own sources and no doubt knew
more than they did; still, their information was confirmed by nondip-
lomats and represented the thought of many European neutrals and
belligerents for whom a neutral conference would offer the hope of a
negotiated peace and the opportunity to exhort their governments to that
end. He conceded that the continuous-mediation plan had its defects, but
at least it was an attempt that might succeed, and something had to be
done before Europe annihilated itself.

Wilson thanked his callers for their visit, but when Lochner took his
polite remarks to mean approval and asked if he might bear the message
that Wilson would act, the president quietly replied, "No, that is for me
to say when the right moment, in my judgment, arrives."

"We have 'put it over,' the plan of 'continuous mediation,'" Jordan triumphantly wrote his wife, after telling Lochner he had never seen Wilson "so human, so deferential, and so ready to listen." With such encouragement Lochner was certain the president would be forced to act if the mediationists kept "pounding away at the doors of the White House—if in no other manner than by continued demonstrations."

But demonstrations cost money, and thus far not one person of substantial wealth had offered to subsidize their peace campaign, though all likely prospects had been asked. Some months earlier Henry Ford had publicly announced he would spend his fortune on peace work, and even though every attempt by the pacifists to get past his office barricade had failed, he was their only hope. "We must get Mr. Ford," Lochner wrote, after seeing the president, "to furnish us unlimited funds" for "an overwhelming series" of meetings. He was sure once he told Ford what the women envoys had learned and what Wilson had said that he could win the millionaire "for the cause," and then the two of them could go to Wilson, present their plan and tell the president "to either get into the game or be forever left out."

Lochner had tried to see Ford, but his most recent request for an interview had been evaded—the manufacturer was out of town. Probably none of the neutral conference advocates would ever have met Ford, certainly not on his home ground, had it not been for the single-minded tenacity and persistence bordering on fanaticism of Rebecca Shelly, a young Midwestern schoolteacher with a particular need for "special heroines." The previous winter when she read in the paper that Jane Addams was leading a delegation to a woman's congress in The Hague she quit her job and bought a steamship ticket with her trousseau money. Mme Schwimmer's oratorical wizardry in the final minutes of the meetings had bewitched her, and she adopted the Hungarian pacifist—"the midwife of my new birth"—as her newest idol. Seeing herself as God's instrument intended to unite Ford's fortune with Mme Schwimmer's divinely inspired plan, Rebecca Shelly spent the fall in Detroit, running downtown street meetings and addressing women's clubs, drumming up support for the early-November peace demonstration. The national organizers at the Woman's Peace Party headquarters had little faith in her judgment and none in her expectation of what she said she could do on "nerve and brass tacks," but they did not stop her, hoping that a public meeting might be the way to reach the unapproachable Henry Ford.

Apparently Mme Schwimmer and Lochner thought so also when they agreed to appear in Detroit, hoping to share the speakers' platform with the peace-minded philanthropist. Though disappointed at Ford's absence they were astounded at the splendid turnout and support for mediation. Even more surprising was the favorable newspaper coverage the peace rally received, with one myopic reporter describing Mme Schwimmer as "a housewife . . . with the happy smile of a contented mother [who] reminds you of a crock of cookies." On the theory that anyone who could produce that publicity could probably accomplish the impossible, the Chicago leadership told Miss Shelly to stay in Detroit and find "Big Money" to continue her good work. "Big Money," of course, was a synonym for the elusive Mr. Ford. It took Rebecca Shelly not quite two weeks and a critical and almost impossible fluke of circumstance to pull it off. By mid-November Rosika Schwimmer had dined with Henry Ford and then telegraphed the bewildered Lochner: "Why are you not coming to Detroit to keep the appointment made for you with Mr. Ford?"

CHAPTER 3

Henry Ford: "War is murder"

ONE LATE-SUMMER DAY in 1915 a young red-headed reporter from the Detroit *Free Press* was sent by his editor to interview Henry Ford and follow up on some recent comments the manufacturer had made on the war. The reporter, Theodore Delavigne, was one of only a few newspapermen who had access to the then publicly reticent businessman, an access won because the young man had once identified an English clock in Ford's office, and Ford's first love had been timepieces and finding out why they ticked.

Together they wandered the domesticated wilds of Ford's acreage in Dearborn. Waste of resources, animate or inanimate, Henry Ford could not tolerate, and he spoke strongly, if inarticulately, of the futility of war and the cost of armaments as a misdirection of man's abilities and energy. He had no understanding or knowledge whatever of the international politics that caused war. To Henry Ford all wars were caused by one group of men wanting what another group possessed. If men could be usefully—which is to say productively—occupied, then the people, having sufficient to their needs and desires, would resist the warmongers' cry that the greener grass was on the other side of the national border. If the men who went to battle were given tractors instead of guns, war and its causes would cease.

As Ford and Delavigne walked through the woods that late-August day, Ford told his interviewer that war was plain, ordinary murder, that he would give his time and substance to educate Americans against military preparedness and educate the rest of the world to use motorized plowshares instead of armaments. Delavigne was stunned at such determination and largesse and asked Ford if his plan was for publication. Ford said yes and told the reporter to put it all in his own words. The entire "interview" was the lead story in the Detroit *Free Press* the next day, bearing the three-column headline HENRY FORD TO PUSH WORLD-WIDE CAMPAIGN FOR UNIVERSAL PEACE, and it was carried in the major papers of the country.

Why Henry Ford, a fifty-two-year-old maker of automobiles, should decide one fine summer day to pledge his fortune to educate the people in the cause of peace and how he finally came to spend almost half a million dollars on a peace expedition to Europe can best be understood—as well as anyone can ever understand what motivated Henry Ford—by examining his character and his early environment, for he was one of those men who never escape or outgrow the first years of life.

Henry Ford was a son of the soil, a paternity he lamented. His love of birds and of their habitat was almost the extent of his love of the land. From his earliest years, Ford's interests had to do with machinery, not with hand plowing and the dulling chores of farm life. "Considering the results," he said about his father's farm, "there was too much work on the place." And, somewhat more succinctly, "milk is a mess."

William Ford, Henry's father, had come from Ireland with his parents in 1847 and had settled in Dearborn, Michigan, near his uncles who had arrived ten years earlier. In 1861, having bought forty acres from his father, William married Mary Litigot, the adopted daughter of his neighbors, and two years later, Henry, the second child but the first of six to survive, was born.

Henry's boyhood home was comfortable and large—a white frame house with six bedrooms, a Sunday parlor, a common parlor and a large dining room and kitchen. The family library included a Bible and hymnal, *Practical Piety II*, *Pilgrim's Progress*, a history of England and a pictorial history of America. Mr. Ford subscribed to a county newspaper, a farm paper and a New York newspaper as well as *Godey's Lady's Book and Magazine* and other home magazines. Though not frequent church-goers, the family belonged to the Episcopal church. William Ford was, at times, a justice of the peace and a member of the school board and of the road commission, and he was sufficiently interested in the technological wonders of his time to visit the Philadelphia Centennial Exposition. And most important to his eldest son, the father was an industrious farmer and carpenter who prospered on the land and thought he followed the most respectable calling a man could pursue.

Mary Litigot Ford was an affectionate, understanding woman, orderly, energetic and vivacious. She taught her children self-discipline, cleanliness, thrift and service to others, and in her son Henry especially she instilled a reverence for the efficacy of intuition.

By the time Henry went to school at seven and a half, his mother had already taught him to read McGuffey's *First Eclectic Reader*. From his parents and the Reverend Mr. McGuffey he learned that hard work, duty and obedience to family, God, country and the elderly were virtuous and that greed, sloth, gluttony, drunkenness and pride were sinful. Ford credited McGuffey with teaching his generation that good quality and proper business methods would yield profits, that one should be ambitious not to win position and power but to excel. The didactic tales and poems in the *Readers* taught, in fact, not that virtue was its own reward but that kindness, honesty and generosity brought rich and prompt material dividends. By serving his fellow man the virtuous would also serve himself.

Practically all of Ford's formal knowledge—and his love of maxims—came from the *Readers*; his geography book served mainly as a desk shield at school to hide his tinkering with watches rather than as a source of information. "There is an immense amount to be learned simply by tinkering with things," he said—more than one could learn in books. From the time a patient farmhand let the seven-year-old boy examine his watch until he left the farm, Ford was investigating or repairing the innards of a timepiece. His mother said he was "a born mechanic," and encouraged his enterprise even at the expense of her corset stays, which he fashioned into tweezers, and her knitting needles, which he filed into screwdrivers. "The first watch I fixed was after Sunday School. . . . I looked in it and saw what was rong [*sic*]." He was thirteen years old. His mother died that spring and, characteristically, Ford recalled her death in horological imagery: "The house was like a watch without a mainspring."

A few months later, while riding on his father's wagon, Ford saw for the first time a vehicle not drawn by horsepower and immediately leaped into the road, ready with a barrage of questions for the operator of the portable steam engine. "That showed me," he wrote later, "that I was by instinct an Engineer."

He certainly was not a scholar. All told he probably attended school no more than six years, including his sporadic attendance for three years after his mother died. Much of his time after his thirteenth birthday he spent firing and running the engine he had seen on the road, which

Clara and Henry Ford and son, Edsel, on the *Oscar II* before departure (Courtesy of Henry Ford Museum).

belonged to a neighbor, and walking back and forth to Detroit for tools. It was during these years that he and his friends built a steam turbine which exploded and burned a large part of the schoolhouse fence. Though William Ford insisted his son do his share of the farm chores he also indulged the boy's obvious mechanical curiosity and competence, permitting him to repair implements and letting him set up a workbench in the kitchen. At night, in his bedroom, Henry literally moonlighted, doing repair jobs on his portable workbench which he quickly dismantled at the sound of approaching footsteps. One day in early December of his seventeenth year, Henry Ford walked the few miles into town and got himself a job with the biggest streetcar manufacturer in Detroit.

Detroit in the 1880s was a busy lake port with ten converging railroad lines and nine hundred manufacturing plants. The years of Ford's youth were prosperous and peaceful years for the country, a time of tremendous industrial growth, of railroad expansion, of mobility and immigration for those seeking to be a vital part of the energy that pervaded the continent. For three years after he moved to Detroit, Henry Ford was part of that world.

He lost his first job in six days, not through laziness or ignorance but because older hands in the shop were resentful when he quickly fixed some broken machinery that had defeated them. Ford's next job, courtesy of his father's influence, was in a machine shop where he mastered all he could learn before moving on to the engine works of a shipbuilding company. For a time he worked at night in a jeweler's shop to make ends meet. In the engine shop he read technical and scientific magazines, and in his boarding house he built his first practical steam engine. Ford's mind and hands were restless with different ideas—a boiler, an eight-day clock, a boat—ideas he would get his friends to work on with him, moving on to something else himself before the job at hand was completed. He had an idea then of mass-producing a thirty-cent watch until he realized "watches were not universal necessities" and he could never make a living manufacturing what few would buy.

In the spring of 1882, at his father's urging, the young inventor returned to the farm. But it was more of a mailing address than a place of employment. Most of the next few years he spent as an itinerant operator and repairman of a portable steam engine in southern Michigan, traveling from farm to farm as a member of a threshing crew. When he was home he was busy as always in his workshop, building a tractor to replace the farm horse. Ford had little training in mathematics and none in engineering; he gained knowledge by reading but mostly by experimenting, becoming as a result a lifelong exponent of learning by doing. One winter he took courses in Detroit in bookkeeping, mechanical drawing and business procedures, having possibly decided even then to follow some form of business life. When his father gave him forty acres of woodland, he farmed only a small part of it, built a sawmill and began a lumber business because by then he needed money to get married.

At a New Year's Eve party in 1885, Ford had sat out two dances with a bright, lively, dark-haired eighteen-year-old girl, Clara Jane Bryant, ex-plaining to her the workings of his newly invented two-dial watch that told railroad and local "sun time." Another time she patiently listened to his detailed explanation of the functions of a Westinghouse engine and suffered a ride on the behemoth. By the next spring they were engaged, but they had to wait two more years to wed because her parents were unwilling to let their daughter marry too young. The interim was a joyful courtship of hayrides and sleigh rides, picnics and strawberry fes-tivals, and for Clara, a St. Valentine's letter assuring her of "the pleasure it gives me to think that i have at last found one so loveing [*sic*] kind and true as you are."

Theirs was a warm, supportive relationship from the first. Clara had the same background as her husband, except that she and her family were staunch members of the Episcopal church. Her father served in the state legislature and was active in church and local affairs. Clara was steady, stolid, thrifty, practical. Ford called her "The Believer" because of her steadfast faith and loyalty, especially during the uncertain early years. By the time of their marriage in April 1888, Henry was doing well at the sawmill, serving neighbors and selling his own lumber to furnituremakers and shipbuilders. When he was not at the mill, he was in his machine shop working on a steam engine that would operate a vehicle. By the fall of 1891, when he was twenty-eight, Ford decided he needed more training in electricity and, with a reluctant but trusting wife, he returned to Detroit. The day they moved he went to work as an engineer with the Edison Illuminating Company.

The next ten years were stimulating and satisfying years for Henry Ford though unsettling for his wife and son, Edsel, born in 1893. At the end of the decade the family moved into its ninth home. Wherever they lived there was a workshop nearby for Ford's after-hours labor. Within two years of his return to the city, he was chief engineer at Edison at triple his starting salary, on call twenty-four hours a day, but with his time his own to work on the gas-powered motor car that had replaced the steam-driven tractor in his interest.

In Detroit, Ford lived and worked among mechanics and engineers—many more able than he—who were also working on motor-powered vehicles. Energetic, honest, sensible, easygoing, he sported a handsome mustache, played practical jokes and enjoyed the camaraderie of consulta-tion and collaboration with his friends on his automobile. Ford was warm-hearted and fun-loving, but also stubborn and obstinate. His friends ad-mired his efficiency, tenacity, ingenuity and mechanical ability and gladly worked with him. Ford was developing in these years his capability of getting others to do the work, guiding them, organizing them, and inspiring them with his optimism and his imperviousness to failure.

At two A.M. on a rainy June morning in 1896, Henry Ford rode out of the coal and wood shed in back of his rented home—after he had taken an ax and hacked down part of the brick wall so that his vehicle could get through the door and out into the world. The carriage, topped by a bicycle seat, rested on a frame mounted on bicycle wheels, with a doorbell set in the top of the steering tiller to serve as a "horn." A friend rode ahead on a bicycle to warn any pedestrians or horses that might be abroad at that hour.

That first run was short and successful. In the weeks spent rebuilding and improving the first model, Ford enjoyed the attention he received as he drove it about the city and out to the family farm. The greatest discouragement came from his boss, Alexander Dow, who not only had no faith in gasoline engines but thought it rather strange that an engineer for an electric company should be fiddling with them in a company shop. But Dow was effectively silenced the summer of 1896 at the company's annual meeting, when he told his boss, Thomas Alva Edison, of Ford's tinkering, hoping Edison would discourage his assistant's foolishness. Instead, the inventor summoned the young mechanic to his side. Ford talked, drew diagrams and talked some more. At the end, Edison, banging the table with his fist, exclaimed: "Young man, that's the thing. You have it. Keep at it!" and Ford remembered that "that bang on the table was worth worlds to me. . . . out of a clear sky the greatest inventive genius in the world had given me a complete approval."

Back went Ford to his shop, sold his first car, took almost two years to build another, patented a carburetor and looked for backing so he could manufacture a quantity-produced, simple, but durable, car. He was not alone. The automobile industry was at the beginning of a boom, building not only luxury cars for the well-to-do, but inexpensive models for everyone else. In the summer of 1899, Ford quit his job and with businessmen as backers, organized the Detroit Automobile Company. It was Ford's first experience working with others who had control over what he wanted to do, and the connection did not last long. One year later, his sponsors $86,000 poorer, the company failed. They had expected seven different models—Ford turned out only a delivery wagon. His backers charged him with excessive expenses; he was provoked by their impatience. Characteristically, Ford was reluctant to go into production with anything less than the perfect embodiment of his ideas.

This stubborn insistence on producing cars his way and at his pace and for his purpose regardless of his sponsors' demands was evident again in Ford's next business association. The Henry Ford Motor Company, incorporated to manufacture a two-cylinder runabout based on Ford's design, dispensed with his services in the spring of 1902, less than six months after it was formed. Once again, the stockholders complained that Ford took too long and spent too much to produce nothing salable. Ford had gotten the financing for that company after he won his first race in October 1901 with his newly built racing car. With it, he had hoped "to make $ where I can't make ¢ at Manufacturing," he had written his brother-in-law. But his backers wanted a passenger car. In addition, Ford was dissatisfied with his share of the company stock and with the head of the machine shop, Henry Leland, who happened to be a well-trained, highly experienced engineer, somewhat more competent than a "trial-by-error" mechanic. Resisting the pressure to produce a less than perfect vehicle, Ford was out on the street again, taking only his name, $900 and plans for another racer.

That summer Ford organized another company with Alex Malcomson, a coal dealer, but they didn't move out of the workshop and into a factory until another racing car, driven that fall by bicyclist Barney Oldfield, brought the publicity and prestige that resulted in increased funds, more partners and a labor force. At last Ford hoped he could build a cheap, useful motorized "family horse."

Companies came and went, but Henry Ford was lucky in his new partners. Some of them gave only financial support, but the Dodge brothers supplied the chassis and James Couzens, Malcomson's bookkeeper, supplied business acumen and encouragement. At the same time, Ford attracted a work crew of exceptionally talented, imaginative and skillful men without whom his company might have folded. Ford's contribution to the business that bore his name was his engine, his determination and his willingness to try anything that might work. A day in the factory was one of improvisation, change and improvement. Ford was in charge, not as a dictator, but as coordinator and co-worker. Though there were disappointments, Ford's buoyancy and patience, his zest for cleanliness, efficiency and accuracy and his opposition to the prevalent practice of piecework rallied the men who helped create his fortune.

The company did very well from the beginning making medium-priced cars. But when Malcomson wanted to build luxury cars, Ford set up a subsidiary that threatened Malcomson's profits in the parent company and the coal dealer sold out. Stockholders, such as Malcomson, who contributed only money and no labor, Ford called parasites who were fair game for financial finagling. With Malcomson and his friends gone, Ford had majority control and the loyalty of the remaining stockholders.

And for Clara, the wandering days in rented houses were over. She reigned in a splendid $300,000 red-brick, stone-columned house with a butler's pantry and servants' dining room, surrounded by landscaped gardens, and she rode about town in an electric car. But most of Ford's tremendous profits went into his new Highland Park plant, the biggest, cleanest, most efficient factory in the world, which opened in the fall of 1910.

Two years before, at the crest of a boom in auto-buying, Ford had introduced the Model T. But it was not until they moved into the mammoth new plant with its facilities for increased production that he could begin to realize his declared goal of making a car his own workers could afford. By 1912, Ford had 96 percent of the low-cost car field, selling the Model T for $500. Two years later a new car, assembled in an hour and a half, rolled out of the plant every twenty-four seconds. In its first full year the company did $1,000,000 worth of business; at the end of its twelfth year, in 1914, it did $120,000,000. During these years Ford had become a hero to the industry, having fought a patent suit through the courts until he won, thus ending the threat of a man who tried to monopolize automobile manufacture. Though others tried to ride to wealth making a cheap and durable car, none rode as far and as long as Ford.

It was process, not invention, that was Ford's singular contribution to the automobile industry. He did not invent interchangeable parts or mass production or the moving assembly line, but he did put all of these processes together. He had the nerve to take risks, to trust his hunches, to try the unorthodox and to experiment with new materials until he got what he wanted. To cut costs he restricted production only to the Model T chassis, and later he eliminated all paint dyes, allowing a customer the choice of "any colour he wants so long as it is black." Ford lowered the price of the car on the gamble that increased sales would more than make up for any loss of revenue caused by the reduced price.

Ford's business philosophy was elemental: buy in large quantities to receive cheaper rates, pay bills promptly to receive cash discounts and build in huge quantities to reduce production costs. And above all, do not get into debt by borrowing, especially from Wall Street. Banks were for *earning* interest on deposits, not for *paying* interest on loans. The parasites of Wall Street produced nothing but paper and lived off businesses in distress. Rather than invest in stocks and bonds, the weapons of capitalists, Ford kept his surplus cash in small-town banks which he considered community-serving institutions. He never called himself a capitalist because he did not make money from money but from his own labor. "I put it to work," he said. "I build and create with it."

Henry Ford was not only the right man in the right place at the right time, but he was the man who got the necessary other right men together with him. He had neither the brains nor the experience to make it alone. Sharing responsibility at the very top with him was James Couzens, a temperamental slavedriver, imperious and pugnacious, who was a wizard in the front office. The two men worked perfectly together, equally committed to the plant and to the business, as long as they stayed in their separate spheres. Where Ford was unsystematic, a rare occupant of his oak-paneled, richly endowed office, unable to sit still even to open his mail, Couzens, the martinet, supervised their advertising and sales in the expanding American, Canadian and European markets, ruthlessly but effectively dealing with dealers. Patient and painstaking though he was, Couzens stopped Ford's endless tinkering with mockups and saw that the car got into production and to the marketplace. Both lived well, but generally did not flaunt their wealth. The single intent of building the business kept Ford and Couzens together. In those developing years the company would not have existed at all without Ford, but it would not have lasted long without Couzens to organize and develop the business operation. Neither sought personal attention but both encouraged publicity of their product in the press, by word of mouth and by jokes about the versatility and vagaries of the Tin Lizzie. As a result, though there were more than half a million Fords on the roads all over the world, loved by drummers and draymen, by the farmer and his city brother, very little was known about the man whose name they bore. That anonymity ended when thousands read their morning papers on January 5, 1914.

Ford and Couzens had been right. With a small unit profit and large-scale manufacture the car cost less and less and sold to more and more people. Net profits were accumulating at an embarrassing rate—the company surplus doubled in 1913—and Ford, though sufficient businessman to wish his company reasonable profits and his fellow stockholders a fair return, thought the $26,000,000 in dividends they had received on a collective investment of $10,000 was excessive, especially for those who did not even work for the company. Having set aside plenty for plant expansion, he felt the men who made the car were entitled to some of the surplus, favoring, as he always did, the man who did the work rather than the man whose money did the work for him. And he thought the public would stop buying the car when they learned the amount of profits the company was making.

There was also the matter of maintaining a stable labor force, which large-scale production required. Because the workers were driven hard to meet the increased output demanded by management, there was a large turnover. The apparent solution was to pay wages that would keep men on the job and unapproachable to labor organizers. It was time to share the wealth.

What actually happened that Sunday morning in early January 1914 in the Ford plant offices will never be known for certain. What is known is that Ford, Couzens and a few others, after some figuring on the blackboard, decided to pay a wage of $5 a day, which was more than double the going rate for unskilled labor. At the same time they changed the work day from two nine-hour shifts to three eight-hour shifts, another innovation. Some of the finer points—that single men and all women had to meet age qualifications and maintain certain behavior standards to participate in profit-sharing—were not publicized. What hit the front pages was the $5 a day wage for an eight-hour day and that profit-sharing, which would cost the company $10,000,000, would be paid as salary.

Before that day it was the process and the product that were known, loved and admired—but not the man. After that day, Henry Ford became an instant folk hero—a St. Francis caring for his followers and feeding autos to the poor. He was revered worldwide; college students voted him the third greatest man ever to have lived, after Napoleon and Christ. The legend that his advertising office and his own pronouncements created fed the needs of those anxious to obtain the good life through material wealth but unwilling to lose their sense of innocence. Henry Ford proved to them that a man could make millions without losing his conscience or the exalted values of the American dream.

The public learned that Henry Ford was a humanitarian employer. A special staff helped his employees save and spend their wages. Believing there was good in everyone, that every man was educable, Ford hired convicts who were carefully screened by the warden at Sing Sing. He also hired Negroes, Jews, the blind and the crippled. Foreign employees who could not speak English were taught the language and American customs so that they would not be victimized by their countrymen—and so that they could understand their plant foremen.

The public learned that orphans on a nearby farm received the benefit of Ford's philosophy of education: more learning was acquired through observation and personal involvement in productive effort than from books, desk-sitting and teacher-watching. In his own schools, he set up the first of his job-training experiments where children learned a skill while they learned to read and write.

The public learned that when Henry Ford said he gave at the office, he meant he gave "a chance and not charity"—that is, he provided a job opportunity. A handout was antithetical to his beliefs in thrift, hard work, self-reliance and the abstemious life. "Aid the man who sweats," he said. It was society's obligation to provide every man a decent living beyond subsistence, but the worker had "to *dig* for it." As for himself and his company, he thought "social justice begins at home."

The publicization of Ford's practical altruism also won the enthusiastic approval of businessmen who, in these peak years of the Progressive Era, were seeking order in their environment and of the social reformers who were seeking a better life for the "teeming refuse" lately deposited on American shores. Small wonder, then, that Ford was considered for the Bull Moose gubernatorial candidacy of his native state just months after the profit-sharing pronouncement or that he never bore the Robber Baron image of Rockefeller, Carnegie and others who also called themselves stewards of their wealth.

Henry Ford, the public learned, was a simple man of the people, clay of their clay, who neither smoked nor drank. That he had over $1,500,000 in his personal checking account, or that he built himself a Scottish baronial mansion of fifty-six rooms, fifteen baths, eight fireplaces and 550 light switches—the entire twelve-hundred-acre estate and its buildings costing over $2,000,000—did not mar the public's adulation of this ascetic common man whose wealth was a just reward. The money was for the plant and improving the motor car so that its cost could be reduced further, and the mansion was not on Fifth Avenue but near his old family homestead. There was a library of rare books, but also a panel-glass window of illustrations from the McGuffey *Readers*. There was an Italian marble-and-walnut fireplace on which was carved "Gather ye rosebuds while ye may," but there was a more modest mantel in the Rustic Room downstairs inscribed with one of Ford's favorite maxims: "Chop your own wood and it will warm you twice."

That first year of Henry Ford as a practicing evangel of social justice in the New Industrialism was a tremendous success. The proof was in the profits: a cash surplus at the end of 1914 of $48,827,032.97.

Of Henry Ford, public benefactor and protector of the common man, the people were well advised. But that persona masked a private man whose behavior was a perpetual puzzle even to those who knew him best and longest. Henry Ford with his simplistic ideas was a very complicated man.

He had a technological mind that could see through machinery to its workings. It was a mind not given to deep thought, introspection or abstract concepts, but to moral absolutes.

He was a solitary man who liked to walk alone through his woods, a quiet man who spoke little, chopped wood to keep in shape and climbed stairs two at a time. Ford was a private person; he had no small talk, or even conversation, except about machines and birds. The little black jot-books, no bigger than the palm of his hand, that he carried in his pockets for fifty years recorded the inner man and his interests. In page after page, year after year, he drew diagrams of machines, tried to improve his spelling and his signature, noted maxims and aphorisms often of life made simple in easy-to-understand but hard-to-practice prescriptions for virtue —"Don't find fault: find a remedy: anybody can complain." Jonathan Swift taught him that "money is the lifeblood of the nation" and Ben Franklin that "the use of money is all the advantage there is in having it." Ford's attempts to understand political economy, premised on the dogma that Wall Street was evil, resulted in such perceptions as "the Present system of finance is the only thing that goes by fits and jerks up and down (*Too mutch of it*) Get rid of some of it and go to work" and "Tax on Large incomes better be left in the hand of the ones who have Earned it—Those who earn know how to spend it they are Leaders." His own business experience taught him: "No Stockholders Money the *Root* of all *Eval* unless used for good purpus," and, not incidentally, "I have been able to make all the money I wanted with out war and every one else can if they will stop and think."

Ford was a shallow man, intellectually arrogant, who did not know much but knew what he liked and never hesitated to say what he thought he thought. He read few books other than Emerson's and Burroughs's essays and little poetry other than Tennyson's "Locksley Hall," because, as he said, books "muss up my mind." Experience was his principal teacher.

He shied away from interviews but enjoyed reading of his glories and his deeds in the press. Though he reveled in the limelight and publicity he created, he was in fact a timid man who was comfortable only with his own kind and never at ease in a crowd or when he had to appear in public. In his first public speech at a dinner in Sing Sing he told the prisoners he was delighted that everyone was there! When he testified before the Commission on Industrial Relations, he submitted a prepared statement replying to written questions, and when he had to answer direct questions, he spoke mostly in mumbled monosyllables and frequently only nodded his head, either affirmatively or negatively.

Ford also avoided reporters, because they bored him. If he was not interested in a person or a subject or an activity he had the attention span of a four-year-old. But a favorable public image was important to the man and the company, so writers, if they were sufficiently winning or influential, were admitted to the presence after a careful screening by Ford's private secretary. The most a writer could get, however, was a brief shotgun splatter of Ford's ideas and long interviews with the secretary, if the latter was so inclined. Even the secretary never knew when Ford would show up and, when he did, if he would stay for a few minutes or an hour. The man who wrote Ford's autobiographies talked with his subject off and on for a month for the first volume and with a Ford assistant for the other two. The result was that virtually everything in print, even under Ford's own name, was written by someone else and frequently approved by his secretary, but never read by Ford.

Ford was often spontaneously kind, extending help despite his injunctions about the evils of charity, but he could be cruel and insensitive. His word, quickly given on impulse, was very often just as quickly forgotten. He operated on his own internal clock and schedule, and it meant nothing to him to break an appointment if something of interest distracted him. He often excused himself for a moment from an interview if he was unduly restless and then darted out a back door and headed for the woods, his workshop or his skating pond. In the shop, in the days when he still moved among the men, he deliberately set workers against each other to see the "fireworks," enjoying the petty ruckuses that inevitably developed, believing they stimulated ideas. If the heat got too hot, Ford simply left the kitchen and let others carry the blame for his callousness.

He never did a thing he did not like. Any unpleasant jobs that had to be done at the factory in terms of personnel or policy were performed by a lesser member of the tough-minded oligarchy that, in effect, ran the company. Thus the victims always assumed Ford never knew what his hirelings were up to and the image of kindness that masked his deviousness and petty cruelty was preserved. At the same time, he disliked men whom he thought were rigid, negative and fearful of trying the untried.

Ford had few friends, and they were mainly men who used their hands as well as their brains and whose accomplishments favored his interests.

Foremost among them was Thomas Alva Edison, whom he idolized, never forgetting the encouragement he had received the first time they met in 1896. Both men had limited schooling in rural Michigan communities, and Edison had the qualities and life-style most attractive to Ford—curiosity, persistence, hard work and moderate living. He also had many of the same attitudes toward the world: a distrust of bankers, an inclination toward anti-Semitism of a generalized sort, abstention from alcohol, endorsement of woman suffrage because women were the custodians of moral values and a belief that the smoking of cigarettes was harmful to one's health because a chemical produced in the burning paper permanently damaged nerve centers and brain cells. As one of his first acts as a benefactor of mankind in matters other than Model Ts, Ford published Edison's pamphlet on the evils of cigarette smoking, entitled "The Case of the Little White Slaver."

As Ford idolized Edison, he revered the naturalist John Burroughs, and was generous to both these friends. He gave Edison the money to reconstruct his factory when it burned down, and to Burroughs, because the naturalist's books pleased him, he gave a free course of driving lessons and a new car every year from 1913 until the old man's death. (His giving away an automobile, Ford once explained, was like someone else giving away a jackknife.) Burroughs was charmed by the "simplicity" of the "earnest, big-hearted, ordinary man" but he was well aware of his "lovable" friend's defects and that he did not have the "great mind" of Edison. "He was a mightly good talker in his own field," he said, but "crude in his philosophy."

By middle age a person's patterns of behavior can be softened or hardened, but rarely completely changed. So it was with Henry Ford. None of the contradictions of his character, evident in his earlier years, had disappeared. He was both modest and vain, sensitive and crass, kind and cruel, persevering and impulsive, naive and cunning. His prejudices and suspicions—the product of his ignorance—he never modified or sought to remove through further enlightenment. Not only was the public beguiled by the accomplishments of the legend; Ford was himself. Believing his intuition and his perseverance were responsible for his success, he was no longer receptive to advice on any matter. He was arrogant, even despotic, but he was also a mischievous child who was sincerely trying to effect the preachments he had learned in school and at his mother's knee.

Those who met him—and they were not many—saw a lean, lithe, wiry man of medium height, his face lined, his hands, his whole body, restless, anxious to be on the move, a man of easygoing charm and a disarming smile. He had the "face of a middle-aged ascetic," a reporter wrote, ". . . but he has the manner of a restless boy." Those who tried to understand him imagined they saw the contradictions of his personality mirrored in his face: one half of it sweetness and light, the other cruelty and darkness. All agreed that he was arbitrary and capricious, a man of quick-changing moods, of great strengths and great limitations. "More interested in things than thought," as his wife's minister observed, he was a man neither of reason nor ratiocination. His restless energy required action, not contemplation. His ideas were hunches, intuitions that he acted on immediately, often with courage and daring, always certain he was right. His thinking was simplistic, in keeping with the verities of the McGuffey *Readers* and the Ten Commandments. And because he understood so little of human behavior and the ways of the world, he thought himself ill-treated when the truths he pronounced were challenged. Ford "is not all good, and he is not all bad," wrote a newspaperman who knew him well, but after January 1914 millions of people thought him the embodiment of wisdom and virtue.

The sound of money talking in America is highly persuasive. It is assumed that those who make a fortune are knowledgeable and competent not only in their own area of expertise but on any matter. When Ford announced he was but the steward of his wealth, which belonged to the people, the public saw him as a simple man of social justice. No one then said that profit-sharing, far from being the keystone of a social-economic policy, was only a higher minimum wage paid from increased profits; that his minions in the company's Sociological Department monitored his workers' lives in the manner of a secret service; or that the monotony of the assembly line was just as deleterious to health as alcohol and cigarettes. That a man of limited education and even less intellectual curiosity was not competent to deliver dicta on world affairs, science, medicine and, indeed, on any topic he fancied escaped notice in the public's willingness to believe that his apparent generosity and success qualified him on all matters.

Even the more sophisticated, considering Ford the spokesman of the New Industrialism as they considered Theodore Roosevelt the spokesman of the New Nationalism and Wilson of the New Freedom, expected Ford to be as informed on matters of social behavior, domestic economics and international politics as he was on the manufacture of an enduring and inexpensive automobile. It was something of a shock when they met the man behind the myth and learned that between their expectations and reality there lay a large and very dark shadow. That there was no form to his personality, no logic to his behavior, that he was unpredictable in thought and action made them wonder at his substantial success and the gullibility of the American public. Colonel House found him "crude, ignorant and with very little general information" and could not understand how Ford had made his fortune. He was astounded that Ford knew nothing of foreign affairs and less about politics, though he rather liked the "wiry and nervous" man's idealism and modesty. Frederic Howe, one of the few social reformers actually to talk to Ford, expecting some intelligent reaction to his own ideas, sat stunned as Ford talked only of autos, tractors and the immorality of parasitic Wall Street bankers.

In the year following the fanfare attendant on the $5 day and his profit-sharing policy, Ford's every action, past and present, was publicly praised. He enjoyed the power of his bulging purse and the attention he received when he tried to diminish his company's profits further by making another price cut and promising a bonus of almost $60 to every buyer if the company sold 300,000 new Model Ts in the coming year. During the previous year, the New York *Times* printed no stories on either Henry Ford or his company; but in 1914 they wrote of the industrial Robin Hood taking from himself and his stockholders to give to the poor, of Ford the benevolent single-handedly rescuing a bankrupt Detroit hospital that he would run for the poor, and of Ford the business counselor advising President Wilson. Of Ford the peaceworker—not a word.

While vacationing in northern Michigan in August 1914, Ford had his secretary send him daily war bulletins, but he made no public statement on the European war. (Privately, he and his wife arranged for Percival L. D. Perry, the Ford plant manager in England, to rent a home for Belgian refugees.) In an interview almost seven months after the war began he touched on practically every one of his interests but mentioned the fighting only in connection with praising Wilson for keeping the country out of it. Not until April 1915 did Ford's views on war reach the public in a one-page story in the New York *Times Magazine*. It was printed as a verbatim account, but the author actually saw Ford for only a few minutes and received most of the material from the director of the company's Sociological Department. Still, it was all Ford: Moneylenders and munitions makers caused wars; if Europe had spent money on peace machinery—such as tractors—instead of armaments there would have been no war; soldiers in the trenches should lay down their arms and let the leaders do the fighting; and, "To my mind, the word 'murderer' should be embroidered in red letters across the breast of every soldier." (In fact, the reporter told Ford that was Jane Addams's sentiment, but since Ford agreed with it, it was attributed to him as well.) As for America, Ford thought the warmongers urging military preparedness were Wall Street bankers anxious to fight Mexico rather than send her the industrial equipment and agricultural experts she needed. As for himself: "I am opposed to war in every sense of the word. I try to be consistent. If war came here and I were offered treble prices to manufacture motor cars for military purposes I would burn down my plant before I would accept an order." The day the article appeared the Fords were entertaining Jane Addams, just before her sailing for the women's conference in Holland. They talked of the war and Miss Addams told her hosts that twenty thousand men were dying each day to gain—or lose— just a few yards of ground. Ford was appalled at such waste of human life to so little purpose.

One can only surmise why Henry Ford spoke out as he did on the subject of war and its causes, and part of the answer is in his background. Twelve members of his father's family were eligible to fight in the Civil War, and not one volunteered. His maternal grandfather had deserted from the British army, and of his mother's brothers who fought, one was killed, the other wounded. It is quite likely that when his mother spoke to him of duty and service she suggested neither could be performed by killing. The Reverend Mr. McGuffey thought war the scourge of mankind and indicated its futility repeatedly in the *Readers*. From Emerson, Ford learned that men of peace are men of industry and that self-help is the means to advance civilization toward permanent peace. The verses in Tennyson's "Locksley Hall" that Ford liked spoke of commerce guided by international law as binding the world together in peace.

Ford believed in those years in a perfecting world. Certainly his own attempts at helping others had been successful and gratifying. Like the social reformers he was soon to meet, he thought that war was anathema to progress. "No animosity for any one," he jotted down one day, "But people who profitt from war must *go*." In June 1915, two months after the *Times* article, Ford called a press conference to announce he would soon build a factory to manufacture his tractor, one of whose several virtues would be to keep the country out of war. "If we keep our people working America will never be dragged into the war. . . . The parasite known as the absentee owner fosters war. New York wants war, but the

United States doesn't. The peoples west of New York are too sensible for war."

Interviewed in New York in early August, Ford again talked of what he and America should do about the war. Apparently he had mellowed since April. It was still against his conscience to manufacture war materiel for the European belligerents but this time he allowed that if the United States went to war he would make munitions for the same reason he "would build a roof over" his house. He admitted that his English company was making ambulances for the British, but not as many as had been asked for, and he had only consented under pressure. Yet an article signed by him appeared in New York newspapers one week later stating, "I would never let a single automobile get out of the Ford plant anywhere in the world if I thought it was going to be used in warfare."* Anyone keeping track of Ford's utterances would have charged him with inconsistency, but his inconsistencies never contradicted his ideology: war was murder, a "wasteful sacrifice of human life and the world's resources," fomented by munitions makers for their own aggrandizement. And that was the limit, the absolute and permanent limit, of his understanding of the cause of international conflicts.

Still, Ford was only speaking and not acting. It was not until the third week in August that the nation learned that Henry Ford intended to put his money where his mouth had been, courtesy of the Detroit *Free Press* reporter who, as it happened, was long-winded, emotional and verbally flamboyant. Delavigne's story went on and on, virtually all of it in direct quotations, beginning on the front page under a sensational headline proclaiming Ford's sponsorship of an international peace program, with the similarly exciting subhead: "Will Devote Life and Fortune to Combat Spirit of Militarism Now Rampant." What followed were the words of Delavigne, but the voice of Ford: "I will do everything in my power to prevent murderous, wasteful war in America and in the whole world; I will devote my life to fight this spirit of militarism."

The article was an attack against those advocating increased military strength in preparation for a war that was never going to come to a country that was protected by her geography. Instead of wasting money on useless armaments, Ford suggested that the United States should dis-

---

* On March 25, 1915, Percival Perry, the Ford Motor Company manager in England, wrote Mrs. Ford: "We have just sold 150 more Ford ambulances to the Government, and a week or two ago we sold a number of our cars to the Admiralty, which we know have been shipped out to the Dardanelles to act in conjunction with the landing of the forces there." The Paris branch also put ambulance bodies on automobile chassis for use in the war.

arm, thereby setting a needed example to the world. Though he had no specific plan for peace, Ford said he would educate the people against the evils of military preparedness in two major ways. First, by teaching children that war was wasteful and that "the preparation for war can only end in war." And second, by manufacturing his tractor and granting fair working conditions, fair prices and honest business operations.

The story was printed all over the country. The New York papers said that Ford was a nice man who worked hard for his money but was not worth listening to on any subject other than automobiles. John Wanamaker, the Philadelphia department-store magnate, on the other hand, sent him a telegram: "I have the same disposition to do anything and spend everything if thereby the waste of the millions of young men that are sinking into graves from lust of bloodshed can be stopped," and he invited Ford to visit him "to talk things over." The pledge caught the eye of hundreds who responded with encouraging letters.

Acknowledging the great support from the public and much of the national press, Delavigne, again in Ford's name, wrote a sequel in early September, this time outlining the plan that would fulfill the promise. One million dollars had already been set aside "to begin a peace educational campaign in the United States and the world." Part of the fund would be a prize for an anti-war history, part would be used to build factories throughout the world that manufactured farm tractors, the "implements of peaceful labor." Workers' thoughts, then, would turn from war to peace as higher wages enabled them to enjoy the benefits of culture and knowledge in their homes. Whatever money was left over from the fund, and any additional money donated by others, would be spent on the "practical suggestions" bound to result from the discussion of peace in the newspapers. Criticism of his ideas did not bother him, Ford said, because that was how he got his education; sarcasm and ridicule were "like the weeds of the field, that, turned under by the plow, make the finest fertilizer in the world."

There was another swipe in the article at the "parasites, these sloths and lunatics" who made war, and at soldiers who were, by definition, "either lazy or crazy." Those preparedness advocates who had suggested that Ford's earlier statements were treasonous and embarrassing to the president were wrong, because Wilson was himself fighting the jingoes, the story said. And Ford's personal position was further refined: if the United States should be attacked "anything that I have is at the disposal of the country for defense. And I would take not a cent of profit," but the country should not go to war to enrich "apostles of murder" or because "some foolish Americans will voyage on ships that are in danger."

A few days later Ford reportedly raised his "endowment for a world peace fund" to ten million dollars, which he, Wanamaker and Edison would decide how to spend. (This pledge may have been made by Ford or Delavigne or an overenthusiastic reporter; it was retracted within the week.)

For the next two weeks Ford was in the newspapers on a different topic almost every day. He talked of his tractor and of his dreams of a vertical industrial empire, and to those who challenged his opposition to a proposed Anglo-French loan, he replied that the belligerents' bankruptcy would end the war. While Delavigne's extended flights had dealt with the intellectual and the ideological, Ford spoke of the actual defense needs of the country: the development of a guided missile that would be so horrendously destructive no country would dare to start a war and, more immediately, a defensive fleet of small submarines to protect the coastline. "It would be no trick at all to build a sub one-fourth the size now in use that could carry a pill at the end of a pole with sufficient explosive power to hoist out of the sea the mightiest dreadnought ever built," said the man who had never seen a submarine.

Ford's comments on naval materiel were not gratuitous. Secretary of the Navy Josephus Daniels had been after him to help solve the navy's problems with airplane and submarine motors. But it was not until Ford received a letter from Daniels the first week in September about curtailing naval expansion—"by far the best letter I have yet received on the subject"—that he went to Washington to meet the man who was as consecrated to peace as he was himself. In his letter Daniels quoted from his own annual reports that the United States should initiate a postwar international disarmament conference and also included the lines from "Locksley Hall," Ford's favorite poem, that spoke of silenced war drums, furled battle flags and world government. But until that time, Daniels pleaded, the country needed Ford's "efficiency" to provide "reasonable precautions" for defense.

In Washington, Ford discussed with the president the possibility of the army using his tractor and with Daniels the possibility of building a gas-powered engine for the navy. After inspecting a submarine in New York, Ford told reporters it was too big and too expensive. He could—if he would—build a smaller one. Though he would not himself make weapons for war, he was glad to advise the government on improving its engines. After all, he explained when asked to reconcile his opposition to war with his offer to help develop military materiel, as long as the country had a navy, it should have the best.

Ford's continuing hodgepodge of statements on war and peace did not disquiet the pacifists. No one could call them "impractical persons" if the world's foremost businessman concurred in their ideals. The old-time peaceworkers saw in Ford a Jeffersonian with Hamiltonian money willing to realize their ideas—willing, in fact, to go beyond their work of disarmament and the rewriting of history books to spreading the word in the press and down every other avenue to reach the people. They were particularly responsive to Ford's statement that he was eager for "the aid and advice of every fair-minded man," and his pledge that for "practical opportunities to further peaceful thought our assistance will be given without stint." One of the first to answer that call was the pacifists' highest-ranking spokesman, William Jennings Bryan, who came to Detroit to help Ford decide how to spend his millions for peace. The former secretary of state gave Ford a complimentary subscription to his magazine, *The Commoner*; a paperweight made out of melted-down Department of the Army swords and shaped like a plowshare, such as he had given the ambassadors who had signed his "cooling-off" treaties; and the gift of his silver tongue at a peace meeting in Detroit, if Ford wanted it. In return, the usually fidgety manufacturer gave Bryan forty minutes of his apparently undivided attention.

Letters offering suggestions and requesting interviews reportedly arrived at Ford's office at the rate of six hundred a day. The few who managed to present their ideas or services in person were told by Ford, through his deputy, that he would spend his money under his own auspices and with people he selected himself.

By the fall of 1915 Ford had accepted the infallibility of judgment that others imposed upon him. His perseverance hardened to stubbornness. The man who used to work side by side with the men in the plant now resented any interference, any questioning of his methods or policies. His new tractor company would have no stockholders. ("I have noticed that an efficient business organization is always built up around one man," he told the writer John Reed.) In early October the Ford hospital opened, run solely by himself and his men. And in the middle of the month, James Couzens resigned as company treasurer.

Couzens's resignation from the business operation was bound to come. As hardheaded and egotistical as Ford, he actively resented the latter's increasing absolutism. In the past year, without even mentioning it to his fellow board members, Ford had arranged for the construction of new plants and buildings. What angered the Canadian-born Couzens most, however, was Ford's peace pronouncements and increasing use of *Ford*

Times, their house organ, for anti-preparedness propaganda. At the same time, Ford was not pleased that his vice president and general manager was using company time to build a political following. The blowup came when Couzens, learning that Delavigne's second peace article "by Henry Ford" was set for the October issue of *Ford Times*, demanded that it be removed. Ford insisted that it stay in, and Couzens resigned. "I have disagreed with Mr. Ford's public utterances on finance, preparedness and about everything else of late," Couzens told reporters. "I cannot be carried along on that kind of a kite. I was quite willing to work with Mr. Ford, but not for him." And he added, "it was through my effort that the Ford Motor Company was built up around one man—Henry Ford."

Couzens and his associates in the advertising department had been responsible for much of the public image of the man, but Ford alone was responsible for the continued publicity of his anti-war remarks and his intention to do another good deed for the world. He thought that newspapers could stop the war if they wanted to and that he could stop it himself in two weeks, "if he could speak to the people through the press" of the belligerent nations. He began his one-man campaign the third week in October in San Francisco, where he had gone with Edison to visit their company exhibits at the Panama-Pacific International Exposition, and continued it at every stop his train made across the country on the way back to Detroit.

In California, Ford said he had started a peace bureau in Detroit to distribute educative materials in the States and to conduct a press campaign abroad that would cause the soldiers to lay down their arms by exposing the people who really started the war.

In Denver, Ford said the war would be over in two months if the newspapers told the people that "the money bags of the world's rich men are being added to at the price of countless lives."

In Chicago, he was interviewed standing on the steps of his private railroad car as it went through the yards. America would not go to war, he said, but if she did he would do his share. His peace plans would follow the peace-propaganda tradition and would include some program for opposing the preparedness advocates in Congress.

Henry Ford returned from his holiday on November 15. He had had a good time at the fair, donning overalls to help assemble four Model Ts. The one millionth Model T was scheduled for production within the month, his new mansion was nearly completed, the company had just declared a $5,000,000 dividend, and his name was in the press almost daily. The limelight that he loved shone upon him brightly.

Ford's extravagant peace statements had won him much additional popular good will. He had not, however, either opened a peace bureau or made any definite plans for a peace campaign. Certainly Ford had not expressed any interest in financing a peace expedition to Europe, much less in participating in one. But then no one had yet been able to get past his private secretary, Ernest G. Liebold, to suggest it to him.

CHAPTER 4

"Something is about to occur"

H ENRY FORD MET ERNEST LIEBOLD in 1910, shortly after Mrs. Ford found a check for $75,000 in a pair of her husband's trousers that she was about to send to the cleaners. Couzens insisted that Ford hire someone to manage his business mail, and Liebold, then an ambitious young bank clerk in his mid-twenties, got the job. From the beginning his duties were undefined, but his industriousness and perseverance in getting any job done without disturbing Ford made him the indispensable nonexpert who could manage anything. When Ford took over a floundering hospital, it was Liebold who saw that construction was completed, hired the personnel and ran it like a factory with doctors punching time clocks and surgeons operating on hernias on Mondays, appendixes on Tuesdays, gall bladders on Wednesdays and so on through the week. Whatever Ford's outside interest, Liebold had a big, grasping hand in it, using his power and influence adroitly and ruthlessly and husbanding an authority that increased by default.

Liebold was a man of strong will and competence, devoted to Ford's solitude, sensitive to who and what would interest him, strenuously aggressive yet subservient to his boss's whims and able to extricate him from the impulsive commitments he made in frequent moments of generosity. Because Ford did not care how these tasks were accomplished and because Liebold had few moral scruples, he performed his job perfectly. Those who tried to penetrate this human shield or to work with him found a profit-minded man with the compassion of a tyrant. At the Ford Motor Company the importance of being Ernest G. Liebold was immeasurable.

But Liebold was no Svengali. Henry Ford could be manipulated, but only in directions he was already headed. And Liebold, always an employee and never a friend, could not control what Ford said and did when he was away from the plant. Thus he learned of Ford's promise to give millions for peace by reading his newspaper. Afterward, he turned aside every single applicant who sought any share of the funds, probably with Ford's tacit approval. Miss Addams, Dr. Jordan, Lochner and Mme Schwimmer had all applied for interviews. Jordan and Lochner had been refused outright; Mme Schwimmer, who went directly to Ford's office, had to settle for a tour of the factory, and Miss Addams was bluntly told that Ford would like to see her but only if she said nothing of money, either "directly or indirectly." Every available avenue of influence to the millionaire had been unsuccessfully pursued by the peacemakers.

Had Liebold not been out of town when Ford finally agreed to see the pacifists the Ford Peace Expedition undoubtedly would never have taken place. However, with Liebold away from his post it was possible for a person with good luck, fortitude, the right connections and a project that interested Ford to see him. For one moment, Rebecca Shelly, the former schoolteacher who had been working for peace since her return from The Hague and trying to arrange a Schwimmer-Ford meeting, had them all. Her good fortune was immediately preceded by another victory won through the reluctant offices of the Reverend Samuel S. Marquis, the dean of the Detroit Episcopal Cathedral, who was, by a happy circumstance, Clara Ford's religious counselor.

In 1906, when he was fifty years old, Marquis became the first dean of St. Paul's Cathedral. Anticipating that elevation, the press praised the rector as "whole-souled, scholarly and able," pallid words to describe the energetic, cultivated, even-tempered practitioner of the Social Gospel who concerned himself with the social and economic needs of the laborers in his parish and, after taking a "health class" himself, taught the power of positive thinking as a means to cure physical ills.

In the spring of 1915, Marquis became a volunteer in the Ford Motor Company Sociological Department, advising on welfare matters. By the fall he was worn out by his excessive endeavors and was about to begin a sabbatical year from his church as head of the Sociological Department when Miss Shelly crossed his path and he agreed to give the invocation at the Detroit peace rally early in November. It was his wife, however, who persuaded him to help Miss Shelly in her quest—at least to the extent of introducing her to Edwin Pipp, the managing editor of the Detroit *News*. Though Pipp could not pierce the walls of Ford's private sanctum, after

Henry Ford and the Reverend Samuel S. Marquis (Courtesy of Henry Ford Museum).

hearing of Mme Schwimmer's vain voyage to America to see the president he telegraphed his Washington correspondent to arrange an interview with Wilson for her and Mrs. Ethel Snowden, an English delegate to the women's Hague conference and wife of a Socialist member of Parliament.

Rebecca's major triumph occurred just a few days later. On November 14, Mme Schwimmer returned to Detroit to give her next-to-last lecture in America. Knowing Ford was due home the next day and that Marquis was going to see him, Mme Schwimmer implored the minister to bring her to his patron. Marquis, however, agreed only to show Ford the reports of the interviews the women envoys had had with foreign officials. When two days went by with no news from Marquis, the women tried again on their own.

Futilely Mme Schwimmer saw the incompetent local National Peace Federation representative, who, she understood him to say, had just arranged an appointment with Ford for Lochner (which is why she had Lochner get on the first train to Detroit). Rebecca Shelly, meanwhile, went to see the editor of the Detroit *Journal*. In despair, she told him of the significance and urgency of Mme Schwimmer's message—no doubt mentioning Miss Addams's close connection with the matter—and of the impossibility of seeing Mr. Ford. Ralph Yonker, a reporter who, like Delavigne, had easy access to Ford, agreed to help and left the room to telephone. In a few minutes he was back: Mme Schwimmer had an appointment to see Ford at the factory the next morning, Wednesday, November 17.

When Mme Schwimmer was escorted into Ford's office he was chatting with Dean Marquis (who promptly returned her documents to her, unread by Ford) and Marquis's college classmate, Frederic C. Howe, commissioner of immigration at Ellis Island and a member of the Henry Street group, who had been talking with Ford about the welfare of his immigrant employees. At lunch they were joined by Yonker; Charles Brownell, Ford's advertising manager; Alfred Lucking, his cautious attorney; and William Livingstone, an elderly bank president whose judgment Ford trusted.

From the first course it was clear to Rosika Schwimmer that she was not among friends, except for Howe and Yonker. Nor was she encouraged when, in the course of the conversation, Ford patted his pocket and announced that he had proof that German-Jewish bankers had started the war. Others present scoffed at the interest the European dignitaries allegedly had in the women's plan for neutral mediation. Despite an appointment for the next day, Rosika Schwimmer returned to her hotel completely despondent.

There were too many people around Ford, she told reporters, for her to share her confidential documents with him. The surest sign of the depths of her hopelessness was her self-pitying—and untrue—remark that she had sold her jewels to come to America in pursuit of her dream. Later, Rebecca Shelly and Louis Lochner, who had just arrived, received the full impact of her deep disappointment: Ford would never be persuaded to finance their efforts or urge Wilson to heed them. Her gloom had no effect on the constitutionally optimistic Lochner, who wrote Miss Wales: "Mme Schwimmer is discouraged as can be. I do not feel that way at all. I just *know* something is going to happen within the next few days. I don't know *what* will happen, but something is about to occur."

By the time Mme Schwimmer arrived at the plant the next morning Ford had already seen representatives of the Industrial Peace Conference and an economist, all of them carrying peace plans in their pockets. To her immense delight she had a private interview, and though Ford still refused to read the women envoys' reports, he appeared to believe whatever she said of their experiences and of the devastation of the war, being particularly distressed by the daily waste of thousands of lives. Wishing his wife to share his concern, he invited Mme Schwimmer to lunch at their home the next day. As he escorted his guest from his office he bumped into Lochner, who, at the suggestion of an assistant secretary, had come out to the factory hoping to keep the appointment that in fact had never been made. When this oversight was explained to Ford, and Lochner was introduced to him as "a victim of circumstances," Ford replied, "You are a victim, are you?" and invited the young pacifist to join them the next day. The secretary had by chance hit on a word that triggered Ford's compassion for those unjustly deprived of a chance, and Ford called Lochner his "victim" ever after.

Much encouraged at finding a millionaire who was not only favorably disposed toward her ideas but who treated her with courtesy, Mme Schwimmer returned to her hotel to find more good news: a telegram informing her she would see Wilson on the 26th, the day before her still scheduled departure for Europe.

The Friday visit was a typical Ford "at home." Mme Schwimmer and Mrs. Ford sat down for a chat and Ford, all dressed up for an outing, took Lochner and Delavigne, who had come with them, for a trip to the tractor factory, talking on the way over of his success in employing ex-convicts, of the evils of liquor and tobacco and of the virtues of his tractor. The monologue continued during a guided tour of the premises with not a word about peace work until Ford, alone with Lochner in a small room, finally asked if the women's plan was practicable. Lochner assured him it was and suggested that Ford receive further confirmation from Miss Addams, George Kirchwey, dean of the Columbia Law School, and other advocates of the plan who were then in New York. He also asked Ford to ask Wilson to support their idea and suggested it would be a noble deed if Ford financed the "practically penniless" Mme Schwimmer's effort to get a neutral European country to call the conference if Wilson would not. Writing to Dr. Jordan and Miss Wales of this encounter, Lochner was cautious but confident. "Mme Schwimmer's plan made a deep and lasting impression on him," he said, and Ford definitely favors "the neutral conference mediation idea" but he is extremely leery "about something being put over on him" and "is naturally afraid that we merely want his money." Though Ford had made no outright promise to back them, the fact that he was going to New York "speaks louder than words." The only discouraging observation he had— and one far more ominous than he then realized—was that Ford's mind "jumps from one idea to another, so that we have quite a job to hold him to the thing in hand."

Mrs. Ford, meanwhile, listened sympathetically to Mme Schwimmer's vivid account of the horrors of war endured by European women, including a detailed description of a young woman surgeon who had aged rapidly as a result of sawing off frozen arms and legs. American women must stop the war, she was instructed, by demanding that Wilson form a neutral conference as the women suggested. Mme Schwimmer's eloquence and sincerity, reinforced by her close association with Miss Addams, for whom Mrs. Ford had great regard, won another convert.

After lunch, the Fords' son, Edsel, entertained the guests with a drum solo and then Ford led a tour of Fair Lane, his nearly completed home. Late in the afternoon, Ford and Lochner saw Mme Schwimmer off to New York, where she was the first to tell Jane Addams, the Woman's Peace Party executive council and the Henry Street group of her triumph with the Fords.

Full of praise for one millionaire industrialist's work for peace, Lochner "tore off the lid from the Carnegie foundation," blasting them for their inaction and calling their failure to help the European peace groups both pitiable and shocking. Thus did he bite the hand that fed him, since the Carnegie Endowment helped finance the American Peace Society, which paid his salary. It was a courageous act for Lochner; he was fairly certain it meant his job, and he had no assurance at all that Ford would back the commission, though he suspected he would, but nothing had been said about future employment for him and he had already borrowed on the insurance he carried for his wife and child.

On Saturday, the pacifists were again invited to the Fords for lunch, with Rebecca Shelly standing in for Mme Schwimmer. Following her leader's instructions, Miss Shelly asked Mrs. Ford to subsidize a Woman's Peace Party telegram campaign to national organizations to instruct their members to ask the President to mediate. On her own, Miss Shelly asked her hostess to pay the bills for a Detroit demonstration the day of the Wilson-Schwimmer-Snowden interview. Mrs. Ford agreed to everything because she had Mme Schwimmer's assurance that the European governments would hail her husband as a hero if he helped stop the war nobody wanted to fight.

On Sunday, just one week after he had returned from the west, Henry Ford was on a train again, heading east. The ride to New York was a strange journey for Lochner, who was treading so carefully he did not dare ask Ford to buy his railroad ticket. Having already noticed the hop-skip-and-jump quality of Ford's mind, he continued to be bewildered as he listened to Ford chatter disjointedly and imperceptively on how to fight military preparedness. Instead of discussing how to implement their peace plan, Ford cheerfully coined epigrams—using Lochner as an applause meter—to "weave" into his interviews. He would announce his plans in New York, Ford confided, to ensure maximum publicity for their action, after he conferred with Miss Addams and her colleagues.

While Ford was thus rambling on about his private venture, Jane Addams, Lillian Wald and Mme Schwimmer were calling upon Colonel House in his New York home. It was a tedious interview at first for the colonel as he listened to "the same old story of trying to get the President to appoint a peace commission jointly with other neutral nations . . . to continue making peace proposals until accepted." He explained—to his own satisfaction only—why the president could not do that officially while advising his guests that Wilson would not object to an unofficial commission. That, at least, was something for the women. And it was not a total loss for House either: "As usual, I got them into a controversy between themselves, which delights me since it takes the pressure off myself." Still, much as he mocked them, House valued Miss Addams's political support, and he asked her to send him a note explaining the uses of the plan she proposed so that he might present it to the president. Once again, she wrote simply and starkly of her conviction:

If this war is to be ended with public negotiations and with discussion on the part of the people themselves of the terms of peace, it can only be done through some such clearing house that a Conference of Neutral Nations would afford. Otherwise the people will know nothing of the terms of peace until they are practically ratified; and the only way popular opposition could then express itself would partake of the character of revolution.

To circumvent the censorship imposed by the dominant military party in each belligerent country, she explained further, those who were unofficially preparing possible terms had to have a public forum. House never forwarded her letter to Washington.

Ford and Lochner arrived in New York early Monday morning and were met by Gaston Plantiff, the Ford company's Eastern branch manager. But Plantiff was much more than that to Ford; he and Percival Perry, his English counterpart, were the only two members of the firm who were close family friends. Up to a point Ford and his protégé had much in common. As soon as he finished school, Plantiff left the family farm in central Massachusetts for the big city, where he worked first in a watch factory and then as a bicycle salesman. Before going to work for Ford in 1905, he had been the assistant manager of Wanamaker's automobile department. His spectacular salesmanship for Ford earned him a $2,000 bonus after his first year, and he received even greater rewards for making over $1,000,000 in sales the next year. That sort of talent naturally endeared Plantiff to Couzens; one fancies that Ford, while certainly not disapproving of such attractive proof of his work ethic, took the ex-bicyclist to his heart and hearth because of the man himself. Plantiff was a great mixer, an habitué of New York's Tenderloin, convivial, congenial, warm-hearted and generous; though he literally drank his fill of the wicked city he still endeared himself to the abstemious Fords. Those who moved in New York's less liquid circles called him "a high liver," but to the newspapermen who really knew him well he was a "corking good companion." Within hours of escorting Ford to the Biltmore, Plantiff was to experience the hazards of Ford's philosophy that a capable inexperienced man was better than an expert in any job any day. By nightfall he was managing a peace expedition instead of an automobile business.

Ford and Lochner lunched the day they arrived with Miss Addams, George Kirchwey and Paul Kellogg, editor of the *Survey*, all of whom were leaders of the Henry Street group, and Mme Schwimmer. After affirming for Ford the need of an American-backed mediatory action, official or unofficial, large or small, they turned to the specifics of when to act and by what means. Mme Schwimmer suggested sending a special ship, thinking again of the peace ship she had wanted to hire the past spring for the American delegates to the meeting in The Hague.* The suggestion probably elicited Ford's first comments of the afternoon. Action that generated publicity was mother's milk to him, and a peace ship which he financed would get front-page coverage all over the world. And, as Lochner observed, for Ford any action beat talking about "scientific commissions"—which quite naturally had been the burden of the conversation thus far.

The luncheon participants, having spent some years in the peace movement, were scarcely prepared for the speed with which their new member put his ideas into action. With the exception of Lochner and Mme Schwimmer, none of them seriously regarded the suggestion of an ocean liner for their delegation. On the contrary, among themselves they talked of the half-dozen or so qualified people who would be willing to go abroad *after* European delegates and a conference site were selected.

Ford, however, returned immediately to his hotel and, using one of his favorite aliases, summoned steamship agents to meet "Mr. Henry." Then, leaving Plantiff and his New York lawyers to deal with them, he and Lochner called on Colonel House, the third peace delegation to call on the president's man in two days. House was astonished that Ford's "views regarding peace were so crude and unimportant," and annoyed that every time he maneuvered the conversation to what interested him—manufacturing and employee welfare—Lochner steered it back to peace. Finally, when Lochner challenged House to act, the colonel summarily replied: "I'm not the Government," to which Ford retorted, "But you're close to it." Summing up the interview for his diary, House decided the poorly educated "mechnical genius" was an easy mark for "faddists who desire his money."

Back at the Biltmore after the interview, Ford checked with Mme Schwimmer and the others on the progress of the ship-renting business, told the newspapermen hanging around that they would have their story Wednesday morning and, accompanied by Plantiff and Lochner, went to Washington to see the president.

When Ford first asked for an interview with Wilson he wanted only to express his support for the women's peace program. By Tuesday morning he was ready to tell the president he was going to act himself. Wilson's reaction to the first request for a meeting was almost an unqualified nega-

---

* At Christmas 1914 Mme Schwimmer read of a ship laden with toys being sent to Europe by a Chicago newspaper, and she had hoped a millionaire would hire a boat for a large delegation to the women's conference.

tive: "Mr. Ford has proved himself so unwise recently that I think this interview ought to be avoided if possible." But his press secretary, Joe Tumulty, was just as explicit: "We could not afford to turn Ford down."

Lochner, in the White House again as amanuensis to a famous American for the second time in ten days, was startled by the contrast between the presidential interviews. Dr. Jordan, wearing a frock coat, stood stiffly until asked to sit down, then dispatched his business formally and promptly. Ford, dressed in a plain business suit, sat down nonchalantly in an easy chair, his left leg dangling over its arm, and commented on the president's splendid physical appearance. That was the result, Wilson said, of exercise and refusal to worry (though he might have given Mrs. Edith Galt, to whom he had just become engaged, some credit). Then Ford and Wilson swapped jokes. The president, after listening to the latest Ford joke about the man who asked to be buried with his Model T because it had pulled him out of every other hole he had been in, responded with a limerick,* and one of them ended the round with the one about the Irishman and his mother-in-law. Finally, they talked of militarism and munitions makers, Ford and Lochner insisting that Germany really wanted disarmament and Lochner observing that as the world became more militarized the people had less opportunity to speak their minds.

From that it was a short jump to the neutral conference for continuous mediation, and Ford landed right on target. He had decided to back the women's plan, he told the president, and was hiring the first ship he could find that could take a large delegation to Europe. Not only did he invite Wilson, his son-in-law Secretary of the Treasury William McAdoo, Mrs. McAdoo and Margaret Wilson, another daughter, but he asked the flabbergasted president to appoint the expedition members. Remarking that Dr. Jordan had already submitted the plan to him, Wilson reaffirmed his disinclination to have anything to do with a multinational conference whose decisions he could not control, nor would he officially sanction their enterprise. To do so would preclude consideration of a better plan that might come along, which had been his rebuttal to every presentation of the idea since the pacifists first crossed his threshold. After reaffirming that their informal commission would not embar-

---

* The president probably recited his favorite limerick:

> For beauty I am not a star,
> There are others more handsome by far,
>   But my face, I don't mind it
>   For I am behind it—
> It's the fellow in front that I jar.

rass the president, the pacifists expressed the hope that it would soon win official approval. Though Wilson refused to help with their guest list, he cautioned them not to ask people all of the same mind. As they left the White House, Ford tersely observed to Lochner, "The President is a small man."

To the waiting newspapermen, Ford reportedly reiterated his promise to spend his fortune, if necessary, to end the war and "militarism," and that Christmas was a good time to begin. Back in New York late that night, after a brief appeal for support at the office of the apostolic delegate in Washington, Ford told his new associates that even though the president withheld his blessing, they were sailing as soon as they had their ship. And that was arranged by midnight.

Of course no ship could be chartered in just a few days for the exclusive use of the peace crusaders. Instead, first- and second-class space was engaged on the *Oscar II* of the Scandinavian American line, departing December 4 on a scheduled ten day crossing to Christiania (now Oslo), Norway, that would probably be delayed a day or two at a British port. The steerage passengers remained as a welcome but ignored ballast and the displaced passengers were either compensated; shifted to the *Frederick VIII*, a newer and faster ship leaving a few days later; or permitted to sail as planned, which a few did. That the peace party was sailing on a ship named for Sweden's exemplar of peacemaking, the democratic king who had presided over the peaceful separation of Norway from Sweden and who had been a popular international arbitrator, was naturally considered a good omen. "If he was alive today he would give you a glad hand and assist you in furthering your cause," wrote Ford's travel agent.

At ten o'clock, Wednesday morning, November 24, Henry Ford met the members of the New York press. By then Lochner knew that the industrialist fidgeted and stammered when confronted by more than two reporters and had summoned Oswald Garrison Villard, the editor of the *Evening Post*, to run interference with him. Villard tried to persuade Ford to hand out a prepared statement, explaining that the local press corps did not treat peaceworkers either accurately or kindly, but Ford refused. He had a way with newspapermen, he said, and would easily win them with his slogan: "We'll get the boys in the trenches home by Christmas." Astounded by such an unexpected lack of plain common sense, Villard pointed out that the *Oscar II* would not reach land until December 16 at the earliest and that it would be impossible, even if the war ended that day, to get the ten million men in the trenches home by

Christmas. Ford agreed only to modify his headline grabber—he would not get them home, just "out of the trenches by Christmas." Then, flanked by Lochner and Villard, Ford stepped into the crowded parlor of reporters and photographers.

Right off he blurted out his plan: on December 4 he was sailing on the *Oscar II*, which he had chartered, accompanied by the "most influential peace advocates," who would help him get the boys out of the trenches by Christmas. Their overall intent was to fight preparedness and crush militarism. To do this they would use the biggest "gun" in the world— the Marconi wireless radio, which, with the help of the press, would blare their message of peace. Not even one percent of the people in Europe wanted war, he said, and he intended "to do the greatest good to the greatest number and certainly getting the men out of the trenches will be accomplishing that."

There followed an insistent stream of questions from the scarcely sympathetic crowd, all of which Ford referred to the two gentlemen by his side. Lochner and Villard carefully explained that Ford was backing the plan endorsed by the women's conference the preceding spring, that they had not yet had time to make complete plans but intended their conference to provide the machinery to implement peace talks when the belligerents were ready, that they had good reasons for thinking the citizens of the warring countries wanted an immediate peace, and they carefully pointed out that the ship was *only* the means of transporting "a delegation of important Americans," but little of this saw the printed page the next day.

Eager to mock and quick to deride any private attempt to end the war by any means, the press found further ammunition to shoot down the project in Ford's diffidence, in his very apparent ignorance of what the war was about, in his simplistic reasons for why he thought he could end it and, worst of all, in the spectacle of Lochner and Villard answering all substantive questions while Ford stood silent between them, giving the impression that the well-meaning but naive industrialist was literally being taken for a rather expensive ride. Writing of that morning after forty years in journalism, Villard remembered it as "so extraordinary that I have no parallel to it in all my experience." And Lochner, also writing years later, in perhaps the understatement of his lifetime, suggested "it was not the best possible start that could have been made."

Ford was right when he said he knew how to hit the headlines. GREAT WAR ENDS CHRISTMAS DAY: FORD TO STOP IT, sneered the New York *Tribune* on the front page above a story that bespoke a literary creativity scarcely commensurate with newspaper canon. The lead superciliously announced, "This is the world's greatest Christmas," apparently forgetting the presumed origin of the day's celebration. Most of the other papers placed their accounts less conspicuously. But even they let the

"The Tug of Peace," *Punch* magazine, London, December 15, 1915.

most sensational of the statements made by Ford speak for their own astonishment and ignored the background information supplied by Lochner and Villard. The Detroit *Free Press* did carry Villard's explanation of the purpose of their conference, but that was on a second page and in the last paragraph. Before that the reader learned that "repeated questions disclosed not the slightest evidence that Mr. Ford has a definite plan as to what he is going to do when he gets to Europe." Basically the same story appeared in the Detroit *Journal* following a statement saying Wilson disapproved, which was an editorial supposition that any peace move at that time would antagonize the Allies and the administration.

"Mutt and Jeff—Back? Back Where? Back to the Front!" by Bud
Fisher, San Francisco *Chronicle*, January 22, 1916.

And Franklin Pierce Adams, in his "Conning Tower," bet Ford "one slightly used run-about against a set of slipcovers" that he would neither stop this war nor all future wars as he reportedly promised.

Day after day increasingly inaccurate, irresponsible and damaging front-page reports followed these first accounts. The tenor of the stories was the result of the newspapers' bias, but a good bit of the inaccuracy was the product of the pandemonium always present in the expedition's cramped headquarters in the Biltmore Hotel. Ford had selected New York's newest hostelry, a modern Italian Renaissance palace, the home away from home of European royalty, to house his latest fancy. Through the marble-walled lobby and down the corridors, hour after hour and day after day, hundreds of supplicants trod the luxuriant rugs, ascended to the seventh floor, and lined the narrow hall to a small suite of small offices rapidly filling up with typists, stenographers, translators, multilith operators and messengers, many of them on temporary duty from the Ford Long Island City office, and none of them able to tell a pacifist from a handsaw. The day of the announcement was prelude to two weeks of confusion and commotion, derision and harassment, exhilaration and exhaustion.

The first telegrams of invitation, sent on the 24th and 25th to 115 people, announced prematurely and erroneously the acceptances of John Wanamaker, Thomas Edison and Jane Addams, and invited the recipients to sail as Ford's guests to join "leading" European men and women "at some central point, to be determined later," there to "establish an international conference dedicated to negotiations leading to a just settlement of the war." Before that, the peace pilgrims would stop at Christiania, Stockholm and Copenhagen. How the conference was to be established and other details would be covered in a letter that was on its way. The last paragraph of the telegram made the pitch for participation:

> With 20,000 men killed every twenty-four hours, tens of thousands maimed, homes ruined, another winter begun, the time has come for a few men and women with courage and energy, irrespective of the cost in personal inconvenience, money, sacrifice and criticism, to free the goodwill of Europe that it may assert itself for peace and justice, with the strong probability that international disarmament can be accomplished.

Ford had told his aides that Wanamaker was going with him, but within a few days the man who earlier had told Ford he would go to the ends of the earth with him in pursuit of peace reneged as the ridicule, the haste in preparations and the haphazard selection of delegates became so quickly evident. Ford's expectation that his friends would stand by his side met the same disappointment. Apparently hoping to get the gang together for an outdoor excursion, he invited Edison, John Burroughs and Luther Burbank. Privately Edison did not think the idea worth anything at all; publicly he said he was too busy. Burroughs's doctor suggested that a winter crossing of the North Atlantic followed by a trek through northern Europe would contribute very little to his eighty-year-old patient's longevity. And Burbank declined for the same reason.

Jane Addams, Rosika Schwimmer and Louis Lochner invited most of the guests that first day. Though Mme Schwimmer overrode her prejudices when it came to asking the best political and international minds, she vetoed many who had not taken her to their hearts. She also invited several socially conscious millionaires just to show them that she had arrived, a tactic that "was very, very obvious" to Lochner. And she asked all the good ladies who had formed the legions behind their bold Boadicea in her battle for American action despite their lack of discernible qualifications. The luminaries invited the first few days were those active in social reform or with some political connection to the Wilson administration. Though Ford forbade invitations to congressmen, wishing their friends on the Hill to stay home to battle the administration's preparedness program, several were asked. Every state and territorial governor was invited, not in the expectation of acceptance, but in the hope that their favorably worded refusals would be good publicity. Suffrage leaders and friends of peace among the clergy and academe were also summoned.

For the next two days Mme Schwimmer, Lochner and Ford were in and out of the Biltmore like so many bouncing balls. Emmy Lochner arrived with her baby daughter to spend Thanksgiving with her husband but did not see him for even "ten uninterrupted minutes." Ever the good lieutenant, Lochner spent Thanksgiving Day with William Howard Taft, the president of the newly founded League to Enforce Peace, who was hurrying across the river and through the town from train station to train station, already two hours late for his holiday dinner in New Haven. For his pains, Lochner was told—though not in so many words—that the expedition was "a fool performance," "a waste of effort . . . that organized emotion would not accomplish anything" and that Taft "would not have anything to do with it."

Ford, meanwhile, combined business with pleasure trying to persuade Thomas Edison to join his expedition and also talking with a real-estate agent about New Jersey property.

Early Friday morning, Ford and Lochner, accompanied by Mme Schwimmer and a small coterie, went to Washington again, this time to participate in the "Mothers' Day" peace demonstration planned to support Mme Schwimmer's and the English suffragist Mrs. Snowden's visit with the president. At the meeting—held in the Belasco Theatre cater-corner to the White House—Dean Samuel Marquis gave the invocation, Lochner said that Ford agreed with Miss Addams that young men fought wars on orders from their elders, Mrs. Snowden called for a permanent and constructive peace and a demand for the war's end by neutral nations, and Mme Schwimmer gave another of her blood-and-guts addresses. When Ford was called upon to speak, he hastily explained he had never spoken in public before and only asked the audience "to remember the slogan 'Out of the trenches by Christmas—never to go back' " before he retired to his seat to the sound of wild cheers. Then the audience of women escorted Mme Schwimmer and Mrs. Snowden to the White House and stood in silent vigil for forty-five minutes while the two women gave the president the just-passed resolutions asking him to "call upon the other neutral nations to appoint representatives to assemble in conference for constant mediation without armistice" and requested that he add them to the thousands of telegrams he had already received. Wilson politely told his guests that he, too, favored mediation, though not by conference, but had no evidence that the belligerents were ready to negotiate. At that, said Mrs. Snowden, "Rosika grew voluble, bitter, insulting," implying that Wilson would not act because America was profiteering from the war.

While taking Marquis to the train station, Ford was listening to a message that his wife had sent her pastor to deliver. Clara Ford had not only been reading about her husband's promise to spend his fortune to stop the war but had received a phone call from him to pack their bags so they could both go to Europe. The message was short and simple: to come home at once and "follow the advice of Dr. Marquis. He is discreet and wise." Her itinerant husband promised to be home by Monday.

In the next twenty-four hours Ford, with Lochner as his mouthpiece, made several calls in Washington, Baltimore and Philadelphia. Supreme Court Justice Charles Evans Hughes half-heartedly promised to study the Wales plan; Cardinal Gibbons, the highest Catholic prelate in America, admired Ford's "roseate view" of world affairs and blessed the undertaking, and John Wanamaker listened to their arguments and then gave Lochner a copy of *Pollyanna*, the story of the fatuous optimist.

Disappointed but not discouraged by these turndowns, Ford and

Lochner returned to New York. With scarcely a minute to spare, Ford boarded the train for home and "Mother," and Lochner plunged again into the turmoil at the Biltmore.

As soon as she returned to her suite in Washington's New Willard, Rosika Schwimmer telegraphed her friends that Wilson had been gracious and she was greatly encouraged. The prestige, power and money that she now commanded in Ford's name had evidently caused her to forget that not a month earlier she was certain the belligerent governments would not "listen to proposals made by unofficial people" and that the European neutral governments would not favor an unofficial conference. Her days with Ford thus far indicated that his money flowed from a bottomless well. Husbands who would not go to Europe without their wives were invited to bring them along. Lola Maverick Lloyd's three children and their governess were invited. Miss Wales's $900 obligation to the University of Wisconsin was paid. Ford wrote a check on the spot to the Woman's Peace Party to cover an $8,000 misunderstanding in his wife's telegram campaign and promised $20,000 in matching funds to the Henry Street group to fight preparedness and $200,000 to Mme Schwimmer for the International Committee of Women for Permanent Peace, whose plan he thought he was sponsoring. Ford was caught in the spirit of the sensational gesture he had made; his new colleagues did not know then that a spontaneous Ford pledge seldom went through his bank.

Rosika Schwimmer thought she was in fairyland. "All I have to do is wave my wand for what I think is necessary for our Peace Mission," she told Lochner, "and lo! it appears." She took her wand to Washington and waved it in the direction of the neutral embassies. The caravan of delegates through the neutral capitals was her idea, aimed at turning out the peace troops at meetings that would be the talk of the Continent. On the strength of her association with European suffragists and her understanding of the interviews she had had with neutral statesmen the preceding spring, she had assured Ford they would be warmly welcomed by the governments, the people and the press, and that their mission would attract qualified delegates eager to serve. To ensure such a reception she combined her industriousness and effrontery with Ford's name and money and told several of the neutral European ministers to Washington to inform their governments that the peace expedition under the direction of Henry Ford and herself was on its way and expected official cooperation. The Danish and Spanish ministers refused to see her, but at the Norwegian and Swiss legations she opened one-thousand-dollar cable accounts so that her messages would not only avoid delays and censorship but receive the imprimatur of diplomatic transmission. Back at her hotel she fired off a salvo of cables to press services, neutral European newspapers and her neutral European friends, instructing the latter to appoint welcoming committees, arrange official receptions, publicize the coming of the pilgrims and advise their respective governments that nothing would be done to embarrass them. In little more than twenty-four hours she spent $900, almost $600 of it on cables and telegrams and over $100 on the four-hour train ride with her two assistants back to New York.

Jane Addams had gone to Detroit on Thanksgiving Day to speak at the Mothers' Day peace meeting co-chaired by Clara Ford. She left New York utterly distressed that "the plan had fallen into the hands of Mr. Ford who had long taken an inexplicable position in regard to peace propaganda" and into the hands of "a group of very eccentric people." Above all she feared that "the offer of a crusading journey to Europe with all expenses paid could but attract many fanatical and impecunious reformers." But when she suggested to Ford that a few properly selected delegates could get to Europe on their own, he insisted a peace ship would get world coverage and the more publicity the better.

Miss Addams did not disapprove of publicity, only of the ballyhoo already attendant on the activities at the Biltmore which was bound to increase as the circuslike expedition proceeded through Europe. As she gathered her warm clothing for the trip she listened to her friends' pleas that she disassociate herself from a doomed enterprise, but she held firm to her resolve. To be exposed to "ridicule and social opprobrium" and "probably never be applauded again" she thought "a small price to pay for a protest against war." It was the conference that mattered. Not that the belligerents would heed its appeals until they were ready for peace, but by publicizing the projected peace settlement the conferees would be conducting open diplomacy and permitting the English and German anti-war groups to learn each other's views. The essential soundness of that endeavor, she was certain, would in a short time eclipse the damage done by the expedition itself. She tried to persuade herself that Ford's wild promise to "get the boys out of the trenches by Christmas" was consistent with Tolstoy's injunction that everyone must "cease to do evil" regardless of the consequences as soon as they realized they were doing it. She even tried to believe that the spectacle was a necessary spot of color for the traditionally "quietistic and much too grey and negative" anti-war movement. But her attempts at stifling her revulsion to the aura of moral adventure generated in New York were not completely successful.

She phoned Lochner "begging him to keep the enterprise in hand," to concentrate on the conference not the conveyance; but propinquity had much to do with the direction of Lochner's attention, and he, after all, was only nominally second-in-command. Almost daily, Miss Addams received complaints either from the members of the executive committee of the Woman's Peace Party in Chicago and New York or from the International Committee of Women for Permanent Peace in Holland charging Rosika Schwimmer with "crude fanaticism and self-exploitation" and asking that their organizations have as little to do with her as possible. However, Jane Addams felt obliged, as she told her Chicago friends, to sail on the *Oscar* if only to temper the pyrotechnics of the expedition's volatile adviser.

Like Miss Addams, Henry Ford was staving off the arguments of family and friends. Clara Ford had been pleased to contribute money and to chair a meeting for a peace drive sponsored by Miss Addams. She could even sustain the temporary presence of the frenetic Rebecca Shelly, who had been sent back to Detroit when word leaked to the reporters that she was engaged to marry a German soldier. But her husband sailing to Europe through mined seas with a shipload of maniacs and free-loaders—as they were called in the papers—was too much. She refused to go with him, fearing they would be torpedoed and Edsel left an orphan, and she pleaded with her husband, as did William Livingstone, Ford's friend and banker, and the Reverend Samuel Marquis, to give up the ship.

Ford countered Marquis's argument "to go slower or to put the matter in a different way" by asking, "Is it right? Am I not doing right, Marquis? Is there anything wrong about trying to do all I can to get the world to try to think of peace?" When the clergyman, perforce, said no, Ford recited the minister's teaching: "What's right cannot fail. . . . It's the only thing I can do and I am plenty able to do it." After three days of this circular colloquy, Marquis went home and packed his bag. "You and I reason about these things intellectually," he explained to some Detroit businessmen, "but Mr. Ford feels them with the heart of a child." Officially the minister went as a peace delegate; Mrs. Ford assigned him the further job of guarding her husband.

Even Livingstone, not constrained by moral argument as Marquis was, had no effect. Neither did Ernest Liebold. He had read about Ford's flight to New York in the clutches of peaceworkers when he was in Denver, thought it might be a temporary aberration and, reasoning that his office knew where to find him, continued his inspection of Ford premises in the provinces. By the time he saw his boss again, he could do nothing. Only once did Ford appear to waver when he phoned his peace managers in

New York and asked if his sailing with them was necessary. Their un-categorical assurance that his absence would signify his lack of faith and guarantee the expedition's failure convinced him he must go, and no one could persuade him otherwise. "Nothing dampens his enthusiasm," a friend remarked, "when he knows he's right."

Ford always followed his hunches, and this hunch had every appealing attribute: it meant action, it was sensational, it defied convention and conformity, it was needed and wanted, it was for the betterment of the common man, it stopped the waste of lives and substance, it struck at the vested interests in government and business that profited from war, it promised glory. The chance to be the world's peacemaker if he was only willing to spend the money was irresistible. Having talked of peace for months, he was overripe for action.

The day after Ford returned to Detroit he hired Theodore Delavigne, the reporter who had initially made him a front-page pacifist, as his domestic peace secretary. Delavigne's ostensible assignment was to speak for Ford against preparedness, but the first service that verbally improvi-dent young man performed in his new role sent several European minis-ters in a panic to the State Department. Courtesy of Delavigne, the papers reported Ford proclaiming:

I have all faith that on Christmas Day the world will see a general strike—that on that day of days war-worn men will climb down from the trenches, throw down their arms and start home. . . . A general strike on Christmas Day, that is what we want.

The statement also raised havoc in the expedition headquarters in New York, where the already harried organizers promptly blamed press ir-responsibility for the gross distortion of their purpose and sent disclaim-ers to the European governments. Later, Lochner complained bitterly that "orders given in New York were countermanded in Detroit" and Ford Motor Company news releases conflicted with those from the Biltmore, but at the time he was neck-deep in much more imperative problems.

CHAPTER 5

"Not the best possible start"

It was bedlam at the Biltmore. A stream of self-proclaimed messiahs, swift-tongued opportunists and inventors anxious to sell Ford a better way to make a motor car jammed the corridors and turned the expedition's suite of five tiny rooms into Liberty Hall. Messengers and mailmen wormed their way down the halls to dump their bags of telegrams and letters onto the desks of an inexperienced and badly managed staff which was trying not only to sift the acceptances from the rejections and the superfluous suggestions from the legitimate inquiries, but also to cope with a mountain of memoranda and miscellaneous instructions reminding passengers to bring warm clothing and passports and informing the press of the supposed latest authentic list of participants. Frantically and unsuccessfully, the staff tried to keep track of those who were "invited and coming, invited and not coming, coming but not invited."

A woman appeared one day with a family recipe for an herbal remedy guaranteed to cure wounded soldiers. Another demanded passage because she had rolled fifteen thousand bandages for the Belgians. The lyricist of "I Didn't Raise My Boy to Be a Soldier" demanded an invitation; the composer of "I Raised My Boy to Be a Soldier" demanded publicity. Newspaper clipping services and film companies, playwrights and poets, a

[78]

minstrel and an impersonator of Charles Dickens's characters, all offered their wares or their presence.

Phony invitations were sent to Dr. Moses Stearns, a perpetual mayoralty candidate in Philadelphia who lambasted Sunday blue laws weekly in the City Hall plaza, and to Dr. Charles G. Pease, president of the Non-Smokers' Protective League. Stearns was tactfully uninvited but threatened to sue Ford for $50,000 to cover the cost of his public embarrassment and the life preserver and water wings he had bought for the trip. The first the organizers heard of Pease was his telegram of acceptance, on which a puzzled Lochner had scribbled: "See Who's Who." The clergyman was a proper Christian who had endeared himself to New Yorkers by hauling off those who smoked on subways into the embrace of the nearest policeman. Though Pease was finally invited, he declined "on account of professional engagements and the feelings of my mother."

The formal letter of invitation to the delegates was sent on November 27, only one week before departure. No more time could be wasted waiting for the government to act, it stated; the people of America on "the greatest mission ever before a nation" must lead. The women envoys had obtained "full evidence" that European neutrals were certain "a mediating conference" would end the war. Because of "diplomatic etiquette," however, the evidence could not be publicly expressed. In Europe, the Americans would be joined by "Norway's valiant sons and daughters," the choicest of Sweden's democracy and Denmark's "harbingers of peace." In six weeks, after many meetings and much publicity, they would reach The Hague, where they would select all the conference delegates and the peace pilgrimage would end. By then, "the moral power of the peace movement will be irresistible." The letter concluded with a brief outline of the plan: the international conference, sitting in a neutral capital, would consist of a small deliberative group of representatives from each neutral country and would be joined by international authorities from the belligerent countries to frame an equitable peace dedicated to the "abolition of competitive armaments."

There is no certain record of who received the first telegrams, the formal letters of invitation and the later invitations that were sent hour by hour as friends suggested names or unknown enthusiasts suggested themselves. There is, however, an exhaustive record of those who declined to go.

Only one of the fifty-one state and territorial governors, plus the lieutenant governor of South Carolina, accepted. Six governors sent representatives and almost forty wired their regrets with suitable expressions of sympathy that were released to the press. Louis B. Hanna, governor of North Dakota, arrived in New York with his sidekick, Sam Clark, editor of a periodical of personal opinion, talking of the necessity for preparedness. He was hardly in the spirit of the mission, but the governor was up for reelection and a free ride to the homelands of many of his constituents was beyond his power to refuse.

Not a single prominent man of business, science, education or national government accepted. Julius Rosenwald, the philanthropic president of Sears, Roebuck, did not think he could be of service; H. J. Heinz, the foodpacker of many varieties, thought the president knew what he was doing and that Ford's commission, in any case, should be composed of statesmen, diplomats and international lawyers. Wanamaker, whom Lochner had gone to see once more, declined with a public statement that Ford had "a mission, a generous heart and a fat pocketbook; but he has no plan to stop the war."

Charles Steinmetz and John Dewey, Louis Brandeis and Robert La Follette, William Dean Howells and Zona Gale, Walter Lippmann and Herbert Croly, all sent their regrets and best wishes, and Vachel Lindsay sent autographed copies of his poems of Lincoln, Buddha and Tolstoy to Ford as tokens of his support. Colonel House spoke only of previous engagements; Mayor Newton D. Baker of Cincinnati—soon to become secretary of war—refused because he was not "wise enough about the causes of the European War or the conditions of possible peace to be of any help" and "for reasons altogether too personal and complicated to detail." Charles W. Eliot, president emeritus of Harvard, in declining told Ford the pilgrimage was "probably fruitless and surely calamitous if peace were brought about on any terms now conceivable." Frederic Howe, having heard through the House grapevine that Wilson appointees were to stay home, simply telegraphed, "All kinds of obstacles prevent my going to Europe. Am sorry." Rabbi Stephen Wise excused himself, and Dr. Felix Adler, founder of the Ethical Culture Society, not only saw little hope that the peoples of Europe wanted their governments to end the war but feared that future American attempts would be jeopardized by Ford's unwanted and unwise action.

Every well-known socialist had been invited and had refused to go. Peace now, they said, would mean only an armed truce till the next time, but a war to the end would exhaust the capitalist nations. The expedition "is not only hopelessly futile but likely to do infinite mischief," Charles Edward Russell warned. Helen Keller wrote Ford a long letter expressing compassion for the worker-soldier in the trenches and advising that her lecture bureau would not let her cancel her engagements. Professor William Hull, an active Quaker pacifist, could not leave Swarthmore College. Eighty-year-old Social Gospel minister Washington Gladden said he would go if his son could accompany him, but then, after receiving that confirmation, was "constrained to decline" because of family illness. Ida Tarbell, the muckraking journalist, did not think they had a chance of success and would not go despite Miss Addams's pleadings. Ford, she later commented, would never have built an engine in such haste and with so little preparation. Feminists Fanny Garrison Villard and Anna Howard Shaw also said no. A leader of the conservative General Federation of Women's Clubs accepted with alacrity but, at the last minute, was suddenly "threatened with pneumonia" and did not sail. Roger Babson, an economist with his own peace plans, could not go, but he and the mayor of Philadelphia had Betsy Ross's granddaughter assist in making an expedition flag.

Katherine Leckie, Mme Schwimmer's lecture agent, took advantage of old friendships and asked Clarence Darrow and Brand Whitlock either to join or endorse the venture. Darrow told her he did not think "it is wise or right for us to interfere," principally because America had thus far done nothing but make money out of the war, and Brand Whitlock, the minister to Belgium on home leave, spent a perfectly hideous evening, according to his account, listening to talk of "this foolish project of Henry Ford and his sublime peace ship." Finally toward midnight Miss Leckie went to phone, he thought, for a taxi. Instead, a few minutes later, there "appeared a rather dowdy little Hungarian Jewess, very dark and grinning through wide separated teeth." Mme Schwimmer made no friend of the acerbic Whitlock, who sat silent through her discourse hoping she would leave.

Congressman Richard Bartholdt, the founder of the American branch of the Interparliamentary Union, the international organization of national legislators, was anxious to go, provided his wife and her nurse could accompany him. With arrangements made, he backed down to save Ford embarrassment since his "pro-German sentiments" were well known in America. Had he been pro-Ally, he bitterly noted, he could have gone with no adverse comment. William Jennings Bryan wanted to go to Berlin and talk the kaiser into ending the war. Joining the Ford Peace Expedition might pave his way—or it might wreck his chances. Upon receiving an invitation, he pointedly suggested that "the success of the trip will depend largely upon the President's attitude" and asked if Wilson was sympathetic. The evasive reply was not satisfactory and Bryan kept his options open: he would remain home to fight preparedness for the time being and was coming to New York to explain this to Ford. At the same time, he arranged for two friends to travel with the party and keep him informed.

The expedition organizers did not grieve excessively over the loss of Bryan. He had a reputation abroad, as Miss Wales and Colonel House had earlier remarked, as a mental lightweight and therefore would not attract the scientific thinkers the conference required. Nor were the leaders at all distressed by the hundreds of rejections from the prominent. They hardly expected every famous liberal American to join them, but thought they lost nothing by asking. Disparaging replies were suppressed, encouraging remarks publicized.

However, rejections from the Henry Street group and from the executive board of the Woman's Peace Party—the supposed American sponsors of the peace plan—if not disquieting to the leadership were certainly disastrous to the mission. One by one, Lillian Wald, George Foster Peabody, Oswald Garrison Villard, George Kirchwey, Crystal Eastman Benedict, Hamilton Holt and Paul Kellogg declared their first obligation was to preserve social reforms at home, which they feared would be destroyed by Wilson's preparedness program. Lobbying members of Congress was thus more imperative than stopping the war through a neutral conference—or so they said. In fact these peacemakers were deeply pained at what had happened to the neutral conference plan and they tried to weave a silver lining for the monstrous cloud created by the peace ship and its populous crew. All would not be lost if, in the end, out of the tumult and shouting, there was created a small commission of qualified international experts from both neutral and belligerent countries that would study the causes of the war and make continual suggestions to the belligerents for a peace settlement in the "spirit of constructive internationalism" till a basis for negotiation was agreed upon. At lunches and dinners, by telegraph and letter, they fed these words of caution and advice to Lochner, the only one of the managers they thought they could reason with. Rosika Schwimmer was always impervious to any arguments but her own, and no one dared tell Ford that his passion for brash publicity was not the way to win friends or influence people. Only one person publicly told their well-heeled gift horse to kindly close his mouth.

The Reverend Anna Garlin Spencer, professor of sociology and ethics at Meadville Theological School and vice president of the Woman's Peace Party, was one of the five people Jane Addams knew who had agreed to go and then declined. Before she changed her mind, Dr. Spencer tried to change Ford's in a letter she released to the New York *Times* in which she said that his publicity-seeking slogan and the haste in sailing were perilous errors bound to result in their not having ten men competent to do the work of constructive mediation. Not at all, Lochner good-naturedly replied, they would certainly attract "at least ten men well known and deservedly trusted" and he hoped Mrs. Spencer would "be one of them." That reply brought Mrs. Spencer to the Biltmore, but her visit with Lochner and Mme Schwimmer confirmed her fears, and she hastily wrote Miss Addams to reconsider her acceptance as she had done herself. Any woman going, she reminded Miss Addams, would be "compromised" by Mme Schwimmer and would be surrounded by "some inferior women" who would be "specially under her influence," as was Mr. Ford.

Mrs. Spencer could not help but realize that whether she went or not was of only perfunctory concern to either of the principal organizers. That was definitely not the case when it came to the refusals sent by David Starr Jordan and Emily Greene Balch. Lochner sent telegram after telegram to his mentor, foretelling doom for the peace venture if it sailed without its "original champion." Trusting that Jordan was beyond the delivery zone of New York newspapers while traveling on a Southern lecture tour, Lochner even wired him that the metropolitan press was "dead in earnest with us." Though he wanted very much to go abroad for peace, Jordan was too jealous of his reputation to affiliate with "a shipload of amateurs" gathered together with such ill-considered haste and publicity and managed by the "emotional and intense" Rosika Schwimmer. "In my scheme," he wrote his wife, "there will be no Schwimming."

Lochner tried flattery with Jordan; Mme Schwimmer used presumption with Miss Balch. The Wellesley College professor declined because she could not "desert" her classes as she had done the previous spring to attend the Hague conference. But Miss Balch was Mme Schwimmer's idea of a perfect delegate, being both an admirer of hers and knowledgeable in international affairs, and therefore her reasons for refusing were inadequate. When she remained steadfast, Mme Schwimmer telegraphed the Wellesley faculty and students to put Miss Balch on the train to New York. Professor Balch, however, remained in Wellesley.

Lochner, on the other hand, resigned his job—before he was fired. In a letter acknowledging the resignation, Henry C. Morris, the president of the Chicago Peace Society, praised Lochner's executive abilities and, noting that he had searched in vain in the newspapers for "a full statement of the objects of the trip," suggested that Lochner release an explicit statement of precisely what their mission expected to accomplish, how they were going to do it and why.

It was a sensible request, perhaps, but its fulfillment was inconsistent with the entire evolution of the scheme. Every statement of the plan thus far—by Rosika Schwimmer in London, the Woman's Peace Party in Washington, Julia Grace Wales at the Emergency Peace Federation in Chicago, the International Committee of Women for Permanent Peace in The Hague and the Henry Street group in New York—were specific and consistent only in the intent of the plan and always general in the means of its execution. There were two distinctly different *styles* of operation: that of a small neutral commission publicizing its work and that of a large-scale conference operating with a great deal of publicity about its existence but not always about what it was doing. Mme Schwimmer favored the latter method and had already purposefully created an aura of intrigue and mystery by telling reporters that she had evidence, which she could not disclose, that certain neutral countries, which she could not mention, approved their action. Following Mme Schwimmer's lead, Lochner repeated only the contents of the letter of invitation to one reporter and told another there was no need for a preconceived plan, the conference would be successful because its "keynotes" were faith and moral suasion, two undefeatable forces to many Americans at that time.

Henry Morris concluded that he had not seen a clear statement because the press was not giving "Mr. Ford fair play or a square deal." His observation was wrong but his conclusion was correct. Had the peace expedition sailed in the first days of the war it might have had the good wishes of the people and the press. By December 1915, though the country still thought itself neutral it was in fact predominantly pro-Ally. The pacifists' petitions to the president and the large attendance at meetings notwithstanding, most concerned citizens believed the president was doing all that could be done to end the war and to protect American interests.

Because the Eastern establishment newspapers could not believe that a man able to make millions with a motor car could be so benighted as to try to stop the war when Germany was winning, they said the industrialist was being duped by the unscrupulous and the incapable who were intent only on their own aggrandizement. Ford was the country rube being gulled by the city slickers. Therefore, though it was Ford who supplied the reporters with most of the ammunition to attack the expedition, he was usually treated kindly. One or two said he was only advertising himself and his motor car, but most pardoned his ignorance and praised his courage and humanitarianism. He "is really a fine, earnest man whose impulses are not sufficiently corrected by education nor by experience outside of mechanics," wrote Mark Sullivan, the editor of *Collier's*. "He rushes in where angels fear to tread," said the humor magazine *Life*. His plan "does his heart and soul more credit than it does his head," said the Boston *Transcript*. Of those who criticized Ford's action while praising his motives, Edgar Guest said it best:

> It may be folly, it may be wrong, and all that critics say,
> And to end the strife and the slaughter grim this may not be the way,
> I've shaken my head in a time of doubt, I confess that I cannot see
> Whether or not it's the thing to do, or just what the end will be,
> But just the same when your ship sets out, I'll cheer for your
>   splendid pluck
> And wave my hand in a fond farewell and wish you the best of luck.

Others who were not so gentle called Ford a knight errant leading a children's crusade, a "mechanical genius of a sweet and loyal disposition with almost boundless ignorance," impractical and maladroit. In an editorial entitled "A Little Child Shall Lead Them," the *New Republic* remarked: "Mr. Ford belongs to the tradition of self-made men, to that primitive Americanism which has held the theory that a successful manufacturer could turn his hand with equal success to every other occupation." Ford was treating the boys in the trenches in the same paternalistic manner he treated the boys in his plant. What was good for the Ford Motor Company was good for America, and what was good for America was good for the world. When told only a miracle could bring him success, Ford retorted: "Miracles are only the aspiration of the many carried out by the few."

The journalists, ignoring the tenets of their trade—reliability and verification—hounded the management of the mission and fed off the cranks and crackpots, the fools and frauds, who were peddling their panaceas in the Biltmore hallways. Every rumor however inconsequential or improbable, every minor gaffe that was derogatory to the enterprise, was printed: the cable sent to a pope who had been dead almost a thousand years; the New York authority who allegedly said Ford and his followers might be jailed for violating the Logan Act of 1798, which outlawed private citizens interfering in foreign affairs; the news that the *Oscar II* was still more than fifteen hundred miles out to sea and would never sail on time, when it was already in port; the rumor that if the ship did sail no European country would let it land because of the threatened strike in the trenches. The wags and wits had their fling at "that wonderful yachting party," the "innocents abroad," and the "jitney peace-excursion." Franklin P. Adams suggested that the party had "stop-over privileges at the Scilly Islands." The most frequent epithets were "grotesquely farcical," "fantastical," "mischievous" and "Quixotic." After reading hundreds of editorials, Mark Sullivan concluded that only half a dozen showed any freshness of mind; the rest were ground out "with coarse irony and crude invective."

Of the conference itself—even of the concept of the conference—there was scarcely a word. Only a very few praised the selflessness and sincerity of the delegates. None even hinted that some who sailed might have made a sacrifice by interrupting their lives for six weeks at such a time and at such short notice. The Philadelphia *Evening Bulletin* at least printed delegate Mary Fels's chastisement of the press:

> It isn't funny, this wave of merriment. . . . rather, it is horrible to think that a nation can laugh against such a frightful background as that of Europe. Instead of making jokes, we should all be on our knees praying for the success of the venture.

The widow of the Fels-Naptha soap manufacturer went on to say she certainly was not crossing the winter seas in wartime for pleasure but fulfilling her duty to arouse her country, which had been passively resigned to years of slaughter, and the world "from its inertia."

A sympathetic rabbi wondered how the foreign press and statesmen could possibly respect a mission that the American newspapers castigated and ridiculed. But the British and French needed no cues from across the sea. Making a rather feeble attempt at double-entendre, a Labour member asked in Parliament: "Have they not a right of asylum here, and cannot we certify them?" And the London *Times* reported daily on the pro-German pilgrims' progress, labeling Ford's antics "the product of megalomania." *The Spectator* called Ford "self-important and boisterous" and laughed at his qualifications for making peace, suggesting that the *Oscar*'s sides carry the letters "S.O.F." to signify that it was both a "Ship of Fools"* and a "Ship of Ford." The French were offended that a "traveling troupe" thought that "simply by making speeches" it

---

* The title of a popular satiric poem of contemporary foibles and follies written by Sebastian Brant, a Swiss professor of canon law, and first published ca. 1496. T. H. Jamieson, in an introduction to a later edition of *Das Narren Schyft*, observed: "Brant's fools are represented as contemptible and loathsome rather than *foolish*, and what he calls follies might be more correctly described as sins and vices."

could persuade nations fighting desperately for survival to lay down their arms. Even so, while the French newspapers chided Ford for his "ignorance," they excused him as a "dupe" of his "illusions" that only munitions makers wanted war. The German press was leery of an American-originated peace drive and treated the attempt as a "manifestation of American eccentricity."

It was all the same to Henry Ford. He was getting just what he wanted: peace talk on the front pages. It did not matter that most called him foolish and unwise; it was not the first time he had gone against the odds certain that he was right. To ensure continued coverage after they sailed, Ford had his assistants ask members of the press to join them on the *Oscar II* and on the European excursion.

Gaston Plantiff, Ford's man in New York, probably selected a few of the New York reporters who were his drinking companions in the Tenderloin. Katherine Leckie, the suffragist publicity agent whom Mme Schwimmer appointed to direct the expedition's press relations, invited many of the women reporters who she knew would be sympathetic to their mission. News film companies eagerly sought exclusive rights to immortalize the hegira for posterity, as did several news photographers. Some journalists sought and received invitations. Several came aboard carrying both press and delegate credentials.

In the end, every major New York City paper and papers in Boston, Philadelphia, Chicago and San Francisco, the three principal wire services and several magazines sent correspondents. Editors of papers in the South and Midwest asked and received accreditation for correspondents, as did editors of fraternal-organization publications and New York-based ethnic papers. Free-lance writers and cartoonists who expressed sympathy for the project or who knew Mme Schwimmer were invited. A few who went served only a very limited readership; some were anxious to be part of the pilgrimage and contrived credentials to get on board, and a few, a very few, went just for a six-week joyride. Because Ford's friends and business associates did not want the hometown folks to read about Ford's folly, they exerted pressure on Detroit newspaper editors and none sent a correspondent except one who sent a suffragist reporter. Instead, the Detroit *News* and the Detroit *Journal* arranged to be represented by New York reporters already booked to sail.

The journalists were invited to observe and report; a group of about forty "live wire" college students—as Ford called them—were invited to observe and learn. On Monday, November 29, with the boat due to leave on Saturday, Lochner sent telegrams to the presidents and some faculty

members of "prominent universities" asking them to recommend under-
graduates, using Rhodes Scholarship criteria, who believed "in international understanding and fellowship." The president of Princeton
University refused outright to name a student because he did not think
"the efforts of individual citizens" would result in proper peace terms.
The presidents of Yale, Wisconsin, Smith and Minnesota said they had no
authority to select anyone; others refused because they either did not
have time or they could not ask students to suspend their studies for so
long a period. Vassar College, its president advised, "does not presume to
dictate individual action of alumnae or students." Lochner's student aide,
Karl Karsten of the Collegiate Anti-Militarism League, also invited a
dozen people he had met the previous spring at the International Student
Conference, many of whom were either in graduate or law school or out
of school altogether.

Of the students who finally came, most were selected on the basis of
their participation in campus activities—only one was a card-carrying
member of a peace society. Several candidates, just begun in the business
world, asked to go as students and were invited on the basis of their
demonstrated interest in peace and international relations. William Henry
Draper, Jr., a go-getting student from New York University, read that
"live wires" were in demand and plugged himself into the Biltmore outlet, first with a letter written on an Intercollegiate Association of
Amateur Athletes letterhead (of which he was American secretary), followed by another missive, this one on an N.Y.U. humor-magazine letterhead (of which he was news editor), promising the editorial columns of
the magazine to the expedition if they would take him along. It was his
chancellor's recommendation, however, that he was a "mixer of good
address" that got him the invitation.

Other students, equally desirous of going, did not have the advantage
of proximity. Hurriedly they borrowed tuxedos and evening gowns and
money from friends and professors, and waited at the depot for the
tickets they were told would be sent but which never were. Several in the
far West left home without fulfilling the required protocols and passport
procedures lest they end up with an invitation finally in hand but no time
to catch the boat. So it was with Paul Fussell, a Phi Beta Kappa senior and
chairman of the Student Welfare Committee at the Berkeley campus of
the University of California. Just a few days before his college president
received Lochner's telegram, Fussell won a debate on whether or not the
Western Hemisphere should organize a league of nations. He was notified
late one morning that the university president had selected him, and
he hastily packed a bag, telegraphed his mother, arranged to miss his

classes and caught the afternoon train, arriving at the Biltmore Friday morning to find his name not on the list! But because he had come so far so fast, an indulgent Lochner sent his passport application to Washington. Even so, Fussell got to the ship only five minutes before it sailed.

Military armies march on their stomachs; missionary armies require paper, ink and duplicating machines for their spiritual sustenance and to spread the gospel of peace. To secure the supplies and personnel to run the machinery, Lochner engaged Rexford Holmes, an alert, energetic stenographer from Washington, D.C., who ran a convention reporting service. Peace meetings were his preference, and Holmes attacked his job with a flourish, suggesting the use of rustproof Navy typewriters for the ocean voyage and ordering 20,000 large envelopes, 565 reams of paper, 1,778 pencils, 36 jars of paste, 30,000 staples, 240 boxes of carbon paper and 5 gross of erasers. He recruited the staff in Washington, though one lucky lady in Taylorville, Illinois, his hometown, received a wire informing her, "You are engaged as English critic and proofreader Ford Peace Party under name Anna Monroe Lovejoy and you do love joy, don't you? . . . Wonderful opportunity." (In addition to Holmes's order, the Ford Motor Company Biltmore staff purchased or rented over $5,000 worth of office machines, furniture, stationery and photographic supplies.)

On Thursday morning, December 2, Ford returned to New York in his private railroad car, accompanied by Clara Ford; his son, Edsel; his banker and adviser, William Livingstone; Dean Marquis; his peace bodyguard, Ray Dahlinger; and his peace secretary, Theodore Delavigne. He told the reporters who besieged him at the Biltmore that his announced intention of "getting the boys out of the trenches by Christmas" was only a rallying cry to inspire a peace move at the optimal holiday season. If the slogan was not effective, then there was always New Year's, Easter or the Fourth of July; the conference would be ready to function as a clearinghouse whenever the belligerents were ready to exchange peace terms. That was evidently all that Ford was permitted to say. Once again, the newsmen complained that he was flanked by two spokesmen—this time Lochner and Delavigne—both so quick with answers that Ford only had a chance to smile and stare beyond them with a faraway look in his eye.

One glance at the flagrant extravagance of the Biltmore operation and Clara Ford, who was still darning her husband's socks, felt a fury she never forgot. Some months later, Mme Schwimmer, having written to inquire if Mrs. Ford ever received the necklace she had sent her in those hectic days, received a "thank-you note" that said in part:

The way Mr. Ford's name and money was used was shameful, and you were the leader. . . . I shudder when I think what might have happened had I not begged Dr. Marquis and Ray Dahlinger to go along to protect him. You and your followers cared not if he died, just so long as he went along to lend his name and provide money to be squandered.

The extravagance was only the crowning frustration. Jane Addams's sudden withdrawal from the mission, which was reported in the paper on Wednesday, December 1, the day the Fords left Detroit, was regarded by Mrs. Ford as an unforgivable betrayal. No one—not the reporters, the Fords nor Mme Schwimmer and Lochner—believed Miss Addams had been taken to a hospital with a severe kidney infection as her friends reported. Miss Addams's absence, preceded by Mrs. Catt's refusal and Miss Balch's inability to go, put them, as Mme Schwimmer delicately noted, "into a very disagreeable position."

On Friday morning Henry Ford and his escort visited the *Oscar II* to inspect the decorations that Mme Schwimmer and Wanamaker's Department Store had wrought. In less than a week the lounge and cabin furnishings were redone in gay chintzes with matching drapes and lampshades and 140 soft pillows were flung about the premises. The ship's library was replaced with books on peace. A dove with an olive branch in his beak hovered over the portrait of King Oscar II at the entrance of the main saloon, which had also been redecorated. The public rooms were transformed with festoons, ferns, palms and flowers, all in red and green to betoken the spirit of Christmas; stuffed doves, olive branches, flags and Easter lilies surrounded the light fixtures. The ladies' parlor was done in the suffrage colors of yellow and white. Each cabin had a basket of fruit and a potted plant.

Wanamaker's charged $1,000 for the rush job. In all, Ford spent $57,000 to send the expedition on its way, including $30,000 for transportation; $6,200 for the two-week stay at the hotel, including nearly $200 in tips given at Ford's orders. There were also the lesser expenses of nearly $2,000 for cables and telegrams, $2,500 to Miss Leckie for her publicity and recruiting services and $1,000 each to the interpreter Holmes engaged as part of the office force and to Mr. Ford's New York lawyers. Because neither Lochner nor Mme Schwimmer had any money of their own, Mrs. Lochner was given $2,500 for expenses while her husband was gone and Mme Schwimmer used Ford money to pay a shopper who bought her a coat, a camera, toilet water, hair curlers, combination underwear, seasick medicine and a few more items, all for less than $100.

Ford went from Hoboken, where the *Oscar II* was docked, to Wall

Street, guided by the banker Livingstone, who hoped that a face-to-face meeting between his old friend and the financial moguls would have a mutually beneficial impression or at least convince the financiers that Henry's anti-capitalist bark bore no relation to his bite. It was not until six o'clock that Ford returned to the hotel, four hours late for his appointment with William Jennings Bryan. Lochner spent those anxious hours listening to the reporters' penny-dreadful reassurances that Ford had at last been kidnapped by the "mysterious, compelling dark influences" that had been trying to persuade him not to sail. Bryan, unperturbed, sat in his suite chatting with the delegates and arranging with a former aide at the State Department, the acting chief of the Citizenship Bureau, to process passports until midnight.

Bryan and Ford conferred in private, and then chatted awhile with reporters. Ford told them he had made his will and had checked and found no Huns hanging from his family tree as had been suggested. "This is the most serious thing that has ever come into my life," he added, "and I never was more sincere than I am at this moment." Bryan then praised Ford's unselfishness and accused the war profiteers of ridiculing his effort. Ford and his crew would return with an olive branch, Bryan said, and he would join them in The Hague to help them find it.

Friday evening, December 3, the "eleven days of Inferno," as Lochner called them, were finally coming to an end. The last two days were particularly harrowing for the organizers as the delegates arrived at headquarters from across the continent. Not being privy to Mme Schwimmer's and Lochner's predilection for signing Ford's name to communications, the guests, having received a telegram and a long letter from their host urging them to come, expected to tread the red carpet into the inner sanctuary. Instead, Mme Aino Malmberg, a highly regarded Finnish nationalist and friend of Mme Schwimmer's, banged on doors until she found someone who would acknowledge the legitimacy of her presence, and the Reverend Charles Aked, who had abandoned a loving congregation in California, was brutishly treated by a motor-company clerk and was about to enter the elevator on the way back to San Francisco when Lochner, appearing in the corridor, soothed the man's easily mangled pride. That sort of administrative ineptitude, plus the newspaper attack, almost persuaded two other delegates of some reputation—Governor Hanna and Judge Ben Lindsey—to cancel on the last day.

Julia Grace Wales and her Oregon friend from the women's conference, Grace DeGraff, arrived in town Friday afternoon and wandered over from their hotel early in the evening to see Lochner, not guessing they should have made an appointment. They caught glimpses of him and Ford making their way through corridors "black" with reporters. The gentle Miss Wales was deeply disturbed at the massive confusion she witnessed. Just the day before she received her invitation, she had written Jordan that, since a conference was improbable, "an unofficial scientific national commission to do preliminary work in a quiet way" working at home until they were ready to meet with a similar commission abroad, would be a good thing. "The grand mistake," she now realized, was the rush to effect their plan. "Modesty, simplicity, sincerity, clearness, reverence in the expression of the aim" would have won them public support, which the Ford-Schwimmer-Lochner circus clearly forfeited. Despite her distress, she thought even then at that literal eleventh hour that it might not be too late "to present our errand to the American public in its deeper and more dignified aspects," and tried without success later that night to find someone in authority who would rephrase her thoughts in a journalistic style appealing to the press.

On the eve of sailing, some of the students from the Midwest, having their first fling at big-city night life, heard a comedian at the Hippodrome tell his straight man that the Ford plants were closing down because "Henry is sending all the nuts to Europe."

Ford spent his last waking hours before he sailed closeted with Marquis and Livingstone. Nothing they said could dissuade him from his belief that what was right would succeed even if it were done in what Marquis called the wrong way.

As Ford was finally dropping off to sleep, two middle-aged women, only a few hours on terra firma after a five-day transcontinental train ride, were boarding the train to Washington. Ada Morse Clark, Dr. Jordan's secretary, who had implored Lochner to find some way to take her along, and Alice Park, suffragist, friend and devotee of Mme Schwimmer's, had timed their trip perfectly from California, arriving just on the eve of departure, thus leaving a safe margin, they thought, to deal with the unanticipated. Both had travelled abroad before but not in the new age of mandatory passports. By the time they learned they needed that important document the last messenger had left with applications for Washington. Undaunted, the women hunted down a photographer and just before midnight caught the last train to the capital.

Perched upon the passport-office doorstep at six A.M., they waited until what they considered a decent hour and then, as Mrs. Park put it, "pried open the passport office with our Western nerve," which is to say the night watchman let them in to use the phone. LeMat, the acting chief of the bureau, agreed to come to their aid if they sent a taxi to his suburban home. Another phone call to LeMat informed him he would be doing a land-office business. Christian A. Sorensen of Nebraska had first called his senator, George Norris, with no luck.* He, H. M. Thomas of Princeton University, and Frank O. Van Galder, the editor of a fraternal paper, were all down at the New Willard hotel when they arranged to meet LeMat at his office. That diligent official caught a ride to town on a passing vegetable truck when his taxi did not arrive.

Sorensen and Mrs. Clark, with passports in hand, returned to the depot just in time to make the last train to New York that could catch the *Oscar II*—if it sailed half an hour late. Kenneth Pringle of the University of Kansas, another last-minute applicant, being both a gentleman and a scholar, delayed his departure by holding his taxi for Mrs. Park, and they arrived just a few minutes after the New York train left. Mrs. Park was too determined a woman to be stopped so close to her goal. She and Pringle caught a train to Philadelphia, trudged through a tunnel, caught another train to Newark and then took a cab to Hoboken. Pringle was detained at the dock for lack of a ticket, but Mrs. Park, who was similarly impoverished, saw her daughter in the crowd, borrowed her coat, blouse and "small bag of tag ends" and headed for the nearest gangplank, where both Mme Schwimmer and Lochner greeted her, observing in their words of welcome that more people had come than they had expected. A word to the wise, though inadvertent, was sufficient to that dauntless soul. She hid on the ship until the pilot boat had returned to shore and then informed the purser that she had neither ticket nor stateroom. Her luggage, too, she explained, had neglected to join her, and she asked him to outfit her from the stock of garments she assumed he kept aboard for shipwrecked passengers.

On Saturday morning, December 4, as Ford made ready for departure, his farewell message was distributed to the press. He was sailing that day, it said, on a mission of good will from which little harm and much good might come. Though he admittedly knew "little of the details," he did know from the reports of the women envoys that his action would be welcomed by most Europeans. And since his effort was the "only serious organized attempt" to end the war, it merited the respect and attention of the world and not the mockery it had received from its detractors who tried to destroy it. The "gang of death-peddlers that would like to see the thing go to smash" were going to be disappointed.

* His son, Theodore Sorensen, had considerably more success on Capitol Hill when he worked for Senator John F. Kennedy many years later.

The newspapermen knew well enough by then that Ford had nothing to do with the handouts which they had been stuffing in their pockets and collared Ford when he left the hotel. With his back to the wall—his favorite position for an interview—Ford quickly glanced over a copy of the release and said he approved it all. "We've got peace talk going now, and I'll pound it to the end," he promised. Did he have a final message for the public? "Tell the people to cry peace and fight preparedness." Then he and his family and friends left for Hoboken in a six-car caravan.

Those who gathered at the river that morning—whether it was three thousand or fifteen thousand as the papers severally reported—were there in the joyous enthusiasm of jubilee and the Fourth of July, in the spirit of Christmas peace and universal good will. They crowded on the ice-cold pier, sitting on the mountains of luggage or standing on the office desks (hastily ordered, delivered and left behind), singing and cheering as two bands—one on the ship and the other on shore—played "I Didn't Raise My Boy to Be a Soldier," "Tell the Boys It's Time to Come Home" and "Onward, Christian Soldiers." Only the reporters came to mock, to see, as one of them wrote, the

> Millionaires, statesmen, inventors and preachers,
>   Sociological pupils and teachers
> With Henry the Peaceful . . . sailing today
>   To see if the war is as bad as some say.

The New York *Times* called it "one of the most picturesque . . . noisy demonstrations" ever witnessed in New York harbor. The New York *Sun* said it was "so grotesque as to be almost beyond belief." The Detroit *Free Press* expressed the weariness and exasperation with the days that went before:

As it was at the beginning of the Ford peace ship plan, so it was at the pier today. Nobody knew where to go, nobody was in charge of anything, nobody knew anything except that here was a ship that Henry Ford was taking to Europe to stop the war, get the boys out of the trenches by Christmas, and lots of other things.

In addition to the Danish flag on the ship's sides to denote its neutrality, there hung a brilliantly colored banner, designed by Mme Schwimmer's friend, the artist Willy Pogany, of a ferocious knight on horseback, lance at the ready ("Paul Revere dressed up like the Tin Man" taunted the New York *Herald*), riding down the cringing figure of militarism. Beneath the rider huge letters proclaimed: STOP THE WAR. At the railing stood the expedition's social director, Lloyd Bingham, wearing a beret, smock and yellow spats, a megaphone in his hands, leading the crowd in cheers. When he spotted a celebrity coming up the gangplank he let loose a "Hip, Hip, Hooray!" and cried the person's name and coaxed him to the rail to make a speech. Ford sported a long, fur-collared

Delegate feeding the expedition's mascot (Mary Alden Hopkins Papers).

coat and black derby and received sustained cheers as he boarded the ship, as did Bryan, who arrived with the mayor of Hoboken. Waiting for the voyagers in one of the lounges were two squirrels in a cage labeled "For the Good Ship Nutty" and another gift, a big box of raisins, inscribed "To Go with the Nuts."

Bryan's visit in Ford's cabin—the bridal suite—was interrupted by a summons to the main saloon, where they both witnessed a wedding between two members of the press. Berton Braley, the folk poet and feature

writer for *Collier's*, had been permitted to bring his fiancée, Marion
Rubincam, a Philadelphia fashion writer, along. Too impatient to wait
until they passed the three-mile limit and with a cavalier disregard for
legal technicalities, they were married with a Pennsylvania license in New
Jersey waters by a minister whose authority in such matters did not ex-
tend beyond the boundaries of Illinois. While Bryan felicitated the bride,
Ford returned to his coterie.

John Burroughs had come to the dock still thinking the "undertaking
foredoomed to failure" and still wishing, nevertheless, to show his friend
his gratitude for past favors by bidding him farewell. Edison, too, had
come to say goodbye. As they stood surrounded by a crowd at the rail,
Ford shouted into the deaf man's ear: "I'll give you a million dollars if
you'll come," but Edison only smiled, shook his head, and walked off the
ship.

Three professional tour conductors were at the pier to get the show on
the sea, issuing tickets at the dock upon presentation of passports and
hoping to prevent stowaways and improperly credentialed passengers
from getting on board. It was first come, first served, with male students
the last to get tickets, so that when the whistle finally blew more than an
hour after departure time, no one knew who had made it and who had
been left on shore. (Provision had already been made for the overflow to
sail on the *Frederick VIII* and rendezvous with the main party in Norway.)

A beatific smile on his face, Ford stood at the rail and threw roses to his
wife and friends. As the ship pulled away from the pier, some on the
upper deck sang a peace song, the crowd cheered and waved handkerchiefs, the bands played, and Bryan stood at the very edge of the dock,
waving his umbrella and crying "Godspeed." When the ship reached
midstream an overeager celebrant jumped off the dock and began to swim
toward the moving vessel. Urbain J. Ledoux, a former consul in Europe,
had promised Lochner he would stay behind to activate the press and
pulpit for peace but changed his mind *after* the last minute. A tug rescued
him from the brine and an ambulance took him to a hospital. (He was
swimming to reach public opinion, not the ship, he told the police, who
fined him $25.) For the reporters, it was a fitting end to the carnival they
had covered.

Paul Kellogg of the Henry Street group tried to show the bright side to
his *Survey* readers: those who went had faith in Lochner's executive
capabilities and in Mme Schwimmer's determination to achieve her goal.
He hoped a week at sea would unite them as a group, and, in any case, the

neutral conference was bound to be beneficial. But to Jane Addams he wrote his valedictory thoughts of the "strong, unwelded personalities, loose ends, mistrusts and bickerings" and of Mme Schwimmer's "understandable but nonetheless disastrous impetuousness and arbitrariness in launching the expedition."

For those on the ship of peace, it was a beautiful day, a calm sea and full dreams ahead.

CHAPTER 6

The "illustrious unknown"

THE IMAGE OF BRYAN waving his umbrella receded; the sound of the cheers, of the singing and of the band dimmed; and the passengers, numb with cold, went below to find their staterooms, get a cup of coffee and write letters home for the pilot to carry back to port.

Besides the potted begonias and the baskets of fruit, the copies of peace songs and the isinglass name badges in their cabins, the members found a note of welcome from Henry Ford asking their forebearance for any discomfort caused by the great rush and assuring them that "this mission is a righteous and an important one, and there is every reasonable expectation that it will reach a satisfactory and a decisive fulfillment." While most people settled in, others had more immediate business to attend to. Mrs. Grace Latus, a Pittsburgh newspaperwoman, hunted for her husband and two children who had stepped off the boat for just a moment before it sailed. She did not see them again until the *Frederick VIII* docked in Christiania two weeks later. (It was not a large loss for the expedition, since only Mrs. Latus had been invited and that presumptuous woman had just brought her family along.) Ora Guessford, a student, searched for her heavy sweater and brand-new, badly needed durable shoes where she had left them in the music room, only to find they had been stolen. Marion Penn, another student, searched for the purser after he discovered on entering his cabin that he was to share it with three young ladies. And the purser received a visit from the bedazzling suffragist lawyer Inez Milholland Boissevain, who had been assigned to a cabin with two other women, and was in absolute need of a single inside cabin to minimize the suffering she endured on any ocean voyage. And finally the purser was confronted by a furious Dean Marquis.

Mrs. Ford had selected the best cabins for her husband and his bodyguards, spiritual and temporal, but when Marquis went in search of his quarters he found that Mme Schwimmer had made some changes, and he was assigned a room "near the coal bin," one deck below Ford. He and Dahlinger were soon transferred to a cabin with only the music room between them and their charge. While Ford was in the wireless room sending messages of thanks to his family and friends, his protectors prepared his cabin. Inside his suitcase they found a model of a Model T, a gift from an admirer. "It did not look good," Marquis wrote his wife, "so we dropped it overboard. We feared the gasoline tank might blow up." They cleared out the flowers, laid out his nightgown and, at some time during the evening, "got Mr. Ford out of the crowd and kept him in his room."

Most of the ship's company, their names pinned to their chests, walked the decks and visited the lounges, seeking celebrities and speaking of the hazards they had overcome to reach the ship, all warmed by the bond that brought them together. They were argonauts on a mercy mission to the world, perhaps to be remembered, as Crystal Eastman Benedict foretold, with John Brown's raiders and Coxey's Army.

For those who knew each other personally or by reputation, their names having appeared together on letterheads of innumerable uplift organizations, it was old-home-week. For most there was the fun of matching the names of those they had heard about with the living flesh. Henry Ford, the star attraction, gave each guest a hearty hello and a handshake. Expecting to be overpowered or ignored by the mighty industrialist, everyone was charmed by his modesty, his friendliness and his sincerity and, depending on their views of the expedition and its leaders, regarded him either as a savior or a put-upon saint.

Easily the most identifiable person was the white-haired, white-bearded seventy-three-year-old gentleman of the cloth whom the passengers came to write of in their diaries, letters and dispatches as "Santa Claus" and "a nice old gentleman" and whose character and abilities they greatly admired. The Reverend Jenkin Lloyd Jones, a kind man of great ego and grand voice, was having a splendid time. He had already been photographed by the movie newsmen while making a speech to the thousands on the dock and had been selected to officiate at the Braleys' impromptu wedding ceremony. Though not keen on a winter voyage and not expectant that the peacemakers "will have much direct influence upon the war maddened rulers," he thought their attempt would bring some hope to the warring peoples and believed that every effort for peace in Europe should be tried. He had been vigorously advising his colleagues of the Chicago Peace Society to act for peace since the war began and had been an advocate of the neutral conference plan with Miss Addams and Louis Lochner since they first heard of it. Jones was a free-lance fighter for righteousness, pleased with his reputation for independence of mind and action and accustomed either to leading his congregation, his settlement house and his adult summer camp or, when persuasion failed, to fighting those in authority who opposed him.

The Reverend Charles F. Aked was as gifted in oratory, as certain of his leadership capabilities and as independent and radical as Dr. Jones, but there was nothing in his manner that would have led his shipboard companions to suppose he too might one day impress them as "a nice old gentleman." They admired his abilities but called the English minister "dogmatic," "pompous," "domineering" and "a stuffed shirt."

As a young lad of twelve in the 1870s, Aked followed his father's profession on the auctioneering box. At nineteen, his pastor talked him into going into the ministry. For eight years he served in village chapels and then was called to Liverpool, where he stayed for almost twenty years. During the Boer War when Aked spoke out against the iniquity of British rule, his church was mobbed and his home wrecked. But nothing ever kept the "Fighting Parson" from speaking his beliefs and working for his many causes. He wrote prolifically on the religious, social and political issues of his time and voiced his views on his several preaching tours in the United States.

In 1907, "the whole country talked about" John D. Rockefeller's engaging Aked to be the pastoral shepherd to the flock of millionaires that prayed with him in a modest edifice on Fifth Avenue. The minister had crossed the Atlantic to improve his health and wealth, believing that American millionaires followed the simple life and desired to do good in the world. Unfortunately, they did not desire to do enough good for Dr. Aked, and when they reneged in 1911 on their promise to build him a bigger church, he went to San Francisco, where his energy and eloquence were structurally rewarded. Before he left, he told his Baptist board of trustees: "I owe something to my own past. It is not immodest to say that

I did a work for Liverpool and for England which makes my ministry here look pitifully small."

Within three months of his arrival in San Francisco, Aked was a recognized leader in the community, and his powerful pulpit personality and innovative programs had greatly increased the membership of the First Congregational Church. In the years following, Aked's nonconformist views and active participation in libertarian, civic and national causes and his crusades against war and social injustice brought him honors and national renown.

The San Francisco minister had been a friend to the peace activists in their efforts to induce a Wilsonian intervention and was one of the first invited to join the peace expedition. The day after Aked received Ford's telegram he told his disapproving church board and his congregation he would be gone for six weeks, and the day after that he was en route to New York, anxious to be among the "devoted enthusiastic lovers of their fellow men" and certain that Ford was doing a far, far better thing than those who "scurry around Wall Street trying to make money out of human agony and death." Halfway across the Atlantic Ocean, his brother minister, Dr. Marquis, remarked that Aked "loves the limelight like a fish loves water. He began by putting himself forward in every way." So he did—and he stayed up front for many months to come.

The Reverend Arthur Weatherly of Lincoln, Nebraska, was very like his fellow Unitarian minister and friend Jenkin Lloyd Jones in his active devotion to reform, but was of considerably less reputation. At first a Congregational minister in Rhode Island, his change to the more liberal Unitarianism was speeded by his church elders' insistence that he stop playing semi-pro baseball on the Sabbath. In 1906, in his early forties, Weatherly accepted a call to Lincoln, where his strong social conscience and recreational activities were welcome. There he participated in social and political reform movements and became a director of the national American Peace Society.

Gentle in spirit, profoundly committed to pacifism no matter the odds or the abuse, Weatherly was a man of stability, principle and good sense, content to join with his fellows for the common good. He would have enjoyed sharing the attention given Jones and Aked on board, but he did not have their strong personalities and he remained in the background, the light of his countenance dimmed by the brilliant glow of his colleagues.

Another officer of a local peace society aboard was a man whose name was then a household word far more significant than the man himself. In the first decade of the century, S. S. McClure had been "among the ten first men who were important on the American scene"; by 1915, though only in his late fifties, he was a has-been.

Sam McClure worked during his youth in Indiana, but only after school so that nothing could interfere with the college education he was determined to have. He was a restless though persistent young man. As Ford was to do some years later, and for the same benevolent reasons, McClure became a successful businessman with an idea that had been abroad for some time. He "invented" the newspaper syndicate service so that farmers could read the popular literature of Kipling and Stevenson in their newspapers. Then, in the depths of the 1893 depression, he began publishing *McClure's,* a magazine of high quality intended to inform the masses and to be sold at a price the common man could afford. Six years later, when he was forty-two, McClure was the head of five magazines, the syndicate service, a lecture bureau and two companies. In six months his empire, though not all of its components, collapsed—and so did he. Impetuous and impatient, his mind constantly ablaze with wild schemes capriciously conceived and discarded, he had been flitting peripatetically across two continents with such speed and force that Kipling called him a "cyclone in a frockcoat."

After McClure regained his health during a year of luxurious living in Europe, he ran his magazine just as he had before. Each time he came back to his office from a trip his great talent for disorganization reversed the process of Creation in the editorial rooms so that "from Order came forth Chaos." Then, in 1906, his major writers quit, fed up with his excessive enthusiasms and chameleon mind, his extravagance and flamboyance, his overbearing manner and his unstable temperament. In 1911 he was forced to sell, retaining only a titular editorship for two years.

Still a hustler, McClure started a lecture bureau featuring two stars, Maria Montessori, the educator, and himself. He also developed a plan for world peace, the result of his longstanding association with the peace movement. On one of his many visits to the Battle Creek, Michigan, sanitarium which he favored for its health-food regimen, McClure shared his plan with a young teacher, Dr. Edward Rumely, and while the hospital restored his health, Rumely restored his ego. McClure was always in need of large and constant quantities of admiration and flattery; Rumely, acting for the German government, was in need at that time of a front man to edit the New York *Evening Mail,* which the Germans were secretly buying. However, he did not mention this to McClure when he offered him a two-year contract.

McClure went to work on the paper at the end of May 1915; within a short time he realized he was a titular editor once more. That summer his name was discovered in the secret papers the German propagandist Dr. Albert left on the New York subway, and his friends cut him on the

S. S. McClure (Courtesy of Henry Ford Museum).

street. By fall, he wanted to quit but could not terminate his contract. Instead, he covered the Mexican revolution. In late November, McClure was back in New York looking for another opportunity to leave town when the invitation from Henry Ford to join the peace expedition arrived.

McClure admired Ford. Not six months earlier he had asked to write the manufacturer's life story and sent, as a sample, his own autobiography (which he had acknowledged in the introduction, though not on the title page, was written by Willa Cather). A Ford secretary replied that the project had already begun. The peace invitation provided McClure with a much desired transatlantic voyage, a chance to inspire and lead and the reassurance that he was not forgotten. To one who met him at that time, McClure was only "a little, grey, shabby, important man, very conceited, and somewhat desperately clinging to the idea of his own value in the world. A man who somehow just missed the trapeze." But to those aboard the *Oscar II* who knew him only by name that first day, S. S. McClure was definitely counted a celebrity.

McClure's dual status as a delegate and a journalist was enjoyed by a dozen others sympathetic to the peace attempt, two of whom were syndicated columnists. John Barry was a Boston-born, Harvard-educated critic, essayist, poet, drama editor and novelist, a delightful dinner guest and raconteur, and a highly civilized gentleman who seemed "to bear the aura of the New England of Emerson, Lowell, Holmes and their times." His friends in San Francisco knew him as straightforward, honorable and persuasive, a practiced mediator "of gentle consideration of everybody else all the time." Then in his late forties, Barry had found his métier in a syndicated column, "The Ways of the World," which he wrote for the San Francisco *Bulletin*. In a chatty, informal style, he discussed literature, art, peace, international government and woman suffrage. Russian-born Herman Bernstein, another delegate-journalist, was a naturalized citizen who had lived in the United States for half of his thirty-nine years and was devoted to its institutions. As cultivated a gentleman as Barry, Bernstein also wrote literary works and had translated Tolstoy, Chekhov and Gorki. He was a man of principle but also an operator of modest political connections and ambitions with some call on the Democratic Party, principally because he was the owner of a Jewish paper, *The Day*, had recently been secretary of the American Jewish Committee and often acted in the interests of world Jewry. The New York *Times* had sent him to Europe four times to report on governmental policies and to interview political and cultural leaders, and he had just spent three months as special correspondent for several New York papers interviewing European statesmen on the possibilities of peace.

Bernstein sent an effusive four-page telegram in reply to Ford's invitation, which was released to the press. His trip through the belligerent countries the past summer, he said, convinced him "that the people everywhere want peace" and that many in the foreign offices, realizing at last that war was not the means to settle their problems wished that President Wilson would initiate mediation.

The Grand Foreman of the Brotherhood of American Yeomen reminded the expedition leaders that eight million men belonged to fraternal beneficiary societies and not one of them had been knowingly invited. He suggested that Harry Carroll Evans, past president of the Fraternal Press Association, a lawyer by training and currently editor of the *Yeoman Shield* in Des Moines, and Frank O. Van Galder, editor of *The Modern Woodman* in Rock Island, Illinois, would "exercise a wonderful influence," and both were invited.

The governor of Mississippi appointed a Southern colonel and newspaper editor as his representative, a man who had been president of the National Education Association, a grand commander of the Mississippi Masons and a fervid member of the Democratic Party since the last years of Reconstruction. Colonel Robert H. Henry, publisher of the Jackson *Clarion-Ledger*, proudly announced his paper was foursquare behind the peace mission.

John E. Jones, a member of the Anti-War Society in Washington, D.C., and owner of a weekly news service for five hundred rural and small-town papers, requested an invitation for himself and his wife, Estelle. Ralph MacBrayne, a man of varied social-service background, came representing his peace sympathies and the Boston *Transcript*. Of the four women delegate-journalists, only two were members of peace organizations, but all were suffragists, social reformers and friends of Katherine Leckie, the mission's press-relations manager.

It is not likely, considering the wide range of reform interests of the assemblage, that there was anyone who had not heard of Denver's Juvenile Court Judge Ben B. Lindsey, certainly one of the best-known members aboard. In a public-opinion poll the year before, the "Kid's Judge" tied with Andrew Carnegie and Billy Sunday for eighth place as the "greatest living American."

As a young man, Ben Lindsey, despite his frailty—at five feet five he weighed scarcely one hundred pounds—held three jobs simultaneously, the one in a law office ultimately leading to a legal career. Though it was a political appointment in 1900 that led to Lindsey's innovative work in the juvenile court, it was his compassion for the deprived and down-trodden unjustly used by society, his understanding that a small boy who stole a few pieces of coal from the railroad yard to warm his family's hovel was not a criminal, and his willingness to trust young wards of the state as they trusted him that made him so exceptional a jurist, known for putting "a little love in the law." But when Lindsey made the adults who contributed to juvenile crime—the gambling-den operators and the saloonkeepers—liable in court and when he attacked political graft and chicanery, he found himself a David, armed only with community support, battling the Goliath of the corporate interests and political machines at every election.

Lindsey loved the political fights and the national and international reputation that grew as he helped write juvenile-court legislation for other states, and lectured on the Chautauqua circuit, and as he developed friendships with the intellectual, social and political elite of Progressive reform. Theodore Roosevelt affectionately called the little judge "the Bull Mouse" when there was talk of Lindsey running for vice president on the 1912 Bull Moose ticket. In 1913, Rosika Schwimmer, always an admirer of humanitarians who not only thought and talked but acted, invited Lindsey to speak before the International Woman Suffrage Alliance meeting in Budapest, and Lindsey, who was eager to study urban conditions abroad, accepted.

But the years of constantly raking the rich lode of muck in Colorado and the continuous political struggle sent him instead to a Battle Creek sanitarium. There he saw his old friend S. S. McClure, who was kind enough to let him read the galleys of his autobiography, and he met Henrietta Brevoort, an interior decorator twenty years his junior ("delicate as a flower and full of the spirit of rebellion," Emma Goldman described her), whom he married the following winter.

In the early fall of 1915, Lindsey, then forty-six, thought of retiring from the court to make some money as a writer and lecturer. Instead he fought and beat the "gang of conspirators" in November. Nonetheless, he was restless and the Ford invitation presented a tempting prospect. Lindsey was no radical pacifist; he believed in limited military preparedness. His only previous connection with the peace movement had been *not* to answer the letter inviting him to become a charter member of the League to Enforce Peace. He even admitted to Roosevelt that the peace venture might be "worse than useless." But when Lindsey talked to Ford in New York of his doubts and dreams and difficulties—he would forfeit nearly

$3,000 in lecture fees in January and February—Ford was "irresistible." Though his friends' counsel almost persuaded Lindsey to change his mind on the eve of departure, he and his wife went, not so much because they believed in the mission but because Ford led them to believe he would compensate Lindsey's lecture agents and finance the Lindseys' dream of establishing homes for European war orphans.

Judson King, another political reformer, had had no previous contact with the peace movement, and his invitation came "like a clear bolt out of the sky." King had vigorously campaigned across the country for initiative, referendum and recall and was the executive secretary of the National Popular Government League. His friend Ben Lindsey called him "one of the sanest, sincerest, constructive radicals in the country." While King was all for the pacifists' "heroic and democratic" attempt and cooperated with the management all the way, he, like Lindsey, saw the expedition as a means of pursuing his interests in Europe.

Louis B. Hanna, the governor of North Dakota, disqualified himself as a pacifist and announced, before sailing, that he planned to visit the war zones. His aide-de-camp, journalist Sam Clark, explained, "We are simply on the sidelines looking on" (which was certainly true of Clark, who was not considered a delegate). Thus the governor pleased those of his constituents who thought he should try to end the war by sailing with the peacemakers and those who thought he should not by dissociating himself from their endeavor.

Lieutenant Governor Andrew J. Bethea of South Carolina, on the other hand, was unintentionally ambiguous. He told Ford it was a privilege to participate in such an "unspeakable blessing to mankind."

Four teachers managed to get away for six weeks in the middle of the school term. Two of them, Florence Holbrook, Mme Schwimmer's disciple from Chicago, and Grace DeGraff, representing the Oregon State Federation of Women's Clubs, had been at the International Congress of Women at The Hague. Another, Katherine Devereux Blake, the daughter of a pioneer suffragist, had been speaking for the New York Peace Society since the war began and had enlisted Dr. Jenkin Lloyd Jones and others in publicizing her children's peace petition, a two-mile-long document that she presented to Bryan at the State Department. For years she crusaded for women's rights in New York schools, opposing minority male control of policy-making positions in a system in which 90 percent of the teachers were women. Miss Blake was impressed by Mme Schwimmer and her plan for peace, and though Henry Ford was paying her way, she clearly considered herself Rosika Schwimmer's guest.

Willis Conant, a politically radical friend of Miss Leckie's, was headmaster-owner of a country school for boys in New York state. M. Stuart Levussove, a middle-aged instructor of descriptive geometry at the College of the City of New York, obtained leave on the basis of his doctor's advice that a sea voyage would cure his persistent throat infection.

Theodore A. Hostetler, a patent-office examiner in Washington, D.C., was a member of the American Peace Society, a trustee of the Washington Bible Society and a vice president of the Anti-Saloon League and was representing the Washington Sunday School Association on the trip.

Of men and women of science or the laboring classes, there were none, and but a handful of people connected with business. There was Ford, of course, and Herman Bernstein, who had founded his own newspaper, and McClure, and Benjamin W. Huebsch, the thirty-three-year-old avant-garde publisher who had helped Mme Schwimmer meet Colonel House. Huebsch published works by American and European radicals and liberals in government, reform and literature—Hauptmann, Gorki and James Joyce among them. His association with House began in 1912 when he published the colonel's anonymous novel; his association with Mme Schwimmer began at a suffrage rally in 1914 where he and his good friend, Mary Fels, were deeply moved by her description of the suffering endured in the European war. Because his publishing house was essentially a one-man operation, Huebsch's participation in the expedition was a sacrifice of profit to ideals. He paid the forfeit willingly, convinced that the war had to end and that the Ford-sponsored plan was the way to do it. "At that time," said a friend, "he was young and energetic and fearless."

Frederick Holt, a temporarily unemployed Detroit businessman, was invited because his wife, Lilian, knew Mrs. Ford. And Mrs. Holt earned an invitation as the reluctant head of the Michigan branch of the Woman's Peace Party. Quite possibly Clara Ford persuaded the Holts to go hoping that the clubwoman and her husband would have a moderating influence.

Mary Fels managed not only her late husband's Fels Naphtha soap interests but continued his philanthropies, especially his support of the single tax. In her own right, she was a charter member of the Woman's Peace Party and a worker for woman suffrage. "A wise little body," Weatherly called her, whose "judgment on practical matters is very good."

Of the women of known suffrage sympathies who committed themselves to peace action, several had national and even international reputations which marked them as leaders rather than willing followers.

Helen Ring Robinson of Colorado was the first woman ever elected to a state senate. She had shared the platform with Jane Addams, Carrie Chapman Catt and other leading suffragists many times and was known in America and Europe for her appearances in support of women's rights. In the Colorado legislature, Senator Robinson concerned herself with women's and children's issues relating to prison, labor and health and was thus an associate of Judge Lindsey. Her message of acceptance expressed her gratitude for the chance to sail on the "Ship of Good Hope" and "render a service in behalf of good will."

The venerable and vigorous septuagenarian May Wright Sewall, while running her Indianapolis school, had organized civic and statewide woman suffrage associations and lectured across the country and in Europe urging women to organize themselves for their own advancement. She was a founding officer of several women's organizations, most notably the National and International Councils of Women. She was also a friend of Rosika Schwimmer, and had met the boat when the Hungarian suffragist first came to America in 1914. Since then, Mrs. Sewall had been in California organizing a women's peace meeting and speaking for the neutral mediation plan of the Woman's Peace Party, of which she was a national officer and chairman of its Northern California Branch. For years she had chaired the Peace and Arbitration Committee of the International Council of Women, and she had been an officer of the American Peace Society and the World Peace Foundation and frequently spoke at national peace congresses, on the same program with Bryan and Carnegie. Her presence on the peace ship served as a reminder to other women of "the historical continuity" of their mission.

Without question the one person among the celebrities the lesser lights were most anxious to see in the flesh was Inez Milholland Boissevain, the young woman who had made the Sunday rotogravure the day she led a suffragists' parade down Fifth Avenue, gracefully sitting on her white charger and wearing a Grecian gown, her dark hair flowing down her back. Her contemporaries ran short of adjectives describing her. One surmises she possessed the beauty of Helen of Troy, the eloquence of Portia, the bearing of a Viking goddess, the resourcefulness of Scheherazade, the courage of Judith and the modesty of Cinderella. They called her "strong-willed in a nice way" and "courageous and uncompromising"; she gave of her "wonderful vitality to the neediest claimants on her sympathy." They spoke of how audiences gasped at her beauty when she took the platform, of her brilliance, of her commanding personality and of her elegance, and John Barry told his readers no photograph did justice to her rich coloring, and he marveled at her friendliness, the good cheer she created about her, her rebellious temperament and her freedom from

Inez M. Boissevain and Louis Lochner (State Historical Society of Wisconsin).

"self-consciousness and vanity." A student remarked at the time, "Cleopatra had nothing on her."

At Vassar College, where she enrolled in 1905, Inez conducted a suffrage-club meeting in a nearby cemetery after the speakers she had invited were not permitted on campus. Later, after the Harvard trustees refused her entrance to their law school because she was a woman, she enrolled at New York University and, outside the classroom, worked for labor reform and woman suffrage. Without entirely forsaking the self-centered life of her class, as a militant radical, earnest and high-spirited, she fought effectively in the state legislature and on the picket line for the weak and ignorant, the poor and neglected. She lived in Greenwich Village among her fellow reformers—the "ethical Bohemia" of the socialists and settlement workers—sharing the mores of the artistic Bohemia as well. At the same time, she went where she was needed for the suffrage cause, always as a leader but a generous and gay one, who never compromised her principles, independence or individuality.

In the spring of 1913 she traveled to England with Guglielmo Marconi (to whom she had been briefly engaged when she was seventeen), his wife and their friend, Eugen Boissevain. She had met Boissevain, a handsome, adventurous, prodigal Dutchman who was making an American fortune, in Greenwich Village; they courted on the ship and, with her customary flair for immediate action, she married him as soon as they reached London. She went to Italy as a war correspondent in the spring of 1915 and was home by September, declared persona non grata by the Italian government for her pacifist articles.

Inez Milholland Boissevain was proud to be among the "selected few" who, she thought, had been chosen for their vision, sympathy and impartiality to participate in the peace pilgrimage. "It may fail," she told reporters, "but the world will be the better for it." Though she was too polite to say so, Miss Wales was relieved when her cabinmate, Mrs. Boissevain, insisted on private accommodations. Her style of dress and unconventionality, her lack of "objection to publicity," were disturbing, though Miss Wales appreciated her "clear, vigorous intellect" and thought her "frank and good-hearted."

Not glamorous certainly, but equally dynamic, was the third occupant of that cabin, Alice Park. Her ingenuity of the last fourteen hours ashore —from getting a passport photo taken late at night to getting on the boat without a ticket—was only par for the course. Born in Boston just before the Civil War, a descendant of Paul Revere and Benjamin Franklin, Mrs. Park took her ancestry seriously, beginning her protestations for justice with a schoolgirl commitment to woman suffrage. After her husband's death she moved to San Francisco from the Colorado mining town where they had been living. Returned to urban life in the late 1890s at a time when even "national purity" seemed realizable, Alice Park became the compleat reformer, traveling from Europe to Hawaii for her causes. She was, quite expectedly, "glad to obey" the call to join the peace crusade and to follow wherever Mme Schwimmer led.

Sitting in the cabin that first night, a "small wiry woman . . . with a rather prim, wrinkled face and humorous eyes," happy-go-lucky, her bosom covered with badges ("a wholesale propagandist," thought Miss Wales), she chattered excitedly awhile, then borrowed a nightgown, pulled a stocking over her eyes and went to sleep, her loud snoring disturbing the slumber of Miss Wales in the upper berth.

Henrietta Neuhaus, a founding member of the absolute pacifist Fellowship of Reconciliation, came at the suggestion of the director of the Church Peace Union, who was a good friend of Lochner's.

Lars Nelson entered the Biltmore headquarters an unknown and emerged a delegate on the expedition. For some time he had been drafting plans for world government and sending them to likely proponents. Seven years earlier, Nelson had been a small-time political functionary in Denver, begging Judge Lindsey for a job and billing himself as a "capable clerk, careful and orderly." He presented himself to the expedition managers, however, as a peace advocate, a Scandinavian expert with helpful newspaper connections to whom he had already sent eulogistic accounts of the expedition, and as a reporter for the *Christian Science Monitor*. They may have questioned his connections, knowing he had emigrated forty-five years before, and they probably knew he was at most a stringer for the *Monitor*, but he was a willing worker at headquarters and, at the least, he could read the foreign newspapers.

That some proportion of the delegates would be foreign-born was to be expected in those peak years of immigration, but they were all either citizens or long resident in America, except for two Finnish friends of Mme Schwimmer's, Aino Malmberg and Elli Eriksson.

Mme Malmberg, a Finnish nationalist and former Socialist member of the Finnish diet, was exiled from her native land. She had made repeated lecture tours in America, speaking for freedom for minority nationalities and, since the war, for peace. International experts called her "exceptionally intelligent and well informed." Writing in *Harper's Weekly* the preceding spring about "The Protected Sex in Wartime," she said she was a pacifist because war was "a senseless, wicked and medieval means of temporarily settling diplomatic or commercial quarrels." Mme Schwimmer sympathized with the difficulties of her friend's exile and had asked Miss Addams to engage the Finnish patriot to organize branches of the

Woman's Peace Party and speak for the neutral conference. Aino Malmberg willingly interrupted her fall lecture tour to join her friend's effort to end the war. As a member of a subject people she was certainly one of the best informed on a principal problem sure to be considered at the peace table.

The Russian authorities had exiled Aino Malmberg, but her young compatriot, Elli Eriksson, had voluntarily left Finland when the war started to see the world. She went first to England on the advice of Mme Malmberg, whom she had met through a travel agent, and there at a suffrage benefit she met Mme Schwimmer. In America the next year, still seeking adventure, the young governess settled near Chicago and renewed her acquaintance with her Hungarian friend. When Mme Schwimmer invited her as messenger and personal caretaker, Elli packed her native costume and came to New York. Frequently wearing her dark-blue dress and lace bodice, her long blond hair braided beneath her cap, always with a merry smile, she soon became the ship's mascot as she ran her errands from the peace staff office.

The eleven members of Mme Schwimmer and Lochner's peace staff—including Elli—were considered working delegates. Mme Schwimmer styled herself "expert adviser" to Ford and the expedition, and Lochner was the general secretary. Katherine Leckie's chief duty as head of the publicity and press bureau was keeping the press corps happy, a task as difficult as any job in Tartarus. As her assistant she brought her friend Elizabeth Watson, a social worker who was a hard campaigner in her fights for prison, child-welfare and labor reform.

The chief writer of state papers and letters to important people was the emotional and erratic Ellis O. Jones, whom a friend described as "a slim, prim, stiff little person, so stiff that he curved backward but he had a smiling eye." Jones was a Greenwich Village habitué, one of the founders of *The Masses*, a committed woman suffragist and, according to Ben Huebsch, "an enthusiast for the peace movement." As an editorial humorist, Jones wrote "the radical things in *Life*" until his unrestrained pacifism cost him his job.

Rebecca Shelly's particular responsibility was the welfare and conduct of the students. "Utterly dedicated and serious," her attentions to her charges, who were only a few years her junior, were never modified by jocularity or friendliness, and she was recognized by them as a "causist who had her mind on her work."

Lola Lloyd's brother, Lewis Maverick, recently out of college himself, served on Miss Shelly's student advisory committee, but mostly he functioned as a jack-of-all-trades, having more energy and enthusiasm than experience in peace matters. He was invited only because he was staying with his sister, who was Mme Schwimmer's most devoted follower.

Insofar as the expedition was concerned, Lola Maverick Lloyd was exclusively committed to Rosika Schwimmer. She had, however, a prior commitment to her children, whose custody was at issue in her pending divorce suit. With the help of her lawyers and Mme Schwimmer, supplemented by Mr. Ford's generosity, she arranged to bring the three oldest, ages seven to eleven, and their governess on the journey.

Two other staff members from Chicago followed their leaders to Europe. Florence Holbrook, the school principal and chairwoman of the club that engaged the Hungarian suffragist for her first Chicago appearance, was as emotionally and intellectually committed as Mrs. Lloyd, as captivated by the magnetism and brilliance of their mentor and as willing to follow wherever Mme Schwimmer led. Alfred Kliefoth, a "man of ability, willing to do small tasks," served Lochner on the peace ship just as he had at the Chicago Peace Society.

Finally, there were Mme Schwimmer's and Lochner's private secretaries: Mrs. Nora Smitheman, a socialist-suffragist, and Mrs. Ada Morse Clark, Dr. Jordan's secretary and Alice Park's cross-country companion of the preceding week. A widow in her forties, Mrs. Clark was a strong woman, a hard-core pacifist with a happy disposition, proper and pious, and, like the others, loyal to the management and eager for all tasks. Time and temperament brought additions and schisms, but these eleven people, working in Mme Schwimmer's cabin or the office next door, were the founding members of what Julia Grace Wales came to call the "Inner Circle."

Of the remaining delegates, one, Lloyd Bingham, a jovial extrovert, was engaged by Plantiff as entertainment director to amuse the group aboard ship and during their European sojourn. Bingham had been a touring actor and a Wall Street broker. In 1903, at thirty-five, he had made his fortune and established his own theatrical company starring his wife, Amelia, a fairly well-known actress. She was on tour and he was at liberty when Ford's invitation arrived. "Wonderful friends," he wrote his host whom he had never met, "I'm with you, body and soul," willing to come, if they wished, as the "ships Gester [*sic*]." The other entertainer aboard, Mary Fulton Gibbons, was a concert singer and a friend of peace whom Mme Schwimmer had met in her travels.

Estelle Jones, Edith Lloyd Jones and Henrietta Lindsey were invited at the request of their husbands, who claimed they shared in their work and convictions. They had no further qualifications, other than intelligence, to fit them as participating members of a peace mission.

At the outset, there were fifty-five delegates on the *Oscar II*, about equally divided by sex. None were from the first rank of American life in international affairs, and only a handful were known outside their special areas. Others called them "negligible women. And negligible men, too" and "genteel mendicants, inveterate notoriety seekers, main-chance reformers, cheap mountebanks, crack-brained philanthropists, boisterous egoists." They called themselves the "illustrious unknown," "devoted lovers of humanity, so moved by the horrors of the war . . . that they had left their homes and their business." Knowing they were not a conventional peace delegation, they exulted in being a "motley crew," representing American "sympathy and good will for bleeding Europe." Marquis compared his fellow voyagers to "an entire American village," and observed that "in great national crises the more prominent people have never come to the front." Several were "self-seekers and grafters," as might be expected in any large and hastily organized group financed so offhandedly, but most were dedicated people who had long been working in the vineyards of reform. Some were willing to be led, some expected to lead. Whatever their virtues, whatever their flaws, the day they sailed they were a happy crew of uplifters certain of the righteousness of their action and confident that new-world democracy would help the decadent governments of the old world formulate an enduring people's peace.

There were forty-four in the press complement: twenty-nine were newspaper or wire-service reporters for American papers, four were foreign correspondents or correspondents for foreign-language papers, six were magazine writers, four were photographers and newsreel cameramen and one was an alleged reporter for a religious news service, a defrocked, free-loading minister whose invitation request had been approved by someone who had his mind on something else. Half of the news contingent came from the New York City area, and more than half of the New Yorkers were sent by local and ethnic papers and national magazines. This geographical imbalance often created resentment between the self-invited reporters from small-town newspapers and those from the large metropolitan dailies and wire services who thought themselves an elite, though most had been raised west of the Appalachians, and treated their confrères as country cousins.

All the major New York City papers, except the *Evening Post*, sent representatives. The senior man was Joseph Jefferson O'Neill, star reporter on the *World*, the prototypical hard-drinking, hard-working newsman, very like his jovial friend and fellow imbiber Gaston Plantiff. Elmer Davis, a Rhodes scholar from Indiana and later a world-famous radio commentator, went as a cub reporter for the *Times*. Two Brooklyn newsmen—George Edward Riis, the prep-school-dropout son of the famous social worker Jacob Riis, who had gone west to become a cowboy and had become a reporter instead, and Jacob Hirsch,* a seventeen-year-old enthusiast who billed himself as a "wide awake newspaperman" willing to do anything in four languages—had talked with Mme Schwimmer at the Biltmore and asked to come. The Chicago *Tribune* sent Carolyn Wilson, an astute, sharp-penned war correspondent just returned from Europe following her arrest for espionage. And the Philadelphia *Public Ledger* sent William C. Bullitt, a scion of Philadelphia society educated at Yale, Harvard and on European sojourns, and a future ambassador. Young "Billy" was caustic, hot-tempered, snobbish, debonair and dashing—and a bright and knowledgeable hard worker.

Some—by no means all—of the reporters questioned the propriety of the expedition or doubted the optimism of its members. Many of the journalists were unknown to the leaders; some were their friends. Besides the delegate-writers, there were socialists, suffragists and those simply sympathetic to the attempt among the press. The organizers assumed that the self-invited free-lance writers and the reporters for the small-town and ethnic papers favored their cause, though they realized a few might be along for the ride. The organizers also assumed, with some cause, that the reporters from the Eastern metropolitan papers and wire services were biased against the peace venture, and that their stories appearing daily for the next six weeks would affect the attitude of those the expedition wanted to influence, especially in Europe.

The twenty-five students, representing a considerable geographic distribution and coming from both private and public colleges, were practically all of the same mind and temper. They were all interested in internationalism, though only two or three called themselves pacifists. Despite the refusal of their college presidents to nominate candidates, students from Barnard, Princeton and Vassar volunteered. Probably the most qualified of all was Edgar Fell, who was working for a doctoral degree, spoke four languages and had served as secretary to the American ambassador to Spain. They were a bright, level-headed, cheerful group mindful of their obligation to observe their elders and participate in events.

---

* Mr. Hirsch changed his name to Burnet Hershey during the First World War.

Three working staffs served the expedition: the Schwimmer-Lochner peace staff, Rexford Holmes's contingent of office workers and Gaston Plantiff's business force. Among Holmes's crew was a Swedish-born interpreter, a newspaper reporter to write news releases and edit the minutes and Van Arsdale Turner, a Library of Congress cataloguer who was put to work in one corner of the press room digging in the barrels of unsorted mail brought from the Biltmore, a job that lasted the entire voyage.

Gaston Plantiff, an anomaly among his charges, was along to pay the expenses of the policymakers and to arrange logistics. With him was his chief clerk in the Ford office, Robert Neely, who was an expert accountant and office manager, several lesser clerks and typists from the Long Island City plant and a junior member of the law firm that had arranged the ship's charter. Three tour directors had been engaged to see that the pilgrims were bedded and their luggage transported in Europe, and a passenger agent with the Scandinavian American line came to handle affairs on the ship. On Henry Ford's personal staff was Ray Dahlinger, from the Detroit office, who guarded Ford's body by day, and James Golden, of the New York office, who guarded it by night.

Four days out to sea the purser finally figured out how many were in the Ford party: 163 adults and three children.* The breakdown until crisis changed the balance was fifty-five members, eleven of them on the Schwimmer-Lochner staff; forty-four members of the press; twenty-five students; thirty-one on the business and clerical staff; and eleven supernumeraries. Four of the latter were wives of newspapermen, one was Frieda Mylecraine, a social worker who was Mrs. Fels's companion and family friend, and another was George Beadle, a Detroit peaceworker who falsely claimed credentials from the *Christian Science Monitor*. Lilian Holt and Dean Marquis arranged his passage, but neither Mme Schwimmer nor Lochner wanted Beadle in the party and he was not a delegate. A stowaway was not yet counted a member of the party; and twenty-three more people, half of them students, followed on the *Frederick VIII*.

Julia Grace Wales, alone in her cabin that first evening, her accident-insurance policy just put away, sat among Inez Milholland Boissevain's flowers and champagne, thinking of the thousands on the pier to whom

---

* Eight first-class passengers of the original sailing kept their reservations and joined the others only at meals.

once more "the adequate thing was not said." It had been another lost opportunity for "the most impressive kind of propaganda." Talking with her fellow passengers earlier, she had realized they were "all going forward in the dark [anxious] to know more about each other and about our enterprise." It would have been clear to anyone that the members may have been qualified to perform their secondary task of electing American delegates to the conference but were not yet capable of performing their primary job of persuasively speaking of the conference's purpose in Europe. Before dinner, Miss Wales tried to see Lochner long enough to suggest they all get "down to [the] real work" of studying internationalism the next day, but Lochner laughed good-naturedly and remarked that Sunday should be a day of rest.

When Ford entered the dining room that first evening everyone rose as the orchestra played "The Star Spangled Banner" in honor of host and country. Dean Marquis, entering beside Mme Schwimmer, commented on how rested she looked. "Yes," she replied, "no telephones. No conspirators." There was no talk of the hazard of their journey; no neutral ship had ever been blown up by mines or torpedoes. Instead, the major topic was the validity of the Braleys' marriage. The lawyers declared it legal, and the press gave an after-dinner dance in honor of the bride and groom.

That night Rosika Schwimmer received William Bullitt in her cabin for an interview. She was reclining on her bed, dressed in a purple kimono covered with a scarlet blanket, eager to speak of her expectations for the conference and of the great welcome they would have in the Scandinavian countries. Her confidence shook the politically aware Bullitt, who sat about the press room the next few days uncertain what to write.

At ten that night, Lochner held a brief press conference, and those reporters whose papers paid cable charges sent back messages that "everything was jolly aboard." That observation probably had little to do with what Lochner said and a lot to do with the case of Scotch stashed in Plantiff's cabin by a friend, the bottle of rye Sara Moore's fiancé gave her at the pier (which twenty-four years later Elmer Davis still remembered drinking) and the fact that the most expensive drink at the bar cost fourteen cents.

In the business office that night, twenty-year-old Isidor Caesar* care-

---

* A schoolteacher Americanized Isaac Caesar's first name to Isidor; a music publisher changed it to Irving when Caesar wrote the lyrics to "Swanee," in emulation of the hit songwriter, Irving Berlin.

fully and conspicuously folded the discarded wrapping paper and picked
up the pieces of twine left on the floor after the unpacking of supplies. At
his father's bookstore, a rendezvous for intellectual East European Jews
of the Lower East Side, he had heard talk all his life of social and political

Jacob Greenberg, the stowaway (State Historical Society of Wisconsin).

injustice. When he read of the Ford expedition, he had a friend at Western Union send a free message requesting a berth and then hurried up-
town for a personal appearance. Determined to make good in the world,
Caesar had himself hired as a stenographer and later solicited newspaper
credentials from *Our Town*, a short-lived socialist weekly. That first
night he hoped that the rich man, Henry Ford, passing by, would see him
tidying up and reward him for his Horatio Alger virtue. Caesar was
recognized, but it was Jake "Squint" Greenberg, his Western Union
friend, who spotted him through the doorway.

Together they had attended Cooper Union lectures, talked of Tom

Paine and Whitman and schemed to get on the peace expedition. But Caesar had a birth certificate, the prerequisite for a passport, and Greenberg did not. However, the twenty-six-year-old messenger had two other assets: a Western Union uniform and chutzpah. Early Saturday afternoon he put on his uniform, typed out a phone message to Inez Milholland Boissevain on a Western Union blank, marked the envelope "Important: Answer by Bearer," took it to Hoboken and, flashing it at an official, walked up the *Oscar* gangplank and looked for a place to hide. He chose a lavatory with a porthole and hid for seven hours, reading the newspaper and magazines he had brought with him. By nine o'clock he figured it was too late to be sent back and he emerged seeking a more comfortable sanctuary. Quite naturally he hunted for his old friend whom he had helped get on board. But Caesar was too frightened of his own standing to return the favor. If anyone learned a friend of his had stowed away, he would never reach the first rung of the ladder he was so eager to scale to success; someone else must discover him. Jake Greenberg wandered down the corridors until he found Ford, who was talking with McClure in the press room. Boldly, nobly, he stepped forward and gave himself up in an impassioned monologue on the necessity for peace and his devotion to Ford's plan. He begged for a chance to work his way over. His honesty, grit and ingenuity won him the privilege of sleeping on the press-room floor that night; his plea for a chance to work got him a pair of overalls, a shirt and an assignment from the captain the next morning to peel potatoes in the hold. Several days later, at the behest of Judge Lindsey and Rex Holmes, Greenberg was put on the office staff.

It had been morning and evening of the first day, and Ford looked about him at his community of old and young, rich and poor, and found it good. Outside his door, James Golden, enshrouded in a shawl, a wool cap on his head, sat through the night. And on the other side of the ship, outside Mme Schwimmer's cabin, Elli Eriksson sat on a campstool, guarding her mistress's rest.

"A veritable floating Chautauqua"

EARLY THEIR FIRST MORNING at sea the band awakened the argonauts with a Sunday hymn. Many took one look at their slanting potted begonias and rolled over in their berths, aware that the six-course dinner of the night before was the last meal they would eat for days. Those who made it down to breakfast ate a "moveable feast," Lewis Maverick remarked, as the ship pitched and tossed in the rough seas. The hale and hearty played tag and quoits while others stretched out on the deck chairs and bundled in steamer blankets trying to fight the miseries of mal de mer. The most popular person on board was Elizabeth Watson, who spooned out 250 doses of Mothersill's Seasick Remedy in the first few days. The more discriminating—Mrs. Boissevain, Mme Schwimmer, Miss Leckie and Plantiff's staff—sipped champagne.

The weather was dreary and bleak for three days. Under gray skies, on heavy seas, the small, slow liner pitched and rolled, her speed cut in half by great waves that battered her hull and poured over the upper deck. On the top deck were the cabins of the leaders and their friends, Mme Schwimmer's office, the smoking room, which was converted into an office, the press room, outfitted with the best equipment, and the music room, which served as the library. The public rooms on the saloon deck below were for rest and rehabilitation. There were unassigned sittings for all meals in the first-class dining room, the second-class facility having been converted into a general meeting hall and smoking lounge. And in a nook of the lounge, hidden behind an open corner, was the bar, the cause of much friction between the tipplers and the Prohibitionists.

Before breakfast each morning a staff member slipped a daily bulletin giving the order of the day beneath each cabin door. Every day at least three meetings were squeezed between three meals and four collations. The ambulatory among the clerical staff started working almost around the clock from the moment they unpacked the paper and set up the equipment, reproducing and distributing the continuous stream of bulletins, programs and statements prepared by Mme Schwimmer's office.

The stalwart and upright—mostly students—bundled up in their long coats and woolen mittens and danced the fox trot and the tango on the afterdeck. Ford, who always enjoyed a sea voyage, chatted with the occupants of "Seasick Row" during his daily constitutional, his body-guard, who cared for him "like a mother," by his side. One day several of the delegates placed a message—"Let us have peace—Ford Peace Party" —in a corked bottle and threw it overboard.

There was a pervasive mood of harmony and positive purpose, a willingness to be helpful, aboard the *Oscar II*. The earnest conversations and the diligence and interest at the frequent and well-attended meetings persuaded the reporters, who had thought the pacifists were acting without a notion of what they were doing, to revise their views. The mirror of this amity was *The Argosy*, the expedition's daily paper, edited by Ben Huebsch. It printed official announcements, but was mostly an outlet for the light verse, short sketches and miscellaneous happy thoughts of the assembled and was a cheerful contrast to the shipping line's paper, which reported war bulletins, stock quotations and forecasts of foul weather. Midweek, *The Argosy* published a ditty which reflected the party's camaraderie and, incidentally, the managers' expected conference site:

Our peace ship party started with a sendoff at the pier,
We don't know where we're going—but we're mighty glad we're here,
It's a seasick sort of voyage, over miles of ocean spray
But we put our trust in Henry and with faith and hope we say:

It's a long way to Copenhagen
It's a long way to sail,
It's a long way to Copenhagen,
But we'll get there, never fail.
Goodbye dear old Broadway,
Farewell Herald Square

It's a long, long way to Copenhagen,
But peace waits right there.

Sunday, December 5, was a free day for most of the passengers. The students met to hear Rebecca Shelly speak of her "spiritual rebirth" at the women's Hague conference and Miss Wales explain her neutral mediation plan. Afterwards, the young people decided to meet twice daily, and did so for the rest of the voyage.

Under Lochner's guiding hand, Ford cabled his thanks to all Americans for cheering their departure, and then the manufacturer spent many happy hours with the men and machinery in the engine room.

Late in the afternoon Dean Marquis read vespers and Dr. Aked spoke lengthily and fervidly of the pacifists' errand, comparing it to the "small beginnings" of Paul's conversions of the people and the Pilgrims' settlement in the New World. Ford took advantage of the arrangements his managers had made for many newspapers to receive free copies of whatever the *Oscar II* cabled and had the sermon sent verbatim to New York and London for further distribution. (Like all cables from the *Oscar II*, it was sent in fifty-word segments to passing vessels which relayed it to shore, at an approximate cost of $3.60 for ten words. Aked's sermon cost over $800 and was then the longest single message ever sent by a ship's wireless.) After dinner the Reverend Jenkin Lloyd Jones addressed the assembly in "thundering tones" on the causes of war and the perfectibility of man through internationalism.

At the evening gathering on Monday, Mme Schwimmer made her first appearance in two days to speak on "The Purpose of This Journey." It was a gallant gesture, since she too was mostly hors de combat because of the turbulent sea. The assemblage waited in wonder to see the person they had heard was a powerful orator, a dynamo of purpose and a learned internationalist. (One student even visualized her as "a row of morocco-bound books entitled *Information about Europe*.") She did not disappoint them. After winning her audience's sympathy by apologizing for her English, which was, in fact, excellent, Mme Schwimmer assured the delegates that the Europeans would welcome their peace initiative. As evidence she cited the universality of the women's congress proposals for a lasting peace, which were similar to those suggested by all the peace societies that had been founded since the war began, and she reported the substance of the women envoys' conversation with the leaders of the belligerent countries. The neutral governments, she explained, had offered mediation when acceptance of such an offer was tantamount to defeat. The mediation conference would act as a clearing house for peace proposals, its doors always open, so that no opponent need suffer loss of face using its services.

Several times Mme Schwimmer referred to secret matters between the neutral and belligerent government leaders and the women's congress deputations, noting that the statesmen said they could confide in the women but not in Colonel House. Regrettably, the documentary evidence she had that the European governments would welcome an unofficial conference would be denied if she disclosed it; instead she promised the delegates they would see her assertions realized before their journey was done.

Caught in the evangelistic spirit she had created, McClure jumped to his feet to give his testimony: "Mme Schwimmer," he cried, "may I say here I go with you, I go with you because I saw those documents and they convinced me!" She thanked him and then tried to end her talk, promising to answer any questions about what they would do in Europe at another time. But the audience would not let her go, and she talked on for a few minutes of the immediate future. The *Oscar II* would probably be held up at Kirkwall, in the Orkneys, while the British inspected the cargo for contraband. In Europe, the peace party would stay about three days at each Scandinavian capital, where large committees were at present arranging banquets, receptions and meetings. At the end, in The Hague, they would be greeted with enthusiasm and sympathy and would return home knowing they had enhanced Europe's impression of the United States. Then, promising again to answer questions the next day, she quickly disappeared amid great applause.

Her performance enthralled the young, the devoted and the unquestioning. Miss Wales recorded the impact of Mme Schwimmer's presence that evening: "In her black hair and eyes, her powerful voice, the solid bulk of her figure, the great strength of her head and neck, the emotional vigor of her speech, she suggested the natural force of the super-woman." And a student reported the persuasive effect of her guarantees of welcome and success:

An infinitely significant and interesting thing which madame said was that she had documents showing in black and white that when the belligerent powers became certain that they had a conference of the neutral powers either officially or unofficially gathered, which represented the best opinion of all neutral nations that they would be willing and eager to send delegates to this conference.

And, he wrote, McClure's endorsement of Mme Schwimmer's documents "substantiated our highest hopes."

Rosika Schwimmer's account, however, was gravely flawed by false-hoods, distortions and omissions caused by her need to dramatize their mission and magnify her role. No government official had endorsed an unofficial neutral conference; she had herself already said that such a gathering would be ignored in Europe. She implied that the members of

Rosika Schwimmer and her notorious black bag on the *Oscar II* (Courtesy of Henry Ford Museum).

her audience were not competent to deal with the complex matters of their pilgrimage by saying nothing of how the neutral conference would proceed to accomplish its aim. She did not even mention the delegates' principal duty of electing American representatives. In relating the history of the mediation scheme, she associated herself with the famous— Miss Addams and Mrs. Catt—but of Miss Wales, whose plan the voyagers were advocating and who was sitting in the audience, she said nothing.

The clearest indication of her autocratic attitude toward those she was to advise—and her most serious misjudgment—was her handling of the "secret documents," which she ostentatiously carried everywhere in a large black handbag and which were no more than the letters and accounts of statements made by the officials the women envoys had interviewed seven months before. They were not secret documents. McClure, Jordan, Lochner and Marquis had seen them. President Wilson and Maurice Francis Egan, the American minister to Denmark, had seen them. And their substance was in the women's manifesto published in the New York *Times* in October.

At the question-and-answer session the next day, the reporters and delegates asked specific questions and Rosika Schwimmer gave evasive answers. She refused to show anyone the "secret documents" even though Dr. Aked said "everybody has a right to see the evidence. . . . [and] know all that is to be known"—and everyone knew McClure had seen them. Instead, Mme Schwimmer demanded blind trust and accused the journalists of suppressing the constructive aims and accomplishments of the pacifists. The antagonism between Rosika Schwimmer and her questioners was so palpable that after the meeting the United Press reporter began his cabled dispatch, "All is not peaceful aboard Henry Ford's ship of peace to-day."

As it happened the gathering was only a curtain raiser to a grander drama played at the general meeting that night. McClure, the featured speaker, read from his press copy of the State of the Union message which the president had delivered that day. In the past year, Wilson said, "the whole face of international affairs" had so changed that he was now compelled to ask Congress to strengthen the armed forces so that the nation could "care for its own security and to make sure of entire freedom to play the impartial role in this hemisphere and in the world which we all believe to have been providentially assigned to it."

The topic Mme Schwimmer's staff selected for general discussion was what reply they, a peace mission, should make to Wilson's advocacy of military preparedness as a national policy, and it "blew up" the meeting.

The absolute pacifists called the president's program "the entering edge of militarism." Others argued that until all nations agreed to disarm simultaneously, each country had to have arms to defend itself and maintain its standing in the council of nations. In any case, they added, the Ford mission should make no statement at all, since Wilson's program had nothing to do directly with the mission's purpose.

"I certainly do not think this message should be received in silence by this assemblage," Ellis Jones replied to that argument, his voice rising as his emotional outburst continued. "This is a reactionary message . . . we must speak out; we are going abroad now on a mission to stop a terrible war among nations. . . . This is not the time to disturb American traditions and prepare us for war." The president, Jones charged, had not specified an enemy and was speaking of false danger; he was "sending our best men into vile barracks and muddy trenches and [was] turning over the public treasury to a lot of profit mongers, who are not actuated by the slightest patriotic impulse whatsoever." McClure spoke almost as excitedly in rebuttal, and then Henry Ford stepped in to end the growing turbulence. At the first sign of a fracas, several reporters asked Ford to comment on Wilson's program, and it was through one of them, J. J. O'Neill of the *World*, who addressed the gathering, that he proposed a cooling-off period of several days. During that time small groups could discuss the matter calmly and compose a reply to the president and Congress that "could be signed by every member of the ship." This suggestion and the effort to end discussion "started some more fireworks," but the motion passed after the meeting decided that only "those who could conscientiously place their names" on the message need sign. Before adjournment, Ford promised everyone a chance to be heard and Miss Holbrook was selected to appoint a committee to write the message.

Peace prevailed. The rough seas calmed at last and the sun shone brightly Wednesday morning as the *Oscar II*, no longer cursed as the *Oscillator II* or the *Horsecar the Second*, entered the gentler waters of the Gulf Stream. The Reverend Messrs. Aked and Jones played leapfrog, Dr. Marquis soared high on a rope-board swing, and Ford took the wheel, all to oblige the news photographers. Later, Mrs. Fels presented the peace flag made by Betsy Ross's kin to Ford and the captain ordered it flown from the mast.

The spirit of good fellowship pervaded the company as passengers with similar interests formed clubs; even the six Joneses banded together. "Every one is organized except the delegation as a whole," Bullitt churlishly remarked. In fact, the most organized group of all was the journalists' Viking Press Club, led by President Joseph J. O'Neill and a slew of officers including six vice presidents and an assortment of committees. One night the club passed a resolution, which they printed in *The Argosy* and cabled to their papers. It began as a *mea culpa*—"We are

The Reverend Charles F. Aked and the Reverend Jenkin Lloyd Jones playing leapfrog (Courtesy of Henry Ford Museum).

simply reporters. . . . We're cynical, perhaps. . . . We're cautious, maybe. . . . Some of us, doubtless, entered upon this expedition tainted with the spirit of jest, looking upon it as a foolish, if not foolhardy, exploit of an ultra-rich idealist"—and ended as a pledge of loyalty—"We realize that this is a serious undertaking, from which good must inevitably come, even if the highest hopes of its projectors may not be fulfilled. . . . We are not here as avowed peace-advocates, peace workers, idealists or theorists. We're simply men and women workers on our job. We wish Henry Ford and associates success."

Toward the end of the Tuesday night meeting, the reporters and the expedition press bureau agreed not to send any stories about the discussion of Wilson's preparedness message until the compromise resolution was approved by the delegates. Though Mme Schwimmer openly abrogated the agreement by sending all of Ellis Jones's speech to American newspapers and nothing of McClure's, the journalists not only kept their word but sent reports praising both the delegates and their effort. Thomas Seltzer, the erudite reporter for the socialist daily *The Call*, cabled that the *"Oscar II* has been converted into . . . a model, up-to-date university" and instructed his office to "print serious reports. Withhold criticism. Seems no fool's errand." The 530-word cable the expedition leaders sent to each of the belligerent powers asking them to call an immediate truce, send their soldiers home, and begin peace negotiations was not only cheered by the delegates but applauded by the New York *Tribune* correspondent as "sane and . . . couched in diplomatic language." Even Elmer Davis had kind words for the delegates, though he stigmatized the mission as "a Chautauqua meeting in a town going to entertain an Elk's convention next week," and other reporters concluded that the delegates were not fanatics on a carnival joyride but idealists trying to improve an improvable world.

One day—and one day only—all three meetings dealt with the function of the expedition. Mme Schwimmer spoke to the students and the many adults who always attended the young people's meetings in favor of total disarmament and the use of international economic boycotts as a substitute for war. Her absolute faith in the efficacy of moral resistance, however, was sharply challenged in a prolonged discussion. Later, Miss Wales explained how her plan for continuous neutral mediation provided for the simultaneous submission of peace proposals to the belligerents, and Mme Malmberg spoke of her arrest and exile as a fighter for Finnish nationalism.

The news that Prime Minister Asquith told Parliament the Allies would discuss "serious" peace terms proposed by a neutral or belligerent power seemed to confirm Mme Schwimmer's assertions and so elated Ford that he offered to bet the *Oscar II* against a penny that the boys would indeed be out of the trenches by Christmas Day.

The sunshine lasted only one day; the amicability it helped engender lasted two days longer—until the resolution on the president's preparedness program was presented for approval Friday night, December 10. Though Ford's solution Tuesday night implied compromise, there had been intimations since that the absolute pacifists would not violate their principles. S. S. McClure, for example, was summoned to Mme Schwimmer's cabin Friday morning and, to his astonishment, was "seriously and kindly reprimanded for preaching preparedness to the students." Ever since the ship left Hoboken, he had been flitting in and out of the public rooms like a windup toy, his vocal chords in perpetual motion. So incessant was his chatter that the students decided his first two initials stood for "Seldom Silent." Mme Schwimmer was kept informed of his constant converse with the students, and when he touched upon the necessity for preparedness, he was haled before her.

A much more apparent indication of what lay ahead was in the announcement in Friday's *Argosy*: every member of the resolutions committee that Florence Holbrook, one of Mme Schwimmer's most devoted adherents, had appointed was an avid anti-preparedness advocate.

Rosika Schwimmer, Lochner and the commmittee had deliberately orchestrated the evening's program to ensure harmony and avoid dissonance, but their scheme was so audacious and obtrusive that only the most obsequious and approving did not feel the heavy hand of a cabal. At the beginning of the meeting, Chairman Alfred Kliefoth, of the peace staff, said discussion after Lochner's address would be postponed. The general secretary took his text from the telegram and follow-up letter of invitation, which, he said, spoke of the peace mission's purpose of ending war and militarism through world federation. Therefore, every delegate, having accepted the invitation, was duty-bound to advise the American government that he opposed increased preparedness.

Dr. Jones, the chairman of the resolutions committee, spoke next to explain a *slight* change in procedure. After conferring with Mr. Ford, Mme Schwimmer and others, the committee had written a platform which, "recognizing the futility of debate, and not wishing to produce any complications," it had decided to present for "any member of the party" to sign by Monday. Those who signed, he continued,

will constitute naturally the body that will then be prepared to proceed deliberately and before we land, to the organization of the delegation simply but efficiently, so that whatever may be done by the delegation after we leave this boat may be done in a deliberative and a democratic fashion.

Then Dr. Aked read the three planks of the platform. The first was a loyalty oath to support Ford and his assistants in the quest for peace, the second endorsed a policy of international disarmament, and the third called on all Americans to oppose the dangerous policy of preparedness:

We declare our opposition to any increase by the United States of her military and naval forces. We are convinced that no good reason can be alleged for the expenditure by use of great sums of money in preparing for war. We, therefore, call upon our fellow citizens in every State in the Union to unite in opposition to a policy that is dangerous to our country and to the world, and to join with all earnest men and women in every land in active preparation for the day of international brotherhood.

With the cheap compassion of one who presumes to speak for unassailably righteous authority, Aked remarked; "If there is anybody who cannot sign the platform we are very sorry." Copies would be available after the meeting, Aked concluded, for the signatures "of those who are with us," and Jones then suggested that the observant should sign in ink "as a matter of dignity, and what may be a matter of important history."

Kliefoth vainly tried to adjourn the meeting at once, but the outraged delegates refused to be silenced. On Tuesday night the delegates had agreed that only those who could "conscientiously" sign the message to the president would be asked to do so; no one had said then that those who did not subscribe would lose their privileges. McClure was the first on his feet, insisting that everyone expected the peace mission would eventually lead to international disarmament, but he could not "be a worker with this party" if he had to "impugn the course laid out by the President." He was willing to sign the first two planks but not the statement that put him "in opposition to our Government."

Judge Lindsey said no one had told him that acceptance of the invitation was contingent on agreement with Ford's preparedness views; he thought the whole procedure was a practical blunder, "bad politics . . . bad policy." Harry Carroll Evans, the representative of fraternal organizations who was so highly principled he would not take a drink even if it would stop the war, affirmed his opposition to preparedness but said he would not "sign the Golden Rule if it was presented as the platform was." Charges of railroading met countercharges. Anyone who would not sign, Lochner claimed, had come for a "joyride." And Ellis Jones angrily told a questioning reporter to keep his "head shut!" People argued up and down the passageways, gathering in small groups around the several spokesmen of the new opposition. The reporters, who had been imbibing their nocturnal libations in the press room during the meeting, collided with the clusters in the corridors, and then retreated to their domain followed by the protesting delegates.

John Barry was sensitive to the depth of feeling among those who, like himself, opposed preparedness but were disturbed by the leadership's blatant move to quell those who disagreed with them. Realizing at once the potential magnitude of the rapidly growing schism, he invited Aked to his stateroom and there explained it was "a violation of hospitality as well as a violation of principle" to impose an additional qualification for membership in the middle of the voyage. Aked suggested they put the matter to Ford, and on their way to his cabin, Barry ducked into the press room begging for a half-hour's grace before the reporters sent their stories. The writers agreed and asked that Ford be brought before them. While the journalists waited, the story continued to break before their typewriters. McClure, whom Elmer Davis was ready to award a medal "for endurance in debate," was still arguing that the third plank was not necessary to their purpose, and the committee's adherents were still insisting that those who would not sign the entire pledge were pariahs. Barry meanwhile vainly tried to explain the trouble to a puzzled Ford, who could not believe anyone aboard was actually unwilling to speak out against preparedness.

At the end of the grace period, Barry and Ford, joined by Aked, Jenkin Lloyd Jones and Mme Schwimmer, entered the press room, where a reporter sat them in the center of the room and, acting as spokesman for his colleagues, gave them "the third degree." The letter of invitation was read into evidence, even though quite a few of the delegates had never received a copy. McClure said he would willingly sign the platform if the key phrase of the letter—that the neutral conference "will be dedicated to the stoppage of this hideous international carnage and further dedicated to the prevention of future wars through the abolition of competitive armaments"—would be substituted for the suggested third plank of the platform, which demanded immediate overt opposition to preparedness. But the committee would not change a word. McClure persisted. At last, Dr. Jones said he had come to be interviewed by the reporters, not McClure, whom he accused of preaching militarism and spreading sedition among the students. And when McClure began protesting these charges, Dr. Jones advanced upon his pacifist brother, shook his fist in McClure's face and shouted, "Go to bed, sir! Go to bed!" Sending a parting shot at Lindsey—a "politician not a pacifist"—Jones stalked out of the room, followed by Mme Schwimmer and Aked. The correspondents turned to their typewriters, Barry contemplated the coming havoc when people read of the disruption over a matter of no consequence to the mission, and Ford stayed seated, still confused, but sociable.

Later that night several correspondents took their stories to the wireless room and found the door locked against them by Mme Schwimmer's order. Inside, the wireless operator was sending the peace staff's account of the meeting, which said the three resolutions "were heartily applauded and . . . rapidly signed." At the peace staff office, the reporters were peremptorily told that expedition stories took precedence over their dispatches. That dismissal sent the reporters back to Ford, who then arranged for the journalists to have priority. But when they reappeared at the wireless room, Lochner would not let them in. Finally, the newsmen's accounts were accepted, but another day passed before they were sent out.

Long after midnight the frustrated reporters returned to their bailiwick. Overhearing a few students confessing they had never favored preparedness until they heard McClure, the somewhat punch-drunk newsmen decided to bring the troublemaker to account in a mock trial for "corrupting the morals of youth."

O'Neill, as chief judge, with Braley and Riis beside him, used a stuffed dove for a gavel and a tobacco tin for a Bible, and convened the gathering. Defense attorney Elmer Davis challenged Braley as obviously incompetent, being newly married. He then charged that the prosecution's student witnesses were patently preparedness-minded since they had thought to bring tuxedos. And a journalist defense witness testified it took McClure months, sometimes years, to pay for manuscripts, a certain sign of his unpreparedness. Sheriff Swain, who had been sent to subpoena Aked, Jenkin Lloyd Jones and Lochner, returned without them because Aked was "busy manicuring his English accent," Jones had "caught his foot in his beard" and broken his leg, and Lochner was "fixing" the wireless. At three A.M. Prosecutor Ben Lindsey delivered his peroration. The jury announced, "The bar is closed" and brought in a verdict of not guilty. While they were still out the judges decided the initial accuser, Dr. Jones, was, as anyone could see, Santa Claus, a character of fiction, and thus incompetent. It was all incompetent, but perfect comic relief after the tension of the night.

Saturday and Sunday were devoted to proselytizing and protesting. All meetings were canceled. Only the students united, but their conclusion that the resolutions were "immaterial to the prime mission of the trip and prejudicial to our success" was rejected by the managers, and they were told to vote individually and affirmatively. Some delegates spoke again of resigning. In an explicit statement in which he labeled the Friday-night proceedings barbaric, Harry Carroll Evans pointed out that nothing in Ford's invitation asked him "to subscribe to a platform in order to qualify" as a delegate, and he called for conciliation.

Evans, an unknown, was ignored by Ford; Aked, at least, had a hearing. Still believing that everyone who accepted the invitation knew Ford's position on preparedness, Aked nonetheless realized that McClure, Lindsey, Mrs. Robinson and others equally well known would generate dangerous publicity by quitting, and suggested a compromise: the platform must stand because it strengthened the expedition's peacemaking position,

Lloyd Bingham (Courtesy of Henry Ford Museum).

but those who did not sign would not forfeit any rights as members.

Ford refused to back down. He could not understand why anyone was outraged by the dictatorial presentation of the platform, dishonored by exclusion from the delegation, or disturbed at being disenfranchised. He told an anxious student that "nothing worthwhile ever went down the stream of time without a ripple" and joked about the "mutiny."

During the weekend, every participant received a long, personally signed letter from Ford that was a justification of Friday's action, not a compromise. The invitation, it said, clearly indicated that every member of the mission was expected to oppose increased armaments and that such a position, publicly stated in an "unequivocal platform," was necessary for the peace mission's credibility in Europe. Those who disagreed with the platform did not have to sign it and were welcome to remain with the party. The letter also insisted that the method of presenting the resolutions was in fact a "democratic" procedure designed to avoid disruption; had it been presented for a vote, the minority would have been bound by the majority, and that was certainly undemocratic. All endorsements were to be handed in by Sunday night.

At the same time the staff followed another road to conciliation by scheduling a fun-and-games show on Saturday night. Lloyd Bingham, the expedition's entertainment director, was on stage at last. Only the students, the reporters and a few of the worldly male delegates had thus far enjoyed the acting manager's hearty, hale-fellow boisterousness. Bingham, who had been ill much of the voyage, was least appreciated by his cabinmate, John Barry, who arranged to have him moved to the sick bay and his clothing and blankets fumigated. But the entertainer was lonely in the infirmary, and though his illness grew worse and his mind wandered during periods of delirium, he moved himself back to his original quarters. On Saturday night, Bingham was lucid and his jokes were a welcome relief to all.

Everyone went to bed that night happy in spirit at least. Probably the happiest man aboard was the Reverend Arthur Weatherly, who had known naught but physical discomfort since the moment the ship left Hoboken. Between his biliousness and his bowels, his rheumatism and his sciatica, he had been in constant misery. At Saturday lunch he spoke of his ailments to the ship's nurse, who happened to be sitting beside him, and she offered to give him a rubdown in his stateroom. "That seemed mighty queer to me," he dutifully wrote his wife, "but by night I was ready for anything." Though bruised and battered by the strenuous Nordic massage, he felt the better for it on the morrow. Even so, he entitled his sermon that day "Blessed Are the Gentle."

By Sunday night, about thirty-five members of the expedition, not all of whom had been originally invited as delegates, had signed the pledge. Most of them considered the disagreement only slightly more disruptive than a similar occurrence at a religious convention. Marquis wrote his wife a few days later of their "little trouble"—not in the platform, "but in the fool way it was introduced." Aked thought it would all blow over in a few days. Julia Grace Wales yearned for Miss Addams—"I think of her daily and indeed almost hourly. We miss her so"—while she tried to minimize the damage of their discord: "All it proves is that we are all human, and that nearly everybody is dead in earnest, and that we all have vital convictions and that some people lacked experience and some people weren't as tactful as they might have been." It took Lochner a few more years to admit that "a tactical blunder had been made. . . . nothing that remotely savoured of 'railroading' should have been done to give substance to the latent dissatisfaction."

Some of the delegates did not favor increased preparedness but would not sacrifice their rights to say so. In a public statement, Herman Bernstein wrote Ford he would leave as soon as they docked in Christiania. Governor Hanna said he would leave then, too, and rejoin the expedition after it left Scandinavia. McClure and Barry assumed credentials as members of the press only. Senator Robinson thought the willingness of the delegates to leave their homes for six weeks to cross the North Atlantic during the winter and to endure financial loss and ridicule in following a "vision of peace and good will" was sufficient testament to their faith in the mission without the "sifting of the souls" demanded by the "self-elected elect." But Judge Lindsey, one of the first to explode at the high-handed proceedings Friday, though still unwilling to sign, was mollified by Ford's request that he stay with the party so that he might later explore the possibility of founding an International Home Finding Society for war orphans. In a letter to his friends, Lindsey tried to counteract the news reports: "If you hear of friction in the Peace Party, don't believe it. There were some differences over non-essentials—but nothing serious—the kind of difference in any such party. But in the bigger mission, we were all united."

It was Judge Lindsey who suggested after the general lecture Sunday evening that laughing at themselves in another mock trial might put the party's spirits back on an even keel. Drs. Jones and Aked were the accused, the former charged with militarism for shaking his fist in McClure's face and the latter with being a German spy as proved by his strong English accent. McClure defended Dr. Jones, his former antagonist, Inez Milholland Boissevain defended Dr. Aked, and Judge Lindsey was the prosecutor. "We had no end of fun," Edith Lloyd Jones wrote home, and it did seem the group had successfully regained its lost Eden.

It was an unresolved question then and thereafter whether the preparedness platform crisis had caused a severe wound in the peace delegation or only an easily healed abrasion, a full-scale row or only a minor disturbance blown up by the biased reporters looking for a story. Certainly the disharmony and distrust between the management and their allies and the metropolitan reporters increased, and the impressions the several components of the expedition had made upon one another thus far were set.

Ford passed up the delegates' daily meetings, but he did attend the students get-togethers, and spoke to them once on the blessings of shorter hours and good pay and the evils of labor unions. The manufacturer spent most of his hours inspecting the ship's machinery or stretched out in the captain's quarters. Johan Wilhelm Hempel had been at sea for forty years and the captain of the *Oscar II* since her maiden voyage eleven years before. An association developed between Ford and himself that lasted until Hempel's death after the war. On the voyage, the captain showed his loyalty to his new friend by monitoring the reporters' cables; Ford showed his appreciation by giving Hempel a Model T sedan.

As an industrial magnate who cared for the common good while making his first millions, Ford had already won the approval of everyone aboard. The man who came to dinner in what one passenger called his "$16 suit" was everybody's friend. His simplicity and sincerity, his friendliness and generosity, "the all-pervading radiance of his personality," as Lochner described it, entranced his guests. Miss Wales, after sitting next to him at dinner one night, called him "the nicest type of American millionaire." He invited students to his cabin, where he talked of lightweight railroad cars and submarines. He promised to support several of the young people who wanted to study international relations in Europe after the war and offered to pay the expenses of a delegate who wanted to remain in Europe to study the war.

The journalists were enchanted by the shy and gentle millionaire with the "dreamy look in his eyes," who seemed "curiously like Lincoln," "a sort of inarticulate Christ," and they marveled that this plainspoken man of "good humor, idealism and shrewd commonsense" was "the dominant industrialist" of the day. Ford's ignorance of European power politics, diplomacy and economy, his lack of interest in the implications of his peace action and the fact that "when his mind gets away from blueprints it is vague and unreliable" astounded the reporters but was excused on the ground that the manufacturer was, after all, only "a mechanical genius with the heart of a child." Unquestionably, Ford's presence and behavior produced the companionable and confident mood that held the mission together in its critical early days.

Ford spoke happily of tractors and "flivverizing the railroads" to everyone, but when he talked peace his listeners soon learned he was at sea figuratively as well as literally. Again he told the reporters what he had been saying for months—war was of, for and by the profiteers and wasteful for everyone else. Once the people were told the truth, they would stop fighting and return to their factories to make plows or to their farms to use them. And he reasserted his commitment of himself and his fortune to ending the war and fighting preparedness. Even if the present mission failed, he said, the psychological effect of the undertaking and the front-page publicity would have some beneficial influence upon the belligerents. Even if it only shortened the war by one day, it would have been worthwhile.

While Henry Ford impressed his followers as a complete democrat and most of the reporters as a guileless innocent, Rosika Schwimmer came across as "a high priestess" possessed of "a tortuous Dual-Monarchy mind" who secluded herself in her stateroom "like a great spider, weaving the web of her plans" under the constant protection of her palace guard. "To reach her presence was more difficult than to embrace the Dalai Lama," Bullitt sneered.

Mme Schwimmer rarely appeared at meetings and never at meals or social hours. Although realizing that as a belligerent subject she was disqualified from delegate status, in her job as expert adviser she decided every single detail regarding programs and policies aboard the ship and made similar arrangements for the European tour. No cable was sent, no letter written, no speaker assigned, without her approval. To some her seclusion merely meant that she was working round the clock in the mission's interest; but to most it meant that she was deliberately avoiding everyone. A few were disquieted when they passed her guarded cabin and wondered why her staff opened the door only wide enough to enter or emerge, and why she had her minions secretly reporting the conversations they overheard in the corridors and public rooms.

Some thought she deliberately taunted the curious by always carrying her black bag, which she said contained the secret documents. Her several public appearances were only to give advice, which she expected to be followed unhesitatingly. Her replies to questions, John Barry noticed, were "a little more adroit than frank." She considered all the voyagers her followers when in fact most of the delegates were following an ideal and the students and reporters were along only to observe or report. Lochner later thought she had failed as a leader despite her considerable personal assets because she was "essentially an autocrat," unable to work with the "honest souls who abhorred the secrecy and intrigue of European diplomacy . . . who followed the banner of Henry Ford precisely because his was an open, frank, public attempt to end the War." When her tactics were challenged, Mme Schwimmer defended her espionage system as her only means of protecting herself against those who were conspiring against her—that is, those who disagreed with her. Anyone who questioned or criticized her was perforce an enemy whom she tried to silence or remove. Resentment grew among the peacemakers as the flow of her ukases increased and people thought themselves "unfairly expected to support by their presence and apparent consent a policy which they could not control and which they could not fully understand."

At the time, Louis Lochner believed in Rosika Schwimmer's methods, having seen the successful results of her will power against great odds, first in The Hague when she turned the conference around and again in persuading Ford to back their enterprise. He was also burdened by his customary deference to his elders and superiors.

The delegates' soundings of each other were largely favorable. Judge Lindsey thought he had never met "a finer body of people for intelligence, and earnestness." Marquis agreed with that opinion but excepted the faddists—"a neurotic lot"—and some of the women who only "blink and twitch and squint." He was, however, dismayed by the peculiar habits of mind of his new colleagues who suspected the motives of those who disagreed with them and who considered facts and figures in an argument the same way, he said, as Christian Scientists regarded doctors. Though Mary Alden Hopkins, a journalist-delegate, generously dismissed the foibles of her fellow travelers with the observation that one does not "become a saint by stepping on a peace boat," Ben Huebsch, years later, admitted that those delegates who were prominent at home could not see beyond their own "importance and . . . ability." Mme Schwimmer shrewdly catered to this group of prima donnas by assigning them to the committees she was obliged to appoint from time to time as a democratic facade.

After the metropolitan reporters' apologia was in effect thrown in their faces at the locked wireless-room door, the journalists turned to their typewriters and wrote out the bitterness of the abused and rejected. Those writers whose editors had instructed them to attack the expedition had their ammunition at last. The stories, though not entirely lies and distortions, revealed a growing distance between the written word and the truth, and a variation of Gresham's Law went into effect as the few accurate and fairminded reports on the mission's accomplishments were lost in the abundance of mockery and malediction.

For certain journalists the schisms resulting from the Friday night
debacle separated the men from the boys, as it were, among the delegates.
The reporters called the large controlling group small-town folks with
small minds, stubborn and stupid, primarily concerned with regulating the

Journalists: S. S. McClure, front row, fifth from left; Elmer Davis,
second row, extreme right; William Bullitt, standing, extreme right,
with his hand on Davis's shoulder.

behavior of their betters. Both Bullitt and Davis, for example, with much
cause chastised the travelers for their hypocrisy and their unwillingness
to prepare themselves for their responsibilities and to acknowledge the
implications of their proposed action. Though they stood for democratic
policies, Bullitt wrote, they "feared democratic control of the peace
expedition. . . . Mr. Ford and his fellow Uplifters set out to 'save' Europe
in the same spirit with which they would have set out to save a fallen
man. . . . They did not think it was necessary to hammer their vague
tenderness into a coherent plan of action by means of a democratic or-

ganization and an open forum, where absurdities could be discussed and killed." They did not realize that "they would be regarded everywhere as pro-Germans; first, because of the presence of Frau Schwimmer as leader of the expedition, second because of their advocacy of peace at the present time."

Charles Stewart's dispatch, which led with "War has broken out aboard Henry Ford's peace argosy," was the most damaging sent on the preparedness-platform uproar because the United Press story not only circulated in the United States but was picked up by the wireless station at Land's End and released to British papers. Joseph J. O'Neill's cable to the *World* began sensationally—"All is not peace on the Peace Ship. War has been declared"—and continued in a martial metaphor for three more paragraphs. Other articles reported the dissenters' objections to the anti-Wilson platform written by "Rosika Schwimmer's associates" and noted that a few "prominent members" would quit the party. Though Ford—and everybody else—was told the contents of the reporters' cables, he refused to censor them, and the managers' only recourse was a message to the president, released to the American press, expressing the hope that Wilson would "not be annoyed by misleading dispatches from newspaper correspondents."

Those delegates who were aware of the disarming effect Ford's amiability and their own sincerity had had upon the skeptical reporters blamed the lost harmony on the attitudes and behavior of their leaders. Senator Robinson criticized Mme Schwimmer's manner. "Even a reporter is human, after all," she said. "You rarely melt him to tenderness and praise by calling him a liar and a brute—even if he is one." And Miss Wales remarked, "If [the reporters] failed to understand, others failed to interpret." Those lost to this grievous oversight she thought "were some of the best brains and some of the best hearts on the *Oscar II*."

The students universally received high marks as "a bright, active group." The clerical staff went unnoticed, largely because its members stayed in their quarters typing and mimeographing their way across the ocean. In addition to the prodigious number of daily circulars prepared—every time the managers drew a breath it seemed they wrote a communiqué—the staff prepared two manuscripts for printing. One was a "Who's Who" of everyone on the expedition and the other was a compilation of favorable comments selected from the barrels of letters and telegrams received at the Biltmore.

The rough weather had so slowed the *Oscar II* that she did not enter the war zone off the Scottish coast until her tenth day at sea. Bulbs, strung on steel casings extending twenty feet over the sides, lit up the ship's name, its country of registry and the painted red field and white cross of the Danish flag. In the crow's nest and in the bow, sailors kept a lookout for floating mines while others swung the lifeboats over the railing and loaded them with food and lanterns. All the Americans were exhilarated by their first encounter with the war they had come to stop.

At five P.M. on Monday, December 13, the ship's engines stopped. It had been dark for two hours and a bright moon shone upon the sea. In the distance the passengers could see the British cruiser that had trailed them like a ghost ship, guiding their course by radio. Off to port a converted liner approached, circled the *Oscar II* and then dispatched a prize crew. To everyone's astonishment, when the "red cheeked pleasingly fat" lieutenant came on board, his first words were "Where is the mutiny?" Stewart's facetious cable had been interpreted literally by the Admiralty, which had almost sent a relief party. The lieutenant took command of the ship, ran up the Union Jack and sent his men to seal off the wireless. Within the hour the *Oscar II* was under way, its course changed for Kirkwall.

It had taken only a moment to assure the British tars there were no mutineers aboard, and while some of the reporters may have chortled at the mischief they had caused, it was no laughing matter to the management.

On Tuesday morning the newly qualified delegates met, as Dr. Jones promised they would, to elect a temporary organization committee to work with Ford and the managers. Parliamentary procedure was exemplary this time. A nominating committee, appointed by Chairman Judson King, the specialist in participatory democracy, was told to present fourteen names for a vote that afternoon. Lochner announced that only delegates would participate in the procedure, which was a great shock to the students who remembered how much a part of the mission they had been when their signatures were demanded to approve the platform. At the afternoon meeting, the administration relented, and the recalcitrant delegates who had not signed the pledge not only voted but were eligible for election. Only one of them, Lieutenant Governor Bethea, won; at least half of the other six winners were old friends of either Mme Schwimmer, Miss Leckie or Lochner. Dr. Arthur Weatherly, a veteran of the committee that had worked with Mme Schwimmer and Lochner on the preparedness planks, knowingly observed that it was "pitiful to see how much importance is put into the offices, which do not amount to anything at all." But at the press club meeting that evening, Inez Milholland Boissevain, the club counsel, announced that a new day of democracy had dawned, and others prophesied the end of the Schwimmer-Lochner domination.

Because the *Oscar II* arrived at Kirkwall after the harbor entrance had already been closed for the night by a gate of mines, it was not until Tuesday morning that the seafarers had their first view of land. About them lay green fields dotted with stone cottages and haystacks. On one side of the harbor stood a great castle, the home of Lord Rosebery, the former prime minister who had just mocked the peace pilgrimage in Parliament. Snow-covered hills lay in the distance, and beyond them, on the other side of the mountain ridge, the British fleet was based at Scapa Flow. Hundreds of gulls, golden in the sunrise, swept past the *Oscar II* as she entered the harbor and joined the other ships at anchorage.

Before Captain Hempel took the mail and cables ashore, he showed the reporters' dispatches to Mme Schwimmer and her staff, whereupon Katherine Leckie headed straight for the press room, her anger barely controlled. There would be a tea that afternoon for the journalists, she announced, but Mme Schwimmer would not attend. Miss Leckie had invited her, but the expert adviser was deeply hurt and insulted by the journalists' resentment of her, and had declined, saying, "It seems that I am said by the newspaper people to be the 'hoodoo' of the peace party." Miss Leckie then gave the reporters a large piece of her mind for treating her benefactress so disrespectfully. The reporters asked to see Mme Schwimmer to clear up the matter, and Miss Leckie went to get her.

Though still angered by Mme Schwimmer's refusal to speak of the official promises of welcome she had darkly hinted her documents contained, the writers nonetheless applauded her heartily when she entered their sanctum. "Don't be hypocritical," she acknowledged graciously, as a preliminary to a tirade. The newspapermen had been against her, she said, before they even boarded the ship. Since then they had told Ford she listened behind doors, peeked through windows and spread "malicious gossip." Someone, she said, suggested that Ford was backing the expedition because she was his mistress. However, she knew how to play that game. She had read all their cables and not only was her espionage system reporting "their malicious gossip," she was entering every item on a card file in her office. As Bullitt remarked: "This did not tend to produce any undue amount of good feeling." At the end the journalists asked once more about the secret documents. Two reporters, whose stories are much the same in substance, quoted two different portions of her reply. Miriam Teichner said only that Mme Schwimmer convinced them that the papers she had "could not be shown without violation of the most sacred of confidences." And Bullitt quoted her as admitting, "I have no documents that will be valuable in any way to this expedition. . . . I have received no suggestion that neutral governments will receive the Ford party. I do not expect that the party will be recognized officially. I propose merely a permanent neutral conference." Her admission that she had only expectations, not assurances, "naturally discredited the whole enterprise," Davis later remarked.

If the reporters congratulated themselves on their two-hour interview in the morning, they had their comeuppance in the late afternoon. Robert Bastian Bermann, who had been editing the meetings' transcripts, learned that morning he was one of the clerical staff to be sent home from Christiania. He opted instead for a quick getaway aboard the eastbound *Stockholm*, about to leave Kirkwall, and by afternoon had the harbormaster's permission to transfer from the *Oscar II*. Amid the cheers and farewells of his shipmates, he shouted back he would be a millionaire as soon as he landed, for he carried with him all the news photographs and movie film. (The result was that the first photographs of the peace expedition seen by the public were of Drs. Aked and Jones playing leapfrog.) When the big-city reporters learned that Bermann was a Washington journalist traveling in disguise and thus was bound to beat their still-to-be censored copy and the stories they had yet to file in Norway, they formed an ad hoc committee that tried, but failed, to get him off the *Stockholm*.

Five of the correspondents found an immediate, and rather bizarre, release from their frustration by bursting into Ford's cabin demanding to see if he was still alive. A tremendous wave had washed over Ford some days before and he had been confined to his room for the past three days with a sore throat and a slight fever. He had appeared briefly on Monday when the British boarded, and the reporters had seen him Tuesday night in his quarters, but, they explained, when J. P. Morgan died in his Rome hotel room several years before the news had been kept from the press for six hours and they did not want to be caught short again.

Late that night, the journalists sought comic relief in the plight of one of the passengers. The Reverend Theophilus E. Montgomery, editor of a religious news service, had lingered in limbo during the entire crossing. He claimed status as a delegate; the managers insisted he was only a member of the press. A reporter, hearing of his dilemma, called a special meeting Wednesday night of the Vacillating Sons and Sisters of St. Vitus, which had been founded just two days before, for the purpose of initiating "Tee Hee" Montgomery into membership. The club name derived from a comment by reporter Max Swain who sensed "venom and poison in the air" and warned his colleagues that they would have St. Vitus's dance if they did not do something to alleviate the tension.

After the candidate sang the club song:

> Raving, raving over the bounding main
> There's many a nut goes off his nut
> With peace upon the brain . . .

and took the oath of allegiance:

> . . . With gibberings and ghoulish squeaks
> I swear that I've been nuts for weeks,
> And promise that I'll always stick,
> And stay a howling lunatic,

he was anointed with insect powder and invested with the insignia of the order: "the wreath of unreason, consisting of a circular paper of pins, point upward, symbolizing the pinheadedness of all members" and "a nut suspended by a scarlet cord from a Star of Bethlehem Peace Button." The audience hailed the ceremony as "a scream from start to finish," but it relieved the hostility only momentarily.

The next days were dead days—gray, foggy, damp. The passengers had lived in cramped quarters for almost two weeks. The heavy seas, recurring seasickness, tensions over the platform and de facto status as British prisoners of war for the past two days all made their "confinement somewhat irksome." With no laundry facilities and the journey already delayed several days, the travelers were running out of clean clothing. There was insufficient drinking water and none for bathing. Land was tantalizingly close but inaccessible.

These conditions contributed to another crisis between the New York reporters and the administrators. The commander of the port, learning that the Americans, especially the correspondents, were disgruntled not only at being detained but at the British censorship of their dispatches, invited Miss Leckie to tour the island in the company of a journalist. She asked John English of the Boston *Traveler*, the writer most favored by the expedition managers for his fair reports. As soon as they returned they were summoned for interrogation in the press room. Miss Leckie insisted that her selection of English was sheer happenstance and added that no New York reporter would have been invited in any case. Not surprisingly, the objects of her wrath thought the members of the press should have picked their own representative. They immediately wrote Ford a letter which first complained that English was incompetent because he had not found out if their cables would be mailed or telegraphed to London and then went on:

We have more confidence in our ability to get all the news and to report that news accurately and intelligibly to all other newspaper men on board this boat than we have in the ability to do so of most of the press representatives from other cities, who do not have to live up daily to the standards required of us.

And they reminded Ford that they represented newspapers that had "considerably more influence on public opinion than those represented by the other reporters of the party." Next time there was a special assignment, they advised, it should be covered by the representatives from the wire services, who would report to the others. Ford gave the protest to Lochner and he showed it to the journalists from the hinterlands, who then tried to impeach the New Yorkers, whom they had elected officers of their press club before learning they were arrogant inebriates.

Finally, on Friday, December 17, the engines turned over and the *Oscar II* was en route again—but not before British officials removed almost eight hundred sacks of parcel post, mostly holding Christmas gifts. The Americans were outraged at this violation of neutral rights and smiled at the irony of the names of the two tenders receiving the confiscated presents: *The Good Shepherd* and *Pax Vobiscum*. Just as the *Oscar II* left the harbor the *Frederick VIII* entered, and both contingents of peacemakers rushed to the rails and cheered and sang to each other as they passed.

Once again there was dancing on the *Oscar*'s deck, while below the teachers talked of excessive military history in textbooks and children playing with toy guns and Miss Holbrook suggested schoolhouses should not be painted the incendiary color red. During the next twenty-four hours the *Oscar II* crossed the North Sea and was in danger of attack by German submarines and damage from British floating mines loosed from their moorings. But the passengers felt only joy at being under way, and the more romantic were entranced by the spectacular beauty about them. "Such a glorious balmy night," a student rhapsodized, "such silver water, such clouds, such stars! Afraid? Nobody but a plain fool could be afraid

even to die in all that glory, water all around, some of it pure silver!"
Alice Park and Julia Grace Wales were not afraid to die, but they preferred to face the prospect quietly and practically in their cabin, not
dancing under the stars. Together they devoured an entire box of candy,

Elinor Ryan, Katrina Brewster, Elizabeth Hall, Ora Guessford and
Nell Reeder, students (Courtesy of Ora G. Weir).

rather than have it wasted in a watery grave, while Mrs. Park "accompanied the ceremony by thrilling tales of the San Francisco earthquake."
Next morning the ship sailed along the picture-postcard coast of Norway,
with a view of pine forests, snow-covered crags and bright blue skies, the
clearest day yet. Even Ford was well enough to come out and enjoy the
sunshine.

As soon as the ship had left Kirkwall, Rosika Schwimmer put the
wireless operator back to work. From New York and during the first
days at sea, she had cabled officials of the European neutral governments
and her associates in the suffrage movement asking them to announce the
coming of the expedition in the press, to arrange receptions and meetings
and to decorate the streets and select national delegations. She also asked
the American minister to Denmark, Maurice Francis Egan, to inquire of
the Danish government if it would welcome the neutral conference in
Copenhagen. Secretary of State Lansing learned immediately of Mme

Schwimmer's cable to Egan and instructed him, and every other American minister to the Scandinavian countries, to inform the foreign offices that the United States government "assumes no responsibility for any activities or negotiations" of the Ford Peace Expedition, and to refer future communications from Rosika Schwimmer to the State Department.

Having received none of the progress reports she had asked for earlier, Mme Schwimmer tried again. She repeated her request to the Norwegian foreign minister and also asked the assistance of the American minister to Norway, Albert Schmedeman, both of whom replied they could not acknowledge or aid an informal peace mission. Mme Schwimmer's attempt to join the International Committee of Women for Permanent Peace, the standing organization of the women's peace congress in The Hague, with the Ford peace pilgrimage met the same failure. No sooner had Dr. Aletta Jacobs received her friend's telegram in late November announcing Ford's promise of $200,000 than she cabled Miss Addams, the ICWPP president, asking if they had to unite with Rosika's latest scheme. The Dutch government, she said, opposed "Ford's invasion" and was taking measures to silence it in Holland. Dr. Jacobs and other officers of the committee as well as the branch leaders in Scandinavia, having already experienced Rosika Schwimmer's steamroller tactics to achieve her ends, hesitated to join any enterprise she headed. Miss Addams replied that it would be best for the ICWPP not to affiliate with the expedition until the entire board could vote, but that she hoped the members would cooperate as individuals as she was doing.

Rosika Schwimmer knew none of this; she had simply assumed that she and money were always welcome for the good of the cause and therefore expected her colleagues to obey her instructions. The fact was, however, that the Ford Peace Expedition was arriving in Europe to implement the ICWPP peace plan without the formal support of the ICWPP. Only one of Mme Schwimmer's friends, Cor Ramondt-Hirschmann, a Dutch suffragist, cabled her, and that was to say that derisive articles in the European newspapers had already damaged the expedition's prospects. And the only promises of welcome came from the Norwegian National Students Association and a ministers' peace organization.

Mocked by the foreign press, rejected by the neutral governments and ignored by the organized peace movement, Rosika Schwimmer and her staff knew, just hours before landing, that the peace mission's reception would not live up to its advance billing, that it would not be cheered at the dock in Christiania as it had been in Hoboken, and they quickly moved to unite the pilgrimage behind them.

First, the staff scheduled a reconciliation meeting after the captain's dinner the last night of the voyage, and then they submitted secret complaints to the newly formed organization committee which they hoped would rid the party of its nemesis, the New York reporters and William Bullitt.

The accusations were anemic, even laughable. Lochner said that the culprits were discourteous, that they accused "that damn Schwimmer woman" of listening at doors when she was only strolling with the captain. Kliefoth complained of overhearing "their many insinuating and disgusting remarks and observations, reflecting on the moral character of Mr. Lochner and Mme Schwimmer." The expert adviser brushed aside as inconsequential the remarks about herself, and blamed the reporters for the expedition's bad press in Europe. Even the wireless operators were permitted to accuse the reporters of fomenting dissension.

The accusations were intended to prove that the newspapermen were disreputable; they only proved that the leaders had learned nothing from their previous attempt to silence opposition and that at the least, they created as much discord as the journalists. As Barry noted about the leaders' tactics in general, "like so many moral enthusiasts, they acted as if the end justified the means."

While these indictments were being readied, the *Oscar II* stopped at Christiansand and about ten Scandinavian correspondents came aboard to interview the peacemakers as they sailed up the fjord to Christiania. "After a thorough examination by Mme Schwimmer," wrote a reporter for a German newspaper, during which she said that the lying American reporters were tools of the militaristic press and were being sent home, the Europeans were taken to Ford's stateroom, where Mme Schwimmer continued to do most of the talking. The Europeans met with their American colleagues only moments after the chairman of the organization committee had told the reporters concerned that secret formal charges were being prepared against them for "unprofessional conduct" preliminary to dismissal. The startled guests were treated to accusations and counteraccusations and later that night had ringside seats at the last flareup of shipboard combustion.

During the first part of the evening the scheduled theme of joyful victory over petty dissension triumphed. At the captain's dinner champagne toasts were made in honor of the Scandinavian journalists, peace, the kings of Norway and Denmark, the United States of America and President Wilson and his bride, who were married that day. As a gesture of propitiation to deviant members, Ben Lindsey was appointed chairman of the last meeting and Herman Bernstein the principal speaker. And for the finale, the Reverend Mr. Aked proposed full membership to everyone who approved a much modified version of the troublesome platform which merely reiterated the delegates "earnest and loyal sympathy with the great purpose" that had brought them to Europe and pledged them "to untiring and consecrated effort to put an end to the present war and to all war, and to establish justice and brotherhood upon the earth." It was approved unanimously.

McClure then rose to tell the unsuspecting gathering of the secret charges even then being readied against certain journalists and asked for an open discussion on the matter. Trying to prevent another blowup, John Barry said that McClure was out of order, and others quickly moved to adjourn the meeting. But Lindsey had been instructed earlier to keep the members together until Mme Schwimmer appeared to welcome them to Europe. The arguments continued, with Mrs. Boissevain observing that "we cannot attempt to pacify Europe until we have pacified ourselves." Finally, Mme Schwimmer appeared, spoke inspirationally of their great mission, and then adjourned the meeting. Too late; within five minutes a small group reconvened the gathering. A split in the party would be disastrous, proclaimed McClure; they must all unite in the spirit of God against secrecy and censorship. But only "the Spirit of the Devil," John English retorted, "was in the New York 'yellows'" who deliberately distorted the truth. The bickering continued until Henry Ford pondered until midnight about whether or not to dismiss the reporters.

The anti-press resolution said that Davis, O'Neill, Swain, Stewart, Bullitt and others had "violated the rights and obligations of hospitality, transgressed the laws of ordinary courtesy, sought to sow dissension among the members of this expedition and to misrepresent its character, purpose and conduct" and recommended that they be recalled by their editors and replaced with reporters "who will not continuously disregard the ethics of their profession." After reading it, Ford listened to Mme Schwimmer's and Lochner's arguments in its favor but refused to act on the committee's recommendations. The company on the *Oscar* was a community, he said, in which differences of opinion were natural and had a right to be expressed—most especially those of the newsmen whose coverage Ford was counting on to help stop the war. Quite possibly the reporters, who had all but sanctified their host, would have soft-pedaled their criticism if Ford had asked them to, but he was not sensitive either to the real issues or to the amount of animosity involved. "Let them row, it will do them good" summed up his understanding of the conflict among his guests.

By the time the peacemakers went to bed that last night at sea, suspicions and schisms had given way once more to détente. All along most of the delegates had been perfectly willing to follow whatever policies and procedures the managers prescribed. They had come not to lead but to follow a leader and his aides; they intended only to serve as a symbol of American concern to the people of warring Europe; they hoped only that their action would help end the war. And when the members of the Ford Peace Expedition debarked at Christiania early Sunday morning, December 19, after two weeks at sea, they were all eager to begin their peacemaking adventure.

CHAPTER 8

"*The winning of our welcome*"

T HOUGH A SMALL WELCOMING COMMIT-
tee came aboard the *Oscar II*, there were no bands at the pier, no crowds
waving handkerchiefs, when the members of the Ford Peace Expedition
debarked at Christiania early Sunday morning.

It was not only the adverse newspaper accounts and the exceptionally
cold weather that kept the people away. Each neutral European country
was in proximity to a belligerent nation more powerful than itself. Norway had both close social and commercial relations with Great Britain
and an English-born queen. Sweden feared a Russian invasion, her conservative majority party favored Germany, and her queen was German-
born. Denmark was tied by trade and royal marriage to the Allies, but
having lost two provinces to German absorption just fifty years earlier,
she walked a taut line of neutrality lest she share the fate of Belgium. All
three countries adhered to a joint policy of strict neutrality, and popular
peace agitation, therefore, was not encouraged.

Despite Henry Ford's renown and popularity, not a single national or
international peace organization endorsed the mission. The prewar peace
establishments on the continent were defunct for the duration, and the
newly formed peace societies were founded only to ensure a permanent
postwar peace, not to end the current fighting.

Thus even had the peace pilgrims come with the best of unofficial credentials they would have had little acceptance and no official encouragement. But to arrive in Christiania looking like "the Salvation Army" and led by "the extremely energetic Mme Rosika Schwimmer . . . who because of her origin can only give the undertaking an unfortunate stroke of German color," as the German and Danish ministers to Christiania remarked, foretold no prospect of even feeble public recognition.

In addition, there had been no time to publicize the first meeting held the night of arrival, not even in the newspapers, and the $1.50 admission charged by—and for—the university student and alumni association that sponsored the meeting was considered a deterrent to a large crowd. Even so, more than five hundred of Christiania's intellectual elite attended, and an equal number stood outside in the bitter cold. The star attraction was not the peace plan but Henry Ford. However, after a snowball fight and an afternoon hike in a sports park, Ford was again confined to his room.

The millionaire manufacturer's absence dampened the audience's enthusiasm from the outset. Nor was their interest aroused during the next few hours while Dr. Jones, who "talked so loud that nobody could hear him," and four other delegates spoke of everything but why they had come to Europe. Finally, Lochner "saved the night" with an exposition of their purpose and their hope that the conference would serve as a clearinghouse after submitting tentative peace proposals based on "humanity and justice" to the belligerents. "We owe it to humanity, we owe it to the belligerents, we owe it to ourselves to say that for us at least the time has come when this horrible butchery shall be ended." The general secretary's speech reassured the audience; it had no effect, however, on the Norwegian press.

Next day the most important paper, the moderate *Tidens Tegn*, spent eight columns advising Norwegians to have nothing to do with the new Ford advertising scheme and telling the Americans they had no business intruding in European affairs. The *Verdens Gang*, a radical paper, welcomed the strangers and, for two pages, admired their purpose but regretted the lack of a plan. In an interview, Jenkin Lloyd Jones blamed the pacifists' bad press on the expedition's newspaper reporters, whom he referred to as the "snakes in our Eden," an epithet the American reporters cherished. The conservative *Aftenposten* said that Ford was charming and possessed of a "lofty idealism" but that the expedition represented quantity not quality, the plan was vague and it was unlikely the desired ten Norwegians would join. An editorial criticized Mme Schwimmer's wasting money on cables that demanded public receptions and concluded "that the inordinate and therefore offensive power which Mme Schwimmer exercises unquestionably harms the aims of the expedition." (Though Rosika Schwimmer refused to acknowledge that her presence was detrimental, she nonetheless kept to her room and told her staff to tell inquirers that she was ill.) Only two papers, the Socialist organ and a publication mostly read by women, praised the expedition without reserve. Two thousand people, however, ignored the newspaper articles and responded to the advertisements that promised a view of Henry Ford at the next meeting for only a seven-cent admission fee.

The pattern of the peace pilgrims' activities was set in Christiania and repeated in Stockholm, Copenhagen and The Hague. First there was the helter-skelter of arrival and setting up headquarters in the best hotel in town. In each city local arrangements committees held public "at-homes" in hotel headquarters and hosted small gatherings and sightseeing excursions. Other friends of peace who were associated with large organizations arranged the nightly meetings and dinners, and every expense incurred by the local hosts was paid for by Ford. (Every expense—except clothing—incurred by the Americans was paid for by Ford, too. "Send the bill to Gaston Plantiff!" was the most popular American phrase heard by cabdrivers, restaurateurs and tourist-site operators while the Americans were in town.) During the pacifists' visit the United States ministers to the neutral countries maintained their official distance but attended the expedition's receptions and invited some members to tea. They monitored every meeting and read every newspaper report before sending deprecatory accounts of their compatriots' activities and reception to the secretary of state.

For the first day or so of each visit the newspapers vilified the members and their mission. Then followed the hastily arranged meetings, the lavish dinners and the greatly appreciated donation of $10,000 to a worthy local cause. By the time the expedition left, the press, while still doubtful that the peace program would succeed, enthusiastically acknowledged the Americans' sanity and sincerity.

In their public speeches the peacemakers readily admitted their protest could not stop the war; they were in Europe principally "to start a counter-force" to violence by publicizing equitable peace terms until the belligerents were ready to utilize the neutral conference to end the war. Above all, they hoped the reception they received in Europe would inspire the neutral governments to convene an official mediation conference which the Ford pilgrims would happily serve.

Such talk pleased the people and the press, but it did not persuade any government leader to recognize, much less sanction, the mission. None saw the peace expedition as the logical outgrowth of the conversations they had had with the women envoys the previous spring, none honored Mme Schwimmer's purported assurances that the peace mission would be welcome, and all said that the Scandinavian governments would act only *after* the United States officially initiated mediation. The repudiation by government officials never daunted the Americans, who saw partial accomplishment of their purpose in the grand turnouts to their meetings and the newspapers' praise of their noble effort. Such modest expectations astonished the resident European diplomats.

As the newspapers had predicted, the pacifists had difficulty finding ten qualified Norwegians—and Swedes and Danes—to join their trek to The Hague. The peace leaders in each country, whom the expedition's leaders had expected to elect the delegations, were as repelled by the traveling Ford circus and Mme Schwimmer's tactics as were their American colleagues who had remained home. In the end, the selection of each national contingent was engineered by the expedition's peace staff.

Tuesday morning, December 21, at the midpoint of the peacemakers' Norwegian visit, the twenty-three members of the expedition's rear guard arrived on the *Frederick VIII*. Almost half of them were students. Three of the seven delegates—Peter Monroe Smock, "the Lincoln of Idaho"; Hampton Steele, a newspaperman; and William M. Wright, a Baptist minister—represented the governors of Idaho, Kansas and Arkansas respectively. Frank Van Galder, of Rock Island, Illinois, was the editor of *The Modern Woodsman*, the largest fraternal-organization paper in the country, and Mrs. Gina Smith Campbell, of Sioux Falls, had been a South Dakota delegate to an exposition in Norway the year before.

The two other delegates, George Fort Milton and Fred L. Seely, were invited at William Jennings Bryan's suggestion. Milton had been an officer in the Spanish-American War and a delegate to three Democratic national conventions and was editor and majority stockholder of the Chattanooga *News*. He joined the expedition because he believed that "it was no more visionary of Henry Ford to say that wars should be settled by moral suasion than it was for Thomas Jefferson to declare that all men are created free and equal." Fred Seely, the former crusading publisher of the Atlanta *Georgian*, operated a mountain resort in Asheville, North Carolina. Knowing nothing of the planned neutral conference, and caring less, Seely went to see if the Ford mission merited Bryan's participation.

Many of the Americans suffered from the grippe and influenza during their Scandinavian sojourn; for one man it was fatal and for another it was the excuse for a diplomatic exit. Lloyd Bingham, the ship's jester, entered the hospital as soon as he landed, but his influenza developed into pneumonia and on December 22 he died, his resistance reduced by a terminal kidney disease that would have killed him in a few months. After a brief memorial service, Plantiff arranged for Bingham's burial at home.

Henry Ford could not get rid of his cold, and he stayed in his hotel room until his final departure. Though unable to visit the Norwegian prime minister, who had agreed to see him provided they talked only of business, Ford did receive several local journalists, Haakon Loeken, the attorney general of Christiania, who joined the expedition, and Christian Lange, the secretary of the old-line Interparliamentary Union, who did not, but said it was a useful conduit for European pacifists. Ford astounded his guests by receiving them dressed only in his nightshirt and by not saying a word of his peace plans while he was quite voluble on the virtues of his motor plow and how it would revitalize postwar Europe.

On Tuesday afternoon Dr. Koren, the expedition's local physician, told Ford he could either go to a health resort in Norway and join the expedition later or he could go home, but he was not well enough to travel with the party to Stockholm Thursday morning. It was not a simple decision for Ford to make—he had not known a single moment in Christiania when he was not being pressured either by Marquis to go home or by Lochner and Mme Schwimmer to stay in Europe. He was still willing to back the conference and still confident in Mme Schwimmer, though Marquis undoubtedly pointed out that the International Committee of Women for Permanent Peace had rejected his offer to realize their peace plan and Mme Schwimmer had no status in Europe as a peacemaker. Ford's body was weak, and his spirit was weakening. He had fought Marquis's arguments in Detroit, Washington, New York and, toward the end of the voyage, on the *Oscar II*. In his isolated, darkened hotel room he was sick and spent by the tensions that surrounded him and very likely unbearably bored. If he remained in Europe, he could only look forward to a lonely stay in a sanatorium followed by three weeks of sitting on meeting-hall platforms, night after night, listening to speeches given in languages he could not understand. He decided to go "home to Mother," even after Lochner and Mme Schwimmer told him that the world would think he had abandoned the expedition and its purpose as soon as it reached Europe.

According to Mme Schwimmer, Ford told her his decision at midnight Wednesday. That left her, she thought, the rest of the night to prepare the statement for his signature that assigned her full authority for running the expedition with financial control reserved to Plantiff until Ford returned. That, she later said, was the division of labor Ford wanted. It may have been.

It was certainly the division of labor Rosika Schwimmer preferred. As soon as she landed she had indicated that she was transferring her management techniques from ship to shore. She instructed the company's mailman to bring her everyone's mail before delivery (an order promptly countermanded by Plantiff's assistant), she had all translations of newspaper reports expurgated, and she alienated the local peace activists. Professor Wilhelm Keilhau, though he arranged the first two meetings, had resented her earlier advisory cable—"a queen's wire to her most devoted subject"—and refused to join the Norwegian delegation.

At four A.M. on Thursday, while Mme Schwimmer and Ellis Jones were writing Ford's letter of authority they learned that their leader's trunks were being sent downstairs. No awkward farewells for Henry Ford—he was sneaking out with Marquis and his bodyguard much as he sneaked out of his office window when he wanted to end a boring interview or avoid an embarrassing confrontation. Mme Schwimmer and Lochner, knowing Ford only as a gentle though stubborn man who had been accessible and agreeable until the last few days, suspected Dean Marquis was kidnapping their leader. When the Ford trio left their rooms, Ellis Jones followed them down the stairs, through the lobby and to the waiting taxicab, demanding explanations all the way. In the street, Jones pulled Christian Raven, the expedition's travel manager, from another taxi and then, with Huebsch at his side, fought Raven and his driver. Amid the melee and the shouts of "Murder!" and "Kidnapping!" Ford left. And Jones and Huebsch, joined by Aked and Jenkin Lloyd Jones, turned first to Dr. Koren and then to Plantiff, who had been watching the scene from the landing, for explanations. The flustered doctor said Ford was leaving to get some uninterrupted rest. And Plantiff retreated before their advance, shouting, "Keep me out of this!"

This wild spectacle took place at so early an hour that none of the other expedition members were awake, and all present decided to say nothing of Ford's departure until the peace party was en route to Stockholm later that morning. Only Plantiff, who kept his silence, knew that Ford hid in the stationmaster's office waiting for the westbound train to Bergen while the main party waited for their special eastbound train to Stockholm.

The Americans, surrounded by mountains of baggage, waited two hours

in the ice-cold station for their train engine to defrost. Even after it
started, the exceptionally cold weather and low-grade coal caused the
train to proceed at a slow pace and the engineers had to stop it continu-
ally so the engine could thaw and the track be cleared. Because they were

Committee on Administration of Ford Peace Expedition. Left to
right: standing, Ben Huebsch, Charles Aked, Ben Lindsey, Rosika
Schwimmer, Frederick Holt, Gaston Plantiff; sitting, Louis Lochner,
Mary Fels, Lola M. Lloyd, Jenkin L. Jones (State Historical Society
of Wisconsin).

due in Stockholm in time for a late dinner, there were no sleeping cars
and not enough food. The travelers endured a twenty-hour nightmare
crossing the Norseland on the coldest night in 130 years. The staff and
the elderly occupied the two heated cars; the rest of the party huddled
together for warmth, and a few of them slept in the overhead luggage
racks. No one had a kind word to say for the experience, and one mem-

ber, infuriated by the lack of one single amenity, was further frustrated by the absence of conductors to complain to.

All along the railroad track people waited for a glimpse of Henry Ford as the train crawled by. Curious delegates were told he was in a private compartment. For hours Mme Schwimmer, Plantiff, Lochner and their friends planned the way and the words with which to cushion the shock of Ford's desertion and assert their leadership without protest. At three A.M. on Friday—only a few hours before the train was due in Stockholm—the reporters, and no one else, were given a mimeographed statement saying that Ford was temporarily absent on doctor's orders and that he had appointed as his surrogates a Committee of Seven consisting of Charles F. Aked, Jenkin Lloyd Jones, Mary Fels, Lola Maverick Lloyd, Ben B. Lindsey, Ben Huebsch and Frederick Holt to serve with Mme Schwimmer, who had complete authority on policy matters, and Gaston Plantiff, who had financial control.

Mme Schwimmer, knowing she had to buttress her reign, had shrewdly staffed the committee with her own allies and the most outspoken of her "enemies," just as she had done so successfully the last troubled days on the *Oscar II.* To Miss Addams she explained that those who hated her would leave the expedition if they knew she was running it. Only two of the reporters—Joseph O'Neill and Elmer Davis—saw the ruse for what it was: "largely theoretical" and "decorative."

The peace pilgrims arrived in Stockholm early Friday morning, December 24, eight hours after the mayor and over a hundred people had abandoned their plan for a torchlight parade through the city. Tired, cold and hungry as the travelers were, they took a few moments to marvel at their luxurious accommodations and wonder at the custom in Swedish hotels where, in the public baths on each floor, a woman sat waiting to scrub down any male who entered the tub. (Elmer Davis convinced the "ferocious" attendant he could bathe himself, but John English told his Boston readers he "felt like a new man" after the ministrations of "an Amazonian size woman.")

The expedition stayed a week in Stockholm, each day more successful than the one before. The liberal press hailed the pacifists with columns of front-page publicity, and the middle-class intellectuals, including Social Democrats, and the upper-class students attended their meetings en masse. Those Swedes who opposed German militarism and who favored the Entente democracies were generally sympathetic to any group, official or not, seeking peace. Carl Lindhagen, the imaginative and energetic mayor of the city and a member of parliament, whom Mme Schwimmer had designated chairman of the reception committee, wrought organizational wonders scheduling the events and arranging the publicity that drew audiences by the thousands. Lindhagen was a passionate reformer of broad interests who had been active for many years in the peace movement and, as an avid advocate of woman suffrage, knew Mme Schwimmer and her colleagues well. The Stockholm mayor's government position, however, did not bespeak much influence, since the Social Democrats who had elected him to the lifetime mayoralty some years before had lost their power to the pro-German Conservatives in the city and in parliament.

"I think it was the saddest Christmas I ever remember, and we all sat around making lugubrious speeches and trying to cheer each other up, but it was a hopeless task." Weatherly spoke for everyone. Those billeted at the Grand Hotel were partly mollified by "the effect of noble housing." A few others were eased by the cordial welcome they received in the reception committee's suite from those kind enough to stop by on that busy holiday afternoon. But the splendid dinner in the Grand Hotel's enchanting Winter Garden restaurant, with fresh flowers surrounding the base of a giant Christmas tree ablaze with lights and miniature Swedish and American flags, only saddened them. And the after-dinner remarks further depressed their spirits.

Plantiff officially announced Ford's departure and then read a telegram he had just received from Ford saying he was having a comfortable journey home. (A few days later, Plantiff explained Ford's condition was due "merely to a nervous breakdown" and influenza.) Then speaker after speaker briefly but effectively reminded them of the happy holidays they had spent at home in years past. Lindhagen's assurance that the American peacemakers were welcome in Europe even without Ford lifted the gloom somewhat, and the news that an administrative committee would serve in Ford's place dispelled the Americans' fears that the expedition was over. By the end of the evening there was a strong spirit of pulling together, even among the metropolitan reporters, who regarded the elevation of their friend Gaston Plantiff as a portent of efficiency and fair play. In the days that followed several of the newsmen served as the co-administrator's kitchen cabinet, and Plantiff, agreeable by nature, highly susceptible to flattery and easily intimidated by the strong-willed, willingly—sometimes too willingly—responded to the social exigencies of his new role.

Despite the growing public acclaim, Mme Schwimmer knew that without Ford or another big American name the expedition would be ignored by the major powers. Someone was needed who would end the rumors circulated by the American reporters of the group's perpetually imminent disbandment, give the pacifists' reputable standing and hold them all together. As George Edward Riis observed, the group "needs a Moses badly." Hoping to lure Ford back to Europe, Mme Schwimmer sent him daily cables overstating their progress, and she and others also wooed Miss Addams and William Jennings Bryan with appeals for their immediate presence. Miss Addams replied she was "desperately disappointed" that her doctors still forbade her sailing but she was doing her best to counteract the unfair newspaper stories. Though five people asked Bryan to come at once, he canceled his boat reservation as soon as he learned Ford was returning and cabled: "Feel without Ford presence opportunity service less than here opposing preparedness program."

Fortunately, there were enough prima donnas on the Committee on Administration, as the "Seven" called themselves, to keep any one of them in check. Thus Aked's plan for quarantining the "undesirables"— the students and all the reporters except the Associated Press and United Press representatives—in a resort until they could catch a boat home was vetoed after Lindsey pointed out there was no way they could compel the press to stay confined. As for the students, Aked settled for their being lectured to on deportment by Ben Huebsch and Judge Lindsey, the juvenile-delinquency expert. Far from being the scandal of Stockholm, as some members charged, the young people were exemplifying the hands-across-the-sea spirit of the Cosmopolitan Club movement Lochner had helped develop in America between college students. Baedeker in hand, but more often escorted by Stockholm students, they toured the Venice of the North while they discussed the causes of war. They also did guard duty outside the committee-room door, ran messages and handed out anti-war literature on the city streets. Faced at night with the choice of sitting through hours of speeches made tedious by paragraph-by-paragraph translation or attending the Royal Opera and late-night cafés with their new friends, they could hardly be blamed for opting for the latter.

The administrative committee took itself very seriously and met at least once a day, even though its most significant act was electing Jenkin Lloyd Jones chairman, Frederick Holt vice chairman and Lochner ex-officio secretary. The members knew that "in the last analysis," Mme Schwimmer and Plantiff, who were invited to attend all meetings, ran the expedition. Because no matter ever came before them that could not be resolved to every member's—and Mme Schwimmer's—satisfaction, the self-important delegates persuaded themselves that they had an effective voice in the regulation of their fellows. The one issue that would have disrupted the harmony—the procedure for electing the permanent American delegation to the neutral conference—was deftly tabled day after day. Their discussions on other matters indicated that the demand for democratic rule that had been made by some members of the committee on the *Oscar II* was only a matter of whose ox was being gored. The administrative committee believed the expedition required not an autocracy run by Mme Schwimmer and not a democracy run by riffraff, but a paternalistic oligarchy run by their highly qualified selves. That Mme Schwimmer and a similar committee on the *Oscar II*, using precisely this strategy for the same purpose, had caused the chaos on the trip over was apparently forgotten.

Only Inez Milholland Boissevain objected when Dr. Jones announced at a general meeting that Ford had himself selected the seven members—a considerable stretching of the truth—to run the expedition aided by their expert adviser, business manager and general secretary. When, she asked, was the policy of running the expedition on democratic lines, which Ford favored, changed? The reply was evasive, no one took up her cry, and the meeting ended in "a love feast."

Next morning Mrs. Boissevain released her ten-page resignation to the reporters and read it at the delegates' daily convocation. "The undemocratic methods employed by the managers of the Expedition" were "repugnant," she said. Such methods had caused "ill-feeling, suspicion, condemnation and dissension" on the ship, prevented the development of a "scientific program" and made the delegates appear "a confused mass of amiably intentioned persons, of vague thinking and no collective planning." Though she thought the present governing body a good one, it had been "selected, not elected," and her conscience bade her resign. She was going to The Hague and would win what support she could for them privately.

Only Mrs. Boissevain's friends begged her to reconsider, some reporters cabled excerpts of her resignation to their papers, and one wrote that "the Ford peace car [had] begun to clatter and jolt and bump" again. Mme Schwimmer was glad to be rid of the troublemaker, Lochner telegraphed a friend in Holland to "disregard" her, and Plantiff, remembering that Ford had once called her a "vampire," credited her desertion to sour grapes because she had not been appointed to the committee. Aked, acting for the subcommittee that reviewed her resignation, set her straight:

she thought the peace expedition was a democratic body; the other members considered themselves guests of Henry Ford "subject to his governing." They were right, she was wrong, and "no good purpose" could be served by further discussion.

S. S. McClure said nothing after Mrs. Boissevain's outburst. Some called him "Strangely Silent" in Stockholm; Dr. Weatherly thought the "vain, conceited egoist" had "talked himself out" on the ship. The loquacious elder statesman sat alone on the train to Stockholm playing solitaire. He was staying with the pilgrimage "as a matter of duty," he wrote his wife, because without him and Judge Lindsey, it would fall apart. After the party left Copenhagen he would go to Germany as a foreign correspondent, using an old passport. Herman Bernstein, as he had promised on the *Oscar II*, left the expedition still convinced that Mme Schwimmer's "secret diplomacy" had destroyed a "splendid opportunity for dignified mediation."

The peace expedition played to standing room only in Stockholm. Thousands were turned away at each meeting, and one gathering, though arranged on only a day's notice, broke all previous attendance records. A Swedish speaker said he had never seen his undemonstrative countrymen so emotionally approving. At a farewell luncheon on December 30, the expedition's managers gave $11,000 to the city's poor, almost $3,000 to Swedish peace societies and a silver service to Mayor Lindhagen, who expressed his gratitude by formally inviting the pacifists to hold the neutral conference in Stockholm. Fifteen hundred cheering people went to the railroad station that evening to see the Americans off on their special train to Copenhagen. "I wish you could have been there to have shared in the joy such a demonstration brought to my heart," Plantiff wrote Ford. "It showed beyond question that the Swedes . . . would stand behind us in whatever we did to bring about peace."

The Stockholm visit had been extended to a week because of two very critical difficulties that would have terminated the tour in Denmark. The first problem was how to overcome the recent Danish ordinance prohibiting foreigners from speaking in public on war and peace. The Americans could still present their programs if clubs and other private groups sponsored their meetings, but Mme Schwimmer's preemptory cablegrams had alienated her Danish friends who could have arranged such gatherings. Several of the feminists had journeyed to Christiania to learn something of what the Americans planned to do, but when Mme Schwimmer plainly expected the Danes to follow her lead blindly, they refused to ask their countrymen to cooperate and, after telling the Americans their adviser's nationality made her a liability to their mission, left for home. Another possible organizer, Olaf Forchhammer, the president of the Danish Peace Society, was offended because Mme Schwimmer had not personally asked his help. With Ford gone the expedition had no cachet at all, he wrote Lindhagen, and the members of his society regarded "the whole expedition and its reception in Kristiania as so complete a fiasco" they would have nothing to do with it. Don't let the Americans come to Denmark, he added, "merely relying on luck."

Forewarned, Mme Schwimmer left for Copenhagen with two aides two days before the rest of the party left Stockholm. After only one conversation, Forchhammer agreed to chair the arrangements committee. Her explanation that the Americans had no specific program because they wanted the Europeans to develop it with them was all Forchhammer needed to know.

The second problem threatening the expedition's life was much more catastrophic. From the day they landed the expedition's leaders had tried unsuccessfully to negotiate passage through Germany to Holland. The alternative was a voyage through the mined and turbulent North Sea. No American minister, however, could alter the Americans' passports for travel through a belligerent country. However, Mme Schwimmer supposed the minister to Denmark, Maurice Francis Egan, was especially sympathetic to the peace mission and would help. He had read her "secret documents" the previous summer and confirmed her decision to ask Wilson to mediate, and when she asked Egan in late November to find out if the Danish government would host the unofficial neutral conference, he had inquired. But after the State Department told Egan to keep hands off any "activities or negotiations" he pursued her plans no further, not even when she cabled that President Wilson's best friends had encouraged and helped Ford. Consequently, Ellis Jones, acting for Mme Schwimmer in Copenhagen and as determined to get to The Hague as she was no matter the hazard, chartered a ship for $50,000 (most of which paid for the insurance premium), even though the shipping line manager remarked, "I would rather prefer that this arrangement is not closed."

The peacemakers had the most cordial reception and the gayest time of their entire trip in Denmark, which was scarcely their expectation when they saw the Copenhagen harbor filled with warships and later checked into the overcrowded city's limited assortment of hostelries. (The reporters' hotel, William Bullitt wrote, "was the sort of place that can [only] be described in French.") The gloom was gone by evening when the Americans dined at the King's Shooting Club, a posh private establishment outside the city. The police chief warned that the Copenhagen celebration of New Year's Eve was so raucous and rowdy that people boarded their windows, and suggested everyone return by private taxi directly to their hotels. Those who later ventured into the city's streets and cafés danced and drank until, as Elmer Davis fondly remembered, Plantiff arrived "at the last moment like Bluecher at Waterloo to take the [$495] check."

The next morning began a continuous week-long round of visits to museums and castles, private gatherings in the homes of the aristocracy, the wealthy and the intelligentsia, and late-night dining, drinking and dancing. "This traveling on Henry is some life!" a student wrote her family on their Iowa farm, having just spent the evening as opera star Lauritz Melchior's guest at the opera, a dinner party and an artists' ball. The students' chaperone, on the other hand, was outraged at "the idea of people dancing within the sound of guns," and the Reverend Dr. Weatherly, having difficulties of another kind, was embarrassed by "the positions in which nude men and women are placed" in modern sculpture. At the same time, the Danes were wondering at the sexual promiscuity they assumed was rampant among the students and married men and women traveling without their mates. But their assumption about the *fredsexpeditionen*, as "peace expedition" translates in the Scandinavian tongues, was incorrect. "The astonishing thing, considering that there were at least a hundred young people there in their twenties," said Elmer Davis, "was that there was so little fornication, which was mostly because there was always something more exciting going on and people were afraid they'd miss it!"

By far the high point of the Danish visit was the reception given by the Cavlings, the owners of *Politiken*, the radical-liberal newspaper which was considered the voice of the government. That so influential a journal should call the peaceseekers "not idealistic fools, but practical idealists" and stand "sponsor for our sanity, sincerity and sense," Lochner wrote, did much to mitigate the denigrating remarks printed in the other papers. In his toast at the gathering, Baron Palle Rosencrantz quoted his "famous countryman, Hamlet, Prince of Denmark: 'The time is out of joint' " and commended the Americans for assuming "the task of setting your time right."

On Sunday, January 2, the managers learned that on the following Friday the German government was sending the entire peace party through the country to Holland in a sealed train. Egan was the expedition's savior, many members having already decided to forego the opportunity of risking their lives on the North Sea crossing. Though enjoined by Secretary Lansing not to officially acknowledge the peace mission, as American minister, Egan was charged with the safety of Americans in Denmark. And permitting over 150 compatriots to depart on a ship probably on its last voyage he construed as a dereliction of duty.

At the *Politiken* reception. Left to right: standing, Ben Lindsey, Henrietta Lindsey, Katherine D. Blake, Gaston Plantiff, Alice Park, John Barry, Ben Huebsch, Elizabeth Hitchcock, Robert Henry, Haakon Loeken; second row, Mary Fels, Edith L. Jones, Helen Robinson, Jenkin L. Jones, Lilian Holt, May W. Sewall; sitting, Louis Lochner, Frederick Holt, Thomas Seltzer (State Historical Society of Wisconsin).

Had any harm come to the peace pilgrims, he advised his superiors at home, the American government would "have suffered the criticisms that the Saracens had to endure when they intercepted the famous Children's Crusade of the Middle Ages."

Egan solved his dilemma by consulting with his good friend Count Ulrich Brockdorf-Rantzau,* the German minister to Denmark, who was known in diplomatic circles for his lack of Prussian zeal and willingness to reason. The Americans' passports carried the warning "not valid for use in other countries except for necessary transit to or from the countries named," which Plantiff, Lochner and then Egan decided could be interpreted by the German government as sufficient authority to visa the passports for travel *through* Germany to Holland. The German government was disposed to help the Americans—or at least not hinder them—and granted the request. Shortly after the Ford mission left the States, the German ambassador in Washington had cabled the foreign office that "the mission is probably harmless" and he saw no reason why its members should not be permitted to enter Germany. Similarly, after the travel arrangements were made, Rantzau confirmed that the expedition was "well-meaning, warmhearted but impractical and completely unfamiliar with European conditions." Several American reporters wondered at the neutral peacemakers accepting the courtesies of a belligerent without official approval from their government and presumed erroneously that the "German spy," Rosika Schwimmer, had negotiated the arrangement.

As was her custom on the expedition, Mme Schwimmer continued to seclude herself in the expedition's office (making only occasional appearances in the reception room), supervising the usual round-the-clock grinding out of instructional bulletins, telegrams and preparations for the next port of call. When Elli Eriksson complained that she could not sleep at night because she was next door to the mimeograph room, Mme Schwimmer admonished her by reminding her that "when one travels one has to learn to endure." Miss Eriksson learned instead to take a taxi to another hotel, where she caught a few hours' sleep in a vacant room. She also caught another reprimand from her employer; there was no escaping Mme Schwimmer's ever-functioning spy network.

Lochner and the staff sorted the many peace proposals and letters, the latter mostly of the "I'll-do-anything-to-return-to-America-

* Brockdorf-Rantzau was then running a spy ring that was trying to find a way to transport Lenin secretly from Switzerland to Russia; Lenin later traveled by sealed train through Germany.

where-I-worked-before-I-came-back-to-the-old-country-to-care-for-my-sick-mother" variety, addressed to Ford and Mme Schwimmer, that were arriving daily. One day an émigré Russian journalist brought Lochner hundreds of clippings from Russian newspapers and explained that because of government pressure the conservative press was "indifferent," the liberal press "unfavorable" and the radical press gave "silent approval," but "news of the Ford Expedition and its idealist aspirations is daily reaching the millions of Russian readers" in the accounts sent by correspondents in Scandinavia. Lochner deduced that such publicity would give the Russians courage to end the war and, several years later, recounting the interview, wrote, "I think it is not asserting too much to say that the Ford Peace Expedition was a contributing factor to the overthrow of Czarism."

Gaston Plantiff considered himself the caretaker of "a bunch of nuts" who regarded him only as the fount from whence all monetary blessings flowed. The cry of "Send the bill to Gaston Plantiff!" became the refrain to the expedition's theme song, "One Peace Delegate Jumped Right Over Another Peace Delegate's Back" (which had been inspired by Jones and Aked's high spirits on the *Oscar II*), sung to the tune of "The Battle Hymn of the Republic." Actually, the rank and file never overstepped the reasonable. Though the reporters happily cabled the news that several women had asked Plantiff if they might charge the cost of new evening gowns, the business manager simply refused and did not even bother to mention the matter in his report to Ford on his difficulties in minding the store. But Lochner, Mme Schwimmer and Miss Leckie, he complained, "have not the remotest idea of the value of dollars and cents and have incurred expenses which [but] for the sake of keeping harmony within the organization, I would never have permitted or authorized." Their incompetence in publicity matters he found "most nauseating." The trio had "printed, reprinted and printed again their 'Who's Who' until I have had to put my foot down in the most insistent way." Perhaps. Plantiff just was not the sort to put his foot down at all, nor was he pinching kroner himself when it suited him to lend and spend. Aside from the customary $10,000 gift to the local peace organization, Plantiff expressed the peace party's appreciation for Egan's help with a $600 contribution to the diplomat's favorite charity, and he frequently picked up the tab for his drinking companions.

Though Ford had set no spending limit and relied on Plantiff to prevent excesses and extravagance, the financial manager was no match for Mme Schwimmer. When she asked for money, he gave. In return he received a sheaf of receipts denoting expenses for "small presents," "small personal tips" and hiring entertainers. Almost a thousand dollars was spent thus on flowers, china and silver gifts of appreciation in Denmark to those who arranged small gatherings, and hundreds were spent on cables and telegrams. Every staff member was on salary, except Lochner and Mme Schwimmer, who had expense accounts. Lochner scarcely used his; Mme Schwimmer extended hers to include outlays to her peace staff. She controlled every action of the expedition, and since she acted on her own authority, often with money already received, Plantiff was left with *faits accomplis* that he was obliged to agree to. Her style was as distressing as her spending: she gave "with a lavish hand," Egan remembered, "after the manner of royal people when they give decorations." And Lochner agreed that her gift-giving made an "exotic impression," though he said she was only following Ford's example. Rosika Schwimmer was impervious to criticism on the subject, believing that every penny she spent was in the best interests of their endeavor and that Plantiff's competence in peace matters was limited to his capacity to sign checks. Egan described the harried business manager as "a very tired businessman," worn out by Mme Schwimmer's persistent ploys "to dominate the movement." He also reported to the State Department—as had the American ministers in Christiania and Stockholm with similar derision—that "the Pilgrimage has had no effect whatever on public opinion in the Scandinavian countries, in improving the prospects for peace in Europe. The tolerant are glad to know that there are so many kindly idealists in the United States and the intolerant sneer at the childishness of the whole preceeding."

As soon as the managers had heard that the party would go through Germany they started the mimeograph machines running night and day turning out a set of instructions that would have warmed the heart of an alarmist. All "written, printed or typewritten" materials had to be mailed or thrown away. No letters, photographs, cameras, opera glasses, gold coins or even "innocent picture postcards" could be taken along. Any violation would result in "appalling penalties," probably "create complications disastrous to the person practicing concealment," and anyone caught would be left behind "to be dealt with in the manner customary in such cases." For the rest of the week the travelers shuttled between their hotels, the post office and the German and Dutch consulates. And newspaperman John English, mindful of German efficiency and thoroughness, carefully removed the printed labels from his medicine bottles.

Almost two hundred people met at the Copenhagen depot on Friday morning, January 7, to leave for Germany and Holland. The expedition had won a few members and lost a few. The additions were some of the Norwegian and Swedish delegates and their staffs. Among the nonvoyagers were Governor Hanna, who had been in the hospital since Christmas Day; Julia Grace Wales and Elli Eriksson, who, as citizens of Allied countries, could not travel through Germany and were therefore designated guardians of the expedition's papers and equipment, which accompanied them on the boat to Holland; and the stowaway, Jacob Greenberg, whose lack of a passport barred his legal entry into Holland from any country.*

Dr. Weatherly stood on the deck of the Danish ferry in a drizzling rain watching the German shoreline at Warnemunde come into view. He too was mindful of Germany's reputation for efficiency and thoroughness and felt "a strange feeling of oppression." Even the sight of the spiked helmets and smartly tailored Prussian uniforms frightened the Americans. The innocents abroad were amazed, therefore, when the Germans spoke to them in English and only asked to see their passports before ushering them onto a splendid train. There was no inspection at all. Nor was the train sealed, the blinds drawn or the windows frosted, as they had been warned. At Hamburg, where the passengers were permitted on the platform, they were deeply moved by the sight of the Red Cross trains bearing wounded, the women in mourning, the profusion of soldiers and the faces of the people in the station, determined but not despairing, sad but not bitter. One of the officers on the train drank beer and wine with the reporters and listened to them sing "We expire with screeches listening to speeches" and "We have come from Sweden, snakes in Schwimmer's Eden."

Even the dinner on the train thrilled some of the Americans. The best meal they had had so far, they said, so delighted were they to be sharing the suffering of the brave German people who endured two meatless days a week. Others, with less emotional palates, described the food—potato soup, potato salad, potatoes and fish, potatoes and omelettes and a side order of potato bread—as merely nourishing.

At the Dutch frontier, which was reached at three in the morning, instead of a humiliating search and quizzing by customs officials, again

* Greenberg spent several days unsuccessfully trying to obtain illicit transportation. After he boarded the *Oscar II* for the homeward trip, he learned he had gonorrhea, and Captain Hempel, who bore the former stowaway no good will, put him off at the nearest port in Norway. By the time Greenberg received proper medical attention in New York, he had lost the sight of one eye. For years afterward, Greenberg stayed in touch with Irving Caesar and Burnet Hershey (Jacob Hirsch).

there was no inspection at all.* Chairman Jenkin Lloyd Jones thanked the German officers for their government's courtesy, and the Germans wished the peacemakers good luck.

The unexpected courtesies, the charm and friendliness of the two convalescent officers in charge, both wearing the Iron Cross and one of them the personification of the picture-book Teutonic knight, and the fact that the train made the journey on time—a curiously common gauge of the meritoriousness of a national government—beguiled the travelers, who still remembered the miseries of their detention at Kirkwall. The German government in making arrangements for the first wartime civilian train had definitely catered to the Americans. It was national policy at that time to regard official American peace attempts favorably, though Wilson was not himself welcome as a mediator, and this policy no doubt extended to overtures sponsored by a man of Ford's reputation. The more questioning and objective members of the Ford party suspected that the Germans "cleverly" arranged for the train to travel mostly at night when they could see nothing and instructed the officers to be courteous and friendly.

During the ride from Bentheim on the Dutch border to The Hague on Saturday morning, January 8, the Americans were entranced by the European landscape. Some described the windmills and canals, the quaint gardens and thatched-roof cottages, others remarked on the entrenchments, the miles of cannons along the frontier and the soldiers marching on the country roads. But all were glad "to see the sun and *feel* it," a pleasure they had had but five times in the thirty-five days since they had left New York.

A large crowd gathered at the railroad station in The Hague to greet the peaceseekers before the weary travelers taxied to their last abode as guests of Henry Ford, curious to know how Europe's traditional city of peace would receive them after what they considered to be a triumphal tour through Scandinavia.

---

* Lieutenant Governor Bethea traveled the same route the day before and was not so fortunate. He had to strip to the skin while the officials examined his body for secret writing and looked between his toes for secret messages.

CHAPTER 9

"A great deal of bitter feeling"

IN THE HAGUE, as in Stockholm and Copenhagen, the large refugee population filled the hotels, and the travelers were lodged all over town. Headquarters was in the suburban seaside resort of Scheveningen at the Hotel Wittebrug, a luxury hotel just across the street from an artillery barracks. The students were at so splendid a hostelry they were sure someone had made a mistake, and the newspapermen were deliberately housed in a vegetarian hotel whose motto, wrote Bullitt, was "Leave meat, tobacco and alcohol behind all ye who enter here." The students' comfort was short-lived—they sailed home on January 11, just three days after they arrived. The rest of the party had one week to conclude its business of publicizing its presence and electing delegates before it left on the fifteenth.

The Netherlands, lying between two belligerents, though strongly pro-Ally, appeared to the Ford delegates as the most cautious and neutral of the nations they had visited because of the constant view of soldiers on the country roads and city streets and siege guns mounted on the land or canal barges. Though Holland bore the same "terror of little nations" as the Scandinavian countries she also had a history of hospitality to peace movements, and the Dutch government did not interfere with the pacifists' right to conduct public meetings.

Many of the Dutch newspapers, insofar as they acknowledged the presence of the pilgrims, suggested that an unofficial action by private propagandists, while it probably would not end the war, did no harm and, as an expression of disinterested humanity, should be welcomed with tolerance and all judgment suspended until after the mediation plan had been presented. Even those papers that were not so friendly did not sneer at the attempt.

Henry Van Dyke, the American minister to Holland and Luxembourg, wanted the United States to enter the war to assure the downfall of German militarism. Curbing his scorn of the amateur do-gooders, he had merely informed the Dutch foreign minister that "the remnants" of the Ford expedition would soon be upon them and that the State Department "does not in any way sanction this gratuitous peace movement." Like the American ministers in Scandinavia, Van Dyke offered the customary courtesies to his countrymen and his legation sent the expected deprecatory report to the State Department recounting public criticism of the apparent lack of a plan and disgust with the pacifists' conspicuous public promenading and extravagance.

The Ford Peace Expedition's business in The Hague was twofold: it expected to acquire a Dutch delegation, and it expected the American, Norwegian, Swedish, Danish and Dutch delegations to select permanent members to the Neutral Conference for Continuous Mediation. In accomplishing these objectives, the peace expedition did not have the cooperation of the organized Dutch peace societies.

Like its sister organizations in the other neutral countries, the prewar Dutch peace society, Vrede door Recht (Peace Through Justice), lay dormant, willing to mediate the war when "a favorable occasion" arrived. But two months after the fighting started in 1914 some of its members organized the Nederlandsche Anti-Oorlog Raad (Dutch Anti-War Society) to devise a "Minimum Program" of practical, durable and just international principles that would be studied by the people and ultimately incorporated into the peace treaty. In April 1915, just a few weeks before the women's conference, ten countries sent representatives to a meeting called by the Raad in The Hague, where they founded the Central Organization for a Durable Peace with headquarters in Switzerland to unite all national organizations interested in working for a peace treaty that would protect the rights of small nations and minority nationalities. Neither the Raad nor the Central Organization for a Durable

Peace was organized to initiate action to end the war. They spoke for the people's right to sit at the peace table and their program emphasized the real—that which would work—rather than the ideal.

Without the imprimatur of the Raad the Ford expedition did not have a prayer of obtaining a worthwhile delegation to the neutral conference, and both Dr. Benjamin de Jong van Beek en Donk, the Raad's organizer, and Dr. Hendrik Dresselhuys, its president, who was also secretary-general of the Ministry of Justice and a member of the Dutch parliament, withheld their society's support. De Jong and Dresselhuys were influenced partly by their American colleagues in the Central Organization who had written of the expedition's "lamentable notoriety." An unofficial conference of neutral nations was not objectionable, but what de Jong spoke of as Mme Schwimmer's "fantasies" and her lack of understanding of European realities—particularly her insistence on postwar total disarmament—kept the Raad officers from joining the crusade.

The International Committee of Women for Permanent Peace headquarters, like the branches in Scandinavia, gave no official help. Though members attended the expedition's functions, the Dutch officers were so bitterly opposed to Mme Schwimmer they refused to serve as delegates. They objected to her manipulation of the executive committee to endorse her visit to Wilson the preceding summer, to her arrogant treatment of their vice president, Dr. Aletta Jacobs, when she was in America and to her refusal to talk about the $20,000 she had promised to send in November and which the officers had already begun to spend. It was only after Dr. Jacobs told the American reporters what had happened that Mme Schwimmer, for the first time in several weeks, talked to the press. She had forgotten to send the money in the rush at the Biltmore, she explained, dismissing her negligence with, "Dr. Jacobs is rich and can afford to pay what she has spent."

The difficulty of obtaining a respectable Dutch delegation to meet with the expedition at the organizational meetings in The Hague was compounded by the Scandinavians' insistence that the delegations issue a joint statement of principles to guide the neutral conference that was consistent with the Scandinavians' more idealistic views. Both the Dutch and the Scandinavians opposed annexation of conquered territory and favored safeguards to protect small nations and subject peoples and international arbitration of disputes, but the Scandinavians, especially the Swedes, wanted the neutral-conference members to pledge themselves to a "Maximum Program" which included the demand for a total disarmament provision in the peace treaty.

Mme Schwimmer and Lochner personally favored the Maximum Program, but perhaps they were aware that the abyss between the Dutch and Swedish programs was unbridgeable and thought the difficulty could be dealt with later in the conference. At any rate, at the first meeting of all the national delegations, Lochner announced there would be no platform, no declarations and no resolutions. The Norwegians insisted that there had to be a public declaration that would justify their journey to The Hague; they could have stayed at home just to elect their delegates. To aid in preparing the statement and to rally support from other peace groups, a Dane wanted "to go as deeply as possible into the thoughts of Henry Ford during the days we are to spend here," and a Swede concurred, saying, "We need most to hear the details about his opinions." Asked to deliver the impossible, Lochner instead gave his standard speech on the history of the expedition, saying, at the end, that there was no need to formally bind the neutral conference to a specific program as he was sure it would recommend a peace treaty "based upon justice and humanity and not upon military advantage." Weasel words, said the Scandinavians; every conqueror declares his peace terms just and humane. The neutral conference would be nothing but "moonshine and wind," said the Norwegian Haakon Locken, unless the Europeans knew it aimed to create a durable peace that would not carry "the germs for new wars."

The argument continued day after day, the Europeans naively patronizing the great, good-hearted Americans as innocents from a distant irenic land who knew only the simple joy of democracy and nothing of imperialism. At the end of the week, on Friday, January 14, the last day all the delegates met together, when the matter of a formal resolution came to a vote, the Scandinavians won with strong American support. Though there were Dutch observers at the meetings, they were not yet organized as a delegation and did not vote.

While the Europeans were concentrating on the platform of principles, the Americans and the expedition managers spent every waking minute, without exaggeration, in a procedural struggle over the selection of the American delegation to the neutral conference. The Scandinavians had persuaded their sponsors to let them select their representatives after they returned home, but the Americans had to do the job before they disbanded. During the week it took the enlightened Americans to elect their representatives they taught the decadent Europeans that the land of popular democracy was, in fact, the land of the political machine. The administration's behavior, wrote Lochner, a repentant participant, was "the most disgusting chapter in the history of our peace crusade."

Mme Schwimmer frequently acted on her own authority in the name of those who had the reputation and position she lacked, but when she told the Committee on Administration that Ford had appointed them to act in his stead she outsmarted herself. Two of the seven members—Lola Maverick Lloyd and Ben Huebsch—were her followers, but the others were independent spirits. She had picked the latter hoping to bind them to her, and they had willingly deferred to her judgment on European matters, but when what they thought of as their own prerogatives came into conflict with her will, a no-holds-barred battle was inevitable. From its creation in Stockholm, the committee had assumed it would decide, with the advice of Plantiff and Mme Schwimmer, the method of selecting the permanent delegation so that they could determine its membership. But as to the best method of selection there was the usual falling-out among thieves; at one meeting the committee considered and rejected five different plans. At last, on January 10, they decided on a procedure. At the American members' gathering the next morning Lindsey presented the committee's two recommendations. The members then suggested two other plans during the discussion period, and three more after lunch. After considerable "animated discussion" of the seven proposals, the plan suggested by Dr. Aked and George Fort Milton, the Tennessee newspaper publisher, was accepted. It provided for two popular elections, the first to select the five delegates and the second to decide five delegates pro tem who would serve until the permanent delegates arrived. It was a simple and democratic scheme, and it endured only through the night.

Early Wednesday morning, at a meeting called to elect a post-expedition peace propaganda committee, Lochner said he did not understand what he had voted on the day before and asked for clarification. Evidently no one else understood either, since discussion only illustrated the "great confusion in the minds of those present." (The minutes of the meeting were no help—Lochner had written them on the bottom half of a Dutch East Indian mailboat schedule.) The only solution was to appoint a committee of Aked, Milton and Lochner to redraft what had already been approved so it could be voted on again.

Actually, Lochner and his management colleagues understood perfectly what had been decided: a voting plan that gave the assembled members complete freedom of choice in determining the delegation without any safeguard by the administrative committee and its advisers. So untenable a procedure was easily remedied with a redrafted resolution that provided for Ford's approval of all delegates and alternates. Since the committee, Mme Schwimmer and Plantiff all spoke with Ford's tongue, they would ultimately control the selection—provided they agreed among themselves.

A copy of the new resolution was distributed to every voting member late Wednesday night after the party returned from its all-day outing in Amsterdam. On the bottom of the sheet was a list of exactly ten nominees, five to be elected as delegates—Ford, Bryan, Miss Addams, Aked and George W. Kirchwey of the Henry Street group (who had just resigned as dean of Columbia Law School to become temporary warden of Sing Sing)—and five as alternates—Judge Lindsey, Dr. Jones, Mary Fels, George Foster Peabody (a philanthropic banker, also of the Henry Street group), and Professor Emily Greene Balch, one of the women's congress envoys to the European governments whom Mme Schwimmer had begged to sail with them. If anyone doubted that these were the people the management expected to be elected, they had only to step outside their hotel rooms to be told by the Schwimmer and Plantiff factions that the candidates were Ford's personal choice and as Ford's guests the members were obliged to vote the straight ticket. The list, Lochner admitted later, was "jammed down the throats of the delegates in the form of an official 'slate.'"

That night Mme Schwimmer sent her acolytes through the hotel corridors empowered to grant voting rights to anyone promising to vote the party line, and Plantiff made the same gift to his staff of clerks and bookkeepers so that they could vote their master's choice. Everybody wanted Ford, Bryan and Miss Addams. In addition, Mme Schwimmer favored Kirchwey, Peabody and Miss Balch, and Plantiff wanted Aked. In Copenhagen, Plantiff had taken the slight liberty of secretly signing the clergyman to a contract, granting him, if elected, a $15,000 salary for his first six months' service renewable at $10,000 for the next six months, plus all living expenses for himself and his wife. "I regard him," Plantiff wrote Ford, "as the head and shoulders of the American delegates . . . and therefore went the limit to have him remain with the conference."

It had not escaped anyone's notice that the nominees from the expedition were members of the administrative committee. "Those of us not too blind to see, realized that the steam roller had been working," wrote John English, the reporter the managers thought was so fair-minded they had made him a member, adding, "it was evident that the administration was not fussy about the method so long as the desired end was reached." The outraged journalist looked forward to the "fireworks" sure to go off on election day.

The administrative committee was alarmed by the suspicion, distrust and outright fury their maneuver had generated. They had thought they could get away with nominating themselves by letting Aked, Milton and Lochner present the resolution as their own work. In an emergency session early Thursday morning, the committee and its advisers were about to withdraw both the slate and the resolution when Harry Carroll Evans, the fraternal-magazine editor who had been so opposed to the railroading tactics of an earlier administrative committee on the *Oscar II*, burst into the room with a startling but pleasing suggestion: withdraw the present plan and let Evans propose that the selection of delegates be left to a committee consisting of Plantiff, Lola Maverick Lloyd and Lochner.

As soon as Dr. Jones convened the general meeting a few moments later he called on Dr. Aked to withdraw the nominations and then gave the floor to Evans. We are not a democracy, the Iowan began, this is not a town meeting. The expedition is a business and Henry Ford has a right to keep a tight hand on it. "I prayed about this before I came here this morning," he went on, and decided that all must sacrifice personal ambition to Ford's pleasure. "Let's don't think of self," he pleaded, let's "delegate our power to someone else," just as we do in the United States, and authorize Plantiff, Lochner and Mrs. Lloyd, consulting with Ford, to appoint all the delegates. As soon as Evans sat down, Barry quickly rose to speak. For the past two days, he said, he had been afraid some such suggestion would be made. To follow Evans's plan would be "the supreme blunder of the expedition," not only exposing the members to further ridicule for disfranchising themselves but causing "a great deal of bitter feeling." ("Think of it," the young stenographer, Isidor Caesar, wrote in his diary, "here were they come together to protest against secret diplomacy, . . . to give expression to a democratic form of life, . . . and asked to sell out the very heart of themselves and their purpose.")

There followed a replay of their days on the *Oscar II*. The same charges of "frame-up" by some, the same willingness to trust the experts' better judgment by others, the same reminders that they were not "a democratic body" but only "an historic houseparty," the guests of Henry Ford. Finally, Plantiff bluntly said he had had all he could take—he was tired of sitting on committees, tired of living in an "insane atmosphere"; Henry Ford would want an open meeting and an honest election and that was what they were going to have.

And so they did, almost. Ford, Bryan and Miss Addams were elected by acclamation, Mary Fels was elected on the fourth ballot, and Charles Aked won the fifth seat after a few more rounds. As it was late in the afternoon, the Americans hastily nominated ten people from whom they would elect the five alternate delegates the next day. Afterward, and at the banquet that night, lobbying for votes by the factions' tacticians and the independent candidates was unremitting. The reporters attributed the nominees' interest to the handsome honoraria of $500 a month plus expenses, but the candidates and their backers thought they were fighting for the success or failure of the neutral conference itself. Ben Huebsch, a spokesman for Mme Schwimmer on the administrative committee, "was convinced that what we were doing was of vital importance, and the world's going to the damnation bow wows if you don't get it done just right."

By the time the Americans met Friday morning, the next to the last day of their travels, several nominees still retained sufficient integrity to express their disgust with the crude ward politicking. State Senator Helen Ring Robinson said the padded election list reminded her of the crooked politicians in Denver who voted goats and sheep as eligible constituents, and she withdrew her name. So did Mrs. May Wright Sewall.

George Kirchwey, Emily Greene Balch, Ben Lindsey and Jenkin Lloyd Jones were elected as alternate delegates by the fifty-four electors on the first ballot. The first two had been touted by Mme Schwimmer; Lindsey was Plantiff's man and Jones probably was also. That left one more position and four nominees: George Foster Peabody, John Barry, Frederick Holt and Harry Carroll Evans. In the fourth round Barry beat Peabody by two votes.

Barry's election was a hard-fought victory for the insurgents who had been fighting against the "conspiracy to railroad the selection" of delegates. The San Francisco pacifist-journalist had been marked as an enemy of "the Schwimmer crowd" ever since the night on the *Oscar II* when he had opposed the undemocratic maneuvers over the preparedness platform. The metropolitan reporters thought his election signified the end of Mme Schwimmer's control by aborting her scheme for "a conference with all the members except herself in absentia." John English praised Barry as "one of the shining lights of the expedition" and was plainly delighted that he had run "the steam roller into a ditch." That was not exactly true, as Dr. Jones kept reminding the Americans; Henry Ford could veto any choice they made.

During a ballot-counting break earlier in the day, the Europeans stopped by to discuss the site of the conference, a detail not yet settled. The Dutch wanted to meet in The Hague, but Mme Schwimmer, those Americans who favored the Maximum Program and the Scandinavians favored Stockholm, and Plantiff, remembering Ford's preference for Holland, reserved Ford's right of final decision. The Dutch lost the argument for tradition to the easy accessibility of Stockholm, the enthusiastic reception the city had given the expedition and the Scandinavians' suggestion that Europe should have as many peace centers as possible. And naturally the Scandinavians hoped—as had the Dutch—that their philosophy would dominate the conference if it met in their stronghold.

The Americans called an emergency meeting on Saturday, January 15, their last morning in The Hague, to rewrite the guidelines to the neutral conference, which they thought had suffered semantically in the English version. As it finally stood, the resolution pledged the neutral conference to devise a peace settlement based on "the abolition of armaments" and a system of international justice that would protect the rights and freedoms of all peoples. Barry's plea that they stand for the practicable position of arms limitation rather than the improbable goal of total abolition was loudly denounced. When the Dutch asked that the resolution not be publicized until they could organize and vote, the Scandinavians recognized the delaying tactic but had to agree, and in the end the resolution was never released to the public at all.

After Dr. Jones banged the gavel for the last time, closing the "Unofficial International Peace Conference, the first of many more to follow," there remained only the farewell lunch, a round of eulogies and Mme Schwimmer's prediction that the descendants of the *Oscar II* voyage would be as proud of their lineage as those of the *Mayflower*.

The Americans sailed for home exactly six weeks from the day they had left. When the ship docked in New York several members gave prepared statements to the press, and others spoke out in the coming weeks. Most claimed the expedition had achieved its purpose of spreading peace talk in Europe and establishing the neutral conference. "It is the idealists," Dr. Weatherly proudly declared, "who have done things in this world."

The chief, but not the only, target of those who thought the mission had failed was Mme Schwimmer. Herman Bernstein and Inez Milholland Boissevain blamed her "system of espionage that should turn Russian bureaucrats green with envy" and her fear that "her idea would be violated by precious fools who meant well but didn't know what they were about." Senator Helen Ring Robinson of Colorado frankly faced the dilemma of Mme Schwimmer's role: there would have been no expedition without her but her belligerent nationality and affinity for intrigue and autocracy inevitably caused dissension among the delegates and disrepute in Europe. They might have succeeded, Mrs. Robinson thought, if Mme Schwimmer had shared her knowledge and alleged secret documents with the Americans and remained in the States.

Others, including the students, criticized the newspaper reporters, and for the last time the reporters attacked the intelligence and qualifications of the delegates, the behavior of Mme Schwimmer and her coterie and the improbability of the entire mission. There was some charity mixed with the acerbity. Arthur Hartzell of the New York *Sun,* who had been among the most mocking, admitted it was not fair to judge whether the pacifists had failed until the neutral conference had had a chance to perform. And Elmer Davis, though he characterized the returning peace pilgrims as "the largest and most heterogenous collection of rainbow chasers that ever found a pot of gold and dipped into it for six weeks," also remarked that "the peace move is now starting."

Mindful of their obligation to proselytize, a few of the members and almost all of the students wrote articles for their local newspapers and spent several months addressing community groups. One student was still giving slide lectures on the expedition fifty years later.

Henry Ford had faced the reporters when he arrived in New York in early January and proclaimed the expedition a success. People were talking and thinking (to use his sequence of words) about peace. Reports of dissension were "tommyrot," mere differences of opinion and nothing more, nor had he lost his confidence in Mme Schwimmer. His absence from the expedition, he assured the newsmen, had no more effect on its continuity and effectiveness than his absence from his business had on the running of his factory. He had not returned unexpectedly, either, never having planned to stay away more than five weeks. Ford had changed his view on one critical matter. Before he sailed he had blamed the war on capitalists, bankers and munitions manufacturers; in Europe he had learned that the men in the trenches were at fault because they picked poor rulers and were too frightened to criticize them. Still, it was proper that he should spend his money in the interests of the Europeans who had helped him make it, and he would continue to do so. Though Ford said he would return to Europe if he was needed, he spoke eagerly of making tractors and automobiles. The neutral conference, he emphasized, merited his financial backing but had only needed his presence to get it launched.

So saying, Ford designated Ernest Liebold, his private secretary with a mind like a balance sheet, overseer of the project he still cared about but no longer wished to fuss with. And Liebold, now that the only non-moneymaking Ford enterprise was on the back burner, began to reduce the flame. Plantiff received the news of the change in command while the expedition was in Copenhagen. "Keep me posted," Liebold advised, and from then on all messages from the home office were signed by the private secretary. In acknowledging Liebold's authority, Plantiff pointedly retained control of on-the-scene operations with his instruction, "Pay no attention to any information coming from anyone connected with this party beside myself."

Mme Schwimmer and Lochner knew that such an arrangement was in force between the manufacturer and his two employees, but they tried breaking through the barrier. Thus Ford, whose preferred reading matter was six-word aphorisms, was the recipient of over forty typewritten pages from Mme Schwimmer, Lochner and the administrative committee as well as Plantiff reporting the end of the expedition. Lochner thanked Ford for the "experience of being the general dumping ground for kicks," and the committee praised his "foresight and courage and initiative." Mme Schwimmer, apologizing for the brevity of her twelve-page account (and promising that Mrs. Lloyd would visit him to fill in the details), told a tale of triumph and claimed she had done her job perfectly. Plantiff's narrative read like a letter from Hercules to the king who commanded him to perform his perilous labors. Whatever the task, he had done it well. Actually he was half out of his mind with the futility of asking Mme Schwimmer to cut her spending and with the persistence of the expedition's petty politicians who fed on him every waking minute.

Easily outdone in argument—or as Huebsch put it, "always willing to agree in order to escape the need for intelligent discussion"—and never certain, having no conviction about and less knowledge of the peace mission, Plantiff was easy prey for Dr. Jones and Judge Lindsey, both men of wisdom and experience, which they were quick to speak of. While angrily condemning Mme Schwimmer for mindlessly spending Ford's money, Plantiff "loaned" McClure, Dr. Jones and several newsmen hundreds of dollars, and he gave thousands to German and other war charities. Plantiff was a man of good will; he was also a man of weak character, wanting to please first Henry Ford and second whoever was confronting him. Often he made rash promises, quickly broken, to smooth his own course. "Poor Gaston Plantiff! The thing made no sense to him," wrote Miss Wales, who watched him tramping the corridors, "waving his arms and muttering to himself." Though he often tried, Plantiff could never drink his sorrows away.

The Neutral Conference for Continuous Mediation was scheduled to convene in Stockholm at the end of February, providing time for the Scandinavians to select their representatives, for the American nominees to cross the Atlantic and for the expert adviser and her staff to set up the working structure of the assembly. It was that last factor that kept the administrative committee and Gaston Plantiff in The Hague. To offset Mme Schwimmer's political shenanigans Dr. Jones and Judge Lindsey, knowing they were not staying long in Europe, had run as alternates.

Once these people had admired their leader's ability and determination, but her unwillingness to share leadership, her demand for unquestioning obedience and her equating of ideas with person had diminished their respect. The refusal of the influential Anti-Oorlog Raad and International Committee of Women to work with the conference as long as Mme Schwimmer was in charge had convinced the administrative committee that she had to be restricted to an advisory rather than a managerial role until they could persuade Ford to remove her. It had taken time for the anger and outrage to override the admiration and appreciation, time for the unsuspecting, the trusting, the patient and the hopeful to admit the immutability of her frailties, time for the strong and willful, as confident of their abilities and rectitude as she was of hers, to realize that she had manipulated them, time for their inevitable anger to express itself effectively. Above all, it took stamina to outlast her endurance in combat, particularly in this matter, for Rosika Schwimmer was no Moses willing to remain in the wilderness while her followers entered the Promised Land.

On Monday, January 17, the committee began its battle, knowing that Rosika Schwimmer, Lochner and the rest of the peace staff might have word from the German embassy at any hour to leave for Copenhagen. She denied their charges that she used the committee as a front while confiding her plans only to her sycophantic kitchen cabinet. And the committee not only rejected her right to dismiss them, since only Plantiff had signed their letters of appointment, but demanded that their notice of dismissal exempt them from responsibility for the expenses incurred during their tenure. The "long and unprofitable discussion" ended with each side retiring to its corner to prepare for the next round.

Rosika Schwimmer, as was her course, disregarded her opposition's arguments and its right to make them and proceeded to entrench her authority. She sent personal letters of invitation to the American delegates urging them to sail at once, and she asked Liebold to work on Bryan, suggesting that the former secretary of state had damaged his reputation by going back on his promise to serve on the conference. She also strengthened her inner circle, retaining those loyal to her on the conference payroll and sending to Budapest for her friend Paula Pogany, to be her first assistant. Finally, she told reporters she was going to appoint Harry Carroll Evans as an alternate after Ford approved her dismissal of John Barry, who had not signed the preparedness pledge on the *Oscar II* and was therefore ineligible to serve. She had apparently forgotten that Evans was as outspoken as Barry against the forced signing and that, in any case, everyone had been welcomed back into the fold the last night on the boat.

Liebold had cabled Plantiff to turn over the finances to a responsible person, to use his judgment "on all matters," and return with the main party on the fifteenth, but Plantiff had stayed behind awaiting Ford's approval of his choice for successor. The man he picked, with the help of his friends, was committee vice chairman Frederick Holt, the Detroit businessman and former neighbor of the Fords currently at liberty, who had impressed his colleagues as a man of "practical insight" devoted to peace and able to stand up to Mme Schwimmer. Plantiff hoped the matter could be settled before Mme Schwimmer left, but on Thursday the peace staff learned they would leave for Copenhagen the next day, and Dr. Jones urged him to act at once. As a temporary measure Plantiff reluctantly appointed Lochner, who reluctantly accepted. The general secretary was admired by everyone for his competence as a junior executive and for his good will and enthusiasm, but no one thought he could stay Mme Schwimmer's financial vagaries.

Mme Schwimmer did not object to Lochner's serving as her "cashier"; she vehemently objected to the phrases in his letter of appointment which gave "the management of this expedition" into his charge and to a paragraph toward the end which explained: "To make your connection perfectly plain, it may be understood that your judgment will be absolutely final on any matter of disbursement" and which recommended that Lochner cable Ford or Plantiff to handle "any embarrassing situation" or "particularly important decision." Ford had appointed her to manage the expedition, she insisted, and what Ford gave only he could take away. Unless the offending words were deleted she would cable Ford of Plantiff's treachery, she told Lochner, demanding that he bring the villain to her room. Though Lochner assured her it was the rest of the letter promising to put him on salary and to send for his family that mattered to him and that he would always respect her advice, she was determined to fight for her unrestricted access to Ford's bottomless purse. The joy of buying flowers for herself and her friends, of sending silver mementoes to the deserving, of renting the most expensive rooms and sending long cablegrams halfway across the world, all in the name of the cause, was no small matter to her, but much, much more important was the power that unrestrained spending gave her. Without it she could advise but not direct the affairs of the neutral conference; she could reign, but not rule.

When Plantiff ignored Mme Schwimmer's summons, Lochner turned to Julia Grace Wales, the last peacemaker among them, to soothe their belligerent colleague. Miss Wales had already vainly implored the alternate delegates to remain in Europe to keep Mme Schwimmer "on the right track." "I myself," she admitted, "objected in a general way to her methods because they seemed to me suspicious, secretive and autocratic and to lack faith in human nature; but I on the other hand, was very anxious not to lack the necessary faith in her." She was therefore happy to oblige Lochner as she hurried to Mme Schwimmer's quarters that last night in The Hague with what she thought was the ideal solution for everyone.

Sensitive to the peculiar status she and Rosika Schwimmer shared as citizens of belligerent countries helping to organize a neutral action, Miss Wales suggested to Mme Schwimmer that they not go to Stockholm while the conference was being organized but live nearby and submit suggestions by mail. However, Mme Schwimmer "argued, with some show of reason," Miss Wales weakly conceded, "there were dangerous elements about and the situation required a strong hand for the present." The dangerous elements, according to Mme Schwimmer, were Mrs. Fels and John Barry, who were elected without her sanction, and those who objected to her intolerance for the unpredictable results of the democratic process.

Mme Schwimmer waited until two A.M. for either Plantiff or his written capitulation to appear. Then she threw her cape over her shoulders, took a taxi to the telegraph office and sent Liebold a cable. Tell Ford, she instructed, that Plantiff had made Lochner sole manager in her stead. She did not feel she should withdraw when she knew she was still useful, nor would she do so until Ford, who had put her in charge, dismissed her himself. Ford had not sent her a word since he left, she complained, but he could not ignore her predicament, and she demanded he reply to her in Stockholm.

While Mme Schwimmer was gone, Lochner, to whom she had shown her cable, persuaded Plantiff that appeasement was the better part of management. Both men were waiting in her room when she returned. "There ensued," wrote Lochner, in a passage he deleted from his published account of the expedition, "one of those scenes between the spirited Hungarian pacifist and the nervous business manager which I had witnessed of late in increasing numbers. Gaston Plantiff inevitably lost out in these encounters. He would splutter and rage and exhaust his picturesque vocabulary. But in the end he would always submit meekly to the dictation of Rosika Schwimmer, who for some reason or other seemed to have a magnetic hold upon him." Plantiff changed the letter, removing the offending paragraph and restricting Lochner's administrative authority to paying the bills and keeping the books. They all parted in peace and Mme Schwimmer went to bed, her virtuosity intact.

Later that day Aked, Barry and the peace conference staff boarded the train for the long ride back to Stockholm. As the train sped across Germany the tensions of the past week disappeared. Lochner and Mme Schwimmer turned quite giddy and sent Plantiff silly telegrams in German at every stop to let him know they were "not nutty yet." The Danes welcomed the pacifists with flowers at the station, children serenaded them at dinner, and that night Lochner wrote Plantiff that "now that we are away from the depressing atmosphere of Holland, and away from those who justly or unjustly are disgruntled, we are all in better spirits than we have ever been." On January 25, after two days of sightseeing by the staff, gift-buying by Mme Schwimmer and attending to business by Lochner, the Americans arrived in Stockholm, their city of peace.

CHAPTER 10

"Long nervous strain unfits Schwimmer"

"THERE IS A GREAT DIFFERENCE between the Ford Expedition which left Stockholm three weeks ago and the Expedition which arrived here yesterday," a Stockholm reporter was kind enough to observe. The returning band of peacemakers personified "American fearlessness" willing to cooperate with "European responsibility." The writer wondered only at the presence of the belligerent national, Mme Schwimmer, "who still keeps her exceptional position as the adviser."

Headquarters, once again, was in the splendid Grand Hotel. A flight of stairs led from the marble-pillared lobby to a long hall and the white-oak double doors which opened into the principal offices. A medium-sized corner bedroom overlooking the king's palace and the parliament across the canal was converted into a conference room and redecorated in the elegance of the Edwardian Age just past. Rose velvet draperies and tasseled valances framed the large windows, maps of the embattled nations and of the world hung upon rich, red-papered walls, and a dazzling chandelier, reflected in a nearly room-high, gilt-framed mirror, lit the chamber. About the room were gold and rose damask overstuffed chairs and sofas and an assortment of rococo tables "of all sizes and shapes" (later exchanged for two long baize-covered tables, surrounded by stolid leather chairs). Leather portfolios, inscribed in gold, lay at each delegate's place. On one side of the room were the library and Mme Schwimmer's suite, on the other was Lochner and Mrs. Clark's office, and elsewhere in the hotel and its annex, in thirteen rooms, were separate quarters for each national delegation and the business and clerical staffs. Between the conference room and Lochner's secretariat was a bathroom not quite completely converted to an office where Mme Malmberg and Elli Eriksson translated articles from the Scandinavian newspapers.

A staff of fifteen, including Mme Schwimmer, Lochner and Robert Buelow, the son of the Ford Motor Company's Danish agent who had been engaged by Lochner to help with the accounts, was ready to serve the expected thirty delegates. Mme Schwimmer's inner circle had contracted but was still secure. Ellis Jones, whom she had promised Plantiff she would send home, was her chief confidant and head of the press bureau, though his sole duties, according to the office manager, seemed "to consist in swaggering about, giving orders, and spying and carrying tales." Ben Huebsch agreed at the last minute to substitute as financial manager while Lochner went to Switzerland in search of delegates. Harry Carroll Evans was on hand to replace Barry as alternate as soon as Ford approved the switch. Mme Schwimmer also retained her Hungarian associate, Paula Pogany, as secretary-companion, and Lewis Maverick, as factotum. Nora Smitheman stayed as office manager and Ada Morse Clark as Lochner's secretary, and Julia Grace Wales, serving without salary at her own insistence, continued to write suggested position papers for the coming conference.

The primary function of the staff was to serve the conference; its secondary function was to serve posterity with a complete record of the peace endeavor. Such was Mme Schwimmer's grand design as she coordinated every detail and assigned every piece of work, ordered publications and inspected the office supply closet, assigned hotel rooms and kept track of everyone's mail, ran the press bureau and ordered books and pencils, wrote the constitution and tried to remove unsuitable delegates. Through her efforts, the library brought over on the *Oscar II* was greatly enlarged with books and periodicals in all languages on the subject of peace and world organization. Thirteen daily newspapers, at least five of which were American, were subscribed to and several clipping services on the continent sent newspaper articles that had any bearing on war or peace policies. News releases on conference business were sent to the world press, and a weekly news review, daily announcements and special papers were distributed to all the delegates once the conference was under way.

Rosika Schwimmer was at her best as a publicist and organizer of large-scale productions, but there was more than method and good management in her efficiency. In setting the ground rules before the conference formally convened she was trying to define its modus operandi under her sole direction, hoping thus to establish her powers beyond challenge. She looked upon the conference as she had the expedition: it was her private

Grand Hotel, Stockholm. The neutral conference's suite was on the left corner, second floor.

fiefdom, the delegates were her vassals, the office workers her serfs, and all of them owed ultimate allegiance to Ford, whose sole surrogate she was. The delegates, on the other hand, like some of their forerunners on the peace ship, thought themselves members of an independent body endowed by a pacifist manufacturer. And Henry Ford, Liebold and Plantiff regarded the enterprise as an overseas branch of the Ford Motor Company. The result was chaos and crises of a dimension and duration not yet experienced, and it began as soon as Mme Schwimmer and Lochner read the telegrams waiting for them at the Grand Hotel.

There was good news—Bryan accepted his appointment but would talk with Jane Addams and Henry Ford before he set his sailing date—and fair-to-middling news—Miss Addams was too ill to cross the ocean until April, and Ford did reply but only to say he would make no decisions until he saw Plantiff—and there was bad, or at least irritating, news from Plantiff.

Still in The Hague with Dr. Jones, Judge Lindsey and the reporters, Elmer Davis and Joseph J. O'Neill, Plantiff was a poor fish in a sea of sharks, persuaded by their argument, which de Jong confirmed, that Mme

Schwimmer would destroy the conference if she remained in charge and if the gathering convened in the domain of the extremist Maximum Program advocates. The difficulty lay in convincing Ford that the peace mission could manage without her and that, in fact, her presence guaranteed its failure. Whenever anyone had questioned her authority she had replied that at her midnight interview with Ford just before he left Christiania he told her, "You decide and Plantiff pays," and, more significantly, if she ever resigned he would stop financing the mission. She said she had offered to withdraw three times, and each time he had made the same response. Because Plantiff was weak-willed and an easy mark and no one wanted the mission to fail, none had dared challenge her word until her blatant electioneering attempt in The Hague.

Accordingly, when another cable from Liebold reaffirmed Plantiff's authority to make "decisions on all matters" and approved Holt as financial co-manager with Lochner, Plantiff's coterie persuaded him to exert his prerogatives and, with the freedom of expression that distance allowed him, he told the expert adviser of his revised conference plans. In deviousness and unscrupulousness he out-Schwimmered Mme Schwimmer.

First, Frederick Holt, the former vice chairman of the administrative committee, whom Mme Schwimmer despised for opposing her, was coming to Stockholm to manage the money and to act as Dr. Jones's alternate. Mrs. Fels, another "enemy," had changed her plans and was going to take her seat at the conference. Therefore, Evans was superfluous and was to be sent home. Secondly, each national delegation was to consist of three, and preferably two, members instead of five and the staff was to be reduced as well. And finally, Plantiff not very subtly suggested that Ford would prefer the conference to meet in The Hague. Rosika Schwimmer knew a cabal when she saw one, and she and Lochner brashly decided that Plantiff, having already delegated his authority (and $43,000) to Lochner, no longer had a voice in conference matters. Mme Schwimmer replied all was well, which was probably true since they had been in Stockholm only one day. Lochner took a somewhat helpful tone, suggesting that sending Evans home would be "embarrassing" since Lochner heard Plantiff ask him to stay and that Ford would be hurt "immensely if we keep going back on our word."

Two days later, on January 27, Lochner and Evans left for Switzerland, via Copenhagen and Berlin. In his briefcase, Lochner carried step-by-step instructions from Mme Schwimmer on how to get conference consultants in Berlin and delegates and publications in Switzerland as well as a warning to beware of Swiss cranks. Looking forward to his great adventure and responsibility, the ever-optimistic young man minimized the problems he was leaving behind in a filial letter to Ford. "Good old Dr. Jones is sore," he wrote, because he was not "chosen a principal delegate," and despite their minor disagreements, Mme Schwimmer and Plan-

General secretary's office, Grand Hotel, Stockholm. Left to right: Ada M. Clark, Ingebord Hammer (stenographer), Louis Lochner, Gaston Plantiff, Haakon Loeken (State Historical Society of Wisconsin).

tiff "parted the best of friends." All the conference needed, what with Bryan coming, was the return of Henry Ford, who, Lochner thought, "could handle the Kaiser more easily than any person" he knew.

Sitting at breakfast in his Copenhagen hotel on the first day of his journey, Lochner's good spirits vanished when Frederick Holt appeared and announced he had already told the Danish committee overseeing the election of delegates about the new procedures. Neither Lochner nor Mme Schwimmer thought Plantiff would act without their consent and certainly not before Holt arrived in Stockholm. But Holt's action and his insistence that Ford had given Plantiff the authority to make the changes so frightened and confused Lochner, unused to such "crookedness" and "double crossing," that he turned to Olaf Forchhammer, the expedition's local organizer, who was also outraged by the high-handed usurpation of collective rights. Together they phoned Mme Schwimmer for advice. It was not an easy conversation. The Scandinavian governments required as a wartime precaution that all international telephone conversations be conducted in the native tongues of the participating countries. In this case, Lochner first talked to Forchhammer in German, Forchhammer spoke in Danish to Buelow who was in Stockholm, Buelow spoke either in English or German to Mme Schwimmer and then translated her reply into Swedish for Forchhammer, who translated it for Lochner. Still, the message came through. Mme Schwimmer and Huebsch would leave for the Swedish port of Malmö at once, where Lochner and Evans should meet them, and then they would all go to Copenhagen and get rid of Holt once and for all.

In Copenhagen, Mme Schwimmer used the same attack plan she had used against Plantiff in The Hague, and with the same successful results. It began the next morning in the cable office, where she and Lochner sent messages to Henry Ford, and it ended that afternoon when Holt presented his credentials—letters from Plantiff and Jones empowering him to dispense funds and serve as Jones's alternate—and Lochner and Mme Schwimmer presented copies of their cables.

In many words, Lochner told Ford of his "great perplexity" at the variety of contradictory orders emanating from their leader. He wondered why Holt was coming to Stockholm when Buelow was now permanent financial assistant and Huebsch was temporary manager, evidently forgetting he had asked for a fulltime business manager before he left Holland. Nor could Lochner understand Holt's and Mrs. Fels's claim that Ford wanted Mme Schwimmer, who had "perfected" their organization to everyone's satisfaction, to remain in the background. The Danes were distressed by Ford's supposed decision to reduce the number of delegates and to change the conference site, and had asked Lochner to get "point blank assurances" of Ford's long-term commitment. Lochner also wanted to know exactly when Ford was coming and "What is Madame Schwimmer's and my relation to be to conference and to each other?"

Rosika Schwimmer sent a report-cum-lecture. Everything had been simply splendid until Plantiff interfered, making a fool of Ford and almost destroying the conference before it began. She could not believe Ford had sent such orders. They had decided, she reminded him, on five delegates—himself, Bryan, Miss Addams, Aked and Lindsey—and it was too late to reduce the number. He had also agreed with her that the conservative peace-movement traditions associated with The Hague made it an unsuitable site for the conference. One could not humiliate the Europeans by altering conditions according to people's whims, she admonished him; everything must be decided collectively. Finally, she said she absolutely would not work with Holt, who blamed her for his failure to win election as an alternate only because she had told him he did not have the proper background to serve.

Holt and Mrs. Fels offered a weak defense. Their claim that they had only *suggested* the reduction of delegates was contradicted by the Danes, and their argument that Ford, not Plantiff or themselves, wanted the changes and the removal of Mme Schwimmer from control was shattered by the absence of proof. True to her promise, Mme Schwimmer then proceeded to eliminate Holt. First she repudiated Dr. Jones's right to appoint his successor and then, firing her ultimate weapon, she threatened to resign if Holt became business manager.

Outnumbered and out of ammunition, Holt and Mrs. Fels withdrew from the battlefield and waited for new instructions from Plantiff. With Huebsch in tow, Mme Schwimmer returned to Stockholm after telegraphing Plantiff that his latest trick had been reported to Ford and warning him the world would call Ford a crazy man if Plantiff continued misusing his name. And the still-distraught Lochner first chastised Plantiff for nearly wrecking the conference before it began and then forgave him his sins.

Rosika Schwimmer thought herself solidly enthroned at last, all her opponents banished from her realm forever. Ford cabled again he had "not lost faith in you or expedition. Am doing all I can to help things here. Expect to leave for Europe in near future. Am awaiting Plantiff's return," which news she triumphantly forwarded to Plantiff, who said he rejoiced at her support from Detroit and informed her he had already ordered Holt to America.

If so, Holt apparently never received the message. On February 2 he and Mrs. Fels arrived in Stockholm, she to present her ideas to her fellow

American delegates before she left for England on private business and he to test the demand for his attendance as alternate delegate and business manager. When they departed four days later to catch the homeward-bound Plantiff at Falmouth, it was as messengers bearing desperate appeals from every quarter for the removal of Mme Schwimmer as conference manager. In the ten days since the peacemakers had returned to Stockholm she had alienated Aked, Miss Wales and some of the European delegates who had begun working unofficially, and she had sown the seeds of a peasants' rebellion among the conference staff.

Persuaded finally that her attempt to remove Barry was a self-defeating act, Rosika Schwimmer acknowledged his legitimacy when she returned from Copenhagen and, hoping to bind the American delegates to her, told Aked and Barry of her victory over Holt and Mrs. Fels. By then, however, Aked realized he had underestimated Mme Schwimmer's lust for power and knew she would never play the unspectacular role of expert adviser.

In his letter to Plantiff, the American delegate complained of Mme Schwimmer's untoward interference in office matters. He did not catalogue her sins, though she had already significantly diminished the authority of Mrs. Smitheman, the office manager, sent her spies among the clerical workers, closed the books to Buelow and tried to force her right-hand man, Ellis Jones, on Aked and Barry as delegation secretary. However, Aked was most disturbed by the effect the Hungarian feminist was having on the caliber of the conference membership. By controlling the money Mme Schwimmer was "filling the Neutral Conference," he wrote, "with persons of inferior type to the exclusion of men and women of superior character and standing, partly of deliberate purpose because these persons chosen will be her own creatures, and partly as the inevitable consequence of her methods and the prejudice she raises—the better class of men and women refusing to take part with us in the work." Plantiff must persuade Ford to remove her and, until then, Holt must handle the funds. To a former colleague on the expedition, Aked lamented, "We breathe an atmosphere of intrigue, personal ambition, antagonism. . . . I do not think I can endure much more of it." But he held on partly because of his contract and his commitment to the neutral-conference ideal and partly because he placed an excessively high value on his own competence.

It was the yielding of principle, not the frustration of ambition, that gravely distressed Julia Grace Wales. Those who met her on the trip admired her integrity, modesty and courage, but even that unassuming soul finally found it necessary to act upon her anguish. Her chronicle of life in Mme Schwimmer's court, which she recorded during those first weeks after their return to Stockholm, recounts the evolution of her resolve to act, not against Rosika Schwimmer—she refused to think in terms of personalities—but in the interests of the democratic conference she had conceived, and which so many others had endorsed. As honestly and dispassionately as she could, she wrote of the pervasive and unnecessary secrecy that surrounded them, of Mme Schwimmer's attempt to send her on a secret mission to Russia, of the office workers' fear that Mme Schwimmer was spying in their rooms and of Mme Schwimmer's inspecting all incoming mail. Miss Wales also wrote of her own "paralyzing feelings," of her fear that she might be disloyally "mixing with an intrigue" if she talked to Mrs. Fels and of her pathetic stratagem of counteracting the "secrecy in the atmosphere" by "always talking loudly and cheerfully." All this was disturbing but endurable. What she could not countenance, what actually kept her awake at night, were the administrative duties Mme Schwimmer had arrogated to herself when she wrote the conference constitution. The control of the funds and thus all executive power, the selection of the consulting experts from belligerent countries and the running of the press and propaganda bureau all resided in the expert adviser. Miss Wales believed that these functions should be democratically, not autocratically, regulated and that the conference itself should receive a regular monthly stipend, and she appealed to Ben Huebsch, putting her argument in business terms, to change Mme Schwimmer's mind. Instead, Huebsch accused Miss Wales of trying to get rid of Mme Schwimmer and of making "mountains out of molehills," a comment, she observed, which men had always "said to the Conscience of woman about rotten business deals from time immemorial."

At last, toward the end of their first week in Stockholm, Miss Wales confronted Mme Schwimmer herself. "It was astonishing how much courage it took to walk in and oppose her," she reported. She took a deep breath and spoke "slowly and firmly and in a loud voice," but after seeing Mme Schwimmer's recent communications from Ford and Plantiff and after hearing Mme Schwimmer's promise to "retire from power as soon as it was safe to do so," Miss Wales capitulated, more at ease than she had been since she left New York. Her new confidence and renewed loyalty lasted twenty-four hours.

The next morning Miss Wales went to the British legation and learned, to her relief, that her passport would not be extended for travel to Russia. Mme Schwimmer's instruction to her to find a loophole or else get a visa for England still did not disturb Miss Wales's equanimity. But that afternoon, Van Arsdale Turner, the conference librarian, asked Miss Wales for a private interview and for two hours she listened to his impressions of the mission's policy and those of others he had talked to, both Europeans and Americans. "It was as if in my mind a dam broke and a flood of previous impressions came down and swept away my confidence in the wisdom and reliability of Mme Schwimmer's leadership," she remembered, and she knew for certain that she could no longer support their leader's programs.

Still stunned by her third turn of mind in as many days, Miss Wales sat through the delegates' first preliminary meeting, only half hearing Aked speak for democratic procedures while her subconscious mind finally released the "accumulation of minute impressions" she had long disregarded. In the evening, she heard Mrs. Smitheman, the office manager, who had once praised Mme Schwimmer for being a "Bonaparte in petticoats," describe the tensions in the stenographic office. The following day Miss Wales told Mme Schwimmer that since their last talk she had learned of things that were so troubling she was moving to a pension, away from the conspiratorial atmosphere at the Grand Hotel. Though Mme Schwimmer patronizingly inquired of Miss Wales's "nervous breakdown" the next time they met, she was in fact quite distraught at the gentle woman's desertion and, bitterly decrying her enemies, complained that no one had confidence in her and everyone was conspiring against her.

Having estranged the American delegation and most of the business and secretarial staffs during their first week in Stockholm, Mme Schwimmer by the end of the second week had antagonized many of the European delegates who had earlier been her advocates. While waiting for at least five delegations from neutral countries to appear in Stockholm so that the conference might officially convene, the delegates present—the Americans and Swedes and, by mid-February, the Danes and Norwegians—met daily in either "informal unofficial" or "formal unofficial" meetings to review the constitution, set up study committees and discuss the policies and procedures of the coming gatherings.

Aked's protestations at the first meeting for the right of the conference to self-government and control of its funds were soon sustained by others equally determined to deny Rosika Schwimmer the prerogatives she demanded, the most immediate of which was selecting experts in the belligerent countries and arranging for their presence at the conference. When a special committee asked her what had been done in the matter thus far, she not only refused to acknowledge their right to invite consultants without her approval but refused to tell them whom she had selected and whom she was sending to invite them. All that, she said, had been decided by Ford and herself in November and arrangements had already been made, a statement that was at best only marginally true. The committee reported to the delegates that their meeting with her "was extremely unpleasant and that it left a painful impression on our minds." Whether the debate that followed the report reflected the rivalry between Mme Schwimmer and Dr. Aked or between the men and women delegates, as a few thought, it was most certainly a rejection by the majority of Mme Schwimmer as their absolute ruler.

Thereafter Lindhagen, Loeken, Aked and others took counsel with Miss Wales, who talked freely with them of the need for "a maximum of democracy, a minimum of secrecy," in conference affairs. Aked listened and cabled Ford on behalf of the American team, asking for "indisputable authority and money" to administer the peace effort. That message, sent in mid-February, was the first word Ford had directly from the delegates that Mme Schwimmer's "presence" and "methods" were terminally pernicious and that she should be dismissed.

Even with the opposition increasing, Mme Schwimmer sent Plantiff cheerful messages that everything was going splendidly, though Fels and Holt had tried to make trouble until Holt was recognized as a power-hungry money-grabber. The only problem was Aked, a convert to the Dutch Minimum Program, who was secretly trying to undermine the Europeans. And signing Lochner's name, she cabled Liebold, saying they needed $50,000, having already spent the $43,000 Plantiff had left them three weeks earlier (Of that sum, Mme Schwimmer sent $4,000 with her special recruiting agents to the belligerent countries and $4,000 to the Swiss delegates for traveling expenses, and she spent $1,800 on cables and telegrams in two weeks, $400 of it in one day.) Though Mme Schwimmer never conceded she was not permitted to spend funds on her own authority or that she ever spent a penny more than necessary, she signed Lochner's name because she knew Liebold did not share her views. The Europeans, as well, attacked her extravagance, some of the delegates remarking that the honoraria she offered were four times what they should be, and at least one Swedish newspaper criticized the conspicuous consumption at the Grand Hotel.

The office staff were "absolutely exhausted by the stifling atmosphere of plot and counterplot, intrigue and secrecy," and wondered at the time and energy Mme Schwimmer spent "on personal grudges and matters of personal gratification." Henrietta Neuhaus, the highly recommended assistant of the director of the Church Peace Union, suffered Mme Schwimmer's petty vindictiveness toward Aked and Barry when their request for her services as American delegation secretary was denied. Though the office staff often worked past midnight and even on Sundays typing all the speeches of the expedition since the *Oscar II* had left Hoboken, Mme Schwimmer chastised them for taking "too many liberties." To guard against abuses she sent her strawbosses Ellis Jones and Lewis Maverick on inspection tours of the workrooms and herself questioned the younger staff members on their co-workers' supposed infidelities.

Even while the beleaguered in Stockholm waited until Plantiff reached Detroit and pleaded their case, they worried that Ford might still be unwilling to act against Rosika Schwimmer. There was yet one person, the second-in-command from the beginning, who could preserve the neutral conference from disaster before it began. "Lochner of the white heart," as a Danish delegate called him, was regarded by all as fair-minded, honorable and competent. And the longer he was gone—the expected ten-day trip stretched into a month—the greater the belief that he was their redemption. Only Mme Schwimmer had been communicating with him—his secretary, Mrs. Clark, having gone to a sanitorium for her health shortly after he left Stockholm. Three weeks later she was back at headquarters, demanding Lochner's address, and writing him, "Everyone believes in you as the salvation of everything." It was meet that Lochner should bear the burden of the troubles; while his colleagues endured he was having the time of his life in Switzerland.

In Berlin, Lochner and Evans heard that S. S. McClure, Governor Hanna, Inez Milholland Boissevain and Judge Lindsey had been there before them and damned the expedition in the German press. They also just missed Colonel House, who had been in Europe since early January in another secret attempt to arrange a Wilsonian mediation based on postwar disarmament and a league of nations, the guarantees the president insisted were required to prevent future wars. Once again House, who prided himself on his abilities as a closet diplomat, was more beguiled than beguiling. (In London, the American ambassador said, they called him the "Empty House.") Each warring-government leader the president's emissary talked to declined immediate mediation, still determined to fight until victory. However, the British foreign secretary, not wishing to forfeit American support and trust, wrote a memorandum assuring Wilson that American mediation would be welcomed when invited and indicating some of the peace terms—restoration of Belgium, return of

Alsace-Lorraine to France and territorial compensations to Germany—
that the Allies understood the president favored. By early March, House
was home, erroneously reporting to Wilson that the long-sought "right
moment" when he would be asked to intervene was almost at hand.

At the German foreign office, Count Montgelas, director of the American section, listened to Lochner speak of the prospects of the forthcoming neutral conference and ask permission for German experts to travel
unhindered to Stockholm. Montgelas discounted the usefulness of citizens
from neutral nations acting in concert, favoring instead a single, skilled
negotiator acting directly with the belligerents at the proper time. As for
travel to Stockholm, while his office might grant such permits, the military authorities would likely veto them.

Not appreciating the import of Montgelas's remarks, Lochner called
upon potential experts, namely Eduard Bernstein, Socialist member of the
Reichstag; Lilly Jannosch, secretary of the German peace society, the
Bund Neues Vaterland (Society for a New Fatherland) and Professors
Ludwig Quidde and Walther Schuecking, all of whom were encouraging
and all of whom were under the surveillance of German military intelligence. Soon after Lochner and Evans returned to their hotel they were
visited by the criminal police, who confiscated their passports and then
returned them a few hours later stamped with the instruction that the
Americans must leave for Switzerland immediately by the shortest route
and that their return trip through Germany was to be equally expedi-
tious. "Mr. Evans and I," Lochner reported, "left mighty quick," on a
night train to Berne.

"I never thought it possible," Lochner wrote Mme Schwimmer some
days later, "that two people could come to a strange country and be
received with such extraordinary sympathy." As the Americans expected,
the government and press at first did not approve the unofficial neutral-
conference plan, but favorable large crowds attended the public meetings
and the Swiss peaceworkers elected a distinguished delegation. Alfred
Fried, the Austrian Nobel peace prize winner living in Berne, first
thought the American-sponsored effort nothing but "confused dilet-
tantism." He was astounded at the popular approval the idea received
when Lochner explained it at mass meetings, considering "how methodi-
cally, impressively and zealously the European press had attempted to
ridicule the Ford undertaking," and was himself all "fire and flame" for
the plan.

Fried was the first pacifist Lochner saw in Switzerland, hoping to engage him as an expert to the conference. Though the Austrian had to decline because travel through Germany meant certain arrest, he introduced Lochner to his peace friends. Foremost among them, and high on Mme Schwimmer's list of desirable delegates, was Joseph Scherrer-Fuellemann, a member of the Swiss National Council and president of the Swiss sections of the conservative Interparliamentary Union and the Central Organization for a Durable Peace, who invited a group to hear Lochner explain the neutral conference's purpose. At the meeting the very formal but "dear old gentleman," Scherrer-Fuellemann, agreed to head the committee to select a Swiss delegation.

While the committee deliberated, Lochner held meetings in the major Swiss cities which were attended by overflow crowds. At each gathering a resolution endorsing the conference's intention of formulating peace terms based on humanity and justice and not military advantage was passed. It was similar to the statement approved in The Hague before the expedition disbanded, except for one critical omission—nothing was said of disarmament, limited or absolute, which might explain why the Swiss peaceworkers endorsed it so enthusiastically.

Lochner also talked to Romain Rolland, the French pacifist-novelist then living in Switzerland, who was ostracized by his countrymen for his outspoken stand against the excesses of the war. Though Rolland would not come to the conference, he did attend one of the local meetings, after which he wrote Lochner of his hopes that their "most noble of missions [would] repay humanity a little for the miseries and the shame of this fratricidal war . . . and help to save European civilization from the gulf toward which it is stupidly rushing."

In trying to fill another assignment, that of getting a Spanish delegation, Lochner had no luck at all. Neither the American nor the French ministers would approve his traveling through France.

At last the day came when Lochner had to return, and on February 23 he and Evans left, accompanied by one delegate, two alternates, two translators and a secretary, with promises from the others to follow.

Foolishly ignoring their passport restrictions, the two Americans spent a day in Berlin visiting pacifists. At dinner, the secret police appeared, took everyone's name, and this time stamped in the Americans' passports: "Further entry into the German Reich is no longer permitted," and prohibited the Swiss members of the peace party from reentering Germany for three months. Lochner promptly wrote Count Montgelas that it was outrageous to expel people just for talking peace, that the military authorities were "politically terribly stupid" and that their treatment of him would scarcely cause him to "sing hymns of praise for the General Staff."

Still, nothing diminished Lochner's justifiable sense of triumph as he continued his journey to Stockholm. Singlehandedly—Evans spoke only English—he had reversed the Swiss peace leaders' attitude toward the Ford mission and generated strong popular endorsement for their unofficial mediation. The only internal trouble that faced the conference as far as he knew was caused by the refractory Dutch peaceworkers who had tried to keep the Swiss from joining. He heard regularly from Mme Schwimmer, but her only references to adversity were such comments as "Fels feels crazy toward me," which could hardly have seemed newsworthy to Lochner after the encounter in Copenhagen. His only warning of real trouble was the not very specific alert from Mrs. Clark that he would be "up against a big fight" as soon as he walked into the Grand Hotel. Mme Schwimmer increased the magnitude of that "fight" with her last flagrant move to entrench her authority before Lochner arrived.

On Tuesday, February 22, Lewis Maverick, a Schwimmer loyalist, gave Nora Smitheman a diagram that outlined the conference hierarchy to be typed and distributed to conference personnel. On the top was Henry Ford and his "personal peace representatives," Rosika Schwimmer and Louis Lochner, both of whom supervised the staff and special agents. Lochner was also financial representative responsible only to Ford, and Lewis Maverick—not Robert Buelow, whom Lochner had engaged—was Lochner's assistant. Apart from this establishment there was the neutral-conference complement with Lochner as general secretary supervising a staff of secretaries, experts, special agents and interpreters. The chart's introduction began: "The following diagram illustrates the distribution of authority in the Conference party, as outlined and worked out in detail by Henry Ford and his personal representatives, Madame Rosika Schwimmer and Mr. Louis P. Lochner." That was a lie and everyone knew it. Mme Schwimmer was trying to commit Lochner to a staff and structure he would be too embarrassed to repudiate before the conference members, and everyone knew that too. Nora Smitheman, after consulting Mrs. Clark and the Norwegian delegate, Haakon Loeken, simply ignored the directive. When Mrs. Clark suggested to Mme Schwimmer that she wait until Lochner returned, she was told to mind her own business.

Two days later Mme Schwimmer called to ask what had happened to her copy and Mrs. Smitheman replied that the chart had not been typed, since Mme Schwimmer had not initialed it in conformance with her own policy that all assignments must be approved by her. Unhoisting herself from her own petard, Mme Schwimmer sent for the document, signed it, and sent it down again, beginning a busy day for the interoffice messengers. This time, Mrs. Smitheman, backed by the members of her staff, wrote Mme Schwimmer she could not "in conscience" have the work done because neither Lochner nor Ford had anything to do with the chart and she did not think Mme Schwimmer had the right to act unilaterally, whereupon Mme Schwimmer ordered her to pick up her severance pay and ticket home immediately. Mrs. Smitheman advised the lady upstairs that since Plantiff had hired her only he could fire her, thus adopting the tactic used by the expert adviser herself in The Hague. Mme Schwimmer had the last word, which she addressed to Mrs. Smitheman at her lodging, informing her she could appeal to Plantiff but in the meanwhile she was no longer connected with the conference. Mrs. Smitheman disregarded the letter and sat quietly in her office doing nothing until Lochner arrived.

To console herself Rosika Schwimmer sent five radiograms in two days to Ben Huebsch, who had just sailed for home, advising that the office had mutinied but she was in good spirits. And to ensure that Lochner heard only the truth of the situation she sent Maverick, Ellis Jones and another staffworker and friend, Mrs. Waern-Bugge, to meet his train at Malmö on February 26. The emissaries from the other side, Van Arsdale Turner and Mrs. Clark, were also at the station to warn their savior not to commit himself until he had heard from every complainant.

For a day and night and another day Lochner served the Americans and Europeans, delegates and staff, as a human wailing wall. He heard of every abuse of power and of judgment, every injustice and indignity, from the controlling of the conference's policy by controlling its purse to the illicit mail delivery and regulating of every detail in office routine. After the accusers finished their oral reports they left Lochner with their written statements consisting of messages already sent to Ford and Plantiff and conference minutes. Ben Huebsch had left Lochner a letter which denied the charge that Mme Schwimmer's craving for power had created a smothering atmosphere of distrust and suspicion. Beware of Aked and Barry, "the snarling clergyman and the amiable person who sneezes when his coadjutor takes snuff," Huebsch warned, and understand that the issue of a free conference is only "a stalking horse" used by Aked to obtain control himself.

On Sunday night Lochner brought the grievances to Mme Schwimmer for compromise and resolution. On one issue, one petty issue, she took her stand and refused to acknowledge the American delegation's right to select its own secretary, though all the other delegations had been permitted to do so. If Lochner gave in to Aked and Barry's request, she would resign. As Miss Wales observed, it was a small point but it epitomized the issue of "autocratic control."

That night Rosika Schwimmer wrote her resignation. When Lochner called next morning to see if she had changed her mind, she said she had not, that she was the maligned victim of a plot and the only way to preserve the conference was to fire the delegates and staff who were conspiring against her. Trusting that her threat to quit the conference would eliminate that opposition either voluntarily, by popular demand or by Ford's edict, she confronted the delegates that morning and told them she was going to ask Ford for her release because she had been told repeatedly since the unofficial sessions began that she was the chief obstacle to the conference's efficient operation. This time her opposition called her bluff. The delegates asked her to remain as expert adviser, but not commander-in-chief. She would not even discuss the offer but, holding her resignation in abeyance, waited for the delegates to repent and offer her the crown.

In the meantime, Lochner took over. Miss Neuhaus was appointed secretary of the American delegation, Ellis Jones (Mme Schwimmer's candidate for the post) was told to leave by the end of the week, and Mrs. Smitheman was reinstated as supervisor of the office staff. That done, Lochner sent Liebold a long and defensive explanation of what he had done and why. "Long nervous strain unfits Schwimmer for authoritative leadership," he concluded, and asked for instructions. The demand for Lochner to act as decisively as he did had been overwhelming and the need obvious; still it was painful for him to initiate the downfall of the person he knew was largely responsible for the existence of their scheme. But he had to end "the tremendous power she had arrogated to herself," he explained to Miss Addams, because the majority of delegates thought her "unfit." Mme Schwimmer herself told him that as "an absolute convert to Autocracy" and having lost "all faith in human nature" she thought the conference should act only in secrecy.

The general secretary had one more difficulty to contend with during the last days of February, just as the conference was officially beginning its work. The day he returned to Stockholm he received a cable from Liebold summoning him home immediately. It was sent just after Plantiff, Judge Lindsey and Dr. Jones met with Henry Ford *and* Liebold and confirmed the cargo of frantic appeals from the Americans in Stockholm, as well as de Jong van Beek en Donk's advice, that Mme Schwimmer's

influence for peace would increase in proportion to her distance from the
neutral-conference table. The newspaper accounts of Ford's meeting with
the returning Americans said Mme Schwimmer would be removed from
power and asked to take "a back seat"; not that she would be fired.
Possibly none dared suggest that course to Ford, knowing he still believed
in her. Certainly Plantiff backtracked. Her "only bad feature," he later
wrote Dr. Jones, "is that she is so suspicious and does not know the value
of a dollar." She was extravagant, not dishonest, and too concerned with
"her own personal reputation rather than the Peace Expedition." However, it was Plantiff's report that the expedition had thus far spent about
$400,000 and the cables Liebold had been getting from Stockholm all
month asking for more money that made Liebold tell Lochner to come
home and caused him to ask, "Who is handling finances?"

The command for Lochner's return stunned all the peaceworkers. No
one, not Rosika Schwimmer nor the delegates nor the staff, wanted him
to leave. His presence held them together. While he was still trying to
sort out the chaos around him, Lochner hastily replied that he was "taking thorough hold of the situation," including the finances. That news,
however, did not inspire confidence in Liebold, and when another cable
followed two days later asking both for money and Mme Schwimmer's
dismissal, Liebold, with Ford's approval, acted.

On March 1, Rosika Schwimmer heard from Liebold that Frederick
Holt, who had not been able to reach England and was still in Norway,
was the new business manager and she was to cooperate with him. That
message, so clearly contrary to her expressed demands, plus the evident
unwillingness of the delegates to acknowledge her leadership, forced her
hand and she officially submitted her resignation to Ford and the conference. The delegates accepted it unanimously. It was another week before
she heard from Ford.

During that time Mme Schwimmer sat isolated in her chambers protected by her powerless defenders, and waited word from Ford begging
her to retain command. Haggard and tired, but still indomitable, she
released her bitter fury in a barrage of cables to her allies in America,
written in the code they had devised to foil the British censors. Lochner
she cursed as a "swell-headed idiot" who had "turned entirely against"
her. To Huebsch she complained that the delegates had forced her to ask
for release even though she had organized the conference perfectly, and
she urged Huebsch to inform Ford personally of her indispensability. Her
directions to Plantiff harked back to her view of the good old days of
their joint ownership. The conference was doing splendid work under

her strict guidance she told him, but he must send Emily Balch and George Kirchwey right away. Not only did she think these delegates were better qualified than either Aked or Barry but she was certain they would acknowledge her responsibility for their appointments by demanding she remain as leader.

On March 8, Mme Schwimmer heard from Liebold that "Mr. Ford expresses to you his hearty thanks for your interest and cooperation," and that he accepted her resignation with regret.

Generals when defeated leave the field, but Rosika Schwimmer remained for several months in the Grand Hotel, unwilling to leave the "battlefield of the peace-champions," as her secretary expressed it, "as long as there is the faintest hope to be able to help the cause." In less luxurious accommodations she lay in bed till noon, cursing Lochner, Aked and Barry for causing her downfall, hearing the news and gossip of the conference from the delegates who were her friends, seeking heart's ease in petty and spiteful delays as she slowly relinquished official connection with the conference.

Many examined her methods and misread her motives. Certain of her wisdom and judgment, the Hungarian feminist practiced a pious hypocrisy, shading the truth in her favor, sometimes slightly, sometimes grossly, to persuade others to her ends. She wanted power not for personal aggrandizement but to ensure that her ideas, which no one was as capable of enacting as herself, were realized. Once obtained, she used power to gratify her ambition and to force acknowledgment of her supreme position. Because she gave unselfishly of herself to what she took to be a common purpose, she considered her behavior—including her flair for high living when she was in the money, her own or someone else's—above criticism and commensurate with the dignity and importance of her work. Because she personalized her principles, merging herself with her goals, she suffered every rejection of her plans as an affront to her person. At such times her compassion for herself was boundless. She had also an affinity for martyrdom—her weapon when she was opposed and her shield when she was threatened. Without the tolerance, objectivity and perspective that would permit her to accept the needs and aims of others, she considered those who did not agree with her as demented or unimportant and condemned them with the outrage of the pure in heart.

Mme Schwimmer was of that breed so totally committed by their minds and emotions to the immediate actualization of an ideal that they know neither moderation nor patience. Impervious to rational self-analysis, impregnably self-confident, demanding absolute submission from her associates and considering all criticism the product of conspirators, she had little staying power in any of the peace attempts with which she had been associated since the day the war began. Each time that she provided the tenacity and leadership to realize an ideal she also supplied the intransigent behavior that caused her associates to force her resignation or dismissal while genuinely regretting the loss of her ability to help in their work. In the case of the neutral conference, Mme Schwimmer blamed her fate on a series of unfortunate coincidences and waited at the Grand Hotel, neither gone nor forgotten, for the American delegates of her choice to arrive and restore her rights.

"It now seems almost incredible," Lochner wrote Ford after the conference was well into its work, "that Madame Schwimmer should so long have tyrannized all of us on the bluff that you had threatened to take your hand off the whole project unless we did everything at her bidding. You may think that we were 'easy marks,' but . . . the idea behind the movement was so great that we were willing even to bear up under her tyranny."

CHAPTER 11

The Neutral Conference for Continuous Mediation

The NEUTRAL CONFERENCE for Continuous Mediation, though far removed from the scenes of battle, was nonetheless aware of the war. Each day bulletins from the conference's press bureau informed the delegates of the action at the front, of the tens of thousands killed, of the few hundreds of yards gained and lost. In the year just ended, two million soldiers had been killed or wounded on the western front in the *Looking-Glass* war that kept both sides running as fast as they could to stay in the same place. The opposing armies were at stalemate when the year began—and when it ended. On February 28, 1916, the day the neutral conference officially convened, the German attack on Verdun that ultimately caused almost 760,000 casualties was seven days old and another spring offensive had begun. The neutral-conference delegates hoped that by fall, when both sides had spent themselves once more, the belligerents would accept mediation. But whether that mediation should be conducted by members of their conference or by officials of the neutral governments was a matter on which the delegates themselves never agreed.

Such a critical disagreement on why they were gathered together was expressed with increasing passion each time a matter for decision came before them. In the very beginning, however, the very, very beginning, though there was confusion compounded and no unanimity, there was at least a willingness among the delegates to work together.

The constitution, for example, once shorn of Mme Schwimmer's authoritarian provisions, was approved quickly. It provided for thrice-weekly meetings, for voting procedures and for the conference chairmanship to be held by each nation on a weekly basis. The full conference was to be advised by an executive committee, a press committee and a committee on expert consultants, each committee to have equal national representation. Sections were created to study questions of nationality and transfer of territory; freedom of the seas, colonies and other international economic questions; international organization; disarmament and propaganda; and to develop peace proposals. A separate committee was to advise the conference on the preferred method of submitting the peace proposals to the belligerents. Despite the quixotic financial arrangements endured by the expedition, no provision was made by the conference to administer its designated funds. The delegates expected Ford to send them whatever money they needed to be spent as they thought best.

The constitution also provided for five delegates from each neutral country, a total of thirty from the countries represented.* In time, each nation had a full complement, except the United States, which had only two representatives during the entire conference. (Mary Fels, who had visited the delegates earlier in the month, never returned to Stockholm but went directly home after attending to her business in England.) Because the Scandinavian countries were frequently represented by alternates, the same twenty-seven people did not sit together throughout the conference. The Swiss delegation's secretary and translator were allowed to serve as alternates for the two members who failed to leave Switzerland with the rest of the delegation.

Of those who did serve at the conference, eight were both jurists and university professors of international relations, economics or the humanities; three were high school teachers, all holding doctoral degrees; six were in government, including several parliament members; four were in business; four were editors or writers; and two were school administrators. Also serving were a librarian, a minister and a retired colonel. One-third of the delegates were women, many of them professionals. Half of the women delegates had attended the women's Hague congress and all of them were leaders in women's reform movements involving suffrage, working conditions and child labor. Every national delegation, except the American, had at least one woman representative. Later, several of the conference members served on their governments' delegations to the League of Nations.

* See Appendix 2 for list of members.

Charles Aked thought his colleagues were "respectable but not eminent," all "earnest men and women" but none of them exceptional, and some even "feeble and useless," their unfortunate selection the fault of Mme Schwimmer. What they lacked in "brain power," he wrote Ford, was only partially compensated by their "spirit of consecration."

Aked's evaluation was preliminary to a plea to Ford to fulfill his duty as a prestigious American delegate and return to Europe. Liebold passed on Ford's words of encouragement to the conference, but whatever attention Ford gave to peace after his return was devoted to his domestic anti-preparedness campaign. It was unrealistic, of course, for the delegates to think that Henry Ford would consent to sit still for days, let alone half an hour, while the conference deliberated such matters as whether Russia should have access through the Dardanelles, and the Americans in Stockholm knew this. They hoped only that he would make an appearance for a week or two as a token of his faith in their work. Ford did plan such a visit in the spring, as part of a business trip to promote his tractor, but probably because of renewed submarine attacks, he never came.

Neither did William Jennings Bryan, Jane Addams or George Kirchwey. Though Bryan originally expected to come for at least ten days he did not intend to serve unless either Ford or Miss Addams did also, and in late January he was told not to make plans without a personal invitation from Ford. When that was not forthcoming by mid-February, despite Rosika Schwimmer's cable sent over Lochner's signature announcing that everyone wanted to elect him conference president, Bryan replied that the preparedness campaign at home still required his attention.

Jane Addams was fairly certain of her course, but she nonetheless consulted Dr. David Starr Jordan, who was one of the first endorsers of Miss Wales's neutral conference plan. Jordan told her not to go because the potential effectiveness of the conference had been irrevocably damaged by the publicity attendant on the expedition. Instead he suggested she wait until she was invited to join a very small group that would work somewhere in Holland, "very quietly, very modestly and very intelligently . . . avoiding as far as possible all notices in the newspapers." While Miss Addams favored Jordan's preference for a small number of competent delegates working without notoriety, she approved the conference's present location and she absolutely opposed a policy that prohibited newspaper publicity. It was the military control of the press, the censorship of news and thought, that had disturbed her during her travels in the warring countries the previous spring. She did not expect the neutral conference to end the war. Its principal function was to publish the peace plans it received so that, for example, English citizens could read the German anti-annexationist's proposals and German citizens could read the program of the English Union of Democratic Control. That way, she hoped, the war would not end in secret diplomacy as it had begun.

Jane Addams wanted very much to come to Europe; repeated cables from Mme Schwimmer, Lochner and Miss Wales and from Aletta Jacobs made it appear that without her presence both the neutral conference and the International Committee of Women for Permanent Peace would founder. She was desperately needed in Stockholm to mediate among the mediators. But instead of improving, her health deteriorated, and her doctor sent her to California to recover. Lochner and Mme Schwimmer were certain her illness was "diplomatic," and that her friends—their enemies—were deliberately spiriting her as far from Stockholm as they could manage. When Miss Addams learned she could not sail in April as she had hoped she sent Emily Greene Balch as her alternate. But Miss Balch did not arrive in Stockholm until the first phase of the conference was over.

George Washington Kirchwey, another alternate, did not come despite the demands of Rosika Schwimmer and her personal emissaries. It may have been that he did not approve of so large a group of uninformed associates, as he told Ford when he first refused the invitation to sail on the *Oscar II*; it may have been he could not be released from his warden-ship at Sing Sing; or it may have been, as David Starr Jordan supposed, that Kirchwey would not serve on a peace mission with the strong-minded Reverend Charles F. Aked.

Certainly Jordan would not; he knew the character and capabilities of his California neighbors, Aked and John Barry, too well, he said, to expect productive results from a peace conference that accepted them as members. Barry was "a nice fellow" but knew nothing of European affairs, and Aked, though possessed of "excellent qualities," was unable to work with other people since he lacked both tact and tolerance. Aked's defects were so well known by his senior deacon that the latter only submitted Aked's resignation and not his request for a leave of absence to the church membership. But his fellow delegates at the neutral confer-ence knew Aked only as highly competent, wise and self-confident, an "expert driver" whose skills as chairman and parliamentarian were so impressive that, ignoring the provisions of their constitution, they elected him chairman for the first two weeks. It took some time for them to learn that the minister who had walked out on John D. Rockefeller because the millionaire had not fulfilled his expectations might be a success as a leader and a failure as a coequal.

During the course of the conference the delegates regretted their lack of a reputable and responsible leader, but it is problematical whether anyone could have persuaded them to compromise more readily or to refrain from discussing every idea in full. Each day twenty-seven people, the men in frock coats, the women often in equally formal attire, gathered in the conference room. They shook hands all around before sitting down to discuss the issues in six languages and a northern Norwegian peasant dialect, all translated by a Finnish baron into German, French and English, while the chairman of the week conducted the meeting according to the parliamentary rules of his native land. Lengthy and disordered discussions on trivia scarred every meeting, often leading the delegates so far afield from the initial topic that once, when an exasperated member called for the previous question, everyone was surprised to learn there was no motion on the floor. Another time the chairman became so entangled in a parliamentary web he had to adjourn the meeting.

The effort to permit equal national representation in every phase of the conference work and to permit everyone to decide everything, though well intended, resulted in mind-boggling chaos that unnerved the most patient and slowed the work to a sloth's pace. It was not, perhaps, that the delegates were petty; but they had a sense of the historic importance of their endeavor and of its immediate significance. Had the members come to the conference with but one concept of their role and one manner of fulfilling it, all would have gone quickly and well. But they had been called together hastily, and it had been assumed that their acceptance of the invitation meant acceptance of the conference's purpose as plainly stated in its title. On the peace ship, this fallacious assumption led to a crisis over the anti-preparedness platform; at the neutral conference, concerned as it was with considerably more critical issues, it caused many more crises and the same vindictive jealousies, charges of conspiracy and emotional cries of mismanagement.

To achieve the *juste-milieu* of the many proposals volunteered was nearly impossible. Despite the daily publicity that appeared during the expedition's trek through the neutral countries relating its intent and expected procedures, some delegates came to the Neutral Conference for Continuous Mediation expecting neither to confer nor to mediate. The preliminary discussions conducted in early February by only a few delegates clearly indicated that each delegate was reluctant—to put it mildly —to consider the reasonableness of any position other than his or her own. A few blamed organizers of the Ford expedition for not working out a specific peace program which would have guided prospective delegates before they accepted membership. Yet, the minimal instructions set forth in the resolution passed by the expedition members in The Hague

Delegates and their associates at the first formal session of the neutral conference. Left to right: standing, back row: Haakon Loeken, John Barry, Ernest Troesch, Baron Walleen, Ernst Wigforss, Nikolaus Gjeslvik, Mikael Lie, Ole Solnoerdal, Carl Lindhagen, Henrietta Neuhaus; second row, Albert Schenk, Hans Larsson, Johan Bergmann, Frederikke Moerck, Helga Frida Steenhof, Anna Kleman, Louis Lochner, Ada Clark, Otto Volkart; seated, Marguerite Gobat, Charles Aked, Helene Berg, Fritz Studer, Clara Ragaz, A. F. Lamm

were ignored. Mayor Lindhagen thought the lack of a specific plan caused the conference to become "embroiled in European peace societies' schisms." He may not have been right on the cause; he was certainly right on the result.

Two opposing philosophies were at the root of all the conflicts. The Swedes, Danes and some Swiss wanted the neutral conference to demand an immediate armistice and to suggest peace proposals that would stand as a monument to what civilized peoples should aspire to. The Dutch, Norwegians and some members of other delegations who belonged to the international Central Organization for a Durable Peace and Interparliamentary Union thought the conference should study the political and economic causes of the war and then prepare a just, lasting and realistic peace treaty.

This critical dichotomy was immediately apparent when the delegates, trying to frame an agenda and determine a modus operandi, discussed the function of the conference. Two Norwegians, Dr. Mikael Lie and Dr. Nikolaus Gjelsvik, both international law consultants to the Nobel Institute, presented the most sensational plan when they suggested the conference adjourn immediately, taking time only to associate itself with the study program of the Central Organization for a Durable Peace. In its stead, they wanted Henry Ford to establish the Ford Institute for International Justice as a watchdog committee guarding the rights of all minority nationalities. The institute would do "permanently useful" work, they argued, whereas the conference would only waste time and money because the war would only end when one side decided the time was "ripe," and then only official mediators would be consulted. Two other Norwegians, Haakon Loeken, the attorney general of Christiania, and Ole Solnoerdal, a labor arbitrator, agreed with their countrymen that the conference would have no role in ending the war. Demanding a truce in the spring of 1916, they said, would make the delegates appear "more stupid than we really are." Loeken, who was pro-Ally, was particularly worried that a demand for immediate armistice unaccompanied by peace terms would result in a peace based only on military advantage.

The Swedes and Danes, expecting the peace treaty to be based on civil equity, called Loeken's argument irrelevant. Many members of this bloc were friends and followers of Rosika Schwimmer who believed, as she did, that direct action, not deliberation, was the function of the conference. Ford said from the beginning he was backing the program of the women's Hague conference, which, these peace activists said, was committed to direct mediation with government leaders

Usually the two American delegates held opposing views. Aked wanted the conference to develop equitable peace proposals; Barry insisted it should stop the war, not reform the world by "teaching and preaching." And Julia Grace Wales, sitting silently in a corner of the office, revised

her plan once more. It would not matter, she wrote, if the neutral conference was not directly involved in mediation as long as its voice was heard
in all the countries by all the people.

On two matters, however, all the delegates agreed: that the neutral
conference had to ensure that the major powers defined and recognized
the rights of small nations and minority nationalities at the peace table,
and that the neutral conference had to get to work. On March 1 the
conference combined these two purposes and appointed two committees
of seven people each, one to frame an appeal to the neutral nations to call
an official mediation conference, the other to formulate tentative peace
proposals for submission to the belligerents.

The neutral-appeal committee spent hours trying to agree on exactly
which countries the conference should appeal to and what it should ask
them to do, and only resolved the matter when the delegates decided to
personally present their petition to the Scandinavian foreign ministers
who were meeting in Copenhagen the weekend of March 9. The members had a whole week to do their work—and they barely made it. Five
versions were thoroughly discussed before one was picked for revision,
and the revision was "no easy matter with a whole committee watching
each word and ready to pounce." On March 9, the committee presented
its final draft to the conference, and then all the delegates spent the day
and most of the night writing the final version, finishing just in time for
the deputation to catch the last train to Denmark. After several more
sessions the delegates decided to send the neutral appeal not only to their
own governments but to the governments and parliaments of every country that participated in the second Hague peace conference of 1907. All
the delegates signed the document except the Norwegians, Drs. Gjelsvik
and Lie, who again called the proceedings a waste of time, a comment Lie
continued to make regularly in the coming weeks.

The appeal to the neutral nations, after noting that almost two years
had passed since the war began and the warring powers still appeared
determined on fighting to a military victory, suggested that history
would condemn the neutral countries "if they remain merely spectators
of the terrible conflagration." By publicizing in the neutral countries
their justifications for fighting, the belligerents had "made the neutrals
judges of their cause"; therefore the neutral governments should act in
conformity with the Hague conference resolution which provided that
uninvolved signatories could initiate mediation between belligerents.

It was a simple request, simply stated. It had been a year since the
women envoys from The Hague had made a similar request and though

the neutral conference delegates hardly expected their plea would be acted upon, they thought, as Aked wrote Ford, "we shall at least have called the attention of the civilized world to the need of intervention. And we shall feel ourselves empowered by a fresh mandate to do the work of an official conference."

At the Scandinavian foreign ministers' meeting in Copenhagen the neutral conference was only one of several peace organizations vainly urging the officials to act. Even though the substance of their appeal was rejected, the delegates thought it had "scored a big triumph" simply by being discussed at all. Official recognition was a far cry from the ridicule and mockery the American pacifists had received in the world press three months earlier.

Recognition, if such it was, was one thing; approval another. The Norwegian and Swedish foreign ministers, when they were later visited in their capitals by conference delegates, said their governments would be happy to mediate but only when the belligerents asked them to. The American minister to Stockholm agreed to accept a copy of the appeal but said he could not send it to the State Department, though he immediately dispatched it to Secretary Lansing.

There was some positive though ineffectual neutral-government action. Lindhagen's bill in the Swedish Riksdag asking the government to call an official neutral conference passed the lower house unanimously but lost in the upper house. A similar bill was introduced in the Norwegian Storting but was shelved for lack of a quorum. The conference representatives, however, had an encouraging interview with the Storting president, who approved of the neutral conference and wondered why the United States did not summon an official convocation. And most significantly, the appeal was printed in full in the papers of the neutral nations and extracts appeared in the belligerent nations' press.

The seven-member committee to draft the appeal to the belligerents had a considerably more difficult and painstaking assignment. Their first action was to send delegations to the ministers from the warring countries in Stockholm to obtain permission for expert consultants to travel from their countries to Stockholm. The French minister, barely able to restrain his indignation, told them no French citizen would accept such an invitation; the German minister was noncommittal; and the British minister, Sir Esme Howard, would not even see them until he had the consent of his government. Several weeks later, when Sir Esme told the delegates they could call, they sped toward the rendezvous in two cars, elated by what they mistakenly took to be official recognition by the British. However,

Howard's instructions were only to accept the petition and inform the peacemakers that this was no time to end the war.

That was also the message brought back by Baroness Ellen Palmstierna and Dr. Naima Sahlbom, whom Mme Schwimmer had sent to Russia and England, respectively, to arrange for conference consultants. Talk of mediation was not permitted in the czar's empire, and though Dr. Sahlbom could speak of it with the British pacifists, they would not endanger the little freedom left to them by publicly supporting the neutral conference.

It was evident that, for the time being at least, if the neutral conference was to have the advice of belligerent citizens it would have to receive it on a catch-as-catch-can basis when possible candidates came to Stockholm on other business. In this manner, in early March, the conference heard Sir Gilbert Murray, a professor of Greek at Oxford, who was on a cultural mission for the British Foreign Office. Murray, a pacifist during the Boer War and until the eve of the current war, spoke of crushing German militarism, not the German people, and concluding the war with a liberal treaty. The Englishman was impressed by the neutral conference and promised to report his findings to Sir Edward Grey, his foreign secretary.

For the rest, the conference's luck was not very good. A German professor and an Austrian archaeologist declined to appear before them; in fact, no citizen of the Central Powers ever accepted an invitation. The delegates did hear from a Russian pacifist and received the advice of the Belgian Nobel peace laureate, Paul Otlet, through the mail. Their most dramatic witness was an Estonian peasant who illegally crossed his native border and skied over snow and ice for ten days to plead the cause of his desperate people, and then begged the conference to keep his name and presence secret until he had time to return home.

Mme Schwimmer's friends tried to have her employed as a full-time expert adviser, but their attempt was foiled by Holt. Their request that she be invited to address the conference was denied because Mme Schwimmer attached the condition that Holt not be invited to hear her speak. In the end, she spoke to the committee preparing the belligerent appeal and was extremely effective, convincing several newcomers that the belligerent leaders were still waiting for the neutral countries to mediate just as they had told the women envoys the year before. Therefore, she said, the conference should follow through and send its personal representatives to the warring governments with peace proposals. Though Rosika Schwimmer made only one official appearance before the delegates, from her quarters in the hotel, which her secretary referred to as the "Isle of St. Helena," she daily influenced those delegates who sought her advice, most of whom were obliged to her for their selection. Mme Clara Ragaz, a Swiss delegate who had never met Mme Schwimmer, admired her intelligence, and conviction and the apparent loyalty of her friends, two of whom, she thought, "would place their hands in fire for her."

Because of his natural inclinations and the confidence placed in him by the home office in Detroit, Dr. Aked tried to fill the leadership vacuum left by Rosika Schwimmer's forced resignation. He was supported in his power plays by Frederick Holt, Plantiff's replacement, who arrived at the conference office from his Christiania hideaway one morning early in March, "fresh as a four-leaf clover, smiling, and ready for business." Acting on Liebold's instructions to cut costs, Holt promptly fired Mme Schwimmer's faithful staff and several typists. All the conference needs, he told his new boss, "is a firm hand and some decision." The delegates, though not as experienced and capable as they might be, he patronizingly added, were earnest and there were signs already that the conference was commanding respect. Holt's words; Aked's opinions.

To his dying day Ernest Liebold was convinced that the pacifists in Europe "were just running around, getting in trouble and spending money." Holt's first report indicating the conference was already at least $8,000 in debt and carrying a monthly budget of $30,000, more than half of which was going to honoraria and delegates' expenses, did nothing to change his mind. Aked was the closest thing to a Ford Motor Company agent attached to the expedition, and Liebold knew nothing of him except that on Plantiff's say-so he was being paid a sizable amount of money and was therefore likely to be a man of good judgment. Accordingly, Liebold instructed Holt to consult Aked on the policy suggestions that Liebold sent almost daily across the Atlantic in Ford's name. (Ford, in fact, was saying nothing, either about the cost or about the work of the conference.) Holt was only a functionary, a go-between, who knew that if he did not obey orders both he and the conference would be ditched. On the one hand there was Liebold, anxious to get Ford honorably separated from a nonproductive money-consuming operation. On the other was Aked, whose holier-than-thou attitude, assumed by dint of his monetary connection with Ford, antagonized those of his colleagues who thought "Aked and his gang were handing the conference over to the do-nothing conservatives." And in the middle was Holt, a man given to pomposity and punctiliousness who intruded in matters seemingly beyond his concern and hectored the delegates when they did not work as quickly as he expected, causing them to call him the "Dictator of our Assembly."

During March Liebold asked Holt and Aked whether the national delegations could be reduced from five representatives to one, whether the conference could be moved to The Hague, a "more logical place," and whether the "time is ripe" for Ford to come over for a visit. Not until May, Holt replied, expecting the conference to complete its major work—the peace proposals—in a few more days.

So Holt and Aked thought at the end of March. The week before, the committee writing the appeal to the belligerents had submitted its draft, and it had taken only two days for the delegates to analyze and approve the basic platform: self-determination for all nations and no transfer of territory without the consent of the people involved, open-door trade in all colonies, an international organization to which nations must apply to peacefully settle disputes and the democratic control of foreign policy in all countries. "By hook and by crook but still with unanimity we suc-ceeded in drawing up a program which in some form should be the basis of our offer of mediation," Mme Ragaz wrote home, expressing, at the same time, grievous forebodings for the work ahead. She understood that the belligerent governments would expect examples of how the peace principles should be applied and that a start had to be made sometime, but she was fearful that "everyone will have their own pet" idea of what each proposal meant specifically and would insist that it be included. "In short, it will be quite a muddle again." She was absolutely right. Her own idea of simply asking each side to state its peace terms was shared by no one, and the suggestions for specific applications were prolific and endlessly argued.

Day after day the delegates were engulfed by the formidable task they had set themselves of creating the perfect instrument for peace. It was easy to agree to freedom of the seas in principle, but did that apply to artificial as well as natural waterways? And did independence rather than autonomy for minority peoples mean "political independence," "national independence," or just plain "independence"? And if Lindhagen's ex-treme position on full rights for minorities was included, a Dutch delegate suggested, then the Japanese in San Francisco could vote that the city should belong to Japan.

The arguments were bitter and were marked by points of order and of personal privilege. Motions were made while other motions were already on the floor. At one such discussion Aked suggested they adjourn to untangle their parliamentary mess, but Mme Ragaz thought he had been outfoxed and only wanted time to advise his faction on the latest maneuver and line up their votes. Two factions formed, each consisting of almost half the delegates, one favoring Aked's conservative inclinations and the other more or less supporting the gentle, good-humored Lindhagen's idealistic program—"headed straight for Utopia," said Barry—which demanded that the neutral conference mediate immediately. Though the activist faction was in the majority, the minority needed to persuade only a few members to win its position or a reversal on a followup vote. And when this was done, particularly on critical matters, Mme Schwimmer's disciples cried out against tyranny by the minority and insisted that those delegates who did not believe in mediation had no place in the conference and should be disfranchised.

On one matter the delegates were unfailingly unanimous—the conference room was too small and the ventilation so poor that their cigar smoke hung heavily about them and made it impossible for them to think clearly. But when they had Holt in and formally inquired about new headquarters he merely expressed his surprise that they were discussing their comfort when thousands of people were dying.

Finally, on April 4, the special committee that had been designated three days earlier to write another draft of the appeal based on the delegates' discussion presented the conference with a choice of Alternative A or Alternative B. The first consisted of a list of major principles and a list of specific applications. The second was a single list of major principles with the relevant applications beneath each one. It took the delegates three days to decide which format to accept.

One of the most heated arguments that delayed a final decision concerned the objects of their peace program. Were they addressing it to the governments and parliaments or the governments, parliaments and peoples? The plan must be kept from the people, Lindhagen insisted, if the conference expected politicians to consider it seriously. But the sole reason for their existence, cried the heretofore silent Lochner, was to direct peace talk to the people. In the midst of the battle Aked suddenly asked if he could make a motion completely unrelated to what they were discussing. After some talk on the matter, the delegates decided he could offer the motion without discussion, whereupon Aked sprung Liebold's new scheme without naming its author. In view of their discursive discussion, he said, the time had come for them to reduce the size of the conference, leaving one representative from each of the six countries to handle all matters until it was necessary for the full conference to meet again. There was no talk, but as Mme Ragaz remarked; "The bomb exploded and the 'cat is out of the bag.' " So she and her allies spoke of the coup d'état they thought Aked and Mme Bakker, a Dutch delegate, both of whom were considered Anti-Oorlog Raad agents, had planned.

Aked's bombshell at least brought the matter previously under discussion—whether they should address the appeal to the people—to a vote. The peoples' advocates lost. That evening the defeated rallied together to try to direct the conference away from the secret machinations preferred by Mme Schwimmer's nominees.

Next morning, April 6, Holt asked for and received permission to address the conference. Wasting scarcely a moment on the amenities, he said that Ford knew about the distrust begun during the reign of Rosika Schwimmer that was still present, defeating and delaying their work. As business manager, he said, he had "full authority to act" for Ford "in all matters." Thus far he had informed their sponsor of the good work done by the delegates but after yesterday's vote against releasing their appeal to the people he wondered whether his "encouragement" was justified. Was it not time, he suggested, after four weeks of deliberation, that they released their "valuable piece of work"? Holt spoke also of Ford's intention to reduce the conference to a "working committee," its members to be selected either by the conference or by Ford, which would study the causes for war and prepare for peace, probably in another city. "A loose harmonious agreement" would bind the larger conference to the new group. But above all else, Holt said, Ford wants "action," and he begged the delegates to "sink your personal difference and pull together in harmony" to get the "great work" done.

Holt really tried to be gracious, but he failed. His demeanor was pompous, his words patronizing. He was arrogating to himself knowledge and authority no one thought he had. Holt won no friends, but he won his point—partially. The vote the day before was reversed; the appeal would be addressed to the people and their governments.

There still remained the matter of which format of the appeal was preferred. Those anxious to mediate immediately voted for Alternative A, which simply listed the proposals and the concrete applications in two separate groups, and an exactly equal number voted for Alternative B, the longer and more explicit and thoughtful presentation. Such a standoff naturally produced a stream of minor textual alterations as each side tried to obtain the winning vote. In the end, the short form won, and again the victory was short-lived.

When the delegates convened the next morning, Lochner warned them they would be laughed at if after a month of continuous discussion they published principles which had taken the women in The Hague only a few days to write, and he persuaded them to reconsider. The vote was reversed, and in the late morning of Friday, April 7, the full conference began its work of revision, starting with Clause 1, Section A, Alternative B.

They finished the job over the weekend and took two more days to rewrite it for final review, and on April 12, six weeks after they had begun, the last draft was approved and signed by every delegate but John Barry, who was "out of sympathy" with the spirit of the document.

The final version of the appeal, Lindhagen wrote, was a compromise between the Maximum Program of the Swedes and the Minimum Program of the Dutch. It was not a dogmatic document, but one that carefully refrained from reorganizing the world and that dealt only with the European peoples. "A Conference composed of Delegates from six neutral countries," the appeal began, founded on the initiative of Henry Ford and representing no government, was sitting in Stockholm working for "an early and lasting peace based upon principles of justice and humanity." Believing that peace could be achieved before both sides devastated each other vying for a military victory if the opponents would agree to "certain universal principles," the neutral conference was submitting for "sympathetic consideration" some of the guarantees that would prevent another war. There followed seven principles and examples of how they should be realized.

The first principle stated that since annexation of territory against the wishes of the peoples concerned invariably resulted eventually in wars of liberation, the peace settlement should provide "that no transfer of territory should take place without the consent of the population involved, and that nations have the right to decide their own fate." Thus, Belgium and occupied French territory should both be restored, the "difficult Alsace-Lorraine question" should be reconsidered, and Serbia and Montenegro should be granted independence. In addition, "the union of the Polish nation as an independent people" should be guaranteed, the Austro-Italian frontier adjusted, Armenia granted autonomy and the several national questions in the Balkans and Asiatic Turkey settled by international agreement.

The second principle recognized that economic competition was another major cause of war which could be obviated by permitting free trade with all colonies, protectorates and spheres of influence, and by internationalizing certain waterways, notably the Bosporus and the Dardanelles. Also, German colonies should be returned, the present occupiers to receive satisfactory compensation, and Germany should be guaranteed trade access to the Near East.

The next four principles urged the recognition of freedom of the seas, parliamentary control of foreign policy to prevent secret treaties and secret diplomacy, the establishment of an international organization to which all nations would agree to submit disputes for arbitration, and international agreements on disarmament. Finally, since the neutrals as well as the belligerents were affected by the war and would be affected by the peace settlement, the appeal suggested that a "World Congress" of representatives of all nations focusing on the political and spiritual freedom of subject nationalities should participate in the peace conference. The concluding paragraph called for an end to "international anarchy" and "an enduring peace for all mankind" through the "institution of an international order of justice."

These principles conformed to those already advanced during the war by most peace congresses and organizations, but the many specific applications of the principles were the first such presentation ever submitted to the belligerent governments. With the exception of the suggestions regarding Germany, every provision suggested was included in Wilson's Fourteen Points address of almost two years later. That fact alone, Lochner later wrote, did "credit to the inexperienced group of pacifists sitting daily around the green table of the Grand Hotel at Stockholm."

The delegates decided they would announce on Palm Sunday, April 16, that they had a tentative plan which they would submit to the belligerents at Easter. The conference still had to decide how to release the document and to whom. Both of these considerations were as important to the delegates as the document itself and provided fodder for further arguments. The secrecy advocates—those who also favored direct mediation and who had first won and then lost an earlier critical vote—tried again for victory. The appeal, they said, must be hand-delivered to the belligerent leaders and its terms kept secret, otherwise the governments would not negotiate. A Swedish delegate said Mme Schwimmer had told her that Ford thought publicizing the peace terms would be harmful and that the document should be released to the people at a later date. But, exclaimed their opponents, the founding philosophy of the neutral conference was based on open diplomacy and open agreements and widespread publicity of all their activities. Taking a leaf from Miss Addams's book when Rosika Schwimmer had suggested the women envoys personally present the Hague resolutions to the government officials, Loeken remarked that the conference deputations could not parade about Europe with sealed envelopes. And Aked contemptuously added that none of the delegates were fit to be envoys, while Dr. Schenk, the Swiss French teacher, remarked that they could not enter the belligerent countries in any case. At that point, Hoejenbos, a Dutch Socialist, countered that they must do something distinctive or they would only have a rewrite of previously conceived peace proposals to show for their six weeks' work.

The arguments grew increasingly spirited as the delegates accused one another of conspiratorial ploys to control and subvert the purpose of their work. Seeking to comfort his more nervous colleagues, Solnoerdal assured them that "in all parliaments there is as much unnecessary argument as in the Neutral Conference," and he suggested they move on to another subject—their future work—before they settled the question before them. But on that matter they were just as divided, and in the end the delegates talked interminably about the instructions they should leave the reduced conference and how they should present the appeal. Finally, exhausted by argument in their stuffy room, the delegates voted. Those who spoke for secrecy first and for the peoples' "right to know" second won, on another close vote.

And again the minority rebelled. That night even Lochner said he could no longer remain with the conference. However, Holt persuaded the young secretary to speak his mind to the delegates before taking action. Next morning, after Loeken opened the meeting by declaring he would resign if they did not reverse the vote of the day before, Lochner took the floor. There was no grandiloquence in his remarks; he was plainly angry and upset by the betrayal of their purpose. He was "simply dazed," he said, when others spoke falsely in the name of Ford the day before. The fact was that Ford's "convictions as to publicity were the only definite thing about his plan." Their sponsor had consistently opposed secrecy and censorship and was even now taking out full-page ads in American newspapers to broadcast his peace views. It was futile anyway for the conference to expect their work to avoid attention. The European press had access to their cablegrams and the Associated Press reporter in the Grand Hotel was well informed on their meetings. "It may be," he conceded, "that by proceeding in a secret way they are beating the devil with his own methods," but he would have no part of it. They were not met as diplomats but as private citizens, the hope of the people. If they "lacked faith in publicity," if they held to a course of acting *in camera*, he would ask Ford to put him "on some other piece of work."

Lochner's reprimand had the desired effect. One after another of the errant delegates recanted, saying they thought the vote the day before had been on something else. Those who held their ground criticized the turncoats, while the moderate members retorted that their every attempt to publicize the work had been thwarted by just a few votes. This time it was Gjelsvik, the Norwegian who opposed the conference's mediating, who tried to ease his colleagues' damaged spirits. Think of how much had been accomplished considering the circumstances, he reminded them—no preparation by the conference's organizers, six languages used daily to express at least six different national views, and, not to be omitted from the catalogue of complaints, they were working "in a badly ventilated room where one became tired and irritable." When it was clear his side would win, Aked called for the vote on whether the appeal would be publicized. The day was won for the open conference by an amazing fifteen to one as quite a few were shamed into abstaining. But still the battle was not finally won. The delegates still had to decide how to transmit the document, and then to select their successors.

That night Mme Schwimmer and her adherents planned the strategy for the coming day. Their object was to regain their supremacy and to keep the conference from being replaced by a small committee, which they regarded as a sellout to the moderates. If they could not win their objectives, they could at least slow down the reorganization until Rosika Schwimmer could be reinstated, which was to say until Emily Greene Balch, Miss Addams's substitute and Mme Schwimmer's fellow envoy of the previous spring, arrived in a few more days.

At the meeting the next day, April 14, the direct mediationists suggested different ways of presenting their appeal to the belligerents, and the tension mounted. By the time someone moved to adjourn late that afternoon there were seven motions before them, all concerned with when to publish and how to deliver the appeal, and all to be discussed the next day and possibly the next day after that. It was too much for Frederick Holt, who, exercising the privilege of attendance granted him at the beginning of the conference, had spent the day at what he expected would be the last meeting. Having already complained to Liebold that the delegates were "prolonging discussion" unnecessarily, he had asked for and received permission to stop "Mr. Ford's hospitality" by the fifteenth, a matter he had evidently not thought necessary to announce. Now the deadline was only hours away and the delegates were still far from the end of their work.

Holt asked permission to address the meeting and then blurted out his fury. Their "deliberations and procrastinations" forced him to speak and to conclude, as Ford had already done, that nothing could be accomplished by so large a group, which was, in any case, too costly. He ended his outburst by telling the delegates that if they did not reduce the size of the conference themselves he would do it for them the next day. Regretting he had to take such a course, he explained he was only following Ford's "positive instructions," and then he left, refusing to answer questions and suggesting they get right to work.

Holt had at least accomplished something—the shocked, insulted and angered delegates were united at last. Dr. Schenk was all for telling Ford what he could do with his money, and continuing the work on their own. Many had already concluded that the conference was much too large and they were grossly overpaid, and had agreed informally to stop abusing Ford's hospitality and return to their homes to do local propaganda for peace after the appeal was finished, and they had appointed a small committee to perform the continuing chores of the conference. They did not need to be told how to behave by Holt.

The delegates called an evening meeting to finish their work in order not to be fired the next day, though Mme Schwimmer told her followers to continue their delaying tactics and demand Holt's credentials of "full authority" from Ford. Barry, meanwhile, was trying to mediate just as he had done the night of the preparedness blowup on the *Oscar II*. In the relative privacy of the staff office he told Holt he had egregiously overstepped the bounds of his position and should apologize.

Holt tried. He had not meant to insult them, he said, when he called them superfluous, and of course his apology went for naught, and he was asked to leave the chamber. After much discussion during which little was achieved in the way of clarity but something in the way of catharsis, the delegates appointed a committee to check if Holt's instructions had really come from Ford. Before they adjourned at midnight, they decided to hand-deliver the appeal to the belligerents' ministers in Stockholm and to mail it to the foreign ministers in their capitals. Later they decided to send it to the neutral governments as well.

Full press coverage was also agreed upon, forced upon them actually by the wily Lochner and Loeken. Without consulting the conference, they sent a copy of the appeal with a Dutch delegate who had been recalled to Holland for military service, and they sent copies to the world's wire services for release the following week.

Over the weekend, two Swiss members, Mlle Gobat, a prominent pacifist, and Mme Ragaz, submitted their resignations to Holt to be effective after the current work was done. Mlle Gobat was plainly disgusted by

"the autocracy, the secret diplomacy, the favoritism which had prevailed
in the Ford Expedition from the beginning." She was attacking Aked, not
Mme Schwimmer. Obviously Ford, "their mysterious King far away,
whom none of them could reach, and who sent from time to time *ukases*,"
which they never saw, had given up the idea of mediation and wanted
instead only a small study group composed of his court favorites. Both
women expressed their resentment at Holt's cavalier treatment of the
delegates and at being chastised for expenses over which they had no
control. Had they been told long ago that the conference was costing too
much, they would have gladly accepted smaller honoraria. "Men and
women who would allow themselves to be treated as the members of this
Conference have been," Mme Ragaz thought, could not possibly work
constructively for peace.

It took three more days—most of it spent in bickering and quibbling—
until the delegates were willing to accept a compromise proposal on the
future work of the conference.

To begin with there were the questions of whether they could "legally"
reconstitute themselves into a smaller body or whether, if they declared
themselves adjourned, they were not in danger of imitating only the first
half of the performance of the legendary phoenix without the capacity to
perform the revitalizing second half of the act. Attorney Loeken, clear-
headed, practical and succinct, assured his colleagues that it was common
practice for a large assembly to adjourn and leave a small committee to
continue its work. It was not so much what the new committee should
do, he said, but who would be around to do it. That question set off a
nearly interminable succession of proposals suggesting who should constitute the committee and how they should be selected. The debate was
further prolonged by an open battle between John Barry and Charles
Aked.

At one point, when the delegates were considering only one member
per country, Barry suggested that the conference, not the national delegations, select the representatives, to which Aked, aware he was unpopular
with the majority, replied, "The Americans were not chosen by the
Conference and the Conference cannot tell us Americans who is to repre-
sent the American people." He did not care, he added, if it took them
"two or twelve days" to settle the matter, he was going to be a member
of the new committee, and he would not abide by any decision that
excluded him. What the good Ford gave him, he informed them in as
many words, they were not going to take away. With Holt, Ford's financial agent, in his corner, of course, it was only a matter of time until the
adamantine Aked wore down his opponents.

Finally, at the thirty-fifth and last meeting, on April 20, Lindhagen offered an acceptable compromise. The neutral conference would adjourn until peace negotiations began. In the meantime a Committee of Twelve, plus twelve alternates, a total of four members from each country, to be elected by the national delegations, would handle all conference matters. A provisional committee, elected at once, would act until the Committee of Twelve was elected.

Gloom, despair, futility characterized the delegates' last hours together. One by one members rose, officially resigned and left for home. Among them were the Swedish professors Hans Larsson and Ernst Wigforss and the Norwegian Dr. Mikael Lie, all moderates, who expected their ideas would be ignored by the new committee just as they had been by the full conference. Aked allowed he too would resign were he "not unhappily bound by obligations." Others praised the work done, but most spoke funereally of how little the conference had accomplished. Lindhagen tried to deliver a proper valedictory, but his words were remorseful. Wounds were not healed; members battled until the last word. The Dutch did not think they could continue working with the Swedes "if things continued as they had been." And the Swedes were sure the Anti-Oorlog Raad would take over the conference and Ford's money, putting the quietus to active work for peace. A Schwimmer disciple tried in vain to delay adjournment.

In the afternoon the delegates wrote the agenda for the Committee of Twelve. The first order of business was to obtain financial and political independence from Ford. Then, with the appeal to the belligerents as their guide, they must continue mediating, offering new peace proposals, working with other peace groups and keeping the people informed. The program passed unanimously. By then, however, there were only nine people left in the conference room. Only the hopeful and stoic remained to ease one another's hearts with homilies. "Never give up anything that is right and true," Loeken said, and Lochner related Ford's words of wisdom: "Nothing worthwhile is ever done without hard work." Monday, said Troesch, a Swiss professor of German, the day after Easter Sunday, would be Resurrection Day for the conference when the interim committee, consisting of himself and Schenk, Loeken and Solnoerdal, Mme Steenhof and Lindhagen, Aked and Barry and Colonel A. F. L. Faubel, a retired Dutch army officer, would hold its first meeting.

The second phase of the Ford peace endeavor was over. The full conference never met again. All the delegates, except those on the provisional committee, went home, angered by the "undignified manner" of their dismissal. Some were without income until their leaves of absence from their jobs, which Mme Schwimmer and Lochner had encouraged them to take, expired. And the Swiss who came through Germany with Lochner could not go home for another month.

Mme Ragaz, who came to Stockholm with an open mind, had been assaulted by the "egotism, lust for power, base greed for money, stupidity [and] weakness" of her colleagues but was wise enough to realize they had "also a lot of sincere good will and fine sensibility and sincere enthusiasm." Still, she thought it would have been easier to negotiate with the belligerent governments than with the cliques and conspiracies fomented by her co-workers.

"The mistake we made in those days of the conference," wrote Lochner, "was that we did not realize that the various methods proposed were not necessarily incompatible with each other; that, in fact, there was a large field for publicity, for popular agitation, for professorial investigation, and for semi-diplomatic mediation." All these could have been pursued simultaneously, he thought, if each task had been assigned to an autonomous commission rather than every word and action approved in daily plenary sessions. He also thought, as did others, that a strong leader, a permanent chairman, would have smoothed their course.

Even so, the Neutral Conference for Continuous Mediation accomplished what it had set out to do: it had formulated tentative peace proposals, submitted them to the belligerent powers for their reactions and released them to the people through the world press. Though the conference was never honored with an official reply from any of the belligerent countries—only Luxembourg and Panama thanked it for the proposals—it was gratified by the publicity the appeal received. The full text was printed in Germany and Great Britain, each country's newspapers accusing the conference of favoring its enemies. The neutral press gave it good coverage as well, the New York papers printing the entire document. Writing in a Russian paper, a professor predicted that the terms of the appeal would be ignored by the belligerents for the moment, but were sure to be considered at the peace conference. The conference leaders expected their demands to be challenged but thought someone had to make a beginning. Lochner proudly wrote home, "We are 'starting something' and that is quite enough."

The appeal was not ill-timed. Just two weeks earlier the German and English foreign ministers caused a slight flurry with statements that sounded to the hopeful like peace overtures. Years later, Colonel House, thinking of his own unsuccessful mediation move during those months, wrote: "I am not sure that we did not make a greater mistake in not going ahead and calling for a peace conference rather than leaving it to the Allies to be the judges."

It was not part of the original plan that the delegates should present their proposals in person to the officials of the warring nations. The activists, inspired by Rosika Schwimmer, were certain that they could gain access to the government leaders as the envoys from the women's conference had, and, promising secrecy, receive each side's reactions to their proposals. Such an effort was tried later that spring and summer by Mme Schwimmer's associates under her direction and failed. Undoubtedly the same fate would have met the efforts of neutral-conference emissaries in April.

In terms of its aims, the neutral conference failed only where it could not have succeeded. During the winter and spring of 1916 no fighting nation was willing to accept official or unofficial mediatory services, not even to the extent of letting its citizens leave the country to address the self-appointed peace delegates.

In its reduced form the conference could still perform its function of continuous mediation. And it could do so in the manner first conceived by Miss Wales, Miss Addams, Dr. Jordan and the members of the Henry Street group, who had supported the idea long before Mme Schwimmer approached Ford with her grandiose plans. The committee could serve as well as the conference as a clearinghouse for peace proposals should the belligerents decide to end the war through such an instrument. It could keep the hope of peace on the tongues of the European people through publicity and propaganda from the Stockholm headquarters as well as through the efforts of the delegates in their home countries. As a study group, it could explore the causes of war and prescribe "scientific" remedies. In its much reduced size and costliness, it could look forward to a less harassed and longer life than its predecessor. As for mediation, there were ways to mediate a war other than by directly negotiating with the opposing parties, and in the months ahead, though they never stopped trying to meet with influential belligerent citizens, the delegates had more success with alternative routes to peace.

CHAPTER 12

"The idea refuses to die"

"I THINK THE REORGANIZATION was necessary," Emily Balch wrote Jane Addams, after several weeks in Stockholm, "but a terrible lot of eggs were broken to make that omelette."

Miss Balch had arranged for a teaching substitute at Wellesley and after meeting with the Fords, Plantiff and several Henry Street peaceworkers in New York, had embarked for Stockholm as Miss Addams's alternate. An expert in international political and economic problems, Professor Balch believed that the conference's prime function was to act as a forum for peace programs developed by the citizens of the warring countries.

Emily Balch and Rosika Schwimmer had become good friends while serving as peace-conference envoys the preceding spring. It was not surprising, therefore, that Mme Schwimmer's friends and foes haunted the new American delegate with their pleadings and explanations the day she arrived. Only after talking with Lochner, Aked and Holt, and only after a special escort arrived, did Miss Balch go to see Mme Schwimmer.

Since early morning, the deposed expert adviser had been decked in her finery waiting in her room, she wrote a friend, as Mme Butterfly had waited for her perfidious husband. The reunion was brief and shattering for both women. Rosika Schwimmer could not understand why Lochner said she was impossible to work with or why anyone thought she had been forced to resign. She would have to wait until Gaston Plantiff returned to redeem her reputation. "Rosika was at her most magnetic," Miss Balch wrote Miss Addams, "interesting and warm"; it was regrettable the conference could not use her "brains and information and enthusiasm without being honeycombed with intrigue and personalities."

Miss Balch also had to cast the determining vote for the second member of the American delegation. Aked and Barry, by then bitter enemies, had each voted for Miss Balch and for himself. She chose Aked, "preferring a plus and a minus to zero."

The provisional committee did "more business in a day than the 30 did in a week." So Miss Balch proudly spoke of the propaganda actions undertaken during the three-week interregnum between the adjournment of the full neutral conference and the formal organization of the Committee of Twelve. A major impediment to their "far-reaching plans"—lack of money—was temporarily removed after Miss Balch cabled Plantiff, "Waste fortunately ended but penuriousness injuring Ford's prestige and limiting results," and he replied with $5,000. The money helped pay for the projects already in the works—an *enquête* sent to European "leaders of thought and action" requesting comments for publication on the conference's appeal to the belligerents; the fees, when requested, for prominent literary friends of peace who were to implore the neutral governments to mediate; and the very successful and spectacular exploitation of the annual May 18 celebrations commemorating the opening of the 1899 Hague peace conference.

On the eighteenth, the Committee of Twelve and its friends in local peace organizations and churches held mass meetings in every major city in every neutral country, except the United States, that was represented at the Stockholm gathering. Tens of thousands signed a resolution asking their governments to mediate and to prepare for an advisory "world congress" of informed citizens at the peace conference. In Stockholm, fifty thousand white plastic peace flowers were sold by students in the streets for war relief and crowds were turned away not only at the main meeting, which attracted over two thousand people, but at overflow meetings as well. Only in the music halls was the neutral conference mocked. In one of the sketches a woman became hysterical at the sound of an offstage shot and was told to relax, that the noise was not from a gun but "only the Ford Conference having another peace meeting!" Such ridicule could hardly dampen the great joy of the peaceworkers at their success. "It goes without saying," Lochner remarked, "that this one demonstration was not sufficient, despite the publicity it received, to rouse the neutral nations to action. But it helped to make articulate a growing public opinion in favor of the principles for which the conference stood."

It also helped to confirm the confidence and self-regard of the newly formed Central Committee of the Neutral Conference for Continuous Mediation, the name the Committee of Twelve gave itself at its first official meeting on May 16. The news releases announcing their existence bragged of their reputability, of the cooperation their peace-day celebrations received from the old-line peace societies and of the arrival of Benjamin de Jong van Beek en Donk, the spokesman of both the Anti-Oorlog Raad and the Central Organization for a Durable Peace, to serve on the Central Committee. Only an accident of birth, the stories implied, connected the Central Committee with its forebears, the Ford Peace Expedition and the Neutral Conference for Continuous Mediation. No longer were the peaceworkers the voice of the uninformed if enthusiastic pilgrims without credentials who had paraded through northern Europe months before. No longer were they that horde of self-styled experts who had spent weeks bickering before writing a peace plan that was ignored by the belligerent powers. They were now people of respectability, neither impetuous nor irresponsible, asking only that nations live in brotherhood. That they were also the same people who had just served on the larger neutral conference was irrelevant because with only two or three exceptions, the members of the Central Committee had all along opposed the conference's aim of active mediation. It was as Mayor Lindhagen had feared and Dr. de Jong had hoped: the smaller the group the more conservative its work.

De Jong explained their new look, and incidentally his willingness to join the Ford pacifists after the managerial demise of Mme Schwimmer and the numerical demise of her sympathizers, in a long public statement that exhorted other peacemakers to join the fight. In its new phase, he explained, the conference would concentrate on the tools of "indirect mediation"—publicity and propaganda. In cooperation with the Central Organization for a Durable Peace it would ask influential citizens to help formulate peace terms and would join the Anti-Oorlog Raad in demanding that the neutral governments mediate. There always had been and always would be skeptics, de Jong cautioned his new colleagues, who would consider their efforts "only the useless amusement of well-meaning idealists," but these people should be ignored. "Nobody can close his eyes to the importance of the fact that persons belonging to six different countries, each with extensive experience in peace work, are together every day talking about what can be done. Never has the peace movement had such an opportunity to make their views the outspoken wish of the peoples." If the conference convinced the peace leaders that it was no longer "stillborn," if it persuaded those who had worked for years in the peace movement that they all were part "of one great big union," and if the conference actually acted as the clearing-house for the belligerent citizens eager for peace, then, he promised his new associates, "something great can *be done!*"

De Jong did not completely dissociate the neutral conference from its past. "Direct mediation" would still be pursued, and in the very manner that Rosika Schwimmer and the Scandinavians favored and which Lochner had derided as antithetical to the mediators' founding articles. "Though the pacifists are fierce opponents of secret diplomacy," the Dutch realist unabashedly wrote, "they are bound, in these times, where the military power in all belligerent countries, without exception, has the supreme power, to use the same means as the adversary." Lochner enthusiastically endorsed de Jong's exposition of the Central Committee's credo, even the sacrifice of principle to expediency. To those who criticized the conference for abandoning its purpose of mediation, he explained, "the direct mediative work must be of a confidential nature." Experience had changed his mind. Not one belligerent government had dealt directly with the neutral conference or let its citizens journey to Stockholm as conference consultants. Eager to embrace the practical program of the European peace establishment, he proudly wrote Ford that the present membership of the conference had "completely won over the Central Organization. You have no idea what this means from the standpoint of Europe. It will now be far easier for us to go on with our work."

To pursue this work, the twelve delegates set up six committees. The Library and Business Committees served the Committees on Mediation, Constructive Peace and Publicity and Propaganda. These major committees submitted project proposals for review to the Committee on Activities and Outlook, which consisted of the chairmen of all the other committees and the conference chairman of the month, and the Committee on Activities and Outlook in turn submitted its recommendations at the weekly meeting of the Central Committee.

The Committee on Activities and Outlook also was the conference's spokesman to the world. In this capacity it sent congratulatory messages to statesmen whenever they spoke for peace and invited the Central Organization for a Durable Peace, the International Socialists Bureau, the International Peace Bureau, the Interparliamentary Union and the International Committee of Women for Permanent Peace to join with the neutral conference in a postwar world congress that would convey "the pacifistic wishes" of the people to the delegates of the final peace conference. Lochner expected the congress "will so worry the life out of the diplomats that they will have to make the peace that will keep the nations from arming for another conflict immediately." However, none of the organizations accepted the invitation and the Central Organization for a Durable Peace was asked to serve alone.

The real work of the Central Committee was initiated and conducted by the Committees on Mediation, Publicity and Propaganda and Constructive Peace. The Mediation Committee saw its prime function as arranging for the exchange of views between each government, belligerent and neutral, and its citizens, and between the officials and citizens of one side and the officials and citizens of the other. For example, opinion-makers in the neutral countries were asked to comment on a plan to speed the postwar healing process by requiring neutral countries to help pay the costs of the rehabilitation of Belgium and other war-torn lands. Another effort required "one responsible person" in each neutral country to interview a prominent citizen on the conciliatory nature of any public statement made by a belligerent official; the neutral conference would then give the interview to the wire services, which would, it was assumed, print it in the belligerent press. Thus, it was reasoned, the neutral "Minutemen" would be alerting the belligerent citizens to the possibility of peace.

Persuading the neutral governments to mediate was the sixth of the seven duties that defined the Mediation Committee's task, and with good reason. In May the Norwegian parliament tabled the resolution endorsing the March appeal to the neutrals. In early June both the Swiss and Dutch foreign ministers said it was the wrong time to convene an official gathering. And the Spanish ambassador in Stockholm told Lochner and de Jong that his majesty was anxious to mediate but was waiting for the right time to act with other neutral nations. As a last resort the neutral conference sent two Swiss Catholics to ask the pope to intercede, but it was a useless journey; the time was not right for him either.

Persuading the belligerent governments to end the fighting, a matter of higher priority on the Mediation Committee's list, was equally unsuccessful. The British and French ministers to Stockholm were not encouraging, but they at least received the neutral-conference delegates. The German minister, as Lochner politely put it after three futile visits, was "reserved toward foreigners." Even the kaiser joked with the American ambassador about the Ford mission.

No belligerent national was ever allowed to come to Stockholm solely to advise the neutral conference, but, by keeping a close eye on the Grand Hotel register and the daily newspapers, the peace delegates managed to hear the opinions of several informed neutral and belligerent transients. In that way they learned of the devastation of Verdun from an American war correspondent, of Finnish and Indian national interests and of the racial problems in Austro-Hungary from visiting scholars, and of Polish relief work from a Rockefeller Foundation representative. A German national, in Stockholm for a Salvation Army conference, told them Germany would never end the war while Britain maintained a blockade, and members of a delegation from the Russian Duma addressed them twice, going to and coming from a conference of the Entente powers in Paris. At the first meeting, Professor Paul Miliukov, a scholar and a statesman who had lectured at American universities and later was foreign minister in the Kerensky government, "made fun of our whole attempt," Lochner wrote, saying that it was really three successive conferences, each of which was useless, and that in any case it was not "sufficiently authoritative" to be recognized by the Russian government.

On the few occasions when the Stockholm delegates were able to send representatives to the belligerent countries as private citizens on private business, they received the same dismal reports brought back by the agents Mme Schwimmer had sent to Russia and England earlier. In mid-May, Aked went to Berlin. His invitation was secured partly because of his protests against the American sale of arms to the Allies and partly because the wife of a visiting ministerial colleague had "high and important connections." For ten days Aked talked with people on every level of German life, from members of the general staff to rank-and-file soldiers and laborers. The German government, he learned, was ready to come to the peace table as soon as her enemies showed "a conciliatory spirit." Many of the people, he reported, were "moderate, reasonable, pacific," wanting only "a united and prosperous Germany, secure from attack, free to develop its own civilization, to feel its limbs and grow" in the eastern "cradle lands of civilization" which would be Germanized in friendly rivalry with the British empire. Only at the very end of his account did Aked acknowledge that this "moderate" view was not the only one heard in Germany, that there was also a "War party." Aked's colleagues, desirous as they were to exploit the implications of his visit, realized it "amounted to next to nothing."

By the end of July the conference heard from two other representatives who had managed to visit England—Professor Otto Jespersen, a philologist and English-language authority at the University of Copenhagen, and Baron Theodor Adelswaerd, president of the Swedish group of the Interparliamentary Union, a former minister of finance and later a substitute delegate to the League of Nations Assembly. Their special assignment was to find out if Britain would join a postwar league of nations, whether she would welcome a nonmilitaristic Germany in such a league and whether the British government was willing to say publicly that her war aims did not include the alteration of Germany's political structure or annexation of her territory. Jespersen and Adelswaerd probably never mentioned these questions to their English friends, who spoke only of the great expectations of the next offensive.

Though unsuccessful themselves at direct mediation, the delegates celebrated with cablegrams, press releases, pamphlets and articles the course taken that spring by the man all the neutral governments looked to for action. In early May President Wilson won a diplomatic victory at great risk when the Germans agreed to halt submarine warfare against unarmed ships following the loss of American lives on the torpedoed French channel steamer *Sussex*. The concession carried a quid pro quo— the United States had to persuade the Allies to ease the blockade. Though Wilson formally ignored the demand, he feared it was only a matter of time before American rights, as he defined them, would be violated again. Because he wanted to end the war, not enter it, he again asked Britain to accept his good offices as mediator, and again he was rebuffed.

By mid-May, Wilson decided the time was ripe for the United States to commit itself publicly to a role in postwar internationalism. In an address to the League to Enforce Peace, the president said America had no interest in the "causes and objects" of the war, but did have a deep interest in its ill effects upon Americans. Then he proclaimed a platform for world peace that expressed the same principles as the neutral conference's appeal to the belligerents and the platforms of other liberal peace organizations. Having declared America's lack of interest in anything but "peace and its future guarantees," Wilson gently and indirectly asked to be asked to "initiate a movement for peace among the nations now at war." Instead of the expected invitation, each side reiterated its determination to fight till victory and denounced Wilson as a morally blind and naive meddler and politician.

But at the neutral conference in Stockholm, the *Sussex* pledge and Wilson's pronouncements provided the perfect food for peace. "Never has the press of the belligerent countries occupied itself so much with peace discussion," wrote Lochner in the introduction to a pamphlet which contained two of Wilson's internationalist speeches, an analysis of the speeches by a neutral-conference delegate, two interviews with neutral citizens solicited by the conference and more than thirty comments on the speech reprinted from the belligerent press.

This neutral-conference document, one in a series of such pamphlets, had a print run of nine thousand copies and was translated into four languages. Most of the neutral-conference documents were reprints of their own work, ranging from Miss Wales's mediation plan to the recent appeals to the neutrals and belligerents and histories of the conference by Lindhagen and Lochner, the last of which was also printed in Esperanto. An article by the German journalist Maximilian Harden, calling for Wilson to end the war, the Germans to end militarism and the belligerents to make a fair and lasting peace, was also reprinted in this first group of nine pamphlets.

In addition to these free publications, the Committee on Publicity and Propaganda mimeographed a daily digest of world news emphasizing the latest reports on peace and war, which was printed principally for those members who could not read the Swedish newspapers. When foreign correspondents and legations asked to be put on the mailing list, the peace delegates shrewdly seized the opportunity to send the ideas of the moderates in each warring country to their enemy counterparts, correctly assuming that copies of local news stories were sent by the diplomats in Stockholm to their foreign offices and were then published in their national press. Thus, the editorials of the London *Economist*, the *Nation* and the *Berliner Tageblatt*, the speeches of Asquith, Grey and Bethmann-Hollweg and the opinions of the people who wrote letters to the editors had a chance to be read in enemy territory. Also, to silence those in other peace organizations who said the conference was doing nothing toward its declared aims as well as to spread peace propaganda wherever it could, the conference published a pocket-sized weekly summary of its plans and successful activities.

Lochner explained the publications program to Ford as simply as he could. "Only to send messengers is not enough," he wrote, "the belligerents are so full of hatred toward each other that we must first get them to see each other in a more favorable light." Therefore, the news they were circulating was effective educational propaganda because "the statesmen of Europe, and the foreign ministers are *only too eager* to receive this information" and are "quite surprised when you show them any evidence that there are people on the other side of the firing line who are just as human as they themselves." And, he added, "in proportion as the people in the belligerent nations read peace news, the strength of the war party slowly breaks down." The source for all the news disseminated by the publicity committee was their own library, which held four hundred books and subscribed to forty-one newspapers and forty-three journals from thirteen countries as well as nine international newspaper-clipping services. The library was open to the public and soon became a popular rendezvous for the local intelligentsia.

Aside from these continuing publications the Publicity and Propaganda Committee routinely sent out news releases, ran a lecture bureau and arranged interviews. The committee also solicited comments on the conference's manifesto calling for postwar international adjudication of disputes and paid well-known European literati for articles praising the conference's efforts. A few endorsements, such as those of Nobel literature prize winner Selma Lagerloef and another popular feminist writer, Ellen Key, were free. When William Jennings Bryan wrote the editor of a Danish youth magazine that each belligerent should state its peace terms publicly since "a nation willing to sacrifice the lives of its people ought to be willing to plainly say what it is fighting for," the neutral conference released the statement to the world press with Bryan's permission. And when a traveling Ford Motor Company employee stopped by the Grand Hotel to carry messages home, he was burdened with three hundred copies of a twelve-page news release detailing the accomplishments, real and anticipated, of the new order. Spectators at the Swedish games held in Stockholm in early July received printed cards reminding them that most of those who had been scheduled to compete in the 1916 Olympics were now performing in the trenches.

Indirect mediation was pursued by deed as well as by words. In early June the delegates held a reception for more than one hundred members of the Scandinavian Peace Congress, which, in turn, passed a resolution calling for an official neutral conference. At the delegates' suggestion the Scandinavian holiday of Midsummer's Day became Peace Flower Day, and at the meetings and festivities thousands of flowers were sold and thousands of people voted for an official neutral conference and a postwar international political organization. Because both the neutral citizens and the European press had responded so splendidly to the conference's participation in the May 18 Peace Day celebrations, the delegates, in early June, began planning for another round of spectacular demonstrations in the neutral countries in early August to commemorate the second anniversary of the war.

The Committee on Constructive Peace, the third working arm of the reorganized conference, was charged with supervising the writing of the peace program, which would be used to educate the people until it was time to submit the plan to the belligerent nations at the peace table. Its method was "scientific inquiry" and its selection of topics for study was coordinated with the ongoing program of the Central Organization for a Durable Peace, which was also securing position papers from international experts. The delegates wrote on the problems of subject peoples in African and Asian colonies; the social, political and economic aspects of indemnities; the possibilities of socialists and nonsocialists working together for peace; the reasons why the neutral countries should have a voice at the peace conference; and the international legal questions to be resolved in opening the seas to free trade.

Recognizing the limitations of both their knowledge and their time, the delegates subsidized the Central Organization for a Durable Peace, asked the Belgian pacifist Paul Otlet to write a comparative study of world governments and planned to ask Arnold Toynbee and other scholars and statesmen to define and resolve the problems that caused the war and oppressed the powerless. It was a grand scheme and a worthy one similar in purpose to The Inquiry, the group of scholars engaged at President Wilson's instruction after the United States entered the war more than a year later.

The designated outside experts wanted money for their labor—at least the committee members thought they would want it—and the thousands of dollars asked for were not available. Discouraged but not defeated, the committee collected and published what it could in its determination to overcome rejection and failure with perseverance and imagination. For example, articles by Walter Lippmann, H. G. Wells and others were reprinted as a neutral-conference document entitled "The Colonial Problem: Suggestions for Solution by Various Writers" and distributed for comment. European peace publications were given subventions for special issues on the conference or its interests.

In such a manner the Central Committee over and over again tried to circumvent the obstacles and disappointments encountered all along the way. Instead of writing an article praising the conference, Romain Rolland, the French pacifist and winner of the Nobel prize in literature, wrote an angry letter expressing his astonishment that neither Bryan nor Miss Addams had yet arrived, his dismay that the neutral conference had not worked with the right European peaceworkers, his disappointment that it was meeting in pro-German Stockholm and his general disgust with the endeavor. Georg Brandes, the Danish literary critic, agreed to write a flattering account of the work for a large fee and then published an anti-war article in *Politiken* without once mentioning the neutral conference. Despite tremendous mailings, fewer than two hundred people responded to the delegates' questionnaire on the belligerent appeal, and, to their amazement, even though they offered to pay costs, the wire services often refused to carry their stories. The local newspapers frequently ignored them as well. Finally, there was the ever present problem of the conference's reach exceeding its bank balance.

The delegates never brooded over what they could not do. They were blind to hazards and defeat and saw only progress, no matter how difficult to measure. They counted their press notices and their interviews, their returned questionnaires and their resolutions passed at meetings, and considered it all growing evidence of the conference's effectiveness as the only agent publicizing the people's plan for peace in the enemies' camps and in the neutral countries. Toward the end of May Lochner wrote Dr. Jenkin Lloyd Jones, "We are constantly moving forward, despite the great difficulties that seem to beset us on every hand. The encouraging thing is that the idea refuses to die, no matter what pressure may be brought to bear in the opposite direction." Toward the end of June a German newspaper listed the neutral conference along with Wilson, the king of Spain and the pope as possible mediators of the war, and Lochner wrote a former staff member, "We are getting more and more official recognition, which of course puts us in a place to get at the people really able to put a stop to this war." Lochner reveled in their respectability and achievements, and was therefore flabbergasted when Gaston Plantiff arrived toward the end of June and told him that Henry Ford was dissatisfied with the work and insisted on critical changes.

Emily Balch had brought the first warnings that Ford wanted the conference reduced to six delegates and that their American peace friends had conveyed their surprise to Ford that they were meeting in pro-German Stockholm. For a time the delegates considered moving the seat of the conference from one neutral capital to another—"We may *itinerate* like early Kings!" Miss Balch feared—but finally decided that as the crossroads of the neutral world, Stockholm was the best place to find belligerent experts. The delegates then thought of sending Lochner to America to enlighten Ford and their friends, but Lochner could not go home unless he was summoned and every plea for recall thus far brought the reply from Liebold that Plantiff was coming soon to resolve all problems.

For two months Plantiff canceled one reservation after another because sailing was "so dangerous," a difficulty that had not deterred Miss Balch and hundreds of other people. Finally, after buying Neversink life jackets for himself and Robert Neely, the accountant who had accompanied him on the *Oscar II*, Plantiff sailed, arriving the third week in June with the dual assignment of taking "hold of things in Stockholm" and checking the prospects for tractor sales in Finland and Russia. Undoubtedly it was the second task that engaged his heart.

Mr. Ford, he told the delegates, was displeased; they were spending too much money on publicity and propaganda and doing nothing actively to end the war. His orders were to move the headquarters to The Hague, where the delegates should quietly seek out informed and influential peace-minded citizens in the warring nations. Lochner was dumbfounded. In March he had written his mentor that their funds should go for *"publicity, publicity, publicity* and for keeping a *few skilled* persons in constant and living touch with the warring governments," and in April that "publicity is the greatest tool that can be used." No one at home had said that was wrong. On the contrary, since Ford had spent thousands of dollars on anti-preparedness advertisements in American newspapers Lochner thought their peace-education propaganda was precisely what Ford expected. In a long letter, which Ford probably never read, he argued for the status quo in Stockholm. The delegates could not stop the war without spending money, he said, and they could not stop it quickly. In any case, publicity was just as necessary as mediation to persuade the powers to stop fighting. Mediation, direct, or indirect, was long hard work requiring "infinite patience," he chided, especially for the Ford delegates who had to overcome the ill repute of the peace-ship extravaganza. The peaceworkers had not abandoned their principles. They were "on the right track," but "drastic changes" would shatter the harmony they had at last achieved and disrupt their work. Instead of cutting funds, Lochner asked Ford to have Wilson arrange for the American participants to travel to belligerent countries and to send Lochner a letter of introduction to government officials.

The general secretary expressed the indignation of all the delegates, none of whom appreciated being told what to do and where to do it, especially by someone far from the scene of activity. Characteristically, Plantiff gave in and agreed not to carry out his instructions until they appealed to Ford; at the same time, hewing to the Ford line, he cabled home: "Shall they continue expensive publicity campaign or quiet mediation by few but more influential with headquarters at Hague?" Before he had a reply, but after he had sent Ford a full and self-serving report, Plantiff left with Neely on their business trip to Russia.

"Everybody has an idea of his own," Plantiff had written, "most everyone has a kick on somebody else and it would take more than a Philadelphia lawyer to decide this thing right." That was vintage Plantiff. In every report he ever sent he presented himself to his employer as the exceptionally competent and sorely beset keeper of Ford's contentious peace flock. In truth, he greatly exaggerated his difficulties with the Central Committee. By and large they were of one mind, all except Charles Aked, whom Plantiff thought was "the leading light in the conference." So he had been when Plantiff left Europe in February; by late June, Aked's colleagues referred to him as "that one bolt . . . still sticking out and disturbing the whole works."

The disaffection between Aked and the others arose over what the minister called the delegates' "drum and trumpet" publicity and propaganda instead of "informal, intimate and private" negotiations with belligerent governments and influential citizens. Directly he realized his policy would not prevail, Aked refused to write articles, make speeches or even attend certain committee meetings. And when Plantiff arrived his protégé hastily explained the futility of the conference's course and derided his colleagues as "a stupid lot." Because Aked's policy of more direct negotiation and less publicity coincided with Ford's, Plantiff almost certainly suggested Aked seek Ford's support in person. On July 4, Aked submitted his "Declaration of Independence" to his associates in which he told them that because their "effort, good in itself, is at present inefficiently done, badly conceived and badly organized," he was going home to discuss the matter with their sponsor. As soon as the Central Committee heard Aked's last words, which he had left for Lochner to read, they sent Emily Balch to act as a truth squad following the derelict delegate's trail to Detroit.

Miss Balch not only caught Aked's boat before it left Europe, but she was often interviewed by the same reporters, each time providing a thoughtful and rational rebuttal to his intemperate remarks. In his weeklong lament to the press Aked called his associates "visionaries and dreamers," "mediocrities" and "cranks," and claimed "it would take the author of 'Alice in Wonderland' to describe the weird discussion" that culminated in the appeal to the belligerents which was denounced everywhere. Not at all, Miss Balch replied, the Europeans did not consider the delegates "dreamers." "Throughout Sweden," she said, "the Neutral Conference is given credit for being a powerful factor in keeping that country out of war when at times the war question was at the boiling point." The Scandinavians had even coined the word "Fordism" to describe the delegates' "radical, constructive" peace work. Dr. Aked, she remarked, "believes apparently that an unofficial body of citizens can get into the regular old diplomatic game of secret diplomacy"; all the other delegates believed "that the forces making for peace are the forces of public opinion."

Ford did not take kindly to Aked's comments; he saw him once, refused to renew his high-priced contract and would not see him again. In his coda, a facetious article on what he had learned about peacemaking, Aked blamed the failure of the peace mission on the abundant and extravagant use of money which "corrupted" and "debauched" his weak-willed companions but said nothing of his own simultaneous service to God and Mammon.

Refuting Aked was only one of Emily Balch's assignments. She also was supposed to convince Ford to send more money, persuade President Wilson that he should instruct his representatives abroad not to discriminate against the conference as they had been doing* and, finally, organize mass peace demonstrations throughout the country on August 1. Miss Balch dined at Fair Lane, but the Fords—especially Clara Ford—believing that Jane Addams had been faking illness ever since the *Oscar II* sailed and still disturbed by Mme Schwimmer's mismanagement, thought they had been led down the garden path and were no longer listening to women peace-workers. A letter from Plantiff, arriving in Detroit just before Professor Balch, suggested that Ford "keep her there, because we don't want any more women connected with this movement." (No matter that on the same page he had also written, "Miss Balch is a hard worker and seems to be well thought of.")

President Wilson saw Miss Balch, at Miss Addams's request, not because he wanted to but because he was in the middle of a presidential campaign as the man "who kept us out of war" and he did not want to alienate peaceworkers. He listened to Miss Balch explain the difference between the "old" and the "new" neutral conferences and told her to put her complaints about unfair diplomatic treatment, namely that American conference delegates were on "a so-called 'blacklist' of citizens to whom no countenance was to be shown," in writing. (Almost a month later the counselor of the State Department, Frank Polk, wrote Miss Balch that he had carefully investigated her charge and found it false. On the contrary,

---

* In February, Dr. Schenk, a Swiss delegate, had been detained at the German border on his way to the conference. A friend told him that a functionary in the German embassy said Colonel House and the American embassy in Berlin had asked the German government not to accommodate members of the Ford mission.

he said, State Department policy was to give "all the assistance that it consistently could to individuals and groups interested in a peace movement.") Her efforts to organize peace demonstrations on August 1 were likewise fruitless.

At the end of August, Emily Balch saw the president again, this time as a member of the American Neutral Conference Committee. Rebecca Shelly and the other former members of the peace expedition who organized the committee first conceived of it as the American branch of the Stockholm conference, but when none of the prominent conservative peaceworkers joined, they turned it into an "ornamental committee" decorated with many prestigious names whose sole aim was urging Wilson to mediate with other neutral nations. Again, Wilson turned down the pacifists' proposal, explaining that he "sympathized entirely with the high objects they had in view" but that the United States would never act with others whose bias might conflict with her fair-minded proposals.

By then, Miss Balch had decided to spend her year's leave from Wellesley working for peace associations, and she set up her own branch of the neutral conference and hired a publicist to circulate the material she received from Stockholm. She also invited members of the radical and conservative peace persuasions to join the conference in educating American public opinion to favor "a speedy and fair settlement" of the European war. John Dewey, Congressman James L. Slayden, the Reverend Washington Gladden, philanthropist Jacob Schiff, journalist John Reed and Mary Woolley, president of Mount Holyoke College, were among those who agreed to help; Walter Lippmann also accepted the call, but only on a confidential basis. Perhaps Miss Balch's most helpful act was an article in the *New Republic* which spoke of the recognition the conference was receiving despite the difficulties of its unofficial status. It had not yet communicated directly with the belligerents, but its educational work was recognized by the governments and it was synthesizing the peace opinion that would ultimately determine the fate of Europe. The neutral conference, she advised, was "making history, if only on the 'little drops of water' principle."

Emily Balch had pursued Charles Aked to Detroit to counter whatever he told the Fords, and a few days later, Rosika Schwimmer arrived to correct the impression Miss Balch had made and to offer Ford the opportunity to finance her International Committee for Immediate Mediation, which, she claimed, was even then conducting secret negotiations in the belligerent countries. Her visit was unsuccessful; the Fords refused to see her. It was then she wrote inquiring whether Mrs. Ford had received the necklace sent before the *Oscar II* sailed and Mrs. Ford returned the gift, writing, "I did not wish to have anything that reminded me of the terrible nightmare of last December," and went on to rebuke Mme Schwimmer for squandering her husband's health and wealth.

Gaston Plantiff returned to Stockholm toward the end of July. During the three weeks' grace provided by his absence, the conference delegates concentrated on the August 1 peace demonstrations, hoping that the results of their grand plans would prove to Ford that publicity and propaganda were the surest roads to peace.

In early July the outlook was not brilliant. Strong popular opposition had already caused the planners to abandon a symbolic five-minute worldwide transportation and work stoppage. No one in the belligerent countries would help, and citizens in the neutral countries either ignored or mocked the scheme for peace demonstrations. The press was totally uninterested, and only the Salvation Army promised cooperation. To overcome the apathy practically all the delegates spent the month at home signing up speakers and arranging meetings.

This time the resolution proposed only that the neutral governments offer mediation "as soon as circumstances permit," a far cry from the previous demands for immediate official action, and also that the neutral countries send representatives to a people's congress at the war's end "to lay the foundations for an organization of states based upon Right instead of Might."

The inoffensiveness of the neutral conference's rephrased demand, the accumulated strains and abuses sustained by the neutrals after two years of war, the anxieties of another winter's fighting in a war apparently doomed to stalemate and, finally, the organizational work done by the delegates turned their seeming failure into a series of successful rallies far beyond their expectation. In every country represented at the conference, except the United States, church congregations, trade unions, fraternal societies and individuals enthusiastically supported the peace action. In Switzerland, 250,000 people adopted the conference resolution at Independence Day celebrations. One hundred thousand peace pamphlets were distributed at Dutch peace meetings. In the cities and villages of Scandinavia the number of participants was equally great, so that all in all, during the several days of meetings the resolution was passed at hundreds of meetings by hundreds of thousands of war-weary people.

Lochner, who addressed ten thousand people at a meeting in Christiania and eight thousand at another in Stockholm, thought the neutral conference's large-scale public demonstrations "converted the peoples and the parliamentarians of neutral Europe to its belief in the necessity for an official Neutral Conference, and kept the Foreign Offices busy explaining why they had not yet listened to the voice of the people." At the least, he concluded, the Ford conference had popularized the idea that the neutral nations should act in concert to end the war.

When Plantiff returned in the midst of the last-minute preparations for the public gathering, his instructions were waiting from Detroit: "Mr. Ford directs conference proceed quiet mediation one representative each country. Conference headquarters at Hague." Such explicit directions left no apparent margin for maneuvering, but Lochner, Miss Wales and even Holt made impassioned arguments for the continuance of the propaganda program. Frustrated and angered by the ignorance that was directing their affairs, Lochner wrote Ford again that they knew what they were doing and were doing it very well. "I cannot for the life of me believe that it [ending the war] can be done through quiet mediation only," he complained. "We need this quiet mediation to get the governments together; we need the publicity and propaganda to get the peoples together; and we need the work that is being done by our committee on constructive peace so that, when the negotiations come, we may be in a position effectively to bring about a better peace than could be done by diplomats, who to my way of thinking are just about the limit."

The changes had to be made, however, before Lochner's letter reached Detroit, and two more cables from Liebold provided the room for compromise. First, Plantiff learned that Aked's meeting with Ford had been "unsatisfactory" and his resignation accepted. Ford, then, he could assume, did not entirely reject publicity. And second, in the early days of August he was told to "use his own judgment regarding everything." The basis for the solution was provided by Senator Joseph Scherrer-Fuellemann of Switzerland, who finally took his seat at the conference just in time to arrange for its dismemberment. With Mme Schwimmer and Aked gone—his principal objections to participation—both he and his fellow delegate, Senator Emil Goettsheim, decided they could attend the conference they had been elected to almost six months earlier.

First, Scherrer-Fuellemann told his new colleagues the neutral conference could never properly mediate the war. The basis it cited in its appeal to the belligerents for its authority to act—the resolutions of the second Hague conference—provided for mediation by neutral governments, not neutral citizens. But the conference could and should contact prominent neutral and belligerent citizens willing to influence their governments to end the war, and the conference delegates should write articles that would educate all peoples to the principles of lasting peace. To perform these two functions a central headquarters was needed as well as delegates in each neutral capital to consult regularly with local workers. Above all, Scherrer-Fuellemann said, mindful of the turmoil and indignities endured by his compatriots, Mme Ragaz and Mlle Gobat, at the end of the first round of meetings in April, the delegates must have three months' notice before Ford terminated the organization. "A sudden dissolution of the Conference," he warned, "would cause the most disagreeable assumption, which should be avoided in all circumstances, and in the interest of everyone."

The Swiss proposal satisfied both Plantiff and the delegates, though it took a week to settle their discrepancies. The demand for three months' notice was reduced to two by the delegates and to whatever was possible by Plantiff, who also insisted that women could not be associated with the group except, of course, as office workers. The conference had asked for Miss Balch's return, but then demurred to a policy most members would have thought unthinkable a few months earlier. Frederick Holt, who had never managed to balance the books to Liebold's satisfaction, was recalled, and the conference was reduced to six delegates with the former members hired as technical staff.

It was money—what the delegates wanted to spend and what Plantiff wanted to give—that was the most difficult matter of all to settle. When Holt took over in March he told Liebold the conference would run on $15,000 a month, based on Mme Schwimmer's commitments. In May he joined Miss Balch in asking for an additional $5,000 for the May 18 celebrations, and every one of Lochner's letters to Ford spoke of costly projects in prospect. Liebold, hoping to kill the conference by attrition until it could be destroyed outright, had suggested to Plantiff that less, not more, should be spent, and Plantiff proposed a monthly budget of $10,000. (In designating Lochner the American delegate pro tem he had also hired him as a Ford Motor Company employee on detached service so that his $500 monthly salary, retroactive to the sailing of the *Oscar II*, would not be borne by the conference.) After a week of trying, even after cutting the delegates' honoraria from $500 to $100, Lochner said no amount of financial contortions could meet their needs with a reduced allotment, and Plantiff compromised by giving him 150,000 kroner (about $42,855) for the next three months. After that, Ford could change the arrangement if he wished, which was fine with the delegates, who expected peace negotiations would begin by November.

All in all, the peacemakers were satisfied with the new arrangement.

Several regretted there would be no more grand-scale public demonstrations. The few activists were disheartened by Ford's high-handed treatment of an international body and distressed by the center of power being in the same city as the Anti-Oorlog Raad. Miss Wales tried to find the bright side, but failed. She distrusted compromise and blamed their continuing difficulties with Ford on the delegates' never demanding "constitutional" rights. Mr. Ford did not understand, she wrote Miss Balch, that business managers were "influenced by what is good for business rather than what is good for peace."

But most of the members thought the new structure and program were probably more effective than the Central Committee. Lochner rather liked the idea of having bureaus in the neutral capitals—"three lightning rods up" ready to attract the thunderbolt of peace. "The future beyond these months is still uncertain," he realized, "but the great and encouraging thing is that so far every trouble has been overcome, and . . . the Conference to-day stands stronger than it ever did before." If indeed the conference stood stronger than ever, it was because it no longer stood— or sat—as a conference at all. Troubles had not been overcome; they had been avoided by the steady sacrifice of principles and goals.

Nine months had passed since the pacifists had sailed on the *Oscar II* for Europe and peace. Of the original crew only Lochner; Ada Morse Clark, his secretary; Julia Grace Wales, still a volunteer in the Stockholm publicity office; and Elli Eriksson, the Finnish girl in search of adventure, remained in Europe to begin the work of the fourth phase of the Ford Peace Expedition.

CHAPTER 13

"A clean sweep of the past"

D URING THE SUMMER of 1916 the warring armies were engaged in an exhausting battle along the Somme that in a few months killed and wounded over 1,200,000 men, equally divided between the two sides. The slaughter would be halted temporarily by the November rains and then resume again in winter.

In the last days of August the German high command, hoping to break the two-year deadlock, again urged the resumption of submarine warfare, expecting such a course to bring the United States into the war but not in sufficient strength to delay victory. Chancellor Bethmann-Hollweg argued against so precipitous and irreversible an action and won a postponement that gave him enough time, he hoped, to arrange for Wilson or another neutral leader to mediate. If the Allies rejected the intervention and the Central Powers accepted it, then, Bethmann-Hollweg reasoned, the United States could hardly side with the Allies and probably would not enter the war at all when unrestricted submarine attack resumed. Partly because of German diplomacy and partly because of war weariness, peace feelers, trial balloons and talk of the possibility of a Wilsonian mediation appeared almost daily in the world press from early September until late fall.

The neutral conference had firsthand evidence of this new mood of peace when the European newspapers saluted the conference's reorganization as an expansion, not a contraction, of its peace activity. In fact the neutral conference as a conference was moribund, its organizational chart stripped almost bare. Though the major committees still existed on paper and the meaningless office of president rotated monthly, in practice each delegate pursued his own interests and Henry Ford was subsidizing established peace organizations, such as the Anti-Oorlog Raad, and individual projects. In Norway, Dr. Mikael Lie directed the slow-moving preparations for the peace conference, listing in his first report the assignment of almost thirty position papers on topics derived from the appeal to the belligerents. In Switzerland, Scherrer-Fuellemann and his colleagues conferred with members of the German and Austrian nobility and with members of their own government—to little effect—and Scherrer-Fuellemann suggested the Central Committee petition a prominent American to come to Europe and mediate in the name of the people. (The proposal was approved and William Howard Taft was selected, but the delegates never agreed on the wording of the invitation and on who was to sign it.) In the Stockholm bureau, Haakon Loeken ran the publicity and propaganda program, Miss Wales did some translating and continued writing proposals as new approaches to peace occurred to her, and Dr. Ernst Wigforss worked on the neutral-conference's newest scheme, an international review.

The idea for such a publication had been bouncing around the conference for months when Lochner wrote Ford in June of his "pet dream," a European newspaper that would "do for peace what the Christian Science Monitor . . . does for the spread of Christian Science." The journal, to be called *Post Bellum*, was to be an instrument of indirect mediation, publishing articles on "the burning actual questions" of the war—nationalism, militarism, imperialism—and the need for an international peacekeeping organization. Lochner and Wigforss hoped the belligerent governments would permit the magazine to be distributed in their countries, thereby permitting an exchange of views among enemies. To obtain commitments and articles, Wigforss sent Dr. Anna Bugge-Wicksell, the secretary of the Swedish group of the Central Organization for a Durable Peace and later a substitute delegate to the League of Nations, and her husband, Professor Knut Wicksell, to England.

In London, though public talk of peace was equated with defeat and the exchange of thought with German nationals was repellent, the futility and burdens of the war eased the Wicksells' task, and within a few weeks they had twenty pledges of cooperation from such peace-minded writers and politicians as Leonard Woolf, whose essay on international government the neutral conference reprinted and sent to members of parliament; Henry Massingham, editor of *The Nation*; Lord James Bryce, a former ambassador to the United States; and the Fabian socialists Sidney and Beatrice Webb and George Bernard Shaw. Radical pacifists Ramsay Macdonald and Philip Snowden, both in Parliament, feared their early association with the publication might frighten the moderates and promised to participate after the magazine was established. The foreign office reviewed Mrs. Wicksell's brief prospectus and found it unobjectionable to British interests. Wigforss was so exhilarated by their changed fortunes that he sent two world-famed Swedish scholars to Berlin and Vienna the end of September hoping they would find similar encouragement.

At de Jong's suggestion the neutral conference sent two highly placed members of the Anti-Oorlog Raad to Berlin to proselytize moderate, internationally minded Reichstag members against the annexation of Belgium and for German membership in a league of nations. The mediationists had been told that Great Britain would probably consider ending the war if Germany agreed to these conditions.

During the first weeks of September, Lochner sat in his office in The Hague's fashionable Hotel des Indes, adjacent to the "beautiful drawing-and-reception room" where he hoped to entertain diplomats and government agents, eager to begin his new duties as bureau coordinator and peace mediator. But after reading his mail each day he had little to do except read the newspaper articles marked by his Belgian translator, dictate letters in French and German to his Luxembourgian stenographer and in English to Mrs. Clark, go over the accounts with his part-time bookkeeper and carry on a correspondence about the proposed journal with Dr. Wigforss. To mask his idleness, Lochner filled his reports to Ford with significant-sounding snippets: the American minister agreed it would be a step toward peace if the conference persuaded Bethmann-Hollweg to state that Germany would not annex Belgium, a German army officer was certain the war party was practically powerless, and the International Socialists Bureau secretary said Ford should "induce" Wilson to mediate.

Mostly Lochner anxiously awaited the call to report in person to Ford which Plantiff had promised to arrange after Lochner learned in late August that Ford had never seen a single one of his letters. Only "the important parts," the money-minded Liebold wrote, had been brought to Ford's attention. If the conference was to continue beyond November, and, more important, if Ford was to finance an international magazine, a people's congress at war's end and other peace projects, then Lochner knew he had to find a way to talk to Ford directly.

His urgency increased toward the end of September when he met Ferdinand Leipnik, a Hungarian recommended to Plantiff by the British minister to Stockholm. Leipnik invited Lochner to meet his important connections in The Hague and share his cloak-and-dagger schemes. Leipnik had been city editor of the pro-German *Pester Lloyd*, dreaming of working on an international newspaper, when Sir Esme was posted to Budapest several years before the war. After the journalist was fired for his "British proclivities" Sir Esme suggested he settle in England, and in August 1914, when he became an enemy alien in his adopted land, Leipnik moved to Holland.

From the day they met, Lochner saw the refugee writer daily, wholeheartedly and unquestioningly accepting all of Leipnik's suggestions and never suspecting that his new friend was a self-appointed British agent. After several talks with the American peaceworker, Leipnik concluded that Ford's peace venture was motivated by "the unsophisticated enthusiasm of an uneducated and warm-hearted man . . . ambitious to acquire fame as a benefactor of Humanity," and he proposed what Lochner understood to be a two-pronged Ford-engineered mediation coup. First, Leipnik guaranteed that Ford and Lochner would be received at the British Foreign Office and later by other members of the Entente. Then Leipnik promised to furnish representatives from the warring countries as guests if Ford would host an international dinner.

This was a bowdlerized version of his plan; Leipnik filed the original with the British Foreign Office. Ford was an egotistical innocent, he counseled, who could be diverted from his "mischievous propaganda" and "his sense of importance" could be satisfied with an invitation to preside over an innocuous gathering of belligerent nationals or a confidential interview with the foreign minister. Leipnik asked for orders but Foreign Office records indicate none were sent.

The British officials had been keeping track of the Ford Peace Expedition since the lieutenant who boarded the *Oscar II* at Kirkwall had notified the port commander, "The ship from stem to stern is impregnated with intellectuality, and everybody seems a pest to everybody else." The Americans' letters and cables had been routinely censored during their hegira, and after the conference settled in Stockholm Sir Esme was in frequent communication. When the peacemakers had asked permission for their representatives to enter England, the Foreign Office had checked with France and Italy to learn their policies on the matter. Several copies of both conference appeals were in the files as well as the observations of Sir Cecil Spring Rice, the ambassador to the United States, who thought the appeal to the belligerents was so well done the Germans must have had a hand in it, especially since Lochner and Rosika Schwimmer had "acted throughout under direct German influence." In early August, Sir Cecil reported that "Ford has practically washed his hands of peace movement," which Sir Esme confirmed with his confidentially received information that Henry Ford realized it was useless to try to stop the war and was sending a small committee to The Hague for the "propagation of permanent peace ideas after the war." In any case, Sir Esme advised, the conference was no longer influenced by Germany and Lochner was merely "an earnest supporter of the cause of Peace."

Leipnik looked upon his schemes as a means of detouring Ford's money and influence from "the grotesque course" of mediation; Locher regarded them as exciting and potentially productive opportunities that Ford could not be allowed to ignore, so that when Liebold's cable came at the end of September telling him to stay where he was for another two months, he resorted to shock tactics. Sir Esme's friend, he cabled Plantiff, had put him on "to something supremely important" which required either Ford's presence in Europe or Lochner's in Detroit. Three days later, at midnight, with only a few hours to catch the boat, Lochner had his orders to come home at once.

In the months since Henry Ford had returned from Europe his outspoken pacifism had brought him honors and penalties. Without trying he won the Republican presidential primaries in Michigan and Nebraska and was asked to head the Prohibition ticket. Two full-page anti-preparedness newspaper advertisements resulted in libel suits brought by the Navy League and the Vitagraph Company. In turn, Ford sued the Chicago *Tribune* for calling him an anarchist because he reportedly threatened to fire any employee who went with the National Guard to the Mexican border. That his utterances resulted in lawsuits was his lawyers' problem— nothing stopped Henry Ford from speaking out when he had something to say, not even when he spoke on opposite sides of the same issue. He lambasted "fool" preparedness parades in the spring and publicly supported the president, who led them, in the fall.

Louis Lochner spent ten golden days in America on his master's business. One day, while Ford was driving through the Dearborn countryside, he told Lochner he had picked him as his permanent European peace representative because he "had no reputation to lose and everything to gain" and would therefore act fearlessly. In speaking of the new direction he wished his European peace work to follow, Ford instructed his deputy to cease engaging in peace publicity for its own sake and concentrate on persuading the kaiser to announce publicly that Germany would disarm after the war. "Tell him I'll back him to the limit," said the self-important philanthropist. Ford then armed Lochner with "corking good" letters of introduction to the heads of all the belligerent governments and arranged for his peace surrogate to receive several other symbols of probity and influence—a new passport permitting him to travel in the belligerent countries, a letter from Count von Bernstorff asking his government to treat Lochner courteously and a promise from Secretary Lansing that American embassies would do the same.

Lochner returned to Europe thrilled by his new status and the promises he had received from his peace patron. In his portfolio, next to his new credentials, he carried a letter from Mr. Ford to the neutral-conference members authorizing Lochner to act for him on peace matters. Though he had not been able to obtain more money for the conference he had Ford's promise that he would continue sending $10,000 a month for the present; permission to pay Leipnik, his "diplomatic adviser," $3,000 for three months' work (the amount Leipnik demanded for his services) and Ford's pledge to continue his peace activities in Europe for another five years. Ford and Plantiff also charged Lochner with keeping all activities under his control, maintaining an all-male conference and staying within his budget.

Scandinavia was Lochner's first stop on the triumphal tour he expected to make of all the bureaus. As soon as he entered the Stockholm office, however, he was told that his few remaining colleagues—and former delegates as well—had been battling by mail and within the branches since his departure. The Swiss and Scandinavians bitterly opposed each other's programs, half the Dutch delegation objected to the men-only ruling, and all the bureaus disagreed on the plans for their future work. Lochner and the Scandinavians wanted each national bureau to run its own program with approval from headquarters, and the Swiss and Dutch favored collective action on all matters.

For a month Lochner tried to placate his adversaries and failed. The recalcitrant Scherrer-Fuellemann called him a "financial dictator," and Mme Bakker van Bosse refused to resign even though Lochner told her Miss Balch and Miss Addams agreed with Ford that no women should serve "in view of the fact that European diplomacy is still run by men." At last, disgusted by his colleagues' refusal to concede Ford's right "to run his own affairs as he pleased," Lochner notified Plantiff that "conditions here necessitate that Neutral Conference be disbanded and International Commission established instead, directly responsible to me. See no other way clear to rid us of undesirable past problems." Within two days approval arrived, and within the week the Neutral Conference for Continuous Mediation began its official metamorphosis into the "educative rather than agitatory" Ford Peace Commission. On December 20, in a formal, almost imperious, letter proclaiming the new regime, Lochner wrote his co-workers that nothing could be accomplished as long as the conference *"continues to exist as an impossible combination of divergent views."* Therefore, he was making "a clean sweep of the past with its many unpleasant features" and creating instead an international commission of several independent departments all responsible to him as Ford's peace representative. The official changeover date was February 1, 1917, though the new program had been in de facto effect since the move to The Hague.

The young and impressionable peace activist had lost none of his enthusiasm and exuberance since coming to Europe, but after a year of mind-wearying and immobilizing haggling and compromise he had come to believe that collective action did not compare to the authority of one-man rule. Tempted by the power that came with his anointment as Ford's peace arbiter and personal envoy to European heads of state, Lochner succumbed. Until his visit home he had believed, as had his colleagues, that the neutral conference's policies and programs were the business of the delegates alone; afterward, he believed they were the exclusive property of the man who paid for them.

Though encouraged in his action by the conference's current elder statesmen, Lochner nonetheless felt obliged to explain, indeed justify, his bold takeover and abandonment of the founding principles of the neutral conference to the former American members of the expedition still steadfastly working for peace. Claiming success for each phase of the work thus far—the neutral and belligerent appeals and then the mass demonstrations alerting the neutral governments their people wanted intervention—Lochner wrote that the time had come for "expertism" rather than "well-meaning" joint consultation. With a delicate allusion to past trials, he explained that under the new scheme he had "liberated" conflicting groups so that "birds of a feather have flocked together, with insulating rooms between them, but with a door from each of them leading into my sanctuary, from which I can . . . soothe and persuade them." And in another letter, after proudly enumerating the conference's recent successes, he cautioned, "I am now in the very queer position of being

forced to ask you not to identify my name with these communications. . . .
The reason is that I have unusual [German] passport facilities now for
travelling into certain of the belligerent countries, and that entails upon
me the obligation of the utmost discretion." The pretty words and mysterious injunction were meant to mask Lochner's abandonment of open
mediation, total disarmament, popular collective action to end the war
and women's right to participate in the conference they had conceived.
Thus, by acceding to Ford's vacuous pacifist whims because they seemed
to suit his momentary needs, Lochner perverted the aspirations that had
inspired and sustained the ideals of the American radical pacifists since the
war's outbreak, and in the end he paid the price expediency usually
exacts.

The prestigious credentials and the self-concerned advice from his respectable senior advisers lured a not too hesitant Lochner down the
garden path, but the way would not have been strewn with diplomatic
perquisites and privileges had it not been for the favorable exigency of
events that greeted the young pacifist when he returned to Europe. In
October and November the British foreign secretary and the German
chancellor made conciliatory speeches, the former's intended to diminish
Lloyd George's bloodthirsty cry that England would vanquish her enemies with "a knockout blow." In mid-November, Bethmann-Hollweg
told the Reichstag budget committee that Germany would join a postwar
league of nations and, in a peace treaty, respect the territorial integrity of
Belgium.

Since the August meeting at the kaiser's headquarters, the American
embassy in Berlin and the German embassy in Washington had been
transmitting word of the chancellor's hope for a Wilsonian intervention
almost daily. On November 20 the German ambassador told Colonel
House that "peace was on the floor waiting to be picked up." Still, Wilson did not act, despite his anger at Britain's continued rejection of the
mediation offer House had made in the spring and her continued flaunting
of American shipping rights; and despite his growing fear that America
would drift into war when Germany resumed submarine warfare, which
he knew was imminent; and despite his telling House several months
earlier "that it will be up to us to judge for ourselves when the time has
arrived to make an imperative suggestion" to the Allies to negotiate.
Anxious and ready as the president was to be the people's peace spokesman, his pro-Ally advisers, House and Lansing, apparently convinced him
to be cautious.

By early December, Bethmann-Hollweg could wait no longer for a neutral move. The German popular mood, the liberal members in the Reichstag and the liberal press as well as the determination of the high command forced him to act, and the fall of Bucharest to the Central Powers gave him the opportunity. On December 12 he publicly invited the Allies to end the war. Germany, he said, had proved she was unconquerable; still, she did not wish to destroy her enemies, whom she was fighting only in self-defense. To end "the flood of blood," Germany offered to discuss peace; if the offer was refused, she would fight to victory, "disclaiming any responsibility for continuing the war."

The timing of the German move delayed Wilson's peace initiative but did not deter it. He had procrastinated, he had been dilatory, but he had been working on his own peace demands—much tempered in several drafts by Lansing and House—and had finished just at the time the Germans made their move. On December 18 he sent his note to the belligerent powers.

It is time, the president said, for the warring nations to state "the precise objects which would, if attained, satisfy them and their people that the war had been fought out," and to state explicitly the guarantees they required against war's recurrence. It appeared to him "that the objects which the statesmen of the belligerents on both sides have in mind in this war are virtually the same" and it might be "that an interchange of views" would indicate "peace is nearer than we know." Wilson was careful to say he was neither "proposing peace" nor "offering mediation," but "merely proposing that soundings be taken" and offering his services "in any way that might prove acceptable." Apologizing for making the demand so soon after the German's peace offer, he explained that the neutral nations felt "the burden and terror" of the war and had to act quickly in their own interests and in those of civilization. "When the war is over, with every influence and resource at their command," the United States would cooperate in a "concert of nations," he promised, to protect the smaller nations and "secure the future peace of the world" for everyone. But first the war must end, and he quietly instructed his ambassadors to the belligerent governments to tell their respective foreign ministers that "it would be very hard for the Government of the United States to understand a negative reply" to his offer.

As expected the neutral governments promised Wilson cooperation, the liberal European press hailed his action and the conservative press decried his interference. The German government applauded Wilson's "noble initiative" but said the belligerents should confer among themselves. The British, instead of replying directly to Wilson, bluntly rejected the Central Powers offer, calling it "less an offer of peace than . . . a maneuver of war," and their general statement of terms made it very clear that peace was not at hand. As the new year began, President Wilson was disheartened and frustrated, but still hoping to end the war.

Louis Lochner, his colleagues and other unofficial peacemakers wandered through this peace drama as it was played in Europe the last months of 1916. Welcomed and courted by government officials, these strolling players knew no more of the script than the parts they were given to play, and what they read in the newspapers. For Lochner the sudden transformation from pariah to messiah was overwhelming. In the spring he had been shown the door at the German legation in Stockholm; in November the minister received him courteously and wished him godspeed to Berlin. The last time he had been in that city he had had a visit from the secret police; this time he presented his card and Ford's letter at the foreign office in the Wilhelmstrasse and the undersecretary of state for foreign affairs saw him at once.

After scanning Lochner's credentials, Dr. Arthur Zimmermann said the kaiser was at the front and unavailable for interviews but would be informed of Ford's wishes. Lochner then explained that Ford would be an effective mediator between the president, whose reelection he had ensured by his endorsement, and the kaiser, whom Ford considered blameless in starting the war. Ford had "special sympathies" for Germany, his spokesman said. After promising that Lochner would hear from the German minister in The Hague, Zimmermann gave the American pacifist special diplomatic credentials to ease his transit to Switzerland and Holland. Two weeks later, on the last day of November, the German legation in The Hague asked Lochner to make an appointment, and though he replied at once, it was another week before the minister, Dr. Friedrich Rosen, received him.

In the middle of that week, on December 4, Lochner, his wife, Mrs. Clark and a few others celebrated the first anniversary of the sailing of the peace expedition by seeing a pacifist play. At Henry's Scandinavian Restaurant in New York some of the reporters saluted the expedition by recalling every reason for its failure. Ford and Plantiff, though they were in the city, did not attend the dinner but sent a congratulatory telegram acclaiming the expedition for starting "a worldwide peace movement" that had not failed because "those who fail are those who quit and we have not got well started yet." The celebrants also mourned the passing of several members, including the belle of the voyage, Inez Milholland Boissevain, who had died the week before. With other women who favored a national suffrage amendment, she had campaigned for Charles Evans Hughes that summer and fall, knowing she was dangerously ill of pernicious anemia, and continued to speak, even after she lost her strength, until her final hospitalization.

On December 8, Dr. Rosen, an experienced diplomat and later foreign minister of the Weimar Republic, gave Lochner Zimmermann's reply: At the proper time the German ambassador in Washington would be given a broad outline of Germany's peace terms which he might, if he wished, give to Ford. Lochner was not pleased with the diplomatic brushoff, but after a long chat with Rosen he believed he had been told Germany's secret peace terms. Four days later, after Germany invited the Allies to end the war, Lochner hurried back to the legation and asked Rosen to give Germany's terms secretly to Leipnik that he might take them to Britain. Rosen agreed provided they met on the neutral territory of the Ford Peace Commission's office with Lochner in attendance as a witness. In the time before that meeting, which was held on Christmas Eve, Wilson asked the belligerents to state their war aims.

"Things have tumbled over each other internationally with dizzying rapidity," Lochner excitedly reported home, crediting the high-level peace activity to the many months of agitation by the neutral conference and the more recent actions taken by its scattered members. Bethmann-Hollweg's declaration that Germany would join a postwar league of nations was "a direct result of our work," he wrote Plantiff, and that "one fact alone," a French-Swiss told him, "is worth all the money that Mr. Ford has put into the Conference." Lochner supposed that Henry Ford and the American Neutral Conference Committee were responsible for Wilson's finally seizing "the bull by the horns" and demanding the belligerents' peace terms. And there was irrefutable evidence that the neutral governments' notes endorsing Wilson's action were the result of the hundreds of meetings and thousands of petitions sponsored by the neutral conference in the spring and summer. The peace demonstrations in Scandinavia and Holland during Christmas week, Lochner added, were "started by us" and so were the statements by prominent neutrals on the German proposal which were printed by the Associated Press in European and American papers. Hoping to provide the president with a groundswell of popular acclaim in Europe, Lochner instructed his bureaus to have local organizations and individuals send messages of gratitude and support to the White House, and "the thing worked like a charm," resulting in messages sent by the many branches of the International Socialists Bureau, constituent members of the Anti-Oorlog Raad and Scandinavian and Swiss organizations that released their messages to the newspapers as well. So many people were working for the neutral conference, Lochner boasted, that it had become "a net-work covering almost the whole of Europe," and he was himself one day summoned to the American legation to be briefed on "confidential matters" and "pumped" on political conditions in Berlin.

The energetic peaceworker thought he was moving as fast as the diplomats during the December peace scramble, but his hopes were on "the big deal," the Leipnik-Rosen meeting. "I know for certain," he wrote Plantiff, just before the rendezvous, "that I am in his [Rosen's] confidence and in that of Berlin, just as Mr. Leipnik is in the confidence of London."

In November the Hungarian Anglophile had told the British minister to The Hague that his protégé had returned from America with an invitation from Wilson asking Leipnik to report in person on "the European Situation." (Possibly Lochner said he could *arrange* an invitation and Leipnik converted the probable into the certain. Or perhaps Lochner did.) At the same time, Leipnik advised the British Foreign Office that he had "urgent and most important information about Wilson's policy" and asked permission to come to London that he might act on their behalf in Washington. The request went through the chain of command at Whitehall up to Sir Edward Grey, the foreign secretary. It caused some surprise, but Grey and the others knew Colonel House and were aware of Wilson's preference for "the views of amateurs as it were as compared with experts." Several vouched for Leipnik's loyalty, particularly as it was noted that "there is no idea of employing him as an intermediary in any negotiating, but simply letting him have our views." Leipnik's request was granted in early December, but he delayed his departure until after he saw Rosen.

With the Christmas Eve meeting at the Hotel des Indes, Lochner finally achieved the underlying aim of the neutral conference: two influential people with direct connections to the highest officials of the opposing governments met for the purpose of mediation. So Lochner understood; but he was only gulled again, this time by both sides. Departing from his custom, Lochner kept no record of what was said at the meeting, though he commented to Plantiff that Rosen "spoke all through in diplomatic language, yet our friend got a complete understanding from it of the point of view of the Central Powers." That "point of view" was doubtless based on Bethmann-Hollweg's statement that Germany would join a postwar league, Zimmermann telling Lochner that after the war every nation would be bankrupt and would have to maintain a disarmament program and Rosen reaffirming Germany's lack of interest in annexing Belgium. All that coupled with Germany's peace démarche, Lochner thought, met Great Britain's demands for ending the war.

Leipnik left for London on December 29 with the understanding that if the English asked him to take their peace terms to Wilson he and Lochner, speaking for the German position, would go to Washington together and tell the president that "the war can stop and men gather around the green table just as soon as the United States agrees to become a co-guarantor of the future peace of the world by joining the proposed league of nations." Pulling off that "stunt," Lochner rhapsodized, would "more than justify every expenditure incurred, even during the days of the barbaric splendor of one Rosika Schwimmer."

Once again Lochner prepared to leave the work in the hands of his European colleagues, certain that he had the confidence of Henry Ford. He had already told Wigforss "to go ahead full steam" on their elaborate plans for an international journal, which, by then, had the additional encouragement of Albert Einstein and Philipp Scheidemann, a leading member of the Reichstag. While his associates attended to Christmas week peace demonstrations, Lochner visited with his German connection and distributed news releases, one of which said Zimmermann had told him Germany would sign a postwar disarmament agreement. General von Hindenburg read the story in the dispatches from Belgium on the last day of December and straightaway wrote an angry letter to Bethmann-Hollweg demanding to know if such an injurious statement had any "foundation in fact." The chancellor replied that Zimmermann had seen Lochner but only to receive Ford's letter to the kaiser and only to say that "the whole world" would welcome Ford's peace efforts at the right time. The story in the newspaper was "in contradiction of the facts" and he had no idea of the source.

It was neither the British nor the Germans who disapproved of Leipnik and Lochner pursuing peace at the White House but Ford, Leibold and Plantiff. Lochner's letter describing the meeting between Leipnik and Rosen did not arrive before his requests for a $5,000 monthly increase and a large amount of money for the magazine and a symposium on the Central Powers peace note. Every letter and cable he sent—and there were many—evaluated activities in terms of value received for money spent, hoping thus to justify the continued life of the peace commission. Never did Lochner report that an action was taken or should be taken because it was intrinsically worthwhile. Always his letters asked for more money promising that "every penny will be turned over twice."

However, while Lochner was explaining to Plantiff that every "political observer" agreed "that now if ever is the time to spend money," Plantiff was telling Liebold that additional money was not needed precisely because "official proceedings" for peace had been initiated at home and abroad. Henry Ford thought so too. The president's demand for peace terms in December had not only increased the industrialist's allegiance to him, it had all but ended Ford's interest in continuing his European operation. Consequently, Plantiff cabled Lochner that Ford did not want him to come and would not send extra funds. Lochner was infuriated and insulted by this patent lack of trust in his judgment following so soon upon Ford's promise of October, and when Leipnik summoned him to England to begin their voyage to the States, Lochner and his wife packed their bags and left, waiting until they were on the Atlantic before radioing Plantiff that they were coming for a short but mandatory visit. Plantiff, in turn, assured Ford that Lochner would not have disobeyed instructions unless his mission was important and Ford met the voyagers at the pier in New York, arranged an interview for them with the president and asked them to Dearborn afterward to hear his plans.

Lochner and Leipnik were squeezed in among the president's appointments on January 16, just before the Master Gravel and Slag Roofers Association delegation. Though scheduled for a five-minute standup chat, Wilson kept them almost half an hour. Lochner, voluble and earnest, recounted his conversations with Zimmermann and Rosen, which Wilson merely punctuated with a nod of his head or a mumbled "yes." However, when Leipnik took over the story as the unofficial bearer of England's demands—principally assurance that the United States would join a league of nations—the president was full of questions. Why did the British doubt the Americans would join a postwar league? Didn't they know that Congress was certain to endorse it? Wilson regarded Leipnik's remark that England would consider Germany's signing a Bryan "cooling-off" treaty as sufficient evidence of her intent to participate in postwar international arbitration as "very significant indeed." After the president was repeatedly reminded of his waiting appointments, he apologized for the brevity of their chat and assured his guests, as they left, "You gentlemen have indeed rendered me a great service."

Wilson was most interested in Germany's sudden willingness to sign a Bryan treaty. Only the day before he had had a letter from House reporting a conversation with the German ambassador in which Bernstorff told the president's confidant that Germany would join a league of nations after the war and sign a Bryan treaty at once. House thought Bernstorff's remarks—which the peace-loving ambassador had extended beyond his instructions—were "the most important communication we have had since the war began and [gave] a real basis for negotiations and for peace." Wilson, though not as optimistic, wrote the colonel of the "very interesting coincidence" that occurred that day:

Two men came in to see me, one of whom is, I believe, the permanent secretary or aide employed by Henry Ford in connection with his perpetual conference at the Hague, and has been going about talking to the Foreign ministers here and there, like the other pacifists, and the other an English Jew (with a very decided foreign twist to his tongue) who says he is on confidential terms with various men, his friends, attached to the British Foreign Office.

Though pleased that the British believed Germany would be putting her "aggressive principles behind her" if she signed the arbitration treaty, Wilson wondered what it all meant in terms of his present peace attempts. He had intimations several days later when House wrote that the "slippery" Germans were probably getting ready to resume "unbridled submarine warfare."

Time was swiftly running out on the president's dream of being the world peacemaker while he was still a neutral head of state. Two attempts to end the war—a public demand for peace terms and an offer to mediate secretly—had failed. On January 22, he made his final move as he stood in the Senate chamber and in an unprecedented act addressed the peoples of the belligerent nations. "Speaking for the silent mass of mankind everywhere," whom he knew wanted peace, he pledged America's involvement in a postwar league that would be "not a balance of power but a community of power" and called for "a peace without victory" because "only a peace between equals can last." Such a peace, he said, would ensure universal democratic government, arms limitation and freedom of the seas.

Several neutral-conference members proudly commented on the resemblance between Wilson's speech and their appeal to the belligerents, in both principle and word. But Lochner, who thought the president's speech proved "we are absolutely on [the] right track," sat in his Detroit hotel room and pondered the unaccountability of fate. During the week since his return and for three weeks thereafter, the spirits of the man Ford had often affectionately called his "victim" soared and sank like a seesaw as he viewed the continued prospects of Ford-financed peace work. He had been welcomed warmly by Ford at the pier but later told by Neely, Plantiff's bookkeeper, that Ford was cutting the conference's funds in half. In Washington, with Leipnik, he had encouraging visits with the president, the ambassadors from Great Britain and Germany and the chairman of the Senate Foreign Relations Committee. Yet two days later in Detroit when Lochner reported Wilson's encouraging words in their interview, to his astonishment, Ford said America should not try to end the war, that the Europeans would do so themselves as soon as they had suffered enough.

Henry Ford's domestic peace interests were more and more centered on the president, especially after Wilson's December peace initiative. His newest objective was educating the American people to endorse Wilson's peace policies, and at the hurried luncheon with Liebold, Lochner and Leipnik he spoke briefly of his plan, intimating he had no further interest in European projects, and then left, after instructing Lochner to amuse himself over the weekend and be on hand for another meeting Monday.

Lochner fled to Jane Addams for consolation and advice, and he also telegraphed his melancholic frustration to Dr. Jordan: "Work never more promising and chances for success never greater than now but sad that my chief's interest seems gone."

Though down and almost out, Lochner was not beaten when he met with Liebold on Monday, January 22. After a three-hour discussion during which Lochner explained why peace propaganda for a league of nations had to be conducted in Europe as well as in America, he persuaded himself he had won Liebold to the "realization of possibilities" and perhaps even a larger allowance. But the next day Lochner saw Ford and Liebold for scarcely ten minutes of unrelenting bad news. Wilson's "peace without victory" speech of the day before had confirmed Ford's resolve to concentrate exclusively on domestic peace education in support of a league of nations, and he told Lochner to remain in America as his private peace agent (Delavigne had been fired through Liebold's offices after the lawsuits). Leipnik was dismissed. When Lochner mentioned Leipnik's singular connections, Ford said he had his manager, Percival Perry, in England and needed no "high-priced" man. Though deeply humiliated at his friend's abrupt dismissal, Lochner held his tongue, mindful, he wrote Leipnik, of "my moral obligations to my European co-workers," and asked for another meeting to plead for the continuance of the European program. He was told to expect a call the next day but after waiting until late afternoon, Lochner phoned the factory and was told to call again on Friday.

Angered and tormented, and thinking of both resigning and enlisting Plantiff in his fight to see the Europeans treated properly, Lochner left for New York. In the next few days before he returned to Detroit for what he hoped would be a "final adjustment" in favor of continuing the European peace work, Lochner nurtured his determination and plotted his course, advised and supported by his friends at the American Neutral Conference Committee. In his more bitter moments, he wrote two recriminatory letters to Ford that catalogued his benefactor's broken promises, neither of which he sent. It would have made no difference if he had. Lochner had entered the limbo of Ford's lost enthusiasms, and he never saw the man again.

On Monday, Lochner was back in Dearborn. Having had enough of Ford's aides' criticism of "matters about which they understood less than a duck about wireless telegraphy," he had decided that the only way to handle Liebold "was not to appeal to any idealism which he does not possess, but to talk hard business facts." To his surprise, after the visit he was on top of the seesaw. Liebold, Lochner wrote his friends, did nothing but apologize for his chief's constantly misunderstood behavior and relay Ford's assurance that the European work would continue if the president approved.

Four days later Lochner was in Washington again to call at the White House. He had asked for the interview a week earlier to speak of "serious matters" he had not wished to mention in the presence of the "foreigner" Leipnik. Lochner spent the time before the meeting preparing his presentation, asking his influential friends to wire their endorsement of his case to the president and pondering the enigma of Henry Ford. "It is a queer fact, but, sad to say, true that so long as we were not taken seriously in Europe, Mr. Ford took us seriously and supported us generously; now, however, that not only the peoples but also the Governments are taking us seriously, Mr. Ford is wavering in his further support," he wrote Dr. Jordan. To both of his sorely missed mentors, Miss Addams and Jordan, Lochner wrote of his "sleepless nights" and the "veritable hell" he had endured since his return to the States. The tension had been unbearable. Though the justice of his cause seemed transparently self-evident, he was fighting for its existence. He thought his weapons of principle and integrity were inadequate against "the enemies of the work" in Ford's camp, and he expected to lose, but in losing, win, he hoped, a new sponsor who would take over the European peace organization, employ a new general manager and let Lochner return to his longed-for status as "a modest cog in the machine."

In the meantime, while there was a reprieve there was hope, and mistrustful as Lochner was by then of Ford's promises, he arrived in Washington eager to present the case of the Ford Peace Commission to the president. However, on February 1, the morning of the interview, the newspapers carried the astounding news that Germany's reply to Wilson's peace overtures was the resumption of unrestricted submarine warfare on neutral as well as belligerent shipping. Expecting the president would have no time for him that day, Lochner called to cancel his appointment. But the gravely perplexed and distraught president desperately needed to hear the encouraging words of the peacemaker and insisted on seeing him.

Wilson had known for months that Germany was planning to launch unrestricted submarine warfare but he had not looked for it in the midst of maneuvers for a negotiated peace, especially when he thought he had shown his impartiality as a mediator. Beyond that, he believed that in giving his recent speech he had done the right thing, and he had, he wrote a friend, "an invincible confidence in the prevalence of the right if it is fearlessly set forth."

Late into the night of January 31 the president listened to Secretary Lansing argue for an immediate break in relations with Germany. He spent the next morning restlessly walking the floor, rearranging his library and finally seeking some surcease in a game of pool with Colonel House. Lansing came by for lunch and continued his argument for a break, but Wilson, equally adamant, was resolved to keep America out of the war. In the early afternoon the president asked the Swiss minister if the neutral governments would join with the United States in the search for peace. (The answer, which did not arrive until after the crisis was over, suggested it was a bit late in the day for Wilson's response to the European neutrals' persistent importunities for joint action, which they had been making since the war began.)

At four o'clock, after House and Lansing left, Lochner entered the executive office. He commiserated with the "haggard and worried" president, expressed his astonishment at Zimmermann's behavior, so contrary to what his Berlin sources had told him to expect, and offered the services of his "modest organization," which Wilson kindly declined. Mindful of his own problems, Lochner then explained why he was there. He handed the president copies of the cables the neutral conference had arranged to have sent to him after his peace note, spoke of their earlier mass meetings in Europe calling for neutral collective action and explained their current propaganda program for a league of nations. Next, he gave Wilson a copy of the magazine prospectus and emphasized the publication's usefulness in obtaining popular acceptance for a postwar international organization. And finally Lochner spoke of the position papers being prepared on the problems most likely to appear on the peace-conference agenda, problems which Wilson had touched upon in his recent address.

All during the presentation Wilson nodded encouragingly and interrupted only to tell Lochner to focus not on the need for a specific league structure but on its operating principles. When Lochner asked, as a lead-in to his final question, what Ford could do to help the president's cause in America, Wilson stressed persuading the American people to commit themselves and their government to the basic concepts inherent in international government. (A politician as well as an idealist, Wilson knew the people had to be educated to the necessity of international government. When he learned that the Carnegie Endowment for International Peace had $1,000,000 it did not know how to spend, he asked several trustees to use the money enlightening the public at home and abroad "with a systematic propagation of the ideas and the implicit programme" embodied in his "peace without victory" address.)

At the end of their interview, in reply to Lochner's critical question about the continued existence of the conference, the president said he knew nothing of its work except what Lochner had told him, but, based on that report, if the conference continued it not only would not embarrass him but it might do some good. Lochner reported Wilson's favorable comments to Liebold, and then went to New York, where he was an honored guest at a Madison Square Garden peace rally.

On February 3 the United States broke relations with Germany. On the fifth, Ford was in Washington keeping a longstanding appointment with Secretary of the Navy Daniels. Afterward, he told reporters that he did not believe war would come but if it did he would put his factory at the government's disposal and would "operate without one cent of profit." When asked how he squared this position with his pacifism, he reminded the reporters, "I never said I would not do all for the country that I was able to do." And he guilelessly added, "I am a pacifist but I want to say to you that a pacifist is the hardest fighter you ever saw when he finally is crowded into taking up arms."

The next afternoon, Wednesday, February 7, in response to a summons from Liebold, Lochner arrived at the Ford Long Island office. His morning paper told him he could no longer hope for a "satisfactory solution" from Ford, but he was not prepared to learn Ford was closing down all of his peace activities as of March 1 and Lochner's services were ended as of that day. Liebold gave Lochner three weeks' terminal pay, expenses for one more day and railroad fare to his hometown and told him to return the next day with a statement of the conference's obligations.

At their next meeting, Liebold and Plantiff looked at Lochner's estimates and ignored them. Lochner expressed his outrage that his European colleagues, to whom he had promised long-term assignments on Ford's written say-so, should be "summarily dismissed as if they were so many hired men." Most of them were professors, he said, and would be without income until fall. Liebold dismissed Lochner's argument that European public opinion had to be developed in support of international government on the grounds that it would be disloyal for Ford to support peace work when his country was about to go to war, and he squelched Lochner's further protests with the irrefutable statement that since neither he nor Plantiff agreed with Lochner there was nothing to discuss. In a frail attempt to preserve his own integrity in the absence of Ford's "moral responsibility," Lochner refused to resign and insisted that he be fired.

Later, Liebold, apparently expecting Lochner to behave dishonorably, telegraphed the White House to say that Louis Lochner no longer spoke for Henry Ford. A week later, Lochner received his notice in the mail along with a legalistic "party-of-the-first-part-party-of-the-second-part" agreement for his signature in which, for the sum of $922.26, he forfeited all future claims, agreed that for three years he would protect Ford against all damages and claims past and future, and he promised to return his letters of authority. The ending had been very quick and very callous, and characteristic of both Ford and Liebold, the one to be absent during unpleasantries and the other to act without compassion or grace.

Liebold handled Lochner with dispatch; it took Robert Buelow, Plantiff's Danish aide, three months to settle affairs in Europe, because all claims had to be referred to Plantiff and Liebold. And the latter, overbearing and unscrupulous, insisted that Lochner had only limited authority to make agreements, none of which were binding for more than thirty days. The Europeans countered with their copies of Ford's letter giving Lochner "full authority" to negotiate in his name with no stipulations, though in arguing for their past-due honoraria, they suffered the indignity of explaining they were not "beggars, that they only wanted fair treatment."

At last Buelow, his patience at an end after weeks of shoddy and dilatory maneuvers by the home office, wrote Plantiff that Liebold was not competent to judge matters properly and an "international newspaper scandal was not far off." Even that advice was ignored, as was Leipnik's threat to attach Ford's property in England if he was not given $5,000 severance pay ("I would see him in hell first," Plantiff explained). But when de Jong threatened to sue for the $2,000 promised the Central Organization for a Durable Peace and produced the documents to prove his case, Liebold was faced with a viable lawsuit and was forced to act honorably, cursing Lochner while he did so for having put him in such an unbearable position. Even so, when the books were finally closed on the expedition and conference (more or less—just but futile claims continued for many years), there was still a balance of $15,000 in the neutral-conference account Ford had set up with Plantiff. In all, Ford spent just over half a million dollars on his peace venture.

Hardly expecting three months of haggling, the first reaction of the European delegates to Ford's withdrawal was both gracious and grateful. Most regretted his decision but understood his reasons and thanked him for his "generous unwearing support and encouragement." However, Mrs. Clark was chastised for having "publicitisitis" by an already disgruntled delegate because she sent a brief notice to the papers announcing the end of Ford's subsidy and the expected continuance of the work through the offices of other peace organizations. It was Scherrer-Fuellemann who had insisted on emphasizing the continuance of the work, contending that "we have not worked as appointees of Mr. Ford, but we are free and independent men who embarked on the idea for peace mediation" which they still intended to pursue. How anyone could "suddenly" consider the neutral conference "Mr. Ford's private property" was "so basically false and so unworthy" it was beyond his comprehension, which showed how much the Swiss delegate had missed by not arriving in Stockholm until August. Other members also regretted a public tolling of the death knell, though, as de Jong remarked, the conference unfortunately had been defunct as an organized body for six months.

Certainly at the time Liebold's cable arrived instructing Mrs. Clark "to incur no further obligations" no members had recently proposed any obligations worth incurring. Lie had arranged a lecture series on postwar international government in Norway, but all of his experts were still working on their position papers and Wigforss was waiting for articles from Russian and Dutch journalists for *Post Bellum*, having received thus far only a chapter from a book by H. G. Wells.

While Buelow was settling accounts in Stockholm, Ada Morse Clark was taking care of conference affairs in The Hague—handling financial affairs without money and mollifying the delegates, two impossible tasks she did with competence. Operating under the Ford Motor Company "a-woman-is-only-a-woman-but-a-good-cigar-is-a-smoke" management policy, Liebold sent the agency dealer in Amsterdam to The Hague to run the conference office, but he only ran up a handsome hotel bill while re-affirming Mrs. Clark's increasingly desperate pleas for funds.

In mid-December, when Lochner had spoken of going with Leipnik to America, his sibylic secretary wrote her former employer, Dr. Jordan, "I am filled with despair at the thought that Mr. Lochner may make another flying trip to America in January, for in connection with this Ford Movement tragic possibilities have always been in order—the unexpected *always happens*." There was much going on about her that made her anxious, including the fact that she was the last American member of the expedition still abroad. She remained at her post, however, partly out of loyalty to Lochner, who had asked her to see that everyone was treated fairly, but principally because she had no money to buy her ticket home. Her anxiety grew with each day's delay, but it was not until mid-May that she was able to leave. And then the prospect of a calm spring-time crossing on a neutral passenger liner was shattered just as she was about to board the ship.

Wanting to preserve the conference records and mindful that all documents were contraband, Mrs. Clark had very carefully instructed Elli Eriksson, the adventuresome Finnish girl she had kept on as an office aide, to pack the files in two sturdy boxes. These Mrs. Clark took to Amsterdam, where she said she saw them buried beneath the floor of the Ford agency's garage. Not until Mrs. Clark was about to go through customs in Rotterdam did Elli bother to mention she had done some independent repacking—Lochner's papers were in Mrs. Clark's trunk, and Mrs. Clark's winter underwear was being preserved for posterity under the garage floor. The befuddled woman confessed all to the authorities and was permitted to sail, but she did not rest easy until she greeted Lochner in New York. Her anxiety was not frivolous; the American chargé d'affaires in The Hague had cabled the State Department that she was bringing home two trunks full of Lochner's conversations with the enemy.

Henry Ford left the pacifists' lives as abruptly as he had entered them, and, following the custom of the eagle on the United States seal during wartime, turned his gaze from the olive branch to the arrows of battle. Once again he publicly pledged his fortune to a worthy cause, that of manufacturing war materiel. In making his announcement while the country was still at peace he was merely jumping the gun, so to speak, on an earlier promise that he would defend the country against its enemies. Quite likely, Ford's skewed understanding of his peacemaking experience had convinced him that war with Europe was inevitable. On the second anniversary of the peace expedition's sailing, Ford was heard to say that the European "aristocracy and capitalists" had begun the war, that France would have invaded Belgium had Germany not done so and that the kaiser had wanted to make peace but his advisers kept Ford from arranging it. Asked, then, if his peace mission had been at all effective, he had replied, "No, I don't think so, because the men who are making money out of this war didn't want peace then any more than they do now."

Those pacifists who had been associated with the peace venture to the very end took Ford's sudden withdrawal philosophically once they finally realized their patron had never understood the continuous-mediation idea nor been committed to the long-term educative peace propaganda he had endorsed so outspokenly in the press. Even so, Lochner had hoped to the eleventh hour that "old Henry" would come through. Completely exhausted by the emotional ups and downs he had endured in the three weeks since his return and gravely shamed by the brutish treatment accorded his European colleagues, Lochner went home to Milwaukee after his dismissal and "into the family garage for an overhaul." After expressing his sorrow to the European delegates and vainly asking socially minded millionaires to maintain the conference's educative program abroad, the forlorn idealist joyfully heeded the call of his peace friends to join the revived Emergency Peace Federation's whirlwind campaign to halt the drift toward war.

Emily Balch shared her younger friend's distress and shame. "Isn't Mr. Ford's fall from grace more complete and sudden than you expected," she wrote Jane Addams. "The hideous disgrace to America in Europe only ones who were there can fully realize."

Not unexpectedly, Julia Grace Wales was fatalistic. Having seen Wilson's "straightforward and unequivocal Utopianism, . . . the shrewdest diplomacy," fail, she accepted Ford's withdrawal as "inevitable" after the break in German relations, and was content that the neutral conference had contributed a "mite . . . to a great world movement." Miss Addams, dismissed Ford as "certainly past finding out" and not worthy of further comment. Characteristically, neither she nor the other radical pacifists wasted their time or energy in bitterness; after defeat it was their habit to resume the struggle. "I suppose we ought to be grateful," she judiciously concluded, "for having had a chance for fifteen months."

The Ford Peace Expedition might have been "a splendid failure" had it not been for the self-important, ignorant participants, newspaper reporter

William Bullitt concluded when he returned home. Every day for nearly six weeks he had pilloried and defamed the peace pilgrims, mocked their motives and jeeringly condemned their intent. And yet—the night that President Wilson and the American Commission to Negotiate Peace sailed for Europe and the Versailles conference, State Department specialist William Bullitt sat in his cabin on the *George Washington*, writing in his diary: "Three years ago today exactly I sailed from New York with another gentleman who planned to bring eternal peace to the world. I am sure that the Ford Party was a more wonderful experience than this will ever be; and tonight I wonder if Wilson will be much more successful than Ford."

Afterwards

Afew days after Henry Ford disbanded his peace mission in early February and pledged his fortune to the war effort he sailed on a Caribbean cruise in his recently purchased steam yacht (which he sold to the government at cost when he returned). Ernest Liebold spent a more modest vacation in the restful mountains of North Carolina.

There was no such respite for Lochner, Miss Balch, Miss Addams, David Starr Jordan, William Jennings Bryan and other pacifists who, under the umbrella of the reactivated Emergency Peace Federation, joined other Ford expedition members to keep the country at peace. From a downtown New York office building and a small Washington office they organized mass meetings, protest demonstrations and parades and vigorously lobbied for mediation and a national referendum on a declaration of war. Women of the Lower East Side, wrapped in shawls, came to their offices with their pennies for the peace compaign, and thousands attended their rallies. However, so strong was the prewar hysteria that mobs of "patriots" stormed the pacifists' meetings and, in Washington, smeared their office door with yellow paint, raided their headquarters and stomped on the corrugated-iron roof of their meeting hall.

Their battle lost when President Wilson asked Congress to declare war in April, a few of the peacemakers continued to act upon their pacifist beliefs, others quietly abstained from further protest, and the remainder joined other Ford expedition members in the war action. Two of the nationally prominent members of this last group who were too old to fight in the trenches fought the war in the government's propaganda agency, the Committee on Public Information (the Creel Committee).

After leaving the Ford expedition in mid-journey, S. S. McClure stayed

abroad until his unfortunate contract with the pro-German *Evening Mail*
expired and then wrote a book for the Creel Committee explaining why
the United States could not make peace with Germany. After the war he
obtained press credentials to cover the Versailles conference, where he
deeply felt his lack of importance. During the 1920s McClure regained—
and soon lost through incompetence—the editorship of his magazine. He
then spent two years in Italy studying fascism, which he lavishly praised
at home. For twenty more years, until he died in 1949, McClure continued to live the life of a has-been, his days centered on his small New York
midtown hotel, his club and the automat. When the National Institute of
Arts and Letters honored him in 1944, most people thought he had been
dead for years.

"If we had no more than the memorable ten days in Germany," Judge
Ben Lindsey wrote on his way home from Europe in February 1916, "our
trip with whatever penalties may come from being with the Peace Pilgrimage was worth it all." What made the days memorable was the royal
treatment the Lindseys received from high German officials to whom
they talked of their proposed Ford-financed relief work for war orphans.
(They soon learned that Ford's interest in this work as well as his promise
to help Lindsey financially in his next election had been nothing more
than idle chatter.)

Not until early November 1917, after the country had been at war for
six months, did Lindsey decide that "the only way to deal with Germany
is to deal with a defeated Germany," and he went abroad as a special
representative of the Committee on Public Information. In a letter home
the former member of the peace expedition described his few days under
shelling in the trenches as "the most wonderful time of our lives."

While Sam McClure suffered the pain of oblivion in the 1920s, Ben
Lindsey endured the trials of a nonconformist at a time when reactionary
forces were zealously guarding the nation's morals. Lindsey's books, *The
Revolt of Modern Youth* and *Companionate Marriage*, which had been
inspired by his experience on the bench, made him a highly publicized
spokesman for the Jazz Age. Though Lindsey carefully explained he had
proposed only that couples agree to a renewable contract for one-year
childless marriages, that birth control be legalized and that sex-education
courses be taught in the public schools, he was accused of advocating free
love and driven from Denver by a "storm of intolerance." A part of that
storm was the successful disbarment proceedings (later nullified) brought
by his longtime political and business enemies, who were joined by the
Ku Klux Klan. The Lindseys settled in Los Angeles and in 1934 the judge

was elected to the superior court, where he turned his jurisdiction into a laboratory for solving social ills and protecting the rights of the unprotected, until his death in 1943.

The Reverend Charles Aked never recovered from what he called "the greatest mistake of my life." After returning from the neutral conference he lectured for a while, but his pacifistic remarks antagonized his audience and his erratic behavior alarmed his booking agents. Unable to realize that he himself was largely responsible for the decline in his popularity, the minister wrote bitterly to Judge Lindsey of "the evil results of our participation in that absurd and disgusting expedition." After the armistice Aked was called to a pulpit in Kansas City, and in 1924 he moved to Los Angeles, where he organized the All Souls Church, holding Sunday services in a succession of movie theaters and then in the Ambassador Hotel. Aked was crippled by arthritis in his later years and continued his preaching from a wheelchair. When he died in 1941, at the age of seventy-seven, his earlier fame and glory were long gone and his perfunctory obituary was only seven lines long.

Aked's fellow ministers on the peace ship, Jenkin Lloyd Jones and Arthur Weatherly, also suffered for their pacifist beliefs during the war, the latter losing his pulpit for his strict adherence to his ideals. In Lincoln, Nebraska, Weatherly watched his Unitarian congregation dwindle week by week, but refused to resign because he had done nothing wrong. At last, in January 1918, he wrote his old friend Dr. Jones, "In the language of the poets 'the jig is up' "—he had been forced from his pulpit by the monied members of his congregation, who refused to pay his salary. Even after the war ended, the gentle pastor continued to pay a price for his integrity as he moved from one church to another when his right to speak his views was denied. At last, in 1929, the superpatriotic passions of his Lincoln church having dissipated, Weatherly was asked to return, and his itinerant days were over.

"We are both whistling in the dark and reaching out for fellowship," Dr. Jones wrote in response to Weatherly's accounts of his troubles. One of the several ways Jones reached out was by purposefully joining every organization he knew of that opposed wartime restrictions on civil liberties, including the Woman's Peace Party (though he disliked "sex organizations"). Still, though Jones fancied he was "living the life of a hermit," he knew that his thirty-seven years in Chicago, his loyal congregation and his editorial control of his magazine, *Unity*, which he opened to all war protesters, made him almost impregnable. Almost. In 1918 the spring and summer issues of *Unity* were suppressed by the Post Office Department for allegedly violating the Espionage Act. In September, when the ban was withdrawn, the elderly Jones lay on his deathbed, his strength depleted by his aggressive "war against war."

Jane Addams, listening to the eulogies during Dr. Jones's memorial service, was disturbed by an obvious omission. "I do not like to have this meeting go by without one reference to the Ford ship," she said, when it came her turn to speak, and then praised the neutral conference as "a gallant attempt." Miss Addams paid a high personal price for acting on her pacifist principles during the war, when public hysteria was exacerbated by newspapers that distinguished between "pacifists" and "patriots." The ostracism, which was expected, and the tailing by secret agents, which was not, were especially difficult for her to endure after so many years of international acclaim. Hoping to regain some of her lost public approbation, she worked "enthusiastically and conscientiously" for the wartime Food Administration.

After the war, as president of the Women's International League for Peace and Freedom (WILPF), the successor to the International Committee of Women for Permanent Peace, Miss Addams found that her internationalism, for which she had been previously honored, now made her the butt of the superpatriots who looked upon pacifism and disarmament as Bolshevist ploys designed to weaken the nation's defenses preparatory to a Russian invasion.* (The Daughters of the American Revolution had already revoked Jane Addams's honorary membership, which, when she received it in 1900, she supposed "had been for life," but then realized "was apparently only for good behavior.") The red-baiting by her countrymen notwithstanding, it was for her leadership in WILPF that Miss Addams was awarded the Nobel peace prize in 1931, four years before her death.

Jane Addams lost her prestige during the war; Emily Balch, her substitute at the neutral conference, lost her profession. Instead of spending her sabbatical year with the neutral conference in Stockholm, Professor Balch spent it in New York working with other pacifists. Realizing that her radical peace activities would embarrass Wellesley after the United States entered the war, Miss Balch asked for another year's leave through the

* In June 1920 the Lusk committee of the New York state senate, which had been charged with investigating seditious activities, published its four-volume report, entitled *Revolutionary Radicalism: Its History, Purpose and Tactics with an Exposition and Discussion of the Steps Being Taken and Required to Curb It*. The volumes, which received national attention, accused Jane Addams, Lillian Wald, David Starr Jordan, Rosika Schwimmer, Louis Lochner and many other peaceworkers of subversive activities and were not publicly discredited until the end of the decade.

spring of 1918, when, as it happened, her contract expired. She had, like Miss Addams, modified her pacifism as the war continued by working for the Food Administration, but Wellesley, where Miss Balch had taught for twenty-two years, refused to reappoint her. Though terribly distressed, Miss Balch would not sue the college for denying her academic freedom, as her friends urged, and instead celebrated losing her job at the age of fifty-two by boldly smoking her first cigarette. She worked as an editorial writer on *The Nation* and then was appointed international secretary of WILPF at its founding meeting in 1919. Miss Balch served officially for only a few years, but devoted the rest of her long and active life to the international peace movement. In 1937 she succeeded Jane Addams as honorary international president of WILPF, and in 1946 she was awarded the Nobel peace prize.

Louis Lochner spent the war years as the executive secretary of the People's Council for Democracy and Terms of Peace, which had modeled itself on the Russian provisional government and which was intent on ensuring a democratic prosecution of the war and the implementation of an early peace. In 1919 Lochner helped organize the Federated Press, an international labor news service, and continued working for it after he moved to Germany following his wife's death during the postwar influenza epidemic. In 1924, he joined the Associated Press's Berlin bureau, becoming its chief four years later. Lochner worked in Germany for twenty-one years, enjoying the cultural flowering of the Weimar Republic—"a musician's paradise"—and enduring the restrictions of the Nazi regime. In 1939 he won the Pulitzer prize for distinguished foreign reporting. Following Germany's declaration of war in 1941, Lochner returned to the United States, where he worked as a reporter and radio commentator before returning to Europe for a brief tour as war correspondent. He retired from the Associated Press in 1946 and wrote a number of books and undertook several short-term assignments for the State Department, the United Nations and the Lutheran church. In his last years, Lochner and his German-born second wife returned to Germany, where he died in 1975 at the age of eighty-seven.

If the principal participants in the Ford peace mission had lined up in 1917 with the absolute pacifists toward the front and those favoring America's entry into the war toward the rear, Julia Grace Wales would have stood toward the end of the line. After Germany's resumption of unrestricted submarine war she thought the United States could not maintain "neutrality without treason to internationalism"—"peace-at-any-price" had not been the neutral conference's operating principle.

Miss Wales continued teaching at the University of Wisconsin, where she received her doctorate in 1926, until her retirement after the Second World War. She died in 1957 at the age of seventy-six in her Canadian home near Montreal.

Several peace expedition members worked for the Ford Motor Company shortly after they returned, but none stayed long. Isidor Caesar, the zealous stenographer, worked in the Long Island plant until he realized, after writing "Swanee" with George Gershwin, that he could make more money as songwriter Irving Caesar. Joseph Jefferson O'Neill, of the New York *World*, headed the Ford news bureau during Ford's lawsuit against the Chicago *Tribune*.

Gaston Plantiff, who served as a one-man employment agency for former members, also acted as the conduit through which Henry Ford received the supply of goods he had personally ordered from Captain Hempel, of the *Oscar II*. The association was equally beneficial to the three men—Hempel received a deluxe Model T with nickel-plated trimmings, Ford had a case of the *Oscar*'s hair tonic, barrels of Danish potatoes and a fur coat, and Plantiff met his future wife in Hempel's home.

Gaston Plantiff was promoted twice while he was monetary caretaker of the peace mission, and he continued to prosper until alcoholism started him on a downhill slide. Ford sent Plantiff to a sanatorium for what turned out to be a short-lived cure. When the Eastern district manager continued to backslide, Ford had him fired, though he never lost his affection for his protégé. Plantiff continued writing to the Fords from his estate in the Adirondacks, where he died in 1934, five years after leaving the company.

Dean Samuel Marquis returned to Detroit in January 1916, having faithfully fulfilled his promise to Mrs. Ford to guard her husband, and took up his duties as head of the Ford company's Sociological Department. His reign over Ford's paternalistic dominion, making certain that employees conformed to what an interviewer called "a smug clergyman's morality," was cut short in 1921 by an executive rival whom Ford supported. Before returning to the service of his church, Marquis wrote a perceptive book-length character study of Ford, designed to destroy the myth of his former employer as a gentle-hearted humanitarian. Ford was as much a malefactor as a benefactor, Marquis wrote, prominent but not eminent. Henry Ford tried to buy up every copy of the book.

In the few years after Ford's return from Christiania he sustained a series of setbacks that either thwarted his will or publicly humiliated him.

In quick succession he was mocked for his pacifist enterprise, criticized for having his son deferred in the draft, fraudulently deprived of a seat in the United States Senate, grievously disappointed when Wilson's plans for disarmament and joining the League of Nations were defeated, sued by his stockholders and gravely humiliated in a libel action. Thus frustrated and shamed, and lacking the wisdom to see beyond the immediate action, his arrogance increased, his spontaneous generosity diminished, his stubbornness turned to meanness and every flaw in his character hardened.

Ford ran for the Senate in 1917 only after President Wilson explained he needed a Democratic majority to pass his postwar international program; and he lost by a surprisingly small margin if one considers he campaigned mostly in absentia in a traditionally Republican state. His platform pledge not to make a penny from the war had great voter appeal, especially after his return of $130,000 to the government was widely publicized.* Ford's victorious opponent, Truman H. Newberry, violated Michigan primary laws, but it was two years before the senator was persuaded to resign, largely on the evidence Ford's agents had collected.

In the fall of 1916, John and Horace Dodge, stockholders in the Ford Motor Company, filed suit against Henry Ford, the majority holder, to make him distribute a portion of the previous year's $60,000,000 *net* profit, most of which Ford planned to use on a new plant. After the "parasites"—as Ford termed his partners whose initial investment made them wealthy—won the suit in December 1918, Ford borrowed heavily from banks and secretly bought all the outstanding company stock.

Ford's next trial, in May 1919, he brought upon himself. In a June 1916 editorial, the Chicago *Tribune* called Ford an "anarchist" and an "ignorant idealist" for allegedly telling his employees they would be fired if they answered the National Guard's call to protect the border against Mexican attack, and Ford sued. His lawyer contended that it was not anarchistic to oppose Wilson's preparedness policy, that many senators and congressmen had done so. The defendant's lawyers argued that Ford was an anarchist because he wanted to fly an international peace flag over his factory and an ignorant idealist because of his many published statements on peace and war.

---

* Ford never made another payment, though his total war profit has been estimated at over $925,000, partly because he did not want government representatives examining his books, as they would have done, and partly because by the time the amount was determined in 1924 he had lost interest in his campaign promise.

The auto manufacturer was on the stand for a harrowing eight days, mostly listening to the defense attorney read his 1915 and 1916 interviews and signed articles, including, of course, Delavigne's peace stories, the anti-preparedness advertisements and even a letter sent to members of Congress written by the expedition over his signature calling munitions makers "patriots for profit." (Ford was permitted to read the articles aloud, but knowing himself to be a slow reader he avoided the embarrassing ordeal, once blaming his hay fever and another time the absence of his eyeglasses.)

Despite intensive questioning, bordering on harassment and entrapment, during which the manufacturer said the American Revolution occurred in 1812 and Benedict Arnold was a writer, Ford repeatedly refused to acknowledge that he was an ignorant idealist. His peace actions were not intended to educate his countrymen, he said, but "to cause them to think," and he was not against preparedness but "over-preparedness." Asked to expound his ideology, he expressed himself in simple-minded maxims. Finally, Ford bluntly told defense counsel that if he ever needed to know anything about American history he "could find a man to tell me in five minutes all about it." Ford won the case and was awarded costs and six cents in damages by the small-town jury of his peers.

The humiliation endured in the *Tribune* trial, the failure of the peace expedition, the successful opposition to world disarmament and all his other frustrations and disappointments Ford blamed on a cabal of international Jewish bankers who were bent on world domination. (His sister insisted he was not anti-Semitic; "he called all the moneylenders of the world 'Jews,'" she explained, "regardless of their religion.") Henry Ford's belief was common to rural people who grew up in a cultural and political atmosphere that was fearful of the unfamiliar and suspicious of what could not be easily understood. Farmers found it comforting to blame "dark forces"—Wall Street "moneylenders" and "international Jewish bankers"—for the perplexities of a world market that kept them under constant obligation to their banks. Or Ford may have heard of an alleged international Jewish conspiracy during his early years in Detroit from the businessmen and bankers who backed his early companies.

In the midst of his tribulations, Ford bought a country weekly, the Dearborn *Independent*, in order to combat his denigrators and educate public opinion with "unbiased news." In May 1920, Ford and Liebold began publishing a series of articles, "The International Jew: The World's Problem," which included an analysis of "The Protocols of the

Wise Men of Zion."* The entire series lasted several years and was published in pamphlet and book form for worldwide distribution. (In support
of the claim of the "Protocols" that Jews corrupted national institutions in
order to dominate them, an article contended that jazz was a Jewish
creation because "the mush, the slush, the sly suggestion, the abandoned
sensuousness of sliding notes are of Jewish origin.")

Associates on the weekly said Ford had wanted only "to expose an
unethical practice to the good Jews" so "they could clean it up," and was
nonplused by the public disapprobation and the boycott of the Model T
that his educational endeavor had caused. However, Ford did not stop
publishing anti-Semitic misinformation until he was sued by Aaron
Sapiro, a Chicago attorney and agricultural economist, for defamation of
character following a series of articles which accused Sapiro of master-
minding a Jewish takeover of farm cooperatives. At the trial, in 1927, the
editor of the Dearborn *Independent* took all the blame. Ford had a minor
automobile accident the night before he was to testify and, while the trial
was delayed, settled out of court, agreeing to make a public apology, to
never publish anti-Semitic articles again and to withdraw the book *The
International Jew* from circulation. The settlement was politic, if not
sincere; it kept Ford out of the witness box and it appeased at least some
of the public who otherwise might have boycotted his brand-new Model
A. At the same time and for the same reason Ford made a similar settlement with Herman Bernstein, a member of the peace expedition.

In 1921, on the sixth anniversary of the peace ship's sailing, Ford had
told reporters he was publishing his "International Jew" series because
"two very prominent Jews" on the *Oscar II* had convinced him that Jews
"controlled the world through control of gold and that the Jew, and no
one but the Jew, could stop the war." A few weeks later he identified
Herman Bernstein as one of the Jews, possibly because Bernstein, a foreign correspondent and editor of short-lived Jewish newspapers, had just
exposed the "Protocols" in his book *The History of a Lie*. Bernstein's
demands for retraction were regarded as publicity-seeking diversions by
Ford and Liebold until Bernstein sued Ford for $200,000 and successfully

---

* The spurious "Protocols of the Wise Men of Zion" were purported to be a plan
to rule the world by destroying Christian civilization through controlling its institutions which was allegedly devised by a group of Jews and freemasons in Basel, Switzerland, in 1897. According to the *Encyclopaedia Britannica* the "Protocols" were first
published in Russia in 1903 and by 1920 had been translated into most Western languages. They were proved to be forgeries, successively, by a London *Times* correspondent in 1921, by Russian historians a few years later and by a group of American
historians in 1942.

attached $65,000 of Ford Motor Company assets. Bernstein withdrew the suit two years later after Ford personally apologized and made a monetary settlement.

In the aftermath of the *Independent* adventure the only one who suffered permanent serious damage was Ernest Liebold, "the spark plug in the Jewish series." His influence with Ford and in the company declined sharply until he was finally fired in the early 1940s. Liebold never doubted the authenticity of the "Protocols," never considered a single penny of the $5,000,000 he encouraged Ford to spend on his publishing venture wasted (though he thought the half-million spent on the peace mission an unredeemed loss—"an uneconomical thing that was useless in the long run") and never stopped believing in an ongoing international Jewish conspiracy to control the world. He also never stopped believing that Adolf Hitler had "retired" all German-Jewish government employees with a "pension."

Henry Ford's other public-education programs of the 1920s and 1930s were conducted for the most part in his two-hundred-acre back yard and were as dogmatically and stubbornly undertaken as his Dearborn *Independent* "course of instruction." Most notable was his attempt in the early 1920s to recreate the past, which, largely thanks to his own efforts, was literally going by the roadside.

For his public museum Ford collected, or more precisely accumulated, as many nineteenth-century artifacts that enshrined farm and village life as he and his dealers could find. In the buildings and displays in Greenfield Village, next door to the museum, Ford memorialized his heroes—Edison, Burroughs, Burbank and McGuffey—and certain historic American institutions. He reprinted and distributed thousands of copies of the McGuffey *Readers*, and when the city of Philadelphia would not sell him Independence Hall, he built a replica. He did all this to combat the moral degeneration caused by jazz, cigarettes and the radio, hoping he could win over the many farm families who were using the Model T not to go to church but to go past it on their way to the movies. And he did it to teach everyone that history was not military heroes and battles and books but tools and commonplace handmade objects.

Also, at that time, Ford's behavior in the factory became increasingly ruthless and remote. He no longer walked among the men or worked with his department heads. When the bank loans he had negotiated to buy out his stockholders came due during the postwar recession, instead of extending them, he dumped automobiles on his dealers, forcing many of them to borrow or declare bankruptcy. Often his executives were fired during their vacations or learned they were no longer working for the company when they found their office furniture smashed or their offices empty. Within a few years many of the company's best workers were gone, some having quit after finding Ford's capriciousness, business methods and factory practices intolerable. Ford trusted few men and never his son, Edsel, an imaginative and greatly admired administrator whom Ford systematically destroyed by rejecting his ideas and thwarting his authority. By the early 1930s Ford had turned the running of the company over to unscrupulous lieutenants and was spending more and more of his time with the children who attended the Greenfield Village schools.

At this time, when the third volume of his autobiography, inappositely entitled *Moving Forward*, appeared, Ford had lost something of his standing as a humanitarian and public benefactor. By the end of the decade his use of violent anti-union tactics, refusal to abide by government procedures, endorsement of Father Coughlin and Gerald L. K. Smith, employment of Fritz Kuhn, the American Nazi Bund leader, and acceptance of a decoration from the German government had destroyed his reputation. Ford was still, however, a public figure, regularly interviewed by reporters, whom he told, on one occasion, that milk was healthy until it was touched by air. (He instructed his houseman to soak razor blades in kerosene and water because the solution made a fine hair tonic, a conclusion he reached after observing the healthy heads of hair on oilfield workers.)

Ford officially retired from the company in 1938 at age seventy-five, after a slight stroke, but resumed its leadership after his son's death in 1943. Two years later, following a visit from the Truman committee investigating war contracts, Ford was forced to resign, and his grandson, released from the navy, took over. In his eighty-third year, after a pleasant day visiting the factory and Greenfield Village, he died. There had been a power failure in the Fair Lane electric plant, and Henry Ford left the world as he had entered it, by candlelight.

From the time of the neutral conference until his death, Henry Ford had publicly expressed himself on world peace. In the early 1920s he had acknowledged the need for armed forces and had hoped "the world will learn a better way some day" when the economic conditions which caused all wars, namely the greed of munitions makers and financiers, were altered. He had continued to believe that if every man had a tractor to till his land and an automobile to take him to visit his neighbors, no one would respond to politicians' appeals to arms or permit the manufacture of war materiel. "The war financiers got theirs," he remarked in 1927.

"What did the rest of the world get?" And in one of his jotbooks he noted: "War is created by a crowd of people who have no country or home except Hadies [*sic*] Hell and live in every country." The revelations of the 1934 Senate investigation of the armaments and banking industries during the World War confirmed his impressions. Ford continued to believe in an international conspiracy of Jewish bankers, which he held responsible for all his woes and the world's troubles, including the belligerent actions of Hitler and Mussolini. Shortly before the Second World War began, Ford commented that Hitler, whom he admired, had at least put the Germans to work.

As the prospect of another world war developed, Ford maintained a strict isolationist position. In September 1940 he joined his friend Charles Lindbergh as a member of the America First Committee. A few months later, in his message to the celebrants of the twenty-fifth anniversary of the peace expedition, he remarked, "Nobody wins and everybody loses in every war," and early in 1941 he expressed the hope that Europe would battle itself to devastation, leaving the United States to devise a durable world peace. But Ford had already indicated that his company would aid the nation defensively, and during the war the Ford plants produced a great variety of armaments.

In his annual birthday statements in the 1940s Ford predicted that Tennyson's prophecy of a parliament of man would be realized after the war in a world federation of nations that would include a United States of Europe having one nationality, one currency and one economy.

Henry Ford never renounced nor regretted his attempt to end the First World War. The condemnation and ridicule he received from the press and his business associates never altered his conviction that he had done what was right, and the evidence indicates he was always proud of his courageous deed. A quarter of his *Who's Who* entry, which was written under his guidance, is devoted to the peace expedition, and in his personal permanent exhibit in the Ford Museum he had displayed a flag supposed to have been flown on the *Oscar II*, a telegram sent under his name to Jane Addams while the expedition was underway and the unused leather briefcase with his name etched on the silver catch above "Neutral Conference for Continuous Mediation," embossed in gold.

Rosika Schwimmer returned to Hungary in the fall of 1916, and in the spring went to Switzerland as the special representative of Count Karolyi, a Socialist member of parliament who was working for an early and conciliatory peace. In the tumult following the downfall of the Hapsburgs, Karolyi formed a new government, and in mid-November 1918 he appointed Mme Schwimmer minister to Switzerland, the first woman to hold a high-ranking diplomatic position in modern times. Within a month she was asked to resign. Though her spending of state funds on a fur coat, an expensive apartment and a chauffeured limousine—all of which she argued were status symbols necessary to a diplomat—was not appreciated by her countrymen, many of whom were starving, Rosika Schwimmer's downfall was not entirely her own fault. She had the misfortune of serving in a country that did not recognize women's political rights, and her usefulness as a conduit to the Americans at the Versailles peace conference was nullified by the anti-Semitic American minister at Berne, who would neither see her nor forward her messages.

Shortly after her return to Hungary the Karolyi government was overthrown by Bela Kun's Bolshevik regime, which was succeeded in August 1919 by the repressive rightist White Terror. Along with others, Mme Schwimmer was harassed as a pacifist and feminist, persecuted as a Jew and denied a passport. In January 1920 she was smuggled by boat to Vienna, where she spent the next months regaining her health, having contracted diabetes, and trying through her American friends to emigrate to the United States.

Rosika Schwimmer returned to America in August 1921, confident that she could resume her remunerative prewar lecture career, despite her friends' explicit warnings that pacifism was then equated with Bolshevism, and Bolshevism was used by many "to cover every sin in the calendar." The country was suffering from a xenophobic public hysteria, largely caused by postwar disillusionment and recession. Superpatriots, who castigated and often libeled anyone who advocated weakening the nation's defenses, condemned Mme Schwimmer as a wartime German spy, a leading member of the Bolshevik Hungarian government and a founder of the pro-disarmament Women's International League for Peace and Freedom. Others thought her the source of Ford's anti-Semitism. Mme Schwimmer told her American colleagues in WILPF to exonerate her, but they were also under attack and advised her to wait with them in silence until times changed.

Rosika Schwimmer's application for citizenship in the mid-1920s was a red flag to the self-styled patriotic organizations as well as the Bureau of Naturalization, and resulted finally in a landmark Supreme Court minority opinion by Justice Oliver Wendell Holmes. The cause célèbre began with her answer on an information sheet to the question "If necessary, are you willing to take up arms in defense of this country?" She replied: "I would not take up arms personally." On other occasions she had also said that she was "an uncompromising pacifist for whom even Jane Addams is not enough of a pacifist. I am an absolute atheist. I have no sense of nationalism, only a cosmic consciousness of belonging to the human family." During her hearing the judge asked her whether she would shoot an enemy soldier to protect an American officer. She said she would not, and her petition was denied. The denial, however, was reversed on appeal in June 1928, the presiding judge remarking that no American law compelled women to bear arms and adding that in any case, "A petitioner's rights are not to be determined by putting conundrums to her."

On the same day that the district court was ordered to grant Mme Schwimmer citizenship, she won a $17,000 judgment against Fred Marvin, the head of Key Men of America, who libeled her in an article based on the Lusk committee's report. (It is of some parenthetical interest that while suing for libel, Mme Schwimmer slandered Louis Lochner in court, saying she would not be surprised to learn he was a communist because he had "betrayed the whole peace ship.")

Warned of her application and alleged background by patriotic organizations several years earlier, the Labor Department was determined that Mme Schwimmer should not become a citizen and asked the Justice Department to take the case to the Supreme Court. When advised that there were no grounds for review—Mme Schwimmer after all was a fifty-year-old woman unlikely to be asked to defend the country with arms—the Labor Department insisted that her qualifying the terms under which she would be naturalized was "the most vital question" that had ever arisen in a naturalization proceeding, and the Justice Department capitulated.

The government argued that Mme Schwimmer, "a clever woman," had admitted she would try to influence the citizenry to adopt her pacifistic views during wartime, and that, having "no sense of nationalism" and not being "attached to the principles" of the Constitution she was not a proper candidate for naturalization. Mme Schwimmer's attorney argued that only men are legally required to bear arms in defense of the country.

Rosika Schwimmer lost her battle for citizenship in June 1929 in a 6–3 Supreme Court decision. In his eloquent dissent, Justice Holmes, an anti-pacifist, said Mme Schwimmer was obviously more than ordinarily desirable as a citizen of the United States and should not be condemned because some of her beliefs "might excite popular prejudice." The most significant principle of the Constitution, he wrote, "is the principle of free thought—not free thought for those who agree with us but freedom for the thought that we hate."

Mme Schwimmer's two-year struggle at least brought a temporary change in her fortunes and a lasting change in the feelings of some of the peace expedition's metropolitan reporters. She published a book of Hungarian folk tales, had several lecture and radio engagements and received considerable favorable newspaper publicity. In a left-handed compliment, Charles P. Stewart, the United Press representative on the *Oscar II*, said Mme Schwimmer was "queer" for thinking up the peace expedition but not "queer enough to be deemed ineligible for American citizenship." Elmer Davis (later a courageous voice of integrity and wit during the dark McCarthy era of the early 1950s) also gave her active support, and the *New York Times*, referring to the recent Kellogg-Briand pact outlawing war, observed that "it is a little anomalous that a country which has renounced war should exclude from its citizenship a person whose chief offense is her opposition to war."

Still, Mme Schwimmer had been so arrogant, demanding, wheedling and self-righteous that once again she had alienated some of those most sympathetic to her plight. Arthur Garfield Hays, of the national board of the American Civil Liberties Union, who represented her privately in the Marvin case on a contingency basis, had difficulty collecting his fee. Mme Schwimmer thanked the American Civil Liberties Union as the only organization that had supported her, but when they asked her to pay part of her legal costs, as she had promised if she won the Marvin case, she reneged. The ACLU helped Mme Schwimmer because it considered the government's denying citizenship to a pacifist a significant civil-liberties issue, but toward the end both the Chicago branch, which organized the effort because Mme Schwimmer filed for naturalization there, and the national board were quite out of patience with their client. In an exchange of letters the leader of the Chicago branch wrote Forrest Bailey of the national office that it was difficult to raise money locally for the Supreme Court suit because "this community is completely tired of the lady" and that for his part he wished the government would "deport" her and his wife wished it would "drown" her, to which Bailey replied, "For my part, I hope she chokes."

When Rosika Schwimmer's name was publicly mentioned in the 1920s she was invariably identified as the woman who had persuaded Henry Ford to finance the peace expedition, and often she was accused of swindling him and of inspiring his anti-Semitism, which allegedly resulted from her falsely promising him the pacifists would be welcomed in Europe. After Ford made his public apologies in 1927 to Aaron Sapiro, Herman Bernstein and the Jewish people, Rosika Schwimmer, whom Ford had never accused of anything, demanded public vindication. To her lawyers in the Marvin case, Liebold explained that Ford could not deny that Mme Schwimmer had swindled him because she never handled any money nor that she had duped him because he always believed her sincere. The reply did not satisfy Mme Schwimmer, and she went public.

In a very long letter, which she released to the press, Mme Schwimmer told Ford that until she had met him her life "had always been rich in accomplishment," she had earned more money than any other woman her age in her profession and her integrity had never been challenged. "It was my good fortune to arouse and fire the youth of many nations. The whole world was my field." During the peace expedition, however, she was accused of using Ford's money for her own aggrandizement, "the clumsiest assertions about my relations with men in general and about my intentions towards you, were whispered" and "the press of America reverberated with fantastic and highly abusive stories" about her. The "overwork, worry and disillusionment" gave her diabetes, and when she returned to America after the war, she was repeatedly blamed as the cause of Ford's anti-Semitism, causing her to be ostracized by Gentile and Jew and blacklisted by the editors and club leaders who had previously welcomed her. Ford had publicly apologized to others damaged by his anti-Semitic attacks but never to her, and she ended her communication with a four-part instruction explaining "exactly what I want from you": the interview she had been trying to get for ten years during which she would present documentary evidence proving his associates destroyed the peace mission, a public refutation of these associates' lies about her, testimony on her behalf in the Marvin trial and the loan of all his peace-expedition records so she could write "the authentic story" of the expedition and conference.

Her brash move brought only a request for depositions for Ford's signature and a letter from Liebold praising her "laudable aims" and asking for "definite facts and details" so Ford could right the wrongs committed against her. She thought the reply unsatisfactory, and in the early 1930s, with another lawsuit pending, she tried again to have Ford repudiate false charges made against her. Mme Schwimmer was suing Upton Sinclair for writing in his book on the movie producer William Fox that at the time of the peace expedition she said Ford was backing the endeavor because she had promised him it would increase automobile sales. Both her lawsuit and the appeal to Ford failed.

At last, in 1936, Ernest Liebold agreed to see her in Detroit. She had written from her hospital bed in Chicago that she was writing a book on the expedition and wanted to talk with him to confirm her negative impression of his role in the endeavor. It may be Liebold saw her because he had little else to do by then, or perhaps he was curious to meet her. In any event he regretted the encounter because she accused him "of everything under the sun" and said that had he not obstructed the peace mission Ford would have subsidized her for life in gratitude for her "immeasurable service."

The next year Ford was asked three times to contribute to a "World Peace Prize" for Mme Schwimmer (to be "at least" the equivalent of the Nobel peace prize, which a new generation of disciples had tried unsuccessfully to get for her), and when he offered only his good wishes, he was asked to give her a separate monetary award.

In 1938, on his seventy-fifth birthday, Henry Ford heard from Mme Schwimmer again. Reminding him that once before she had offered him a once-in-a-lifetime opportunity, she wrote she was now giving him a birthday present rarer than any other he would receive: the opportunity of halting the coming European war by financing (not participating in) a world constitutional convention. Her idea of a world government, comprising a democratic, nonmilitary federation of nations similar to the United States, was like the one Ford later endorsed, but though she wrote him several more times, he never replied. Her last communication with Ford was a letter to Henry Ford II, after the war and after the old secretariat had been purged, asking him to present her scheme personally to his grandfather.

Rosika Schwimmer spent the twenty years between the Supreme Court decision and her death helping European refugees—Albert Einstein called her his "saving angel"; hoping to establish a world center for women's archives, but alienating those who supported the project; propagandizing her world government program, which she and Lola Maverick Lloyd had developed together; gathering materials for her regrettably but not surprisingly biased account of her pacifist activities; and trying to resume her career as a writer and lecturer. From time to time she published an article or was invited to speak, but from the day she returned to the United States in 1921 until her death she was, as she wrote a friend, forced to live on charity.

That Rosika Schwimmer had to be a financial burden is perhaps problematical. She might have obtained employment as a translator or tutor in the nine languages she could read instead of sharing her sister's income or permitting Lola Lloyd, and then Mrs. Lloyd's children, to support her. (Count Karolyi, for example, the president of the Hungarian republic Mme Schwimmer served as minister, lost his multimillion-dollar fortune when he was exiled and had to pawn his clothing to buy food until he found work as a journalist and his wife got a job as a dressmaker's model.) Apparently Mme Schwimmer never thought of earning her living except as a speaker, writer or organizer, and Mrs. Lloyd was always proud to aid her principled and courageous friend.

Rosika Schwimmer lived for many years in New York City, with her sister and her assistant, in a comfortable apartment amid a clutter of newspaper clippings, pamphlets, books and papers. In the hallway hung a large framed photograph of the *Oscar II* as it sailed from Hoboken bearing the peace expedition, and in a living-room corner lay the notorious black bag that had held the alleged secret documents. Until her death in 1948, Mme Schwimmer actively directed her acolytes, her strength of will as undiminished as her belief that the world had been unjustly deprived of her exceptional abilities and the realization of her ideas.

The Ford Peace Expedition and the Neutral Conference for Continuous Mediation lived on in the memories, and in a few cases the marriages, of its participants. It was also preserved in their letters, diaries and scrapbooks and in the records, stored and long forgotten, of the Ford Motor Company and the War Department. In the 1920s a dramatization of the undertaking was staged in Europe, and the expedition was occasionally mentioned in newspapers, especially during interviews and on anniversaries.

The surprise wedding ceremony on the *Oscar II* that began the peace pilgrimage was followed by four more marriages among members who met their mates either on board or during the European sojourn. Gaston Plantiff was introduced to his future wife in Copenhagen by the ship's captain, publisher Ben Huebsch met his Swedish wife at a soirée in Mme Schwimmer's drawing room, and two students, Elinor Ryan of Ohio State University and Walter Hixenbaugh of the University of Nebraska, met on board ship. In 1941, Mrs. Hixenbaugh wrote Henry Ford "to acknowledge the debt I and my family owe you," and to tell him that "one of our time-worn family jokes is that our sons are the only *tangible* results of the Ford Peace Expedition."

In 1927, an Associated Press dispatch from Berlin, almost certainly written by Lochner, reported that a German drama, "The Peace Ship," told the story of how the well-intentioned Henry Ford, beset by angry voyagers who had been aroused by the newspapermen and Dean Marquis, was reinspired by a fanatical female peace advocate who later died in Norway. After learning that the United States had gone to war and that

Ford's afterthoughts on the peace expedition, and other jotbook notations, in his own hand (Courtesy of Henry Ford Museum).

he had been castigated in the American press, Ford returned home, a bitterly disillusioned man.

The neutral-conference records and the two-hundred-book library left in Stockholm were shipped to the Ford Motor Company in Dearborn after the war, where they were stored and soon forgotten. The material in the Hague headquarters which Mrs. Clark consigned to the Ford agency manager in Amsterdam had rather a bizarre, not to say fateful, career. Mrs. Clark's report that she saw the papers buried in the agency garage may not be entirely true—in writing of her adventures she tended to favor a dramatic construction of events when a truthful one was too prosaic—and it is possible that the Ford agent only told her he would bury the papers.* Plantiff tried to recover the material after the war, but the agent was so evasive Plantiff thought he must have been a United States spy. Whatever the case, in 1917 someone understood to be "the secretary of Mr. Ford's peace expedition" turned over the records to the Military Intelligence Division of the War Department's Office of Chief of Staff. In June 1918 an officer, suspecting that "there may have been some German wolves among the sheep," ordered the material analyzed. However, the staff was insufficient to explore the material's counterespionage potential, and an installment of fourteen boxes was sent by diplomatic pouch to the United States for review. The rest of the material, including seven volumes of news clippings, was probably sent later and lost at sea. In Washington, Captain Schmuck of military intelligence found nothing more damning in the documents than a Berlin librarian's request for neutral-conference publications, and the material was turned over to the War College for forwarding to Henry Ford. Instead it languished in the army's files for thirty-six years until it was routinely transferred to the Library of Congress.

Someone somewhere remembered the anniversary of the sailing of the peace ship every year for at least fifty years. Often the remembrance was no more than a letter to Henry Ford from one of the participants thanking him for the opportunity.

On the twenty-fifth anniversary in December 1940, the Overseas Press Club celebrated the event with a luncheon honoring the "survivors." The gathering had been planned as a satiric look backward, but the sudden death of one of the reporters and telegrams from Elmer Davis and William Bullitt, both of whom were in the hospital, and most especially the

---

* Mrs. Clark did take her office keys home with her and later donated them to a Second World War scrap drive, an ironic happenstance, reminiscent of the fate of the *Oscar II*, which a Scottish shipyard sold as scrap iron to the Japanese in the 1930s.

presence of Sam McClure and Mme Schwimmer, solemnized the occasion. Only a line from Henry Ford's congratulatory telegram—that he had "learned a great deal on that voyage"—brought laughter. Mme Schwimmer, after correcting the preceding speakers and announcing she was about to enter the hospital, talked of her attempts to stop the war that culminated in the expedition. Denying she had ever acted improperly or censored the reporters' dispatches, and accusing others of spying on her and of kidnapping Ford in Christiania, she declared the expedition a "perfect success" and the neutral conference a failure, destroyed by Ford's associates, who still were thwarting his superhuman efforts to communicate with her. Though Mme Schwimmer's comments were marked with bitterness, those present knew the difficult path her life had taken and, as the Ford company's man-on-the-spot reported, she "presented her case very favorably and left everyone convinced of her sincerity and of the good intentions of the entire venture."

Henry Ford's observation in his message to the celebrants, "that with the oceans full of warships we can afford to remember that there was once a 'peace ship,' " was virtually the only reminder at the luncheon that the world was again at war. The Detroit *Free Press*, however, in a nostalgic editorial, "A Vain but Noble Voyage," remarked: "We do not laugh any more, nor joke, when that unique argosy is mentioned. We mourn rather the disappearance of times when men could still believe in progress in human enlightenment, and thought that even those in the throes of bloodlust might be led to reason."

This revised view of the peace expedition became quite popular. It reflected a reevaluation during the 1930s of the causes of the First World War as the failure of the League of Nations to restrain military attack and the Senate war-profits investigations made it evident that the war had not made the world safe for democracy, nor possibly had it even been fought for that purpose.

In 1935, on the twentieth anniversary of the sailing, a New York newspaper blamed the war on those who "lust for power," and mocked "the realists, the great statesmen, the hard-headed editors and men of affairs" who had been "engaged in saving civilization with bayonets." The editorial praised the "unselfishness" and "nobility of purpose" of the expedition and lamented the "scorn and derision it had received." That same year, Walter Millis, in *The Road to War*, still critical of the pacifists' impetuosity, wrote that "today one can only admire the soundness of their instinct and the courage of their convictions." The journalists, he thought, destroyed "one of the few really generous and rational impulses of those insane years." And in *The Shape of Things to Come*, H. G. Wells wrote a nine-page summary of the peace mission, which he called, in a rather great stretch for metaphor, "a tin-whistle solo by way of overture to the complex orchestrations of human motive in the great struggle for human unity that lay ahead."

Merle Curti, a historian of the American peace movement, commended the neutral conference for coordinating neutral peace activities in Europe and for its effective propaganda which popularized liberal peace terms in the belligerent countries. Journalist Mark Sullivan, in a chapter-length review of the expedition, praised it with faint damning as "in essence a not necessarily infeasible idea" whose expectations had been grossly and viciously distorted by the press, and Ray Stannard Baker, still believing the poorly organized effort deserved the ridicule it had received, conceded that "the fundamental concept behind the movement represented a large body of earnest, if naive, American opinion."

In general, Miss Balch's belief in September 1916 that the conference was "making history if only on the 'little drops of water' principle" and Dr. Jenkin Lloyd Jones's view that the peace venture would be remembered for "what it attempted, not by what it achieved," represented the thinking of the delegates at that time and in later years as well. The participants also regretted that the hastily organized and circuslike European tour overshadowed the more serious and significant conference, and many thought that had Jane Addams gone with them she would have restrained Mme Schwimmer and the reporters.

In his vindication of the peace mission, *America's Don Quixote: Henry Ford's Attempt to Save Europe*, published in 1924, Louis Lochner lambasted the reporters and Ford and claimed that the conference persuaded the neutral governments of the need for an official mediating body, made European government leaders more responsive to their constituents' demand for peace and kept Sweden from entering the war. Twenty-six years later, he remarked, "I still think that we might have gotten somewhere with the mission if we had been given more time." Julia Grace Wales ruminated on the experiment after the Second World War and concluded that the expedition was "an idealistic gesture" that had outlived its "absurdities." The "idea of Continuous Mediation as a method of applying moral force," she thought, had been made "commonplace" in the United Nations. (Neither Miss Balch, Miss Wales nor Lochner had misgivings about entering the Second World War, regarding Nazism as an intolerable menace.)

The Ford expedition had its intended educative effect upon the student members, who maintained lifelong commitments to internationalism thereafter. In later years, William H. Draper praised the peace attempt for focusing the world's attention on the possibility of peace, and Paul Fussell valued it as the people's spokesman, acting in place of the diplomats who had tried neither to prevent the war nor to end it.

The European delegates' long-range view of the effectiveness of the peace move ranged from Mme Bakker van Bosse's comment, fifty years after the event, that "Mr. Ford might just as well have flung the money he spent on the conference into the sea," to Mayor Lindhagen's kindly thought that the expedition "brought a light in the dark, and it was a witness that it is not the dance around the dollar that is the symbol of the New World."

The Neutral Conference for Continuous Mediation did not end the First World War, it did not inspire neutral governments to mediate the conflict, nor were its services officially sought by the belligerent powers. The Versailles peace conference did not write the just and durable peace treaty the neutral conference had proposed, and the League of Nations did not function as the neutral conference had hoped it would. That is not to say, however, that the pacifists' action was foolhardy or without purpose and accomplishment, or that it was unable to achieve its major goal because the idea of neutral mediation was bizarre, the peace plan irresponsible or even the timing premature.

For some years before 1915, official neutral mediation had been an internationally recognized diplomatic procedure and since the outbreak of the war one that had been strongly advocated by liberal peaceworkers. The Ford pacifists realized the efficacy of official recognition and hoped that the neutral nations would take over their effort once its popularity and usefulness had been proved. They had acted only because the diplomats would not, and in so doing, had created a new expression of the peace movement which was the very essence of Progressive political idealism.

The peace program which the conference submitted to the warring nations was a distillation of previous plans, but the first one publicized among the warring peoples in their newspapers. The principles in the Appeal to the Belligerents were embodied in Wilson's peace plan of 1918, which was later the basis for the Central Powers' surrender. The mass meetings, publications and other propaganda techniques the conference used to publicize the political, social and economic problems that needed to be resolved and to educate the people to the necessity for a postwar international peacekeeping organization helped accomplish in Europe what President Wilson tried to accomplish later in the United States. The conference's Committee on Constructive Peace, whose members prepared position papers in collaboration with the Central Organization for a Durable Peace, was similar in intent and membership to The Inquiry, the group of scholars and lawyers that President Wilson had assembled in the fall of 1917 to define the United States' positions at the peace table.

The expedition extravaganza and the neutral conference were criticized at the time by peaceworkers who believed in the neutral mediation plan— and by those who did not—for killing the prospects for any future dignified and informed mediatory effort. However, other unofficial peacemakers saw belligerent government leaders, often secretly, all during the war, and the reason they failed had to do with the belligerents and not the Ford peaceworkers.

Pro-Ally sympathizers also criticized the peace mission for its bad timing. But the Ford pacifists' action to end the war was predicated on an equitable peace that recognized the needs and rights of peoples and disregarded the gains or losses incurred on the battlefield. If a neutral intervention might have affected the course of the war, then it was President Wilson and the Congress whose timing was off. Had Wilson publicly offered mediation two years before he did, as Secretary of State Bryan and other mediationists had urged, and had Wilson and Congress pursued a policy of strict neutrality (which would have prohibited unsecured foreign loans, restricted American travel on belligerent ships and challenged the blockade), then the war would probably have been shortened and the victors' need for economic and national vengeance at the peace table greatly reduced. Certainly by the time Wilson forsook his policy of secret negotiations and proclaimed the neutral nations' right to know the belligerents' war aims, no belligerent could accede to mediation and survive.

Speculation aside, one incontrovertible condition obtained that prevented the success of any mediatory effort unaccompanied by the capability of affecting the course on the battlefield. Throughout the conflict both sides lacked the will for reconciliation or the desire for a negotiated peace.

Even so, the Ford Peace Expedition and the Neutral Conference for Continuous Mediation if only by their existence made a significant contribution. Unquestionably the attempt in personal diplomacy would have been better served if Henry Ford had had better judgment, greater knowledge and more patience; if Rosika Schwimmer had had more regard for the truth, less certainty of her own infallibility and a willing-ness to confine herself to her assigned role of expert adviser; if the news-papers had behaved responsibly; if the peace mission's leaders had selected the American members more carefully, explained the purpose of the mis-sion more fully and provided for the selection of European delegates who at the least believed in the purpose of the conference; and, finally, if Ford's surrogates had not regarded the gathering as a time-wasting, money-losing branch of the Ford Motor Company.

However, the participants' ineptitude and errors, pride and frailties, do not dispel the nobility of their purpose or the virtue and validity of their action. Out of the determination of a Canadian college instructor and a Hungarian feminist, out of the conviction of social reformers who saw their perfecting world threatened by the outbreak of war and out of the chance encounter one summer afternoon between an anti-war millionaire and a newspaper reporter, citizens of six neutral nations participated in an unofficial and public diplomatic attempt to formulate a lasting people's peace. Despite the ridicule and condemnation of the press and the dis-approval of their friends, despite the self-destructive intrigue and or-ganizational squabbles, the peaceworkers persisted in trying to end the war and preparing the world for a compassionate peace treaty.

The neutral conference was unique in providing the means for hun-dreds of thousands of neutral citizens to ask their governments to mediate the war, for trying to transmit the ideas and hopes of opinion leaders of one side to the other and for conducting an educative propaganda cam-paign that informed many Europeans of the reasons for open diplomatic negotiations and a league of nations. These were its short-range achieve-ments; of more lasting significance was the deed itself. Never before had a gathering of neutral citizens, acting in the name of the people, asked warring nations to stop fighting and settle their disputes, not on the basis of military conquest, but according to the principles of justice and hu-manity.

The Ford pacifists had courage, imagination and, as Miss Wales later wrote, "sentiments that will persist in the human heart and continue to demand fulfillment in a better world order." The continuance of these sentiments, of the aspirations of those who dream of what the world should be, was, she thought, the main hope for the survival of mankind.

Chronology

Rosika Schwimmer's call for neutral mediation, London	*August 1914*
Woman's Peace Party founded in Washington, D.C.	*January 10, 1915*
Julia Grace Wales's plan for neutral mediation conference presented at Emergency Peace Federation, Chicago	*February 27–28, 1915*
International Congress of Women, The Hague	*April 28–May 1, 1915*
Women's conference envoys visit European government leaders	*Spring 1915*
Henry Ford pledges his fortune to peace	*August 21, 1915*
Henry Ford announces he will send peace expedition to Europe	*November 24, 1915*
Voyage of the peace ship *Oscar II*	*December 4–19, 1915*
Ford Peace Expedition disbands at The Hague	*January 15, 1916*
Neutral Conference for Continuous Mediation begins	*February 28, 1916*
Appeal to neutral governments and parliaments	*March 1916*
Appeal to belligerent governments, parliaments and peoples	*April 1916*
Neutral conference ends first phase	*April 20, 1916*
Central Committee of the neutral conference convenes	*May 16, 1916*
Ford Peace Commission announced	*December 20, 1916*
Henry Ford ends peace activity	*February 7, 1917*

Participants in the Ford Peace Expedition

DELEGATES

On *Oscar II*

Charles F. Aked
John D. Barry
Herman Bernstein
Andrew J. Bethea
Lloyd Bingham
Katherine Devereux Blake
Inez Milholland Boissevain
Willis G. Conant
Grace DeGraff
Louise Eberle
Harry Carroll Evans
Mary Fels
Henry Ford
Mary Fulton Gibbons
Louis B. Hanna
Robert H. Henry
Elizabeth Hitchcock
Florence Holbrook
Frederick H. Holt
Lilian S. Holt
Theodore A. Hostetler
Benjamin W. Huebsch
Edith Lloyd Jones (Mrs. Jenkin)

Estelle Jones (Mrs. John)
Jenkin Lloyd Jones
John E. Jones
Judson King
M. Stuart Levussove
Benjamin B. Lindsey
Henrietta Brevoort Lindsey (Mrs. Benjamin)
Lola Maverick Lloyd
Ralph MacBrayne
Samuel S. McClure
Aino Malmberg
Samuel S. Marquis
Lars P. Nelson
Henrietta A. Neuhaus
Alice L. Park
Helen Ring Robinson
Lou Rogers
May Wright Sewall
Julia Grace Wales
Mary W. Watkins
Arthur L. Weatherly

On *Frederick VIII*

Gina Smith Campbell
Virginia Lynch
Frederick L. Seely
P. Monroe Smock, representing the
  governor of Idaho

Hampton A. Steele, representing the
  governor of Kansas
Frank O. Van Galder
W. M. Wright, representing the
  governor of Arkansas

PRESS

On *Oscar II*

REPORTERS

Daniel Bidwell, Connecticut Valley and Massachusetts newspapers
Meyer C. Block, New York *Jewish Morning Journal*
Marian Bowlan, Chicago *Journal*
Berton Braley, *Collier's Magazine*
William C. Bullitt, Philadelphia *Public-Ledger*
Jesse Cleveland, Spartanburg (S.C.) *Herald*
Charles P. Cushing, *Leslie's Weekly*
Elmer Davis, New York *Times*
John English, Boston *Traveler*
Edward F. Graham, Brooklyn *Times*
Arthur Edmund Hartzell, New York *Sun*
Jacob Hirsch (Burnet Hershey), Brooklyn *Eagle*
Mary Alden Hopkins, free-lance magazine writer
Elon H. Jessup, *Harper's Weekly*
Benjamin Karr, Cleveland *Leader and News*
Florence L. Lattimore, *Survey Magazine*
Grace Druitt Latus, Pittsburgh *Dispatch*
Alice Lawton, New York *Sun*
Paul S. Leahy, St. Louis *Globe Democrat*
William Prescott Lecky, Richmond *Journal*
Helen Bullitt Lowry, International News Service
Ernest L. Mandel, *Amerikai M. Nepszava*
Theophilus E. Montgomery, Union Press Association
Sara Moore, New York *Evening Mail* and United Press
Gertrude Steinman Oliphant, free-lance magazine writer
Joseph Jefferson O'Neill, New York *World*
Theodore N. Pockman, New York *Tribune*
George Edward V. Riis, Brooklyn *Eagle*
Boris Schumacher, *Jewish Daily News* (New York)
Alexander W. Schulz, *Staats Zeitung* (New York)
Lella Faye Secor, Seattle *Post-Intelligencer* and Everett *Herald*
Thomas Seltzer, *The Call* (New York)
James R. Stanton, New Jersey newspapers
Thomas W. Steep, Associated Press

Charles P. Stewart, United Press
Maxwell H. Swain, New York *Herald*, Sunday department
Miriam Teichner, New York *Globe and Commercial Advertiser* and Detroit
  News
Carolyn Wilson, Chicago *Tribune*
Marion Weinstein, *The Day* (New York)
Hiram N. Wheeler, Quincy, Illinois, no publication specified

PHOTOGRAPHERS

Nelson Edwards, International News Service
Burt G. Phillips, Underwood & Underwood
Lawrence J. Darmour, Mutual Film Corporation
Joseph Rucker, Universal Moving Picture Company

On *Frederick VIII*

Robert Doman, *Morning Telegraph* (New York)
George F. Milton, Chattanooga *News*

STUDENTS

On *Oscar II*

Edward A. Adams, University of Iowa Law School
Katrina M. Brewster, Vassar College
William Henry Draper, Jr., New York University
Edgar T. Fell, Johns Hopkins University
John P. Frazee, University of Wisconsin
Paul L. Fussell, University of California, Berkeley
Ora Guessford, Drake University
Elizabeth B. Hall, Barnard College
Walter A. Hixenbaugh, Jr., University of Nebraska
Donald R. Jones, University of Pennsylvania
Lee E. Joslyn, Jr., University of Michigan
Emil H. Molthan, Williams College
Will F. Noble, University of Nebraska
Marion Penn, Purdue University, 1911
Charles F. Phillips, Columbia University School of Journalism
Kenneth W. Pringle, University of Kansas
Nellie M. Reeder, Wellesley College graduate school
Elinor C. Ryan, Ohio State University
Christian A. Sorensen, University of Nebraska Law School, 1915
Harrison McClure Thomas, Princeton University
Samuel A. Trufant, Jr., Tulane University
Earl W. Tucker, Syracuse University, M.A.
Bruce S. Williams, Johns Hopkins University

Francis Stirling Wilson, Dartmouth College
George Wythe, University of Texas graduate school

On *Frederick VIII*

Mark M. Abbott, University of Minnesota
John Neal Campbell, Vanderbilt University
Bruce Davis, Yale University
Roberta Du Bose, Vanderbilt University
Helen Heberling, University of Iowa
Albert J. Hettinger, Jr., Stanford University
David Ernest Hudson, University of Missouri and Harvard Law School
Emil Hurja, University of Washington (also representing governor of Alaska)
Lue C. Lozier, University of Missouri
Donald M. Love, Oberlin College
Lamar Tooze, University of Oregon

SCHWIMMER-LOCHNER STAFF

Ada Morse Clark
Elli Eriksson
Ellis O. Jones
Alfred M. Kliefoth
Katherine Leckie
Louis P. Lochner

Lewis A. Maverick
Rosika Schwimmer
Rebecca Shelly
Nora Smitheman
Elizabeth C. Watson

FORD STAFF

George Bowman
J. Van Devanter Crisp
Ray Dahlinger
James D. Golden

Lenore Kauffman
Robert S. Neely
Gaston Plantiff

BUSINESS AND CLERICAL STAFF

Thomas J. Baldwin
Robert B. Bermann
Annie G. Black
Neil J. Burkinshaw
Isidor (Irving) Caesar
Harry C. Coffman
Salvatore Demma
Lida H. Dorian
Bertrand Emerson, Jr.
Richard B. English
Jacob Greenberg

Skelton C. Higgins
Charles Hill
Rexford L. Holmes
Laura Jaker
Axel Johnson
Mary Martin
Christian Raven
Emmett C. Scott
Mary P. Seaford
Alvin A. Seldner
Fred E. Sniffen

Julia S. Stevens
Van Arsdale B. Turner

Marie L. Wisinger

SUPERNUMERARIES

On *Oscar II*

George Beadle
Marion Rubincam Braley (Mrs. Berton)
Samuel H. Clark
Dorothea Hansen
Mrs. Axel Johnson

Jessie Lloyd
Mary Lloyd
William Bross Lloyd, Jr.
Frieda Mylecraine
Alice B. Stewart (Mrs. Charles P.)
Emily May Swain (Mrs. Maxwell H.)

On *Frederick VIII*

Mr. Latus and two children

Delegates to the Neutral Conference for Continuous Mediation and Members of the Committee of Twelve (Central Committee)

Some of those listed below served on the conference only during its first period from the end of February until April 20, some served only on the Committee of Twelve (Central Committee), some served on both, and some, though elected, served on neither.

Names marked with an asterisk were members of the Committee of Twelve; names marked with a dagger never came to Stockholm.

DENMARK

Dr. Helene Berg (b. 1869), inspector of domestic economy in state schools; member of board, Dansk Kvindesamfund; Socialist candidate for the Riksdag.

†*Severin Christensen* (b. 1867), pediatrician; vice chairman, Danish Henry George Foundation.

Henni Forchhammer (b. 1863), president, Danish National Council of Women; later delegate to League of Nations.

Olaf Forchhammer (b. 1881), civil engineer; president, Copenhagen Peace Society; president, Bureau for Maintaining International Cooperation; member, International Council, Central Organization for a Durable Peace.

†*Eline Hansen* (b. 1859), supervisor in domestic science, Danish state high schools; president, Danish Woman's Suffrage Association; member, Danish National Council of Women; member, Dutch Anti-War Society (NAOR).

*Kristoffer Markvard Klausen, member and first vice president, Riksdag Folketing; member, executive committee, Danish Socialist Party.

A. F. Lamm (b. 1856), retired banker; former president, Copenhagen municipality.

†*Johanne Petersen-Norup*, bank employee; president, Young People's Association (PAX); member, executive board, Danish Peace Society; member, Dutch Anti-War Society (NAOR); member, International Committee of Women for Permanent Peace.

Carl Thalbitzer (b. 1876), editor and publisher, *Finanstidende* (*Financial Times*).

*Dr. Frederick Weis (b. 1871), professor of plant physiology, Royal Agricultural Academy; member, executive committee, Liberal Party.

THE NETHERLANDS

Dr. C. Bakker van Bosse (b. 1884), lawyer; member, executive council, Dutch Anti-War Society (NAOR); member, Netherlands National Council of Women; president, Hague section, Woman Suffrage Society.

*Benjamin de Jong van Beek en Donk (b. 1881), lawyer; general secretary, Dutch Anti-War Society (NAOR); member, international council, Central Organization for a Durable Peace; member, International League of Peace and Liberty.

Clasine A. de Jong van Beek en Donk-Kluyver (b. 1884), vice president, Netherlands National Council of Women; Dutch member, Peace and Arbitration Committee, International Council of Women; assistant secretary, Dutch Anti-War Society (NAOR); later delegate to the League of Nations and United Nations.

A. F. L. Faubel (b. 1865), retired colonel, Dutch colonial army; leader, Free Masons' Society, Dutch East Indies.

Jan Feith (b. 1874), journalist and editor, *Algemeen Handelsblad*; executive member, Dutch Literary Union.

Jan Hoejenbos (b. 1875), town councilor, The Hague; member, executive board, Socialists' Labor Party; assistant director, Central Bank of Labor Party; member, Dutch Anti-War Society (NAOR).

†*Cor Ramondt-Hirschmann*, president, Dutch section, International Committee of Women for Permanent Peace; first secretary, Netherlands National Council of Women.

†*Dr. Romeyn*, town councilor, The Hague; secretary, government housing council.

†*H. van Biema-Hijmans*, president, Netherlands National Council of Women; president, Society for Mutual Protection of Women; member, International Council, Central Organization for a Durable Peace.

Dr. van Leuwen, member of parliament, Social Democratic Party; town councilor, Utrecht.

Dr. Jan Wolterbeek Muller, professor of international law, University of Rotterdam.

NORWAY

†*Carl Bonnevie* (b. 1881), lawyer; former member of parliament; member, executive committee, Norway's Peace Union.

Dr. Nikolaus Gjelsvik (b. 1866), lawyer; professor, international law, University of Christiania; legal adviser, Nobel Institute; president, Norske Samlaget.

†*Eugene Hanssen*, pastor; member, commission on social welfare.

†*Herman Lie* (b. 1869), assessor, town court, Christiania.

Mikael Henriksen Lie (b. 1873), lecturer in science of law, University of Christiania; legal adviser, Nobel Institute.

Haakon Loeken (b. 1859), attorney-general, Christiania; former mayor, Trondheim; member, executive committee, Radical Party; member, Central Organization for a Durable Peace; later president, Norwegian League of Peace.

Frederikke Moerck, principal and owner, private school; former president, Woman Teacher's Union; member, executive board, Norwegian Woman Suffrage Association.

†*Fanny Schnelle*, member, municipal council, Bergen; member, International Council of Women.

†*Thomas Segelcke-Thrap* (b. 1861), lawyer; director, Christiania county jail; prison reformer.

Ole Solnoerdal (b. 1869), lawyer; general secretary, Radical Party; labor-management arbitrator.

SWEDEN

Johan Bergmann (b. 1864), archaelogist and historian; president, International Bureau, Temperance Movement; professor, Stockholm high school.

Johan Hansson (b. 1879), manager, Swedish Co-operative Publishing House.

Anna Kleman, former president, Woman's Suffrage Society; president, Swedish section, International Committee of Women for Permanent Peace.

Dr. Hans Larsson (b. 1862), professor of philosophy, University of Lund.

Anna Lindhagen (b. 1850), municipal inspector, childrens' institutions; president, local branch, National Woman Suffrage Association; member, International Committee of Women for Permanent Peace.

Carl Lindhagen (b. 1860), life-mayor, Stockholm; member of parliament, Socialist Party; president, Swedish Peace Society.

†*Oesten Unden* (b. 1886), professor of international relations, University of Lund; later delegate to League of Nations.

Ernst Johannes Wigforss (b. 1881), lecturer in economics, University of Lund; former town councilor, Lund; later Swedish minister of finance.

†*Carl Winberg*, member of parliament.

Frida Steenhof (b. 1865), social reformer.

SWITZERLAND

†*Dr. Franz Bucher-Heller*, president, Lucerne court; president, Swiss Peace Society.

†*Dr. Auguste Henri Forel* (b. 1848), professor emeritus, international law.

Marguerite Gobat, librarian, International Peace Bureau; general secretary, World Union of Women for Peace; member, International Committee of Women for Permanent Peace; daughter of Albert Gobat, winner of Nobel peace prize, 1902.

**Dr. Emil Goettisheim*, lawyer; member of Swiss National Council (parliament); judge, federal court.

†*Hermann Greulich* (b. 1842), member, Swiss National Council; member, International Council, Central Organization for a Durable Peace.

Clara Ragaz, president, Association of Swiss Women's Societies; member, executive board, International Committee of Women for Permanent Peace; member, Consumer's League.

†*Dr. William Rappard* (b. 1883), professor, political economy, University of Geneva; later Swiss delegate to the League of Nations.

Dr. Albert Schenk (b. 1873), professor of French, Berne High School; secretary, Swiss Association for a Durable Peace.

**Joseph Scherrer-Fuellemann* (b. 1847), lawyer; member, Swiss National Council; president, Swiss section, Interparliamentary Union; member, International Council, Central Organization for a Durable Peace.

Dr. Fritz Studer, lawyer; member, Swiss National Council; president, Swiss Socialist Party; member, International Council, Central Organization for a Durable Peace.

Ernest Troesch (b. 1879), professor of German, Berne High School; secretary, Swiss Association for the Study of the Bases of a Durable Peace Treaty; town councilor, Berne.

UNITED STATES

†Jane Addams
*Charles F. Aked
*Emily Greene Balch
John Barry
†William Jennings Bryan

†Mary Fels
†Henry Ford
†Jenkin Lloyd Jones
†George W. Kirchwey
†Benjamin B. Lindsey

Notes

Abbreviations:

Acc. Accession
ACLU American Civil Liberties Union
BT Boston *Traveler*
CPS Chicago Peace Society
DAB *Dictionary of American Biography*
DFP Detroit *Free Press*
DI *Dearborn Independent*
FA Ford Archives
FO Foreign Office
FPE Ford Peace Expedition
FPP Ford Peace Plan
ICW International Congress of Women
ICWPP International Committee of Women for Permanent Peace

IWSA International Woman Suffrage Association
MS Manuscript
NA National Archives
NAW Notable American Women
NCCM Neutral Conference for Continuous Mediation
NY New York
NYT New York *Times*
PPL Philadelphia *Public Ledger*
RG Record Group
SCPC Swarthmore College Peace Collection
SFB San Francisco *Bulletin*
TC Transfer carton
WPP Woman's Peace Party

Sources not listed in the bibliography are cited in full below.

CHAPTER 1: *"The best people"*

The most useful works on the history of the American peace movement, before and during the Progressive Era, are Beales, *History of Peace*; Curti, *Peace or War*; Herman, *Eleven Against War*; Marchand, *American Peace Movement*; Osgood, *Ideals and Self-Interest*; Patterson, *Towards a Warless World*; and Whitney, *American Peace Society*.

1 On the pier: *NYT*, Dec. 5, 1915, 1:1; NY *Herald*, Dec. 5, 1915, 1:1; NY *World*, Dec. 5, 1915; and Dailey, "Henry Ford—And the Others," 313–17.
1 "The boys out of the trenches": NY *Tribune*, Nov. 25, 1915.
3 "Conservative lawyers": Frederic C. Howe, quoted in Millis, *Road to War*, 8.
4 Bryan: *Memoirs*, 386–88; Bryan to Harry Walker, January 20, 1915, Bryan Papers, LC.
4 "The enormous impetus": *Proceedings*, National Arbitration and Peace Congress, (NY, 1907), 39.

4 Demand for armaments: Arthur H. Dadman, *Book*, Fourth American Peace Congress, (St. Louis, 1913), 234–38, 242.

4 Jordan: "The Impossible War," 67.

4–5 Bartholdt: *Book*, Fourth American Peace Congress, 101–6.

5 "The peace movement": Holt to Archibald E. Stevenson, June 9, 1920, Hamilton Holt Papers, Rollins College Library, Winter Park, Florida.

5 Europe, 1914: Fay, *Origins of the World War*, 1:39–47; Millis, *End to Arms*, 41–43.

5 "That such an archaic": Addams, *Peace and Bread*, 1.

5–6 American reaction to war: May, *End of American Innocence*, 361; Link, *Struggle for Neutrality*, 6–7.

5 Belligerent government replies: *Papers . . . Foreign Relations, 1914, Supplement*, 48–50, 60–61, 79–80.

6 Peace parade: *NYT*, Aug. 30, 1914.

6 "The greatest neutral": Lochner, *Don Quixote* draft MS, Lochner Papers.

CHAPTER 2: *The Idea: "A stroke of genius"*

Biographical information on participants in the Ford Peace Expedition mentioned in this and other chapters is also in "Henry Ford's Peace Expedition Who's Who," Christiania and Copenhagen editions, 1915, Box 11, FPP Papers.

7 Lloyd George interview: Lloyd George, *War Memoirs*, 1:50.

7 IWSA appeals: *Jus Suffragii*, Sept. 1, 1914, 159.

7–8 Schwimmer plan: *Ibid.*, Oct. 1, 1914, 174–75.

8 "Idiots": notation on letter from J. A. Poynton, Carnegie's secretary, Aug. 20, 1914, Schwimmer Papers.

8 "I am quite sure": Schwimmer to Jacobs, Aug. 21, 1914, Schwimmer Papers.

8 Resignation: Schwimmer to Catt, Oct. 25, 1914, Schwimmer Papers.

8 Retains title: *Christian Science Monitor*, Sept. 8, 1914; announcement, Box 4, Maverick Papers.

9 "Mission of urging mediation": Schwimmer to Catt, Aug. 22, 1914, Schwimmer Papers.

9 Passage to United States: *Ibid.*

9–10 Schwimmer biography and character: *NAW*; Bainbridge and Maloney, "Where Are They Now?" 23–29; "Rosika Schwimmer: World Patriot": *Christian Science Monitor*, Aug. 11, 1914; lecture bureau brochures, Schwimmer Papers; and Robe C. White to J. G. Sargent, Jan. 23, 1926, General Records of the Department of Justice, RG 60, File No. 38-23-147, NA.

10 "The best paid": Schwimmer to H. T. Upton, Dec. 8, 1914, Schwimmer Papers.

10 "Magnetic personality": *Jus Suffragii*, Jan. 15, 1912, 3.

10 "Shouts of laughter: Snowden, A Political Pilgrim," 42–43, 49.

10 "A great leader": Catt to Schwimmer, June 24, 1913, Catt Papers.

10 "I have always championed": Pethick-Lawrence to Addams, Dec. 1, 1915, Addams Papers.

10–11 Schwimmer interviews: *Christian Science Monitor*, Sept. 4, 1914; *NYT*, Sept. 6, 1914; and *NY Sun*, Sept. 8, 1914.

11 Europeans complain: *Jus Suffragii*, Nov. 1, 1914, 183, and Jan. 1, 1915, 228.

11 IWSA mediation petition: Catt and Schwimmer to Wilson, Sept. 14, 1914, Wilson Papers.

11 Catt leaves: Catt to Schwimmer, Sept. 17, 1914, Catt Papers.

11 "Carry great weight": Schwimmer, "The Women of the World," 9–10.

11 "Would lose no opportunity": *NYT*, Sept. 19, 1914.

11 Wilson denial: *NY Tribune*, Sept. 22, 1914.

11–12 Administration mediation policy: *Papers . . . Foreign Relations, 1914, Supplement*, 98, 99, 100–102, 104, 146; Bryan to Wilson, Aug. 25, Dec. 1 and 17, 1914, Bryan Papers; House to Wilson, Aug. 1 and 5, 1914, Wilson Papers; Bryan, *Memoirs*, 389–90; Link, *Struggle for Neutrality*, 200–203, 206–17; Baker, *Neutrality*, 37–50.

11 House biography and character: *DAB*; George and George, *Wilson and House*, 113–32; Seymour, *Intimate Papers*, 1:16, 45, 115, 147, 194–95.

11 "The little gray man": Creel, *Rebel at Large*," 248.

11 "Enjoying all the optimism": Millis, *Road to War*, 26.

12 "I hate to harp": House to Wilson, Aug. 5, 1914, Wilson Papers.

12 War status: Baldwin, *World War I*, 47, Esposito, *Concise History*, 81; and Graves, *Goodbye to All That*, 100, 140.

12–13 Churchill, *World Crisis*, 2:1.

13 "The sensibilities": Hendrick, ed., *Life and Letters of W. H. Page*," 1:416–17.

13 New peace organizations: *Enforced Peace*, (New York: League to Enforce Peace, 1916), 6–8; "Towards the Peace that Shall Last;" Addams, *Peace and Bread*," 2–6.

13 Leckie biography: *Who's Who, 1928–29*; Leckie to Addams, Jan. 27, 1915, WPP Papers.

13–14 Schwimmer's speeches: Washington *Times*, Sept. 18, 1914; Chicago *Tribune*, Nov. 23 and 26, 1914 and Dec. 21, 1914; Minneapolis *Tribune*, Nov. 28, 1914; St. Paul *Pioneer Press*, Dec. 1, 1914; Chicago *News*, Dec. 5, 1914; *NYT*, Dec. 8, 1914; Washington *Star*, Dec. 14 and 16, 1914; Alice Henry, "War and Its Fruits," 357–58 and Degen, *History of the WPP*, 31–37.

13 "Unstrung and nothing short of hysterical": Lochner to Jordan, Dec. 22, 1914, Jordan Papers.

13 "What a competent": *Unity*, Dec. 24, 1914, 259.

14 "Constructive peace": Pethick-Lawrence, *My Part*, 208–10.

14 WPP origins and platform: Degen, *History of the WPP*, 40–46, 61–62.

14 "Their usefulness": Linn, *Jane Addams*, 105.

14 Addams biography and character: *DAB*; Linn, *Jane Addams*; Farrell, *Beloved Lady*; Davis, *American Heroine*; Addams, *Newer Ideals of Peace*; Addams, *Second Twenty Years*; Lasch, *New Radicalism*, 3–37; "Jane Addams Memorial Number," *Unity*, July 15, 1935; and Baldwin Reminiscences, 2:109–111.

15 Jones biography and character: *DAB*; William Crow, *Wisconsin Lives of National Interest* (Appleton, Wisc.: C. C. Nelson, 1937), 101–4; Richard H. Thomas, "Jenkin Lloyd Jones: Lincoln's Soldier of Civic Righteousness," Ph.D. dissertation, Rutgers University, 1967; and Jones to A. G. P. Secner, Feb. 7, 1917, Jones Papers.

15 "Chicago's maid-of-all-work": *Unity*, Nov. 28, 1918, 148.

15 "The enlightened few": Minutes, Forty-first Meeting, CPS, Oct. 8, 1914, CPS Papers.

15 "Spiritual" parents: Lochner to Addams, Feb. 19, 1917, Lochner Papers; Lochner to Jones, April 24, 1917, Jones Papers.

15–16 Lochner biography and character: Lochner, *Always the Unexpected*, 7–43; typescript interview, Box 10, bibliography of articles, Box 11, Clark, "Candle in the Dark," unpublished MS, Box 52, all in Lochner Papers; and Jordan, *Days of a Man*, 2:676.

16 "An effective public speaker": Annual report, CPS, 1914, CPS Papers.

16 Emergency Peace Federation: Taylor, "Chicago Peace Convention," 95–96; "Platforms and Resolutions of the National Peace Conference," *Survey*, March 6, 1915, 597–98.

16 Wales biography and character: Louise Kellogg, "Brief Sketch of the Life and Work of Julia Grace Wales," unpublished MS, Wales Papers; Trattner, "Julia Grace Wales," 203–13; A. Letitia Wales to author, Feb. 26, 1967 and Kate H. Zimmerman to author, July 11, 1966.

16 "An excellent, logical brain": Lochner, *Always the Unexpected*, 53.

16–18 Wales plan: "Mediation Without Armistice: The Wisconsin Plan," Wisconsin Peace Society Papers.

18 "A sort of Joan of Arc": George Nasmyth to Addams, Jan. 15, 1915, WPP Papers.

18 "Kindly helpfulness": Aylward and Addams to Wilson, March 4, 1915, Wilson Papers.

18 "A stroke of genius": Jordan to Wilson, March 6, 1915, Wilson Papers.

18 "With all my heart": Wilson to Aylward and Addams, March 6, 1915, Wilson Papers.

18 Memorandum: Aylward to Wilson, March 16, 1915, Wilson Papers. I am obliged to Russell Smith, Library of Congress Manuscript Division, for the information on President Wilson's filing system.

18 Reception of Wales plan: Wales, "Record of the Wisconsin Peace Plan," typescript, Wales Papers.

18 ICW call: *International Congress of Women Report*, xxxvii–xl, 7; the *Report* includes verbatim proceedings and other related information.

18 Invitation to WPP: Jacobs et al. to Addams, Feb. 22, 1915, Addams Papers.

18 Schwimmer-WPP relationship: Leaflet, Shaw lecture bureau, Schwimmer Papers; Schwimmer to Dear Ladies, March 22, 1915, to Executive Committee, March 26, 1915, and to Addams, April 4, 1915, all in WPP Papers.

19 ICW committee assignments: Lochner interview.

19 Lloyd biography: Sam Houston Dixon, *The Men Who Made Texas Free* (Houston: Texas Historical Publishing Co., 1924), 265–71; *National Cyclopaedia of American Biography*.

19 "A sort of saint": Lochner to Betty Lochner, Oct. 26, 1940, Lochner Papers.

19 Holbrook biography: Annual Report, CPS, 1915, CPS Papers; *Unity*, Nov. 12, 1914, 169–71.

19 Lochner role: Lochner, *Always the Unexpected*, 52.

19 Voyage: Balch journal, Box 6, Balch Papers; Wales to Committee, May 15, 1915, Wales Papers.

19 "The whole enterprise": Addams to Lillian Wald, March 26, 1915, Wald Papers.

19 "A certain obligation": Addams to Balch, March 26, 1915, Balch Papers.

19–20 Balch biography and character: "Emily Greene Balch—Brief Sketch of Her Activities and Writings, 1945," typescript, Balch Papers; Randall, *Improper Bostonian*, 70–118; Elizabeth Stin Fainsod, "Emily Greene Balch," *Bryn Mawr Alumnae Bulletin*, May 1947, 1–3; Lochner interview.

20 "Only the plainest": *NYT*, Jan. 10, 1961.

20 "We know we are ridiculous": Journal, Balch Papers.

20 "Dragged into the pit": Addams et al., *Women at Hague*, 17.

20 Dutch hear shells: Crystal E. Benedict, "Now I Have To Do It," *Survey*, Oct. 9, 1915, 47.

20–21 War status: Baldwin, *World War I*, 54–55.

21 "Invite suggestions": *Ibid.*, 154.

21–22 "Only Madame Schwimmer": Hamilton to Mary R. Smith, May 5, 1915, Addams Papers.

22 Addams and Balch reluctance to visit statesmen: Hamilton to Louise deK. Bowen, May 16, 1915, Addams Papers; Addams et al., *Women at Hague*, 107.

22 Lochner as advance man: Lochner to Wilson, June 25, 1915, Wilson Papers.

22 "Feasible proposition": Addams et al., *Women at Hague*, 107.

22 Grey interview: *Ibid*, 94–95.

22 Von Jagow interview: Jacobs, Schwimmer, Macmillan memorandum, Aug. 13, 1915, Addams Papers.

22–23 Bethmann-Hollweg interview: Randall, *Improper Bostonian*, 171.

23 Austrian prime minister's interview: Addams et al., *Women at Hague*, 96.

23 Other European interviews: Randall, *Improper Bostonian*, 174–76; Jacobs, Schwimmer, Macmillan memorandum.

23 "I have grown": Balch to Addams, June 8, 1915, Addams Papers.

23 Modus operandi: Wales to Committee, June 4–14, 1915, Wales Papers.

23 German attitude and "formal though friendly": Balch to Lochner, June 1, 1915, Wilson Papers.

23–24 Schwimmer interview with German minister: Brockdorf-Rantzau to FO, Aug. 10, 1915, Collection of Foreign Records Seized, 1941–, Records of the German Foreign Office Received by the Department of State, RG 242, T-120, Roll 2502.

24 "To no great purpose": Balch notes, typescript, Box 5, Addams Papers.

24 "Was worth all the others": Balch notes.

24 Russian, Swedish, Dutch interviews: Randall, *Improper Bostonian*, 190.

24 "An unsentimental": Wales to Committee, June 4–14, 1915.

24–25 "Germany would find nothing": Jacobs, Schwimmer, Macmillan memorandum.

25 "British government": *Ibid*.

25 "Gravely, kindly": Addams et al., *Women at Hague*, 110.

25–26 Envoys' impressions: *Ibid.*, 22–23, 83, 91, 94–97.

25 "Revolted against war": *Ibid.*, 21.

25 "In our name": *Ibid.*, 67.

25 "Deceived themselves": *Ibid.*, 68.

25 "Smashed to dust": *Ibid.*, 21.

25–26 "Bodies, and bits": Gibbs, *Realities of War*, 84.

26n "Victory": Edwin Dwight, *Life* April 8, 1915, 614.

26 "The unscrupulous power": Addams et al., *Women at Hague*, 91.

26 "We do not wish": *Ibid.*, 98.

26 "Irrational and virulent": Addams, *Second Twenty Years*, 131.

26–27 American reaction to war: Link, *Struggle for Neutrality*, 554–628; Millis, *Road to War*, 209–20; and Peterson, *Propaganda for War*, 139–90.

27 Bryan resigns: Bryan to Wilson, May 12 and June 9, 1915, Wilson Papers; Bryan to Wilson, June 5, 1915, Bryan Papers.

27 Lansing's views: Lansing, "Consideration and Outline of Policies," memorandum, July 11, 1915, Lansing Papers.

27 House advice: House to Wilson, May 25, 1915, Wilson Papers.

27 "Had fastened": House to W. H. Page, Aug. 4, 1915, Page Papers.

27 "Not quite candid": House to Wilson, July 17, 1915, Wilson Papers.

27 Wilson interviews: Balch to Addams, Aug. 17 and 19, 1915, Addams Papers; Lochner to Mrs. George Rublee, July 19, 1915, Lochner Papers; and Wales to Committee, May 14, 1915, Wales Papers.

27 Lansing interview: Balch to O. G. Villard, Sept. 28, 1915, including memo on

Lansing visit, Aug. 31, 1915, Villard Papers; Lansing to Wilson, Sept. 1, 1915, Lansing Papers—Princeton.

27–28 Wilson's moralism: George and George, *Wilson and House*, 11–12; Baker, *Neutrality*, 278–79.

28 Schwimmer returns to America: Minutes, ICW meeting, Aug. 18, 1915; Jacobs to Addams, Sept. 8, 1915; and Macmillan to Addams, Jan. 14, 1916, all in Addams Papers.

28 Schwimmer chastises Addams: Addams to Kellogg, Sept. 24, 1915, Wald Papers.

28 Henry Street meeting: Minutes, Sept. 27, 1915, Kellogg Personal Papers.

28 "We so wholeheartedly": Addams, *Second Twenty Years*, 134.

28 Wales pamphlet: Wales to H. E. Cole, Oct. 7, 1915, Wales Papers.

28 Chicago meeting: Chicago *Tribune*, Oct. 2, 1915.

28–29 Hague envoys' manifesto: *NYT*, Oct. 16, 1915.

29 Lochner's attitude: Lochner to Balch, Sept. 14, 1915, Balch Papers; Lochner to Jordan, Oct. 1, 1915, Jordan Papers.

29 San Francisco peace congress: *Advocate of Peace*, Nov. 1915, 243–45; *Unity*, Oct. 28, 1915, 134–35.

29 Peace rallies: Lochner to Mrs. Glendower Evans, Nov. 5, 1915, Lochner Papers; Addams, *Peace and Bread*, 28; and Lochner, *Don Quixote* draft MS.

29 Schwimmer's plans: Lochner interview; NY *Tribune*, Dec. 12, 1915, V:5. "Nothing can be done": Jordan to Lochner, Oct. 26, 1915, Wales Papers.

29–30 House scheme: House diary, Oct. 8, 1915, House Papers; Link, *Confusions and Crises*, 101–7; and Osgood, *Ideals and Self-Interest*, 199–211.

30 "This is the part": House to Wilson, Nov. 10, 1915, Wilson Papers.

30 Jordan's changed attitude: Lochner to Jordan, Nov. 2 and 5, 1915, Jordan Papers; Madison *Cardinal*, Nov. 10, 1915.

30 White House interview: Lochner, "White House Interview," memorandum, [Nov. 12, 1915] Lochner Papers.

31 "We have 'put it over' ": Jordan to Jessie Jordan, Nov. 12, 1915, Jordan Papers.

31 "So human": Lochner, "Additional Data Regarding Interview" [Nov. 13, 1915] Lochner Papers.

31 Lochner's reaction: in Alfred Kliefoth to Wales, Nov. 12, 1915, Wales Papers.

31 Lochner's recommendations: Lochner, "Additional Data."

31 Shelly biography and character: Shelley to Franciska Schwimmer, Oct. 27, 1956, Shelley Papers; quotation and other personal information from interviews. Rebecca Shelly changed the spelling of her last name, adding an "e" to the second syllable, some time after the peace expedition.

31 Shelly attitude and activities: Shelley interviews; M. Hyers to L. Holt, Oct. 26, 1915, Michigan Branch, WPP Papers.

31 "Nerve and brass tacks": Shelly to Lochner, Oct. 21, 1915, Lochner Papers.

32 "A housewife": Detroit *News*, Nov. 6, 1915.

32 "Big Money": Lochner to Shelly, Nov. 6, 1915, Lochner Papers.

32 "Why are you not": Lochner, *Don Quixote*, 10.

CHAPTER 3: *Henry Ford: "War is murder"*

The following sources were used consistently in this chapter for biographical information on Henry and Clara Ford and for information on his business affairs, and are cited only when used in quotation: Clancy and Davies, *The Believer*; Ford and Crowther, *My Life and Work*; *Henry Ford: A Personal History*; Ann Hood, "The

Boy Henry Ford," typescript, Acc. 653, FA; MacManus and Beasley, *Men, Money and Motors*; Marquis, *Henry Ford*; Merz, *And Then Came Ford*; Nevins and Hill, *Times, Man, Company*; Olson, *Young Henry Ford*; Richards, *Last Billionaire*; Ruddiman, "Memories of My Brother"; Simonds, *Henry Ford*; Sorensen, *My Forty Years* and Sward, *Legend of Henry Ford*.

33 Delavigne-Ford relationship: Detroit *Journal*, Nov. 29, 1915.
34 HENRY FORD TO PUSH: *DFP*, Aug. 22, 1915.
34 "Considering the results": Ford and Crowther, *My Life and Work*, 22.
34 "Milk is a mess": Olson, *Young Henry Ford*, 15.
35 "There is an immense amount": Ford and Crowther, *My Life and Work*, 23.
35 "A born mechanic": Olson, *Young Henry Ford*, 20.
35 "The first watch": *Ibid.*, 22.
35 "The house was like a watch": *Ibid.*
35 "That showed me": *Ibid.*, 23.
37 "Watches were not universal necessities": Ford and Crowther, *My Life and Work*, 24.
38 "The pleasure": Nevins and Hill, *Times, Man, Company*, 107.
39 "Young man": Ford and Crowther, *Edison As I Knew Him*," 5.
40 "To make $": Olson, *Young Henry Ford*, 153.
40 "Family horse": Nevins and Hill, *Times, Man, Company*, 225.
41 Automobile sales: *Ibid.*, 387–489; *Ford Times*, June 1914, 390; June 1915, 387 and July 1963, 27.
41 "Any colour he wants": Merz, *And Then Came Ford*, 101.
42 "I put it to work": Detroit *News*, Nov. 15, 1915.
42 Impact of Model T: Sullivan, *War Begins*, 61–72; Wik, *Grass roots America*, 48–50.
42–43 Profits and labor problems: Ford and Crowther, *Today and Tomorrow*, 160–61; Liebold Reminiscences, 232; *The Ford Plan*.
43–44 Ford as folk hero: Leuchtenberg, *Perils of Prosperity*, 187; May, *End of American Innocence*, 137–38; Pound, "The Ford Myth," 41–49; Liebold Reminiscences, 224; Greenleaf, *From These Beginnings*, 18–19, 178–79; Wiebe, *Search for Order*, 164–76; *NYT*, Feb. 6 and 7, 1914; Sullivan, *War Begins*, 58; Stidger, *Man and His Motors*; and Reed, "Industry's Miracle Worker," 10–12, 64–68 and "Why They Hate Ford," 11–12.
44 Ford maxims· jotbooks, Box 7, Acc. 572, FA; Detroit *Journal*, Jan. 7, 1914; Stidger, *Man and His Motors*, 89.
44 Bank balance: Statement, Dec. 31, 1915, Highland Park State Bank, Box 12, Acc. 2, FA.
44 Ford home: Greenleaf, *From These Beginnings*, 178–79; "Henry Ford's Fair Lane," visitor information sheet, Fair Lane, Dearborn campus, University of Michigan; and Dearborn *Press*, July 16, 1966.
44 Cash surplus: *Motor Age*, Nov. 1914. The 1914 surplus was almost $21 million more than in 1913 and $34 million more than in 1912.
45 Ford maxims: Jotbooks, Box 7, Acc. 572; Boxes 20 and 21, Acc. 23 and Box 13, Acc. 1, all in FA.
45 Ford's reading: Liebold Reminiscences, 1331.
45 "Muss up my mind": Benson, *New Henry Ford*, 330.
45–46 Ford's testimony: NY *Herald*, Jan. 23, 1915.
46 Ford interviews: Liebold Reminiscences, 23, 1240–41, Cary, "Henry Ford," 5–6; Ford testimony, State of Michigan, in the Circuit County of Macomb: *Henry Ford vs. The Tribune Company et al.*, Transcript of Record (*Tribune Trial Record*) 6056, Acc. 53, FA.

46 "Fireworks": Smith Reminiscences, 42.

46 Behavior at factory: Black Reminiscences, 50; Liebold Reminiscences, 1337; Pipp, *Both Sides*, 59, Stidger, *Man and His Motors*, 48 and Rankin Reminiscences, 61–62.

47 Ford-Edison friendship: Ford to Edison, June 27, 1911, Edison Archives, Edison National Historic Site, West Orange, New Jersey; Edison to Ford, April 26, 1915, Box 46, Acc. 1, FA and Matthew Josephson, *Edison: A Biography*, (New York: McGraw-Hill, 1959), 437, 463–66.

47 Ford-Burroughs friendship: Clifton Johnson, ed. *John Burroughs Talks; His Reminiscences and Comments* (Boston: Houghton Mifflin Co., 1922), 326–27, 334–35; Clara Barrus, ed., *The Heart of Burroughs Journals*, (Boston: Houghton Mifflin Co., 1928), 272–74; and Josephson, *Edison*, 431.

48 "Face of a middle-aged ascetic": Cary, "Henry Ford," 6.

48 "More interested in things": Marquis, *Henry Ford*, 57.

48 "Is not all good": Pipp, *Real Henry Ford*, 40.

49 "Crude, ignorant": House diary, Oct. 2, 1915.

49 Howe-Ford meeting: Howe, *Confessions of a Reformer*, 246–47.

49 Bonus plan: *Ford Times*, July 1914, 511.

49 News stories: *NYT*, Jan. 6, June 10 and July 10, 1914.

49–50 Ford's early reaction to war: Liebold-Ford correspondence, August 1914, Box 70, Acc. 62, FA; Perry to Clara Ford, Dec. 5, 1914, Box 145, Acc. 1, FA; and St. Louis *Post-Dispatch*, Jan. 27, 1915.

50 Ford's views on war: *NYT*, April 11, 1915, 5:14; Edward Marshall testimony, *Tribune* Trial Record, 7128.

50 Ford-Addams visit: Addams to Jordan, April 12, 1915, Jordan Papers; Sullivan, *Over Here*, 164.

50 Emerson's influence: Ford, Preface to Hapgood, *Wisest Words*.

50 "No animosity": Jotbooks, Box 15, Acc. 62, FA.

50 "If we keep": Detroit *News*, June 18, 1915; *NYT*, June 19, 1915.

51 "Would build a roof": *NYT*, Aug. 9, 1915.

51 "I would never" and "wasteful sacrifice": NY *American*, Aug. 16, 1915.

51n "We have just sold": Perry to Clara Ford, March 25, 1915, Box 145, Acc. 1, FA; Nevins and Hill, *Expansion and Challenge*, 63.

51–52 Ford-Delavigne interview: *DFP*, Aug. 22, 1915.

52 Wanamaker telegram: *NYT*, Sept. 5, 1915, 2:1.

52 Response to statement: *NYT*, Aug. 23 and 24, 1915; Liebold to H. Woodhouse, Sept. 24, 1915, Box 5, Acc. 292 and Clipbooks, Aug.–Sept. 1915, Acc. 7, FA.

52 Second statement: *NYT*, Sept. 9, 1915.

53 Increased pledges retracted: *NYT*, Sept. 15, 1915.

53 "It would be no trick": *NYT*, Sept. 18, 1915. During the Civil War a ship of the Confederate Navy, the *Hunley*, attached a "pill" to a spar and sank a Union ship by ramming it and pulling a lanyard to detonate the device. It also sank itself. (Arch Whitehouse, *Subs and Submariners*, [Garden City, N.Y.: Doubleday, 1961], 24–34.

53 Ford-Daniels correspondence: Daniels to Ford, Sept. 8, 1915 and Ford to Daniels, Sept. 13, 1915, Daniels Papers.

53 Ford's comments on war materiel: *NYT*, Sept. 23 and 24, 1915; NY *Herald*, Sept. 23 and 24, 1915; and San Francisco *Examiner*, Oct. 19, 1915.

54 "Impractical persons": *Advocate of Peace*, Oct. 1915, 215.

54 Ford-Bryan visit: Bryan to Ford, Sept. 16 and 23, 1915, Box 8, Acc. 572,

FA; *NYT*, Sept. 15, 1915; and Mt. Clemens (Mich.) *Leader*, Sept. 15, 1915. Ford office response to suggestions: *NYT*, Sept. 21, 1915; Liebold to Burroughs, Sept. 8, 1915, Box 130, Acc. 1, FA.

55 "I have noticed": *Tribune* Trial Record, 6063–64.

55 Couzens statement: NY *Herald*, Oct. 13, 1915.

55 "If he could speak": San Francisco *Examiner*, Oct. 19, 1915.

55 "The money bags": undated article by Richard Milton in unidentified Denver newspaper, Clipbooks, Acc. 7, FA.

55 Chicago interview: Detroit *News*, Nov. 15, 1915.

55 Ford at the fair: San Francisco *Examiner*, Oct. 22 and 23, 1915.

CHAPTER 4: *"Something is about to occur"*

Lochner, *Don Quixote*, 10–45 and the *DFP*, *NYT* and Detroit *News*, Nov. 15–30, 1915 were used consistently in this chapter, in addition to the sources listed below, and are cited only when used in quotation.

57 "Something is about to occur": Lochner to Wales, Nov. 18, 1915, Wales Papers.

57–58 Liebold biography and character: Detroit *News*, March 5, 1956; Nevins and Hill, *Expansion and Challenge*, 12–13; Liebold Reminiscences, 74, 528, 578, 653, 731; Greenleaf, *From These Beginnings*, 40–41, 53–56; and Black Reminiscences, 18.

58 Pacifists rebuffed: Jordan to Ford, Sept. 9, 1915, Jordan Papers; Lochner to H. C. Morris, Sept. 15, 1915, CPS Papers; Lochner to Ford, Nov. 6, 1915, Lochner Papers; WPP Assistant Secretary to L. Holt, Oct. 26, 1915, Box 7, Michigan Branch, WPP Papers; Schwimmer, "Humanitarianism of Henry Ford," 10, and E. Dowling to Mrs. F. McMullin, Sept. 14, 1915, WPP Papers.
Marquis biography and character: *DFP*, Nov. 15 and 22, 1915 and June 22, 1948; *NYT*, June 23, 1948; Nevins and Hill, *Expansion and Challenge*, 13, 33; Detroit *News Tribune*, July 12 and Nov. 15, 1908; *Tribune* Trial Record, 1827–28; Detroit *News*, Nov. 22, 1915.

58 "Whole-souled, scholarly and able": Detroit *News Tribune*, April 15, 1906.

59–60 Pipp intercession. Bushnell, *Truth About Ford*, 78–81; Shelley interviews.

60 Schwimmer-Ford meeting arranged: Shelley interviews; Shelley to Mercedes Randall, May 1, 1957, Balch Papers; Marquis's notes, Acc. 63, FA; Schwimmer, "Humanitarianism of Henry Ford," 10; Mabel Hyers to Lilian Holt, Nov. 6, 1915, Michigan Branch, WPP Papers; Richards, *Last Billionaire*, 30–31; and Bainbridge and Maloney, "Where Are They Now?" 24.

60–61 Schwimmer-Ford meeting: Schwimmer, "Humanitarianism of Henry Ford," 10; Detroit *Times*, Nov. 18, 1915; Howe, *Confessions of a Reformer*, 247–48; Olson, *Young Henry Ford*, 160; and Detroit *News*, Nov. 17 and 18, 1915.

61 "Mme Schwimmer is discouraged": Lochner to Wales, Nov. 18, 1915, Wales Papers.

61 "A victim of circumstances": Lochner, *Don Quixote*, 12.

61 Wilson appointment arranged: Schwimmer, "Humanitarianism of Henry Ford," 9–10.

62 "Practically penniless": Lochner to Wales, Nov. 21, 1915, Lochner Papers.

62 Lochner's impressions of Ford: Lochner to Jordan, Nov. 20, 1915, Jordan Papers.

62 Schwimmer-Clara Ford meeting: Detroit *Journal*, Nov. 20, 1915.

62 "Tore off the lid": Lochner to Wales, Nov. 21, 1915, Lochner Papers.
63 Shelly-Clara Ford meetings: Detroit *Journal*, Nov. 20, 1915; C. Ford to Ellen Starr Brinton, April 28, 1948, Box 3016, Acc. 285, FA.
63 House comments: Seymour, *Intimate Papers*, 2:96.
64 "If this war": Addams to House, Nov. 23, 1915, House Papers.
64 Plantiff biography and character: Nevins and Hill, *Times, Man, Company*, 273, 342, 499, 585–86; *Ford Times*, May 15, 1908, 10; *NYT*, Oct. 19 and 21, 1934.
64 "A high liver": Huebsch Reminiscences, 161.
64 "Corking good companion": NY *World*, Dec. 13, 1915.
64–65 Ford-Henry Street group meeting: Addams, *Peace and Bread*, 33; *NYT*, Nov. 26, 1915.
65 "Scientific commissions": Lochner, *Don Quixote*, 20.
65 "Mr. Henry": *Ibid.*
65 House-Ford-Lochner meeting: *Ibid.*, 21; Seymour, *Intimate Papers*, 2:96–97.
65–66 Wilson and Tumulty comments: Memos attached to Lucking to Tumulty, Nov. 20, 1915, Wilson Papers.
66–67 White House meeting: Lochner notes, n.d. Box 4, FPP Papers. Ford first heard the joke he told in Denver, on his way home from the Pan Pacific Exposition (Denver *Express*, Nov. 13, 1915).
66n Wilson's favorite limerick: Sullivan, *Over Here*, 171.
67 "The President is a small man": Lochner, *Don Quixote*, 25.
67 Passage arrangements: H. Jacobsen to A. Hirsh, Dec. 7, 1915 and Jacobsen to Ford, Nov. 27, 1915, enclosed in T. M. Crisp to Hirsh, Dec. 8, 1915, TC 18, Acc. 79, FA; and NY *World*, Nov. 29, 1915.
67 "If he was alive": C. Leidich to Ford, Dec. 1, 1915, Box 53, Acc. 1, FA.
67–68 Ford press conference: Villard, *Fighting Years*, 302–5.
68 "Most influential peace advocates": NY *Tribune*, Nov. 25, 1915.
68 "To do the greatest good": *NYT*, Nov. 25, 1915.
68 "A delegation of important Americans": Villard, *Fighting Years*, 304.
68 "So extraordinary": *Ibid.*
68 "It was not the best": Lochner, *Don Quixote*, 27.
68 "GREAT WAR ENDS": NY *Tribune*, Nov. 25, 1915.
69 "Repeated questions": *DFP*, Nov. 25, 1915.
69 Wilson disapproved: Detroit *Journal*, Nov. 25, 1915.
71 "One slightly used": NY *Tribune*, Nov. 25, 1915.
71 Biltmore Hotel: *NYT*, Dec. 26, 1913.
71 Invitation: Ford to Wales, Nov. 25, 1915, Wales Papers.
72 Ford's friends decline: Burroughs to Lochner, Nov. 29, 1915 and Burbank to Ford, Dec. 2, 1915, FPP Papers.
72 "Was very, very obvious": Lochner interview.
72 "Ten uninterrupted minutes": E. Lochner to Wales, Nov. 26, 1915, Wales Papers.
72 Taft reaction: W. H. Taft to Horace Taft, Nov. 29, 1915 and W. H. Taft to Gus Karger, Nov. 28, 1915, Taft Papers.
72 Ford visits Edison: NY *World*, Nov. 28, 1915.
73 "Mothers' Day" demonstration and Wilson interview: Partial transcript of meeting, FPP Papers; Snowden, *Political Pilgrim*, 45–48.
73 Clara Ford sent Marquis: Breuer, "Henry Ford and The Believer," 124.
73 "Follow the advice": Lochner, *Don Quixote*, 43.
73 "Roseate view": NY *Tribune*, Nov. 28, 1915.

74 Ford called his wife "Mother": Lochner, *Don Quixote*, 10.

74 Presidential interview: Schwimmer to Addams, with notation of other recipients on draft copy, Nov. 26, 1915, FPP Papers.

74 "Listen to proposals": Schwimmer to P. Kellogg, Oct. 27, 1915, Schwimmer Papers.

74 Ford's generosity: Wales to E. Lochner, Nov. 27, 1915, Wales Papers; Chrystal Macmillan to Presidents of Norwegian, Swedish and Danish Committees, Dec. 7, 1915, Addams Papers.

74 "All I have to do": Lochner, *Don Quixote*, 66.

74 Schwimmer assurances to Ford: Ford and Crowther, *My Life and Work*, 244–45.

74–75 Schwimmer visits to neutral ministers: Paul Ritter to Schwimmer, Nov. 30, 1915; H. Bryn to Schwimmer, Nov. 30, 1915; Ford to Ritter, Dec. 2, 1915, and Ford to Bryn, Dec. 3, 1915, all in FPP Papers. Eighty dollars was spent on cable charges at each legation and the remaining funds later returned to the Ford Motor Company.

75 Schwimmer expenses: Expense account and bills from New Willard Hotel, Nov. 27, 1915 and portion of McAlpin Hotel bill, Nov. 20–29, 1915; C. R. Brown to Mr. Moore, Dec. 6, 1915 and Frank Howard to D. K. Haight, Dec. 10, 1915, all in TC 18, Acc. 79, FA.

75–76 Addams's attitude toward Biltmore activity: Addams, *Peace and Bread*, 34–40.

76 Opposition to Addams's sailing: Louise deK. Bowen to L. Wald, Dec. 1, 1915, Wald Papers; "Jane Addams Memorial Issue," 205.

76 Complaints against Schwimmer: Anna Garlin Spencer to Addams, Nov. 29, 1915, Spencer Papers; Jacobs, Macmillan and Manus to Addams, Nov. 27, 1915 and Crystal E. Benedict to Addams, Dec. 3, 1915, WPP Papers; Jacobs to Addams, Dec. 4, 1915, Addams Papers; Farrell, *Beloved Lady*, 166; and Spencer to H. Thomas, Dec. 2, 1915, FPP Papers.

76 Opposition to Ford's sailing: Shelley interview; Breuer, "Henry Ford and The Believer," 124; C. Ford to E. S. Brinton, April 28, 1946; Marquis, address at The Hague, Jan. 16, 1916, Box 4, Acc. 79, FA; Marquis, address to Board of Commerce, *Detroit Saturday Night*, Jan. 15, 1916, 25; and Liebold Reminiscences, 253–56.

77 "Nothing dampens his enthusiasm": NY *World*, Dec. 4, 1915.

77 "I have all faith": *NYT*, Nov. 30, 1915.

77 "Orders given in New York": Lochner, *Don Quixote*, 43.

CHAPTER 5: *"Not the best possible start"*

In this chapter, all inquiries, proposals, invitations, refusals, criticisms and other material concerned with organizing the Ford Peace Expedition that are not otherwise noted are in Boxes 1–4, FPP Papers or the *NYT*, Nov. 26–Dec. 5, 1915; NY *Tribune*, Nov. 27–Dec. 5, 1915; NY *Herald*, Nov. 27–Dec. 5, 1915 and NY *Evening Post*, Dec. 2–4, 1915, and are cited only when used in quotation.

78 "Invited and coming": Fussell interview.

79 Pease invitation: *PPL*, Dec. 3, 1915; Pease to Ford, Dec. 5, 1915, FPP Papers.

79 Letter of invitation: Ford to Invited Delegates, Nov. 27, 1915, FPP Papers.

80 "A mission, a generous heart": NY *Tribune*, Dec. 1, 1915.

80 "Wise enough": Baker to Ford, Nov. 30, 1915, FPP Papers.

80 "Probably fruitless": Eliot to Ford, Nov. 28, 1915, FPP Papers.

80 "All kinds of obstacles": Howe to Lochner, Nov. 27, 1915, FPP Papers.

80   "Is not only hopelessly": Russell to Ford, Nov. 29, 1915, FPP Papers.

80–81 Keller letter: Lochner, *Don Quixote*, 231–32.

81   "Constrained to decline": Gladden to Ford, Nov. 28, 1915, FPP Papers.

81   Tarbell refusal: Tarbell, *All In A Day's Work*, 309–13.

81   "Threatened with pneumonia": G. W. Mead to Ford, Dec. 4, 1915, FPP Papers.

81   "It is wise": Darrow to Leckie, Nov. 29, 1915, FPP Papers.

81   "This foolish project": Whitlock diary, Nov. 27, 1915, Nevins Papers.

81   "Pro-German sentiments": Bartholdt to Ford, Nov. 30, 1915, FPP Papers.

81   "The success of the trip": Bryan to Ford, Nov. 29, 1915, FPP Papers.

82   Bryan as mental lightweight: Wales to Lochner, Nov. 17, 1915, Lochner Papers.

82   "Spirit of constructive": Kellogg to Lochner, Dec. 3, 1915, FPP Papers.

82–83 Five changed their minds: Addams, *Peace and Bread*, 37.

83   Spencer refusal: Spencer to Lochner, Nov. 26, 1915 and Lochner to Spencer, Nov. 28, 1915, FPP Papers; *NYT*, Nov. 30, 1915; and Spencer to Addams, Nov. 29, 1915, Spencer Papers.

83   "Original champion": Lochner to Jordan, Nov. 27, 1915, FPP Papers.

83   "Dead in earnest": Lochner to Jordan, Nov. 28, 1915, FPP Papers.

83   "A shipload of amateurs" and "emotional and intense": Jordan, *Days of a Man*, 2:682.

83   "In my scheme": Jordan to Jessie Jordan, Nov. 29, 1915, Jordan Papers.

83–84 "A full statement": Morris to Lochner, Dec. 2, 1915, FPP Papers.

84   Neutral mediation plans: Chicago *Herald*, Nov. 27, 1915; *The Call*, Nov. 28, 1915.

84   "Mr. Ford fair play": Morris to Lochner, Dec. 2, 1915.

84   Pro-Ally sympathy: Link, *Struggle for Neutrality*, 7–43.

85   "Is really a fine": Sullivan, "The Last Word," Dec. 3, 1915, 12.

85   "He rushes in": *Life*, Dec. 9, 1915, 1150.

85   "Does his heart": quoted in "Henry Ford in Search of Peace," *Literary Digest*, Dec. 11, 1915, 1333.

85   Guest poem: *DFP*, Dec. 3, 1915.

85   "Mechanical genius": *Collier's*, Jan. 1, 1916, 1.

85   "A Little Child": *New Republic*, Dec. 4, 1915, 112.

85   "Miracles are only": "Henry Ford in Search of Peace," 1335.

85–86 Newspaper and magazine comment: NY *Sun*, Dec. 1, 1915; Chicago *Herald*, Dec. 1, 1915; *The Call*, Nov. 28, 1915; "Henry Ford in Search of Peace," 1333–36; *DFP*, Nov. 27, 1915; and *Life*, Dec. 16, 1915, 1195.

86   F.P.A. comment: NY *Tribune*, Nov. 29, 1915.

86   Sullivan comment: "The Last Word," 12.

86   "It isn't funny": Philadelphia *Evening Bulletin*, Dec. 3, 1915.

86   Rabbi's observation: Joseph K. Krauskopf, "Henry Ford and His Mission of Peace," address, Dec. 19, 1915, Box 53, Acc. 1, FA.

86   "Have they not": *Parliamentary Debates*, House of Commons, Fifth Series, 76:991.

86   "The product of megalomania": *Times* (London), Dec. 1, 1915.

86   "Self-important and boisterous": *Spectator*, Dec. 4, 1915, 776–77.

86n "Brant's fools": Alexander Barclay, translator, *The Ship of Fools* [New York: D. Appleton, 1874], 2 vols.

86   "Traveling troupe": *Le Temps* (Paris) in Outlook, Feb. 2, 1916, 252–53.

87   "Manifestation of American eccentricity": *SFB*, Dec. 7, 1915.

87   "Live wire": NY *Tribune*, Nov. 28, 1915.

88 "Prominent universities": General Form No. 1, Karsten Papers.

88 "The efforts of individual citizens": J. G. Hibben to Lochner, Nov. 29, 1915, FPP Papers.

88 "Does not presume": H. N. MacCracken to Lochner, Nov. 29, 1915, FPP Papers.

88 Karsten's invitations: Correspondents of the League, Men Anxious to Cooperate, typescript list, n.d., Karsten Papers.

88 "Mixer of good address": Chancellor, New York University to Lochner, Nov. 30, 1915, FPP Papers.

88-89 Students' arrangements: Tooze to author, April 20, 1967; Hettinger and Lozier interviews; Abbott Reminiscences and Fussell to author, June 9, 1966.

89 Supplies bills: TC 18, Acc. 79, FA.

89 "You are engaged": Holmes to A. Colegrove, n.d., Box 2, FPP Papers.

89 Ford press conference: *DFP*, Dec. 2 and 3, 1915; NY *World*, Dec. 4, 1915; *The Call*, Dec. 3, 1915; and Lochner, *Don Quixote*, 42.

90 "The way Mr. Ford's": C. Ford to Schwimmer, Aug. 12, 1916, Evans Papers.

90 Reaction to Addams's withdrawal: Lochner to Ford, Sept. 7, 1916; Mrs. William (Harriet) Thomas to A. G. Spencer, Nov. 30, 1915, WPP Papers; and *The Call*, Dec. 1, 1915.

90 "Into a very disagreeable": Schwimmer to Balch, Nov. 1915, Schwimmer Papers.

90 *Oscar II* decorations: *PPL*, Dec. 4, 1915; NY *Sun*, Dec. 4, 1915; and Gomme interview.

90 Expenses: bills from Mrs. Lewis Middleton, Dec. 5, 1915; John Wanamaker Company, Dec. 6, 1915; H. Jacobsen to A. Hirsh, Dec. 7, 1915, and Crisp, Randall and Crisp, Dec. 6, 1915, all in TC 18, Acc. 79, FA; Hirsh to Liebold, Dec. 24, 1915, Box 8, Acc. 572, FA; Biltmore Hotel bills, December 1915, Box 54, Acc. 62, FA and Wales to Lochner, Nov. 27, 1915, Wales Papers.

91 "Mysterious, compelling": *NYT*, Dec. 4, 1915.

91 "This is the most serious": *Ibid.*

91 "Eleven days of Inferno": Lochner, *Don Quixote*, 29.

91 Delegates' reception at Biltmore: *Ibid.*, 39.

91-92 Wales at Biltmore: Notes, Dec. 4, 1916, A. L. Wales Papers.

92 "An unofficial scientific": Wales to Jordan, Nov. 24, 1915, Wales Papers.

92 "Henry is sending": M. M. Abbott to author, May 24, 1967.

92 Ford-Marquis conversation: Marquis, *Henry Ford*, 19-20.

92-93 Clark, Park and others' passport arrangements: Lochner, *Don Quixote*, 33-34; Clark-Grose, "Experiment in Unofficial Diplomacy," unpublished MS, Grose Papers; Brooklyn *Eagle*, Dec. 5, 1915; and Park Reminiscences.

93-94 Ford's farewell message: NY *Evening Post*, Dec. 4, 1915.

94 "Millionaires, statesmen": J. F. Kennedy, "They're Off!", unidentified newspaper clipping, scrapbook, Evans Papers.

94-96 Newspaper comments on *Oscar II* departure: *NYT*, Dec. 4 and 5, 2:1; NY *Sun*, Dec. 5, 1915; *DFP*, Dec. 5, 1915, 1:1; NY *Herald*, Dec. 5, 1915, 1:1; NY *World*, Dec. 5, 1915; Newark *News*, Dec. 5, 1915; and Philadelphia *North American*, Dec. 7, 1915.

96 "Undertaking foredoomed": Burroughs to Lochner, Nov. 29, 1915, FPP Papers.

96 "I'll give you": NY *Herald*, Dec. 5, 1915.

96-97 Kellogg's expectations: *Survey*, Dec. 11, 1915, 301; Kellogg to Addams, Feb. 7, 1916, Jordan Papers.

CHAPTER 6: *The "illustrious unknown"*

Biographical information not otherwise cited is in *Henry Ford Peace Expedition Who's Who.*

98–99 Departure and first evening: Mylecraine diary, Dec. 4, 1915, Mylecraine-Cornick Papers; Tucker to Dear Brethren and Sistren, Dec. 4, 1916, Tucker Papers; Turner interview; *SFB*, Dec. 13, 1915 and Jan. 22, 1916; *BT*, Jan. 17, 1916; NY *Tribune*, Jan. 9, 1916; *PPL*, Jan. 7, 1916; Detroit *News*, Jan. 6, 1916; Guessford-Weir interview; Braley, "Grafters Aboard—As Guests of Mr. Ford," *Ohio State Journal*, Feb. 20, 1916, 4:8; and Wales to family, Dec. 4, 1916, A. L. Wales Papers.

98 "This mission": Ford to Dear Friends, n.d., Box 8, FPP Papers.

99 Marquis's report: Marquis to wife, Dec. 16, 1915, Acc. 63, FA.

99 Benedict's prediction: Benedict to Addams, Dec. 3, 1915, WPP Papers.

99 "Santa Claus" and "a nice old gentleman": Tucker and Turner interviews; Huebsch Reminiscences, 146; and *Unity*, Nov. 28, 1918, 143, 148.

100 "Will have much direct": Jones, "A Conscience Call," *Unity*, Dec. 2, 1915, 213.

100 Aked's personality: Huebsch Reminiscences, 144; Maverick and Wythe interviews; and Evans to family, Dec. 24, 1915, Evans Papers.

100–101 Aked's biography: *NYT*, Feb. 18, 1907 and Aug. 13, 1941; NY *Herald Tribune*, Aug. 13, 1941; "One Hundredth Anniversary Directory," First Congregational Church of San Francisco, 1949, 20–22; and Millard, "Heterodox Preacher," Sunday magazine, Los Angeles *Times*, Dec. 5, 1937, 9, 14.

100 "The whole country": Huebsch Reminiscences, 162.

100 "I owe something": *NYT*, March 6, 1911.

101 Aked and peace expedition: *SFB*, Nov. 29, 1915; Aked to Lochner, Nov. 28, 1915. FPP Papers.

101 "Loves the limelight": Marquis to wife, Dec. 16, 1915.

101 Weatherly biography and character: John Weatherly to author, Nov. 23, 1973; Wittke, "Echo of Ford Peace Ship," 258.

102 "Among the ten": William Allen White, *Autobiography* [NY: Macmillan, 1946], 386.

102–104 McClure biography and character: McClure, *My Autobiography*; *NYT*, March 23, 1949; May, *End of American Innocence*, 69; Ellen Moore, Introduction to *Success Story* by Peter Lyon, viii–xiii; Frank Luther Mott, *A History of American Magazines, 1885–1905* (Cambridge: Harvard University Press, 1957) 4–5, 589, 592; Mark Sullivan, *The Education of an American* (NY: Doubleday, Doran Co., 1938), 193–99; Will Irwin, *The Making of a Reporter* (NY: G. P. Putnam's Sons, 1942) 148–50; Lincoln Steffens, *Autobiography* (NY: Harcourt, Brace, 1931), 361–63; 535–36; Lyon, *Success Story*, 337 ff.; Lynch, "Leaders of New Peace Movement," 629–38; W. H. Taft to McClure, Dec. 4, 1915, TC 18, Acc. 79, FA; and McClure to William Archer, July 30, 1915 and McClure to Hattie McClure, Oct. 25, 1915, both in McClure Papers.

102 "From Order": Ellery Sedgwick, *The Happy Profession*, (Boston: Little Brown, 1946), 142.

104 McClure and Ford biography: McClure to Ford, June 28, 1915 and G. S. Anderson to McClure, July 7, 1915, both in McClure Papers.

104 "A little grey": Whitlock diary, Jan. 31, 1916.

104 Barry biography and character: *NYT*, Nov. 4, 1942; San Francisco *Chronicle*, Nov. 4, 1942; Field-Wood interview; and Coggins Reminiscences.

104 "To bear the aura": Hazel J. Achenbach letter, Sept. 5, 1953, Barry Papers.

104 "Of gentle consideration": May Wright Sewall to Friends in Hoosierland, Dec. 16, 1915, Sewall Papers.

104–105 Bernstein biography: *DAB*; *NYT*, Sept. 1, 1935; "Biography of Herman Bernstein," typescript, n.d., Box 923, Acc. 285, FA; and NY *Sun*, Oct. 18 and 24, 1915.

105 "That the people": Bernstein to Ford, Nov. 26, 1915, FPP Papers.

105 "Exercise a wonderful influence": William Koch to Ford, Nov. 30, 1915, FPP Papers.

105–106 Lindsey biography and character: *NYT*, March 6, 1943; Steffens, "Ben B. Lindsey"; Lindsey, "The Beast and the Jungle"; Denver *News*, Dec. 20, 1903; and Denver *Post*, Dec. 31, 1903.

105 "Greatest living American": Larsen, *The Good Fight*, 7.

106 "A little love": *Ibid.*, 54.

106 "The Bull Mouse": Emporia *Gazette*, April 2, 1943.

106 Lindsey and IWSA: Lindsey to Harvey O'Higgins, June 27, 1913 and Anna Shaw to Lindsey, Aug. 5, 1912, Lindsey Papers.

106 "Delicate as a flower": Goldman to Lindsey, April 17, 1931, Lindsey Papers.

106 "Gang of conspirators": Lindsey to Henry P. Harrison, Nov. 18, 1914, Lindsey Papers.

106 "Worse than useless": Lindsey to Roosevelt, Nov. 27, 1915, Roosevelt Papers.

106–107 Lindsey joins expedition: Lindsey to Ford, Nov. 28 and 29, 1915, FPP Papers; Lindsey to Harrison, March 24, 1915 and Lindsey to R. Neely, April 5, 1916, Lindsey Papers.

107 King biography: *NYT*, July 5, 1958; Judson King, *The Conservation Fight: From Theodore Roosevelt to Tennessee Valley Authority* (Washington, D.C.: Public Affairs Press, 1959), v–vi, xv.

107 "Like a clear bolt": King to A. R. Hatton, Dec. 3, 1915, King Papers.

107 "One of the sanest": Lindsey to King, April 22, 1915, Lindsey Papers.

107 "Heroic and democratic": King to Ford, Dec. 2, 1915, FPP Papers.

107 Hanna and Clark background: Wilkins, "North Dakota and the Ford Peace Ship," 384, 389.

107 "We are simply": *Jim Jam Jems*, Jan. 1916, 8.

107 "Unspeakable blessing": Bethea to Ford, Nov. 29, 1915, FPP Papers.

107 Blake biography: "Lillie D. Blake," *NAW*; Blake to Jones, Oct. 17, 1914, Jones Papers; announcement, NY Peace Society lecture bureau, Box 52, Lochner Papers; *Jus Suffragii*, Oct. 1, 1914, 177; and speech draft, Blake Papers.

108 Levussove background: *Register of the Associated Alumni of the College of the City of New York* (New York, 1924); Chester Wright to A. Hirsh, March 24, 1916, Box 54, Acc. 62, FA.

108 Hostetler biography: Washington *Post*, Nov. 7, 1948.

108 Huebsch biography: Huebsch Reminiscences, 1–60; May, *End of American Innocence*, 290–91; Huebsch to House, Sept. 12, 1914, House Papers; and Huebsch to Schwimmer, Dec. 4, 1914, Huebsch Papers.

108 "At that time": Gomme interview.

108 Frederick and Lilian Holt background: F. Holt to Plantiff, June 13, 1917, Box 55, Acc. 62, FA; correspondence between L. Holt and WPP staff, Fall, 1915, WPP Papers.

108 "A wise little body": Weatherly to wife, Dec. 31, 1915, FPE Papers (the repository of all Weatherly letters to his wife).

109 Robinson biography: *Jus Suffragii*, Dec. 1, 1913, 41 and Aug. 1, 1914, 156; *Literary Digest*, Feb. 15, 1913, 367–69; and Denver *Post*, July 10, 1923.

109 "Ship of Good Hope": Robinson to Ford, Nov. 26, 1915, FPP Papers.

109 Sewall biography and character: *NAW*; NY *Tribune*, July 7, 1899; Indianapolis *News*, July 23, 1920; Sewall to Addams, Dec. 24, 1915, WPP Papers; Curti, *Peace or War*, 116; Whitney, *American Peace Society*, 246–47, 251, 333.

109 "The historical continuity": Wales to family, Dec. 26, 1915, A. L. Wales Papers.

109–11 Boissevain biography: *NAW*; *Woman's Who's Who, 1914–1915*; Eastman, *Enjoyment of Living*, 298–99; Irwin, *Making of a Reporter*, 341; Harriet Blatch and Alma Lutz, *Challenging Years: Memoirs of Harriet Stanton Blatch* (NY: G. P. Putnam's Sons, 1940), 108–9; NY *Tribune*, Nov. 2 and 27, 1915; *NYT*, Sept. 28, 1915 and Nov. 27, 1916; and Rochester *Democrat and Chronicle*, Nov. 27, 1916.

109–10 Boissevain character: Gomme interview; Howe, *Confessions of a Reformer*, 242; *SFB*, Dec. 6, 1916; and Nell Reeder to family, Dec. 29, 1915, Reeder Papers.

111 "Ethical Bohemia": Eastman, *Enjoyment of Living*, 266.

111 Boissevain's expectations of expedition: *The Call*, Dec. 2 and 3, 1915; *NYT*, Dec. 4, 1915.

111 Wales on Boissevain: Wales to family, Dec. 4, 1916.

111–12 Park biography: unpublished autobiography, typescript, Park Papers; Park Reminiscences.

112 "Glad to obey": Park to Ford, Nov. 25, 1915, FPP Papers.

112 "Small wiry woman": Wales to family, Dec. 4, 1916.

112 "Capable clerk": Nelson to Lindsey, Oct. 30, 1908, Lindsey Papers.

112 Malmberg biography: *The Call*, May 2 and 9, 1915.

112 "Exceptionally intelligent": Memorandum of Persons Having Information in Regard to Special Subjects, Jan. 28, 1918, Document No. 991, American Commission to Negotiate Peace, Records of The Inquiry, RG 256, NA.

112 "A senseless, wicked": May 8, 1915, 436–38.

112–13 Schwimmer aids Malmberg: Schwimmer to Addams, Feb. 16, 1915, WPP Papers.

113 Eriksson biography: Eriksson-Hyyrylaeinen to author, Sept. 23, 1968.

113 "A slim, prim": Eastman, *Enjoyment of Living*, 398.

113 "An enthusiast" and "the radical things": Huebsch to Schwimmer, Dec. 2, 1915, FPP Papers.

113 "Utterly dedicated": Love interview.

113 "Causist who had her mind": Guessford-Weir interview.

114 Lloyd's travel arrangements: Maverick interview; notes, Box 3, Maverick Papers; and Providence *Journal*, Dec. 28, 1965.

114 "Man of ability": Maverick interview.

114 Clark biography: Grose, "Experiment," Lochner interview.

114 "Inner Circle": Wales to family, Dec. 4, 1916.

114 Bingham biography: NY *Herald*, Dec. 23, 1915; *NYT*, Dec. 23, 1915.

114 "Wonderful friends": Bingham to Mr. and Mrs. Ford, Nov. 25, 1915, FPP Papers.

115 "Negligible women": Dailey, "Henry Ford—and the Others," 316.

115 "Genteel mendicants": Philadelphia *Evening Bulletin*, Dec. 6, 1915.

115 "Illustrious unknown": NY *Sun*, Jan. 30, 1916.

115 "Devoted lovers": Robinson, "Confessions," 225.

115 "Motley crew": Lochner, *Don Quixote*, 51.

115 "An entire American village": Detroit *News*, Jan. 11, 1916.

115 "Self-seekers and grafters": Robinson, "Confessions," 225.

115–16 Press complement: all communications regarding invitations and acceptances are in Boxes 2–4, FPP Papers.

115–16 O'Neill biography: *NYT*, April 18, 1940; Liebold Reminiscences, 299; Gene
116 Fowler to Liebold, n.d., Box 5, Acc. 62, FA.

116 Davis biography: *NYT*, May 19, 1958.

116 Riis biography: Brooklyn *Eagle*, Dec. 5, 1915.

116 "Wide awake newspaperman": Hirsch to Lochner, Nov. 27 and 28, 1915, FPP Papers.

116 Bullitt biography: *NYT*, Feb. 16, 1967; Washington *Post*, Feb. 16, 1967; and Wyth interview.

116 "Billy": W. H. Page to Grant-Smith, Aug. 19, 1916, Page Papers.

116 Hirsch biography: Hershey interview.

116 Students' attitudes, activities and arrangements: information was obtained primarily in interviews and correspondence with Mark M. Abbott, Roberta Du Bose Barton, Paul Fussell, Ora Guessford Weir, Helen Heberling Smith, A. J. Hettinger, Walter Hixenbaugh, Elinor Ryan Hixenbaugh, Donald R. Jones, Donald M. Love, Lue C. Lozier, Will C. Noble, Kenneth Pringle, Nell M. Reeder, Lamar Tooze, Earl W. Tucker, Mrs. Francis Stirling Wilson (diary and letters of her husband) and George Wythe.

117 Turner's job: Turner interview; Turner to Ford, Dec. 1, 1915, FPP Papers. Expedition complement: There is an assortment of lists specifying who went and in what capacities, none of which is correct. Assuming that the proper tally was 166 persons for whom Ford paid passage as advised by Halvor Jacobsen (Jacobsen to A. Hirsh, Dec. 7, 1915, TC 18, Acc. 79, FA), I have devised a list based on documents, diaries, letters and other evidence including lists and correspondence in the FPP Papers, the passenger list published by the shipping line, a cablegram from the Scandinavian American Line to Johnson and Company, n.d., Box 5, Acc. 79, FA, and signatures of passengers in Box 1, Maverick Papers. I am assuming that the stowaway was not counted a member of the expedition on the date Ford was notified of the total count and that Ford paid for the passage of Alvin Seldner who had originally been sent to the Biltmore headquarters to help out and then sailed with the party. See Appendix 1 for list of members on *Oscar II* and *Frederick VIII*.

117 Supernumeraries: Mylecraine-Cornick interview, Paula Pogany to Huebsch, March 30, 1916, Maverick Papers; and Hirsh to Lochner, Dec. 8, 1915, FPP Papers.

117n First-class passengers: *BT*, Jan. 13, 1916.

118 "The adequate thing": Wales to family, Dec. 4, 1916.

118 "Yes, no telephones": Noble, "A Student's View," 305.

118 First night on board: NY *World*, Dec. 5, 1915; Ford Expedition notes, Sorensen Papers; and Davis Reminiscences, 4.

118 Schwimmer-Bullitt interview: *PPL*, Jan. 7, 1916; Turner interview.

118 "Everything was jolly aboard": NY *World*, Dec. 5, 1915.

118 Liquor: Richard A. Picard to author, Oct. 18, 1973; Davis to Moore-Eastman, Dec. 28, 1949, Moore-Eastman Papers; and *NYT*, Jan. 3, 1916.

118–20 Caesar-Greenberg encounter: Caesar, "Account of Jacob Greenberg, Stowaway on the Peace Ship," and Caesar, "How I Stopped World War I," 4–16, unpublished manuscripts, Acc. 167, FA; Rex Holmes, unpublished MS, Box 10, FPP Papers; and *The Call*, Feb. 6, 1915.

118 Caesar biography: Caesar interview.
120 Ford's feelings first night: NY *Sun*, Dec. 5, 1915; NY *World*, Dec. 5, 1915.
120 Guard duty: *BT*, Jan. 14, 1916; Eriksson Hyyrylaeinen to author, Sept. 23, 1968.

CHAPTER 7: *"A veritable floating Chautauqua"*

121 "A veritable floating Chautauqua": Hopkins, "Ford Peace Dream," unpublished MS, Hopkins Papers.
121–22 Conditions during early days: *PPL*, Jan. 7, 1916; NY *Tribune*, Jan. 9, 1916; Guessford diary, Guessford-Weir Papers, Dec. 5, 1916; Bowman interview; Daily Bulletin, Dec. 6, 1915, FPP Papers (the repository of all Daily Bulletins), *BT*, Jan. 17, 1916; and Davis Reminiscences, 29.
121 "Moveable feast": Maverick diary, Dec. 5, 1916, Maverick Papers.
122 *Oscar* routine: Weatherly to wife, Dec. 6, 1915, FPE Papers; Mylecraine diary, Dec. 6, 1915; *Oscar II* price list, Tucker Papers; *The Call*, Jan. 5, 1916; *Argosy*, Dec. 7, 1915, FPE Papers (the repository of all copies of the *Argosy*); and Daily Bulletins.
122 "Seasick Row": Reeder interview.
122 "Like a mother": Marquis to wife, Dec. 16, 1915.
122 "Let us have peace": *Argosy* files.
122 "Our peace ship party": *Argosy*, Dec. 8, 1915.
123 "Spiritual rebirth": Notes, Guessford-Weir Papers.
123 Aked and Jones addresses: TC 3, Acc. 79, FA.
123 Cable costs: Atlantic *Daily News*, Dec. 7, 1915, FPP Papers.
123 "A row of morocco-bound books": Noble, "A Student's View," 307.
123–24 Schwimmer speech: Bulletin, Dec. 6, 1915 and "Mass Meeting of the Ship's Company," Dec. 6, 1915, TC 3, Acc. 79, FA; Maverick diary, Dec. 6, 1915.
124 "In her black hair": Wales to family, Dec. 4, 1916.
124 "An infinitely significant": Hixenbaugh in Omaha *State Journal*, Jan. 9, 1916.
126 "Secret documents": Jordan, *Days of a Man*, 2:676; Lochner, *Don Quixote*, 68; Egan, "Mr. Ford's Peace Party," 9, 22–27; and *NYT*, Oct. 16, 1915.
126 Schwimmer's handbag: Lochner to author, June 9, 1966.
126 Schwimmer interview: Syracuse *Post Standard*, Dec. 9, 1915; Brooklyn *Times*, Jan. 1, 1916; and NY *Sun*, Dec. 9, 1915.
126 "All is not peaceful": Washington *Times*, Dec. 8, 1915.
126–27 General meeting, Dec. 7: Address of the President to Congress, Dec. 7, 1915, *Papers . . . Foreign Relations, 1915*, ix, xx; Weatherly to wife, Dec. 6–12, 1915; Fussell diary, Dec. 7, 1915, Fussell Papers; E. Jones speech, Box 17, Acc. 62 and Minutes, Dec. 7, 1915, Box 4, Acc. 79, FA: NY *World*, Dec. 9, 1915; *PPL*, Jan. 8, 1915 and Guessford diary, Dec. 7, 1915.
127–28 Dec. 8: *NYT*, Jan. 3, 1916; Davis Reminiscences, 3; Wythe interview; Detroit *News*, Jan. 7, 1916; and *PPL*, Dec. 21, 1915 and Jan. 9, 1916.
128 "We are simply": *Argosy*, Dec. 11, 1916.
129 Jones's speech cabled: *Ibid.*, Dec. 8, 1915.
129 Press reaction: Seltzer's cable, Box 4, FPP Papers; *The Call*, Jan. 5, 1916; NY *Tribune*, Jan. 9, 1916; Detroit *News*, Jan. 12, 1916; *NYT*, Dec. 21, 1915; and Brooklyn *Eagle*, Jan. 6, 1916.
129 Speeches: Schwimmer address, Dec. 9, 1915, TC 3, Acc. 79, FA; Fussell and Guessford diaries, Dec. 9, 1915; *BT*, Jan. 10, 1916; and Detroit *News*, Jan. 8, 1916.

129 Asquith speech: *Argosy*, Dec. 9, 1915; Newark *Evening News*, Dec. 9, 1916; and *PPL*, Jan. 8, 1916.

130 "Seriously and kindly": Pasadena *Star*, Jan. 15, 1916.

130 "Seldom Silent": Love and Weir interviews.

130–31 Speeches, Friday night meeting: Minutes, Dec. 10, 1915, TC 3, Acc. 79, FA.

131–33 Reaction to platform: *BT*, Dec. 10, 1915 and Jan. 11, 1916; *NYT*, Dec. 21, 1915 and Jan. 3, 1916; Noble, "A Student's View," 310; *PPL*, Dec. 21, 1915 and Jan. 6, 1916; *SFB*, Dec. 31, 1915; Brooklyn *Eagle*, Jan. 4, 1916; *The Call*, Jan. 5, 1916; Chicago *News*, Jan. 15, 1916; NY *Tribune*, Jan. 9, 1916; and Resolutions, Box 4, FPP Papers.

133 Mock trial: *BT*, Jan. 12, 1916; trial transcript, Box 10, FPP Papers; *PPL*, Jan. 6, 1916; NY *Tribune*, Jan. 9, 1916; and NY *Globe*, Jan. 6 and 12, 1916.

133 "Immaterial to the prime mission": Fussell diary, Dec. 11, 1915.

133 Evans statement: draft, Evans Papers.

134 Aked plan: "Reasons for and against the retention of the declaration as it stands," Box 8, FPP Papers.

134 "Nothing worthwhile": Tucker interview.

135 Ford statement: Ford to Dear Friend, Dec. 11, 1915, FPP Papers.

135 Bingham's illness: *SFB*, Sept. 9, 1916; Park Reminiscences; and Noble, "A Student's View," 314.

135 "That seemed mighty": Weatherly to wife, Dec. 6, 12 and 13, 1915.

135–36 Members' reactions to disagreement: *BT*, Jan. 12, 1916; Hopkins interview in newsclip, Bangor, Maine newspaper, Hopkins Papers; Marquis to wife, Dec. 16, 1915; Wales to family, Dec. 4–18, 1915, A. L. Wales Papers; Lochner, *Don Quixote*, 73–74; Bernstein to Ford, Dec. 12, 1915, FPP Papers; Brooklyn *Times*, Jan. 1, 1916; Chicago *Journal*, Dec. 20, 1915; Robinson, "Confessions," 225; *NYT*, Dec. 21, 1915; and Lindsey to Miss Gregory and friends, Dec. 17, 1915, Lindsey Papers.

136 Second mock trial: *PPL*, Jan. 8, 1916; *BT*, Jan. 13, 1916, Guessford diary, Dec. 12, 1915; and Edith Lloyd Jones to family, Dec. 13, 1915, Jones Papers—Chicago.

137 Ford and Hempel: Brooklyn *Times*, Jan. 1, 1916; *SFB*, June 21, 1916; *BT*, Jan. 11, 1916; *Argosy*, Dec. 10, 1915; Gerda Thorsen to author, Jan. 1, 1968; and Maverick diary, Dec. 8 and 10, 1915.

137–38 Impressions made by Ford: Spartanburg (S.C.) *Herald* clipping, n.d., Mylecraine-Cornick Papers; Lochner, *Don Quixote*, 75; Wales to family, Dec. 26–27, 1915, A. L. Wales Papers; Tucker and Fussell interviews; Noble, "A Student's View," 310–11; Evans to wife, Dec. 13, 1915, Evans Papers; NY *Tribune*, Jan. 9, 1916; *PPL*, Jan. 9 and 31, 1916; *NYT*, Jan. 4, 1916; and Wythe interview.

138–39 Impression made by Schwimmer: *PPL*, Dec. 19, 1915 and Jan. 31, 1916; Davis, "Henry Ford's Adventure with the 'Lunatic Fringe,'" *NYT*, Oct. 4, 1925, 3:3; NY *American*, Jan. 30, 1916; NY *World*, Dec. 20, 1915; Fussell, Mylecraine-Cornick and Wythe interviews; Lochner, *Don Quixote*, 66–69; *BT*, Jan. 13, 1916; Wales, Notes on voyage, n.d., A. L. Wales Papers; and San Francisco *Call*, Nov. 27, 1918.

139 Delegates' impressions of each other: Lindsey to Miss Gregory and friends, Dec. 17, 1915; Marquis to wife, Dec. 16, 1915; Hopkins, "Ford Peace Dream"; and Huebsch Reminiscences, 140.

139–41 Reporters' reactions: *PPL*, Dec. 14, 1915 and Jan. 31, 1916; Brooklyn *Times*, Dec. 13, 1915; NY *World*, Dec. 13, 1915; and NY *Sun*, Dec. 14, 1915.

141 "Not be annoyed": Ford to Wilson, n.d., Box 4, FPP Papers.

141 Delegates' impressions of press: Robinson, "Confessions," 225; Wales to family, Dec. 4, 1916.

141 "A bright, active group": Marquis to wife, Dec. 16, 1915.

141 Compilation of comments: *The Voice of America; Short Selections from American Letters*, (Copenhagen, 1916) FPP Papers.

142 British board *Oscar*: Evans, *Yeoman Shield*, Feb. 1, 1916; Edith Lloyd Jones to family, Dec. 13, 1915, Jones Papers—Chicago; Guessford diary, Dec. 13, 1915; NY *World*, Dec. 13, 1915; *NYT*, Jan. 3, 1916; and Noble, "A Student's View," 312–13.

142–43 Tuesday-morning meeting: Minutes, Dec. 14, 1915, Box 4, FPP Papers; Weatherly to wife, Dec. 14, 1915; and *BT*, Jan. 14, 1916.

143 Kirkwall harbor: F. Stirling Wilson to mother, Dec. 15–17, 1915, Stirling Wilson Papers; Fussell and Mylecraine diaries, Dec. 15, 1915; and Weatherly to wife, Dec. 14, 1915.

143–44 Schwimmer visits reporters: Detroit *News*, Jan. 15, 1916; *PPL*, Jan. 8, 1916; and *NYT*, Oct. 4, 1925, 3:3.

144 Bermann leaves: Detroit *News*, Jan. 15, 1916; Guessford diary, Dec. 15, 1916.

144 Photograph of Jones and Aked was published in major newspapers on Dec. 28, 1915.

144 Ford illness: *PPL*, Dec. 9, 1915; Lochner, *Don Quixote*, 63–64.

144–45 Vacillating Sons and Sisters: Maverick diary, Dec. 15, 1915; account of proceedings, Tucker Papers; *NYT*, Jan. 3, 1916; *PPL*, Jan. 9 and Feb. 1, 1916; and *BT*, Jan. 17, 1916.

145 "Confinement somewhat irksome": Weatherly to wife, Dec. 16, 1915.

145–46 Reporters' protest of English: *SFB*, Jan. 29, 1916; Davis et al. to Ford, Dec. 16, 1915, FPP Papers; and *NYT*, Jan. 3, 1916.

146–47 Kirkwall-Norway crossing: NY *Herald*, Dec. 30, 1915; Sewall to Dear Friends in Hoosierland, Dec. 16, 1915; Fussell diary, Dec. 17, 1915; *BT*, Jan. 17, 1916; *NYT*, Jan. 3, 1916; Reeder to family, Dec. 22, 1915, Reeder Papers; Wales to family, Dec. 26, 1915; Marquis to wife, Dec. 18, 1915; and Weatherly to wife, Dec. 18, 1915.

147–48 Schwimmer cables and State Department reaction: Schwimmer to Bryn, to Moerck and to A. Schmedeman, all Dec. 7, 1915, Schwimmer Papers; to S. Bergman, Dec. 4, 1915, American Legation, Sweden, Records of the Foreign Service Posts of the Department of State, RG 84, File No. 711, NA; to Egan, n.d., enclosed in Egan to E. de Scavenius, Nov. 28, 1915 and Lansing to Egan, Dec. 4, 1915, both in American Legation, Denmark, RG 84, File No. 711; to Ihlen, Dec. 17 and 18, 1915 and Ihlen to Schwimmer, Dec. 18, 1915, both in Norwegian FO Records, Ford Peace Expedition file; to Schmedeman, n.d. and Schmedeman to Schwimmer, n.d., in Schmedeman to Secretary of State, Dec. 29, 1915, General Records of the Department of State, RG 59, File No. 763.72119/113, NA.

148 Jacobs-Addams correspondence: Jacobs to Addams, Dec. 4, 1915 and Addams to Schwimmer, Feb. 18, 1916, Addams Papers; Jacobs, Macmillan and Manus to Addams, Nov. 27, 1915, WPP Papers; Addams to Jacobs, n.d., FPE file, WPP Papers; and *NYT*, Dec. 15, 1915 and Jan. 6 and 20, 1916.

148 Responses to Schwimmer's demands: Ramondt to Schwimmer, Dec. 17, 1915 and W. Keilhau to Schwimmer, Dec. 17, 1915, FPP Papers.

149 Charges against reporters: *SFB*, Jan. 27, 1916; dossier, Dec. 18, 1915, FPP Papers.

149 Norwegian reporters visit: *Frankfurter Zeitung* article, n.d., enclosed with

translation in American Embassy, Vienna to Secretary of State, Dec. 22, 1915, RG 59, File No. 711.9; *PPL*, Jan. 9, 1916.

149-50 Last night on ship: *BT*, Jan. 18 and 19, 1916; *PPL*, Jan. 9, 1916; Chicago *News*, Jan. 15, 1916; *SFB*, Dec. 31, 1915; Guessford diary, Dec. 18, 1915; and NY *Globe*, Jan. 4, 1916.

CHAPTER 8: *"The winning of our welcome"*

152 "Winning of our welcome": Hopkins, "Ford Peace Expedition in Scandinavia," unpublished MS, Hopkins Papers.

152 Arrival in Christiania: Lochner, *Don Quixote*, 80.

152 Neutral countries' political situations: *PPL*, Dec. 29, 1915 and Jan. 9, 1916; *NYT*, Jan. 3, 1916; Chattanooga *News*, Jan. 20, 1916; Lucius to FO, Dec. 22, 1915, RG 242, T-120, Roll 2077; Pasadena *Star*, Feb. 15, 1916; and *Papers . . . Foreign Relations, 1914, Supplement,* 159-61.

152 Prewar peace organizations' status: "Forces for Peace in Europe," unpublished MS, TC 7, Acc. 79, FA.

153 German and Danish ministers' reports: Oberndorff to FO, Dec. 21, 1915, RG 242, T-120, Roll 2077; Krag to Danish FO, Dec. 21, 1915, Danish FO Records, FPE file.

153 First Christiania meeting: Brooklyn *Eagle*, Jan. 3, 1916; NY *World*, Dec. 21 and 22, 1915; *PPL*, Jan. 9, 1916; NY Globe, Jan. 13, 1916; and Lochner, *Don Quixote* draft MS.

153 "Talked so loud": Keilhau to Seely, Dec. 26, 1915, Acc. 63, FA.

153-54 Norwegian press reaction: Report, Hopkins Papers; *NYT*, Dec. 21, 1915; Lochner, *Don Quixote* draft MS; and *PPL*, Jan. 10, 1916.

154 Expeditions' activities: Lochner, *Don Quixote*, 80-108; Weatherly letters to his wife; Fussell and Guessford diaries; *BT*, Jan. 19 and 25, 1916; Schmedeman to Secretary of State, Dec. 29, 1915, RG 59, File No. 763.72119/113.

154 Norwegian press changes view: *PPL*, Jan. 10, 1916; Oberndorff to FO, Dec. 23, 1915, RG 242, T-120, Roll 2077, NA.

154 Delegates' speeches: Robinson, "Greetings to the Women of Norway," Dec. 20, 1915 and Lindsey, "Why We Are Late," Dec. 22, 1915, TC 3, Acc. 79, FA.

154-55 Government leaders' reactions: *NYT*, Dec. 23, 1915; Schmedeman to Secretary of State, Dec. 29, 1915; Krag to Wallenberg, Dec. 21, 1915, Swedish FO Records, FPE file; and Oberndorff to FO, Dec. 22, 1915, RG 242, T-120, Roll 2077.

155 Selecting European delegations: Lochner, *Don Quixote*, 82-83; W. Keilhau to F. Seely, Dec. 26, 1915 in Seely to Marquis, Jan. 20, 1916, Acc. 62, FA; and NY *Tribune*, Jan. 31, 1916.

155 *Frederick VIII* contingent: H. Jacobsen to A. Hirsh, Dec. 10, 1915, TC 18, FA; biographical information in Boxes 1-4, FPP Papers and "Ford Who's Who," Copenhagen, 1915.

155 "Lincoln of Idaho": Hiram T. French, *History of Idaho* (Lewis Publishing Co., 1914), 2:820.

155 "It was no more": Milton, "Impressions of the European War," Box 53, Acc. 1, FA.

155 Seely biography: *NYT*, March 15, 1943.

155-56 Bingham's death: Plantiff to Ford, Jan. 11, 1916, Box 8, Acc. 572 and Plantiff to Frimann Koren, Jan. 1, 1916, TC 18, Acc. 79, FA; *SFB*, Sept. 8, 1916.

156 Ford in Christiania: Lochner, *Don Quixote*, 81; NY *Sun*, Dec. 23, 1915; NY *Herald*, Jan. 4, 1916; and Krag to Wallenberg, Dec. 21, 1915.

156 Ford's health: Marquis to Seely, Jan. 25, 1916, Acc. 63, FA.

156 Schwimmer's management tactics: Turner interview; Keilhau to Seely, Dec. 26, 1915.

157 Ford's departure: C. Ford to Schwimmer, Aug. 12, 1916, Evans Papers; Lochner, *Don Quixote*, 86–91; "Statement of Events Connected with Mr. Henry Ford's leaving the Ford Expedition," n.d., Maverick Papers; and Koren to Plantiff, Dec. 30, 1915 and Neely to Koren, Jan. 3, 1916, TC 18, Acc. 79, FA.

157–59 Train ride to Stockholm: Stirling Wilson, Maverick and Weir diaries, Dec. 24, 1915; *BT*, Jan. 22, 1916; Lozier interview; Reeder to family, Dec. 29, 1915; J. E. Jones, Adair (Iowa) *News*, Feb. 25, 1915; and Lochner, *Don Quixote*, 91.

159 Statement to the press: n.d., Box 4, FPP Papers.

159 Schwimmer selects committee members: Schwimmer to Addams, Jan. 26, 1916, Addams Papers; NY *World*, Dec. 25, 1915; and *NYT*, Dec. 25, 1915.

159 Arrival in Stockholm: *The Call*, Jan. 22, 1916; Lochner to Ford, Jan. 6, 1916, FPE Papers; Hettinger interview; Tooze diary, Dec. 24, 1915, Tooze Papers; Davis Reminiscences, 1; and *BT*, Jan. 22, 1916.

159–60 Stockholm reception: *Unity*, March 23, 1916; Lochner, *Don Quixote*, 93; and Plantiff to Ford, Jan. 11, 1916, Box 8, Acc. 572, FA.

160 Christmas Eve dinner: Weatherly to wife, Dec. 24, 1915; Sewall to Dear Friends in Hoosierland, Jan. 10, 1916, Sewall Papers; *SFB*, Dec. 27, 1915; and Fussell diary, Dec. 24, 1915.

160 "Merely to a nervous breakdown": Minutes, Box 8, FPP Papers.

160 Plantiff and reporters: NY *World*, Dec. 25, 1915.

161 "Needs a Moses": Brooklyn *Eagle*, Jan. 18, 1916.

161 Ford, Bryan and Addams urged to come to Europe: Schwimmer to Ford, Dec. 27, 1915, Schwimmer Papers; cable messages, Boxes 4 and 8, FPP Papers.

161 "Feel without Ford": Bryan to Ford party, [Dec. 27, 1915] Box 30, Bryan Papers.

161–62 Administrative committee meetings: Minutes, Dec. 1915–Jan. 1916, Box 9, Acc. 79, FA.

161 Students' activities: Fussell, Guessford, Stirling Wilson and Abbott diaries, Dec. 26–28, 1915; Fussell interview.

162 General meeting, Dec. 26: *BT*, Jan. 25, 1916; Weatherly to wife, Dec. 26, 1915; and *PPL*, Dec. 27, 1915.

162–63 Boissevain resignation: Box 4, FPP Papers; *PPL*, Dec. 27, 1915.

162–63 Reaction to Boissevain departure: NY *Tribune*, Dec. 27, 1915; Schwimmer to Ford, Jan. 15, 1916, Box 9, Acc. 79, FA; Plantiff to Ford, Jan. 11, 1916; and Lochner to B. de Jong van Beek en Donk, n.d., Box 4, FPP Papers.

163 McClure in Europe: *BT*, Jan. 27, 1916; Weatherly to wife, Dec. 20, 1915; McClure to Hattie McClure, Jan. 4 and 5, 1915, McClure Papers.

163 Bernstein departure: NY *Tribune*, Dec. 30, 1915; NY *American*, Dec. 25, 1915.

163 Swedish welcome: *PPL*, Dec. 29, 1915; Lochner to Ford, Jan. 6, 1916; and Lochner, *Don Quixote*, 95.

163 Gifts: Plantiff to Lindhagen, n.d., Box 5; Schwimmer to Lochner, Dec. 29, 1915; and Lindhagen to FPE, Dec. 30, 1915, all in FPP Papers.

163 Departure from Stockholm: Weatherly to wife, Dec. 31, 1916; Plantiff to Ford, Jan. 11, 1916.

163–64 Danish difficulties: Lochner, *Don Quixote*, 96–97; T. Daugaard and C. Tybjerg to Plantiff, Dec. 27, 1915; Tybjerg to Schwimmer, Dec. 28, 1915, and Forchhammer to Lindhagen, Dec. 23, 1915, all in FPP Papers.

164 Schwimmer in Copenhagen: Forchhammer speech, Jan. 3, 1916, TC 3, Acc. 79,

FA; *NYT*, Jan. 1, 1916; Oberndorff to FO, Dec. 20, 1915, RG 242, T-120, Roll 2077; Egan to Secretary of State, Jan. 7, 1916, RG 59, File No. 763.72119/116; *Papers . . . Foreign Relations, 1915, Supplement*, 78–79; Schwimmer to Egan [Dec. 7, 1915], Danish FO Records, FPE file; and C. M. T. Cold to Ellis Jones, Dec. 30, 1915, TC 19, Acc. 79, FA.

164 "Was the sort of place": *PPL*, Feb. 1, 1916.

165 "At the last moment": Davis to Moore-Eastman, Dec. 28, 1949. Moore-Eastman Papers; Davis Reminiscences, 10.

165 "This traveling on Henry": Reeder to family, Dec. 29, 1915.

165 "The idea of people": Reeder interview.

165 "The positions": Weatherly to wife, Jan. 2, 1916.

165 "The astonishing thing": Davis Reminiscences, 17.

165 *Politiken* reception: newsclip, Iowa City *Republican*, n.d., Heberling-Smith Papers; Lochner, *Don Quixote*, 100; Lochner to Ford, Jan. 6, 1916; and Rosencrantz speech, Jan. 4, 1916, TC 3, Acc. 79, FA.

165–67 Travel arrangements: Egan, "Mr. Ford's Peace Party," 27; Egan to Secretary of State, Jan. 7, 1916; Lochner, *Don Quixote*, 102–4; Bernstorff to FO, Dec. 7, 1915 and Brockdorff-Rantzau to FO, Jan. 13, 1916, RG 242, T-120, Roll 2077; NY *World*, Jan. 4, 1916; and Washington *Times*, Jan. 4, 1916.

167n Brockdorff-Rantzau spy ring: Gustav Hilger, *The Incompatible Allies: A Memoir-History of German-Soviet Relations 1918–1941* (NY: Macmillan, 1953), 85; Brockdorf-Rantzau correspondence, Jan. 2, 1916 ff., RG 242, T-120, Roll 2077.

167 Schwimmer runs operation: *SFB*, Feb. 3, 1916; Eriksson-Hyyrylaeinen to author, Sept. 23, 1968.

167–68 Incoming correspondence: Boxes 4 and 5, FPP Papers.

168 Impact on Russia: "The Attitude of the Russian Press Towards the Ford Expedition," Jan. 3, 1916, FPP Papers; Lochner, *Don Quixote*, 101.

168 Plantiff's relations with delegates: Chargé d'Affaires, Netherlands to Secretary of State, Jan. 18, 1916, RG 59, File No. 763.72119/125; Braley, "Grafters Abroad," Ohio *State Journal*, Feb. 20, 1916, 4:8; NY *World*, Jan. 4, 1916; Plantiff to Ford, Jan. 11, 1916; Plantiff to Egan, Jan. 6, 1916 and account book, TC 18, Acc. 79, FA.

168–69 Schwimmer expenses: Account and receipts, Dec. 1915 and Jan. 1916, TC 18 and 19, Acc. 79, FA; Egan, "Mr. Ford's Peace Party," 23; and Lochner, *Don Quixote*, 122.

169 Egan on expedition: Egan, "Mr. Ford's Peace Party," 23, Egan to Secretary of State, Jan. 7, 1916.

169 Travel preparations: Sewall to Dear Friends in Hoosierland, Jan. 10, 1916; Bulletins, FPP Papers; Brooklyn *Eagle*, Jan. 24, 1916; and *BT*, Feb. 21, 1916.

170 Scandinavian delegates with expedition: Lochner to German Consul General, Jan. 5, 1916, FPP Papers.

170 Hanna's illness: St. Joseph's Hospital bill, Jan. 18, 1916, TC 19, Acc. 79, FA.

170 Wales's journey to Holland: Recollections, n.d., A. L. Wales Papers.

170n Greenberg's biography: Scandinavian American Lines to Lochner, Feb. 1, 1916, FPP Papers; Greenberg to Lindsey, June 5, 1916, Lindsey Papers; and Caesar and Hershey interviews.

170–71 Journey through Germany: Weatherly to wife, Jan. 8, 1916; Stirling Wilson and Abbott diaries, Jan. 7, 1916; Fussell, "A Trip Through Germany," Pasadena *Star*, Feb. 10, 1916; *BT*, Feb. 7, 1916; *PPL*, Jan. 30, 1916; Birnbaum, *Peace Moves*, 94–95, 98; and NY *Sun*, Jan. 9, 1916.

171n Bethea's encounter: Brooklyn *Eagle*, Jan. 30, 1916; Hostetler diary, Jan. 7, 1916, FPE Papers.

171 Arrival in Hague: J. E. Jones, Adair (Iowa) *News*, Feb. 25, 1916; Reeder to family, Jan. 12, 1916, Reeder Papers; and *NYT*, Jan. 9, 1916.

CHAPTER 9: *"A great deal of bitter feeling"*

172 "Leave meat": *PPL*, Jan. 30, 1916.

172 Students' departure: Stirling Wilson diary, Jan. 8, 1916.

172–73 Dutch political position: J. E. Jones, "The Truth About the Henry Ford Peace Expedition," FPE Papers; Pasadena *Star*, Feb. 15, 1916.

172 "Terror of little nations": Hopkins, "Return of Ford Peace Expedition," unpublished MS, Hopkins Papers.

173 Dutch press: Lochner, *Don Quixote*, 111–12; *PPL*, Feb. 1, 1916; and *SFB*, Feb. 16, 1916.

173 American legation attitude: Van Dyke to J. Loudon, Dec. 31, 1915, RG 84, Netherlands, File No. 711.5/11; and Chargé d'Affaires to Secretary of State, Jan. 18, 1916, RG 59, File No. 763.72119/125, both in NA.

173–74 Dutch peace societies: Protocol of Vrede door Recht, Oct. 29, 1914, Van Dyke Papers; C. A. de Jong van Beek en Donk-Kluyver, "The Basis of Permanent Peace," *Jus Suffragii*, Feb. 1, 1915, 233–34; B. de Jong van Beek en Donk to Ford, Feb. 5, 1916, Box 53, Acc. 1, FA; NY *Sun*, Jan. 12, 1916; and *NYT*, Jan. 21, 1916.

174 ICWPP and Schwimmer: Jacobs to Addams, Dec. 4 and 23, 1915 and Macmillan to Addams, Jan. 14, 1916, Addams Papers; *NYT*, Jan. 21, 1916.

174 Scandinavian peace plan: Report of Eighth Northern Peace Congress, Varberg, Sweden, TC 1, Acc. 79, FA.

175 International delegates meetings: Minutes, Jan. 9, 10, 13 and 15, 1916, TC 3, Acc. 79, FA and FPP Papers.

175 "The most disgusting chapter": Lochner, *Don Quixote*, 114.

176 Administrative committee meetings: Minutes, Jan. 10–17 [*sic*], 1916, Box 9, Acc. 79, FA.

176 American members' meetings: Minutes, Box 8, FPP Papers.

176 Lochner's minutes: Box 14, FPP Papers.

177 "Jammed down the throats": Lochner, *Don Quixote* draft MS.

177–78 Electioneering: *Ibid.*; A. Park to K. D. Blake, Jan. 18–24, 1916, Blake Papers; Plantiff to Aked, Jan. 5, 1916, TC 18, Acc. 79, FA; and Plantiff to Ford, Jan. 11, 1916.

177 "Those of us": *BT*, Feb. 10, 1916.

178 "Think of it": Caesar diary, Jan. 13, 1916, Acc. 167, FA.

179 Reaction to railroading: *BT*, Feb. 11, 1916; *PPL*, Jan. 31, 1916; *SFB*, Feb. 17, 1916; Weatherly to wife, Jan. 14, 1916; and *NYT*, Feb. 9, 1916.

179 "Was convinced": Huebsch Reminiscences, 143.

179 Barry's election: *SFB*, Jan. 14, 1916; *NYT*, Jan. 15, 1916; *PPL*, Feb. 1, 1916; and *BT*, Feb. 7, 11 and 12, 1916.

180 Farewell lunch: *NYT*, Jan. 16, 1916, 2:3, 4.

180 "It is the idealists": Newsclip, n.d., Worcester *Telegram*, FPE Papers.

180–81 Schwimmer criticized: Bernstein to R. Lansing, Feb. 28, 1916, RG 59, File No. 763.72119/132; NY *Tribune*, Feb. 6, 1916; and Robinson, "Confessions," 225.

181 Reporters' criticisms: NY *Sun*, Jan. 30, 1916; *NYT*, Jan. 16, 1916.

181 Student slide lecture: Love interview.

181 Ford's return: *The Call*, Jan. 3, 1916; NY *Tribune*, Jan. 3, 1916.
182 Liebold-Plantiff relationship: Liebold to Plantiff, Jan. 4, 1916, Box 39, Acc. 2 and Plantiff to Liebold, Jan. 7, 1916, TC 18, Acc. 79, FA.
182 Reports to Ford: Lochner to Ford, Jan. 6, 1916; Committee on Administration to Ford, Jan. 10, 1916 and Schwimmer to Ford, Jan. 15, 1916, Box 9, Acc. 79, FA; and Plantiff to Ford, Jan. 11, 1916.
182 "Always willing": Huebsch to Schwimmer, April 18, 1916, Maverick Papers.
182 "Poor Gaston Plantiff": Wales to family, Jan. 15, 1916, A. L. Wales Papers.
183 Administrative committee maneuvers: *NYT*, Feb. 25, 1916.
183–84 Schwimmer's tactics: Schwimmer to G. Kirchwey, Jan. 26, 1916, Schwimmer Papers; Schwimmer to Liebold, Jan. 6, 1916, TC 18, Acc. 79, FA; Maverick diary, Jan. 17, 1916; and *NYT*, Jan. 21, 1916.
184 Liebold's instructions: Liebold to Plantiff, Jan. 12, 1916 and Liebold to Hirsh, Jan. 19, 1916, Acc. 2, Box 39, FA.
184 Holt's character: *Unity*, March 23, 1916, 53; Park to Blake, Jan. 18–24, 1916.
184–86 Schwimmer contretemps: Lochner, *Don Quixote* draft MS; Plantiff to Dear Sir, Jan. 20, 1916, FPP Papers; Schwimmer to Plantiff, Jan. 25, 1916, Box 9, Acc. 79, FA; Schwimmer to Addams, Jan. 26, 1916, Addams Papers; Wales MS, n.d., A. L. Wales Papers; and Schwimmer to Liebold, Jan. 20–21, 1916, Maverick Papers.
186 Return trip to Stockholm: Lochner to Plantiff, Jan. 21, 1916, Box 9, Acc. 79 and Lochner to Plantiff, Jan. 22, 1916, Box 54, Acc. 1, FA.

CHAPTER 10: *"Long nervous strain unfits Schwimmer"*

All communications mentioned in this chapter that were sent by Lochner, Liebold, Plantiff, Ford and Schwimmer to each other from Jan. 20 through Feb. 28, 1916, unless otherwise cited, are in Box 9, Acc. 79; Box 39, Acc. 2 and Box 53, Acc. 1, FA and in Lochner and FPP Papers.

187 "There is a great difference": *Dagens Nyheter*, Jan. 26, 1916, Tucker Papers.
187–88 Grand Hotel description: Clark-Grose, "Experiment": Chicago *News*, March 28, 1916; Lochner to Levussove, Jan. 28, 1916 and list of rooms and office assignments, Box 13, FPP Papers.
187 "Of all sizes": Lochner to Balch, March 14, 1916, FPE file, WPP Papers.
188 "To consist": N. Smitheman to Plantiff, Feb. 17, 1916, Lochner Papers.
188 Office staff: Lochner to Plantiff, Jan. 22, 1916, Box 54, Acc. 1, FA; Wales to family, n.d., A. L. Wales Papers.
189 Bryan and Addams replies: Addams to Lochner, Jan. 23, 1916, Addams Papers; Plantiff to Lochner, Jan. 23, 1916, FPP Papers.
189 Schwimmer's role and offers to withdraw: Kliefoth to Addams, Feb. 23, 1916; Schwimmer to Addams, Jan. 26, 1916, Addams Papers; and Wales, Chronology of Events from Return to Stockholm until early March 1916, A. L. Wales Papers.
190 Schwimmer's instructions to Lochner: attached to Schwimmer to Ritter, Nov. 29, 1915, FPP Papers.
191–93 Copenhagen encounter: Harry C. Evans statement [Jan. 28, 1916], FPE Papers. Holt and Fels in Stockholm: Mylecraine diary, Feb. 1 and 5, 1916; Holt to Plantiff, Feb. 4 and 5, 1916, Box 9, Acc. 79, FA; Caesar diary, Jan. 30, 1916 and Feb. 2, 1916.
194 Schwimmer courts Aked and Barry: Schwimmer to Aked and Barry, Feb. 5, 1916, Maverick Papers.

194 Schwimmer alienates American delegates: Aked to Plantiff, Feb. 5, 1916 and Aked to E. Hitchcock, Feb. 4, 1916, Box 53, Acc. 1, FA; Wales, Chronology.

194–96 Wales-Schwimmer relationship: Eriksson-Hyyrylaeinen to author, Sept. 23, 1968; Wales, Chronology; and Caesar diary, Feb. 5, 1916.

196 Preliminary meetings: *SFB*, March 18, 1916; bulletins, minutes and announcements, Box 9, FPP Papers and TCs 1 and 2, Acc. 79, FA.

196–97 Schwimmer alienates European delegates: Wales, Chronology; Report of Committee of Experts, Feb. 19, 1916 in Lochner, *Don Quixote* draft MS; Wales to Lochner, Feb. 25, 1916, Lochner Papers; and Aked to Ford, Feb. 13, 1916, Box 53, Acc. 1, FA.

197 Schwimmer expenses: Kliefoth receipt, Jan. 15, 1916; entries in voucher book, Jan. 31, 1916 and Feb. 21, 1916; and Buelow to Plantiff, March 7, 1916, TC 18, Acc. 79, FA; "Delegates Protest on Honoraria," in Lochner, *Don Quixote* draft MS; and *Svenska Dagbladet*, Jan. 31, 1916.

197–98 Office staff reaction: Caesar diary, Feb. 6, 8 and 13, 1916; [Turner] to My Dear Boy, n.d.; Wales to family, Feb. 15, 1916, draft; "Aked's Testimony"; Smitheman to Plantiff, Feb. 17, 1916; Turner to Lochner, Feb. 29, 1916; Buelow to Lochner, Feb. 28, 1916; and Clark to Lochner, Feb. 20, 1916, all in Lochner Papers.

198 Lochner's reputation: Clark to Lochner, Feb. 20, 1916.

198 Lochner and Evans in Germany: Lochner to Schwimmer, Feb. 6, 1916 and Lochner to Huebsch, Feb. 14, 1916, FPE Papers; Evans to Schwimmer, Feb. 5, 1916 and Evans to Schwimmer, Feb. 5, 1916, Maverick Papers; *SFB*, Jan. 29, 1916; Montgelas to Lochner, n.d., Box 5, Addams Papers; Lochner, *Don Quixote*, 128–30 and draft MS; and Lochner to Montgelas, Feb. 1, 1916 and Montgelas to Lochner, Feb. 2, 1916, RG 242, T-120, Roll 2077.

198 "Empty House": W. H. Page diary, Feb. 9, 1916, Page Papers.

198–99 House's negotiations: Wilson to House, Dec. 24, 1915, House Papers; Link, *Confusions and Crises*, 101–41; and Woodward, "Great Britain," 45–58.

199–200 Lochner and Evans in Switzerland: *Neue Zurich Zeitung*, Feb. 25, 1916; *Die Menscheit*, Feb. 16, 1916; Lochner, *Don Quixote*, 131–36; Lochner to Emmy Lochner, Feb. 8, 1916, Lochner Papers; and Stovall to Secretary of State, Feb. 16, 1916, RG 59, File No. 763.72119/127.

199 "I never thought": Lochner to Schwimmer, Feb. 19, 1916, Lochner Papers.

199 Fried's impressions: Diary, Feb. 8 and 16, 1916, in Alfred H. Fried, *Mein Griegstagebuch—das 2. Kriegsjahr* (Zurich, 1919), translated in Lochner to author, April 6, 1966.

200 Rolland's impressions: Neutral Conference press bureau to J. Petersen-Norup, Feb. 27, 1916, TC 18, Acc. 79, FA.

200–201 Return through Germany: Lochner, *Don Quixote*, 136; Lochner to Montgelas, Feb. 24, 1916, RG 242, T-120, Roll 2080.

201 "Fels feels crazy": Schwimmer to Lochner, Feb. 5, 1916, Schwimmer Papers.

201 "Up against a big fight": Clark to Lochner, Feb. 20, 1916.

201–202 Schwimmer attempts to secure authority: Diagram, Feb. 22, 1916 and Clark to Schwimmer, Feb. 24, 1916, Maverick Papers; Wales, Chronology; Turner memorandum; Turner to E. C. Scott, Neuhaus to Smitheman, all Feb. 24, 1916 and Schwimmer-Smitheman correspondence, Lochner Papers.

202 Schwimmer cables Huebsch: Feb. 23 and 24, 1916, FPE Papers.

202 Lochner reception: Wales, Chronology; communications from Aked, Turner, Smitheman, Buelow, Wales and Huebsch, Feb. 1916, Lochner Papers.

202–203 Lochner-Schwimmer meeting: Caesar diary, Feb. 29, 1916; Lochner to Ford, March 9, 1916, Schwimmer Papers; and Wales, Chronology.

203 Schwimmer offers to resign: Minutes, Third Session, First Formal Meeting, Neutral Conference, Feb. 28, 1916, Box 2, Acc. 79, FA; Lochner, *Don Quixote* draft MS; Schwimmer to Chairman and Members of Neutral Conference, Feb. 28, 1916 and Lochner to Ford, March 1, 1916, Lochner Papers; Wales, Chronology; and Schwimmer to N. Sahlbom and M. Lofgren, Feb. 28, 1916, Schwimmer Papers.

203 "Long nervous strain": Lochner to Liebold, Feb. 28, 1916, FPP Papers.

203 Lochner takeover: Smitheman to Office and Business Force, Feb. 28, 1916, Schwimmer Papers; Lochner to E. O. Jones, Feb. 29, 1916, FPP Papers; and Lochner to Addams, March 14, 1916, Addams Papers.

203 Lochner summoned home: Liebold to Lochner, Feb. 25, 1916, Lochner Papers; de Jong to Ford, Feb. 5, 1916; NY *World*, Feb. 25, 1916; *PPL*, Feb. 27, 1916; Plantiff to J. L. Jones, March 27, 1916, Jones Papers; Schwimmer to Huebsch, Feb. 27, 1916, FPE Papers; and Wales, Chronology.

204 "Taking thorough hold": Lochner to Liebold, Feb. 26, 1916, Lochner Papers.

204 Schwimmer submits resignation: Liebold to Schwimmer, Feb. 29, 1916, Box 39, Acc. 2, FA; Wales, Chronology.

204 "Swell-headed idiot": Schwimmer to N. Kelley, March 2, 1916, Schwimmer Papers.

204–205 Schwimmer tries to retain command: F. Pogany to Yale University Press, March 5, 1916, FPE Papers; Schwimmer to Plantiff, [March 5, 1916], Maverick Papers.

205 Schwimmer resignation accepted: Liebold to Schwimmer, March 7, 1916, Box 39, Acc. 2, FA.

205 Schwimmer's post-resignation behavior: Pogany to Huebsch, March 30, 1916, FPE Papers; Schwimmer to Lochner, March 11, 1916, Lochner Papers; Lochner to Ford, March 13, 1916, FPP Papers; Pogany to Cor Ramondt, March 22, 1916, Schwimmer Papers; and Maverick interview.

205–206 Schwimmer character: Sophie Ramondt to author, Nov. 4, 1967; Lochner, *Don Quixote* draft MS; Wales to family, Feb. 15, 1916, Lochner Papers; and Schwimmer to Addams, March 1916 and Balch to Addams, April 24, 1916, Addams Papers.

206 "It now seems": Lochner to Ford, March 30, 1916, FPP Papers.

CHAPTER 11: *Neutral Conference for Continuous Mediation*

Subjects discussed during conference meetings are in Minutes, Neutral Conference for Continuous Mediation, Feb. 28–April 20, 1916, Box 2, Acc. 79, FA, unless otherwise cited.

207 Status of war: "Daily Review," March–April, 1916, Box 1, Acc. 79, FA; Baldwin, *World War I*, 72, 78.

208 Fels returns home: Mylecraine diary, March 24, 1916.

208 Biographical information on European delegates: Box 9, FPP Papers; Box 5, Acc. 79, FA; and Lochner, *Don Quixote*, 237–40.

209 "Respectable but not eminent": Aked to Ford, Feb. 13, 1915, Box 53, Acc. 1, FA.

209–10 American delegates asked to come to Europe: Aked to Ford, March 9, 1916, Box 8, Acc. 572, FA; Lochner to Ford, March 13, 1916, FPP Papers; Bryan to brother, Dec. 25, 1915, Bryan Papers, Occidental College Library, Los Angeles, California; Seely to Marquis, Jan. 20, 1916 and Marquis to Seely, Jan. 26, 1916, Acc. 63, FA; Lochner to Bryan, Feb. 6, 1916 and Hirsh to Lochner, Feb.

11, 1916, Lochner Papers; Jordan to Addams, Jan. 19, 1916, Addams Papers, Addams *et al.*, *Women at Hague*, 92; *Survey*, Jan. 15, 1916, 444; Addams's statement, Commission for Enduring Peace hearing, Jan. 11, 1916; Addams to Lochner, Jan. 24, 1916, Lochner Papers; Schwimmer to Addams, Jan. 26, 1916, Addams Papers; Lochner to Addams, Jan. 26, 1916, FPP Papers; Addams to Schwimmer and to Lochner, both Feb. 18, 1916, Addams Papers; Kirchwey to Ford, Dec. 3, 1915 and Schwimmer to Kirchwey, Jan. 26, 1916, FPP Papers; Schwimmer to Huebsch, Feb. 27, 1916, FPE Papers; and Jordan to Addams, Feb. 18, 1916, Jordan Papers.

210 Barry and Aked characterizations: Jordan to Lochner, Feb. 28, 1916 and Jordan to Addams, Feb. 18, 1916, Jordan Papers; and *SFB*, Feb. 15 and April 1, 1916.

211–12 Conference characterization: Lochner, *Don Quixote*, 138; "Daily Review," March 29 and 31, 1916; Caesar diary, Feb. 18, 1916; Lindhagen, *På Vikingastråt*, 14–32; Wales, "A Condensed Statement of My Experience with the Ford Conference," unpublished MS, Wales Papers.

213 Delegates' proposals: "The Berg Plan," Feb. 25, 1916, FPP Papers; Solnoerdal, "Remarks on Miss Helene Berg's Proposal," TC 4; Gjelsvik and Lie, "To the Conference," Feb. 28, 1916, TC 1; Steenhof, "Proposal for Immediate Action," TC 3; O. Forchhammer, "Why We Are Here," TC 4, all in Acc. 79, FA; and *SFB*, April 8 and May 16 and 19, 1916.

213–14 Wales revision: Wales, "The Unofficial Neutral Conference for Continuous Mediation," TC 7, Acc. 79, FA.

214 "No easy matter": *SFB*, April 3, 1916.

214–15 Neutral appeal: "To the Governments and Parliaments of the Neutral States Represented at the Second Hague Conference," TC 8, Acc. 79, FA; Lochner, *Don Quixote*, 141–42.

215 "We shall at least": Aked to Ford, March 9, 1916, Box 8, Acc. 572, FA.

215 Scandinavian governments' reaction: Lochner, *Don Quixote*, 143–45; *Politiken*, March 12, 1916; *NYT*, March 12, 1916, 1:5 and June 18, 1916, 1:3; newsclip, *Fredsbladet*, March 15, 1916, TC 1, Acc. 79, FA; I. Morris to Secretary of State, March 15, 1916, RG 84, Sweden, File No. 711; and Ragaz to family, March 26, 1916, Ragaz Papers.

215–16 Visits to representatives of warring countries: *SFB*, April 3 and 4, 1916 and May 26, 1916; Ragaz diary, March 3, 1916, Ragaz Papers; and Lochner to Ford, March 30, 1916, FPP Papers.

216 Sahlbom-Palmstierna missions: Ragaz diary, March 7, 18 and 20, 1916.
Conference consultants: Lochner to Balch, fragment, March 14, 1916, WPP Papers; Wales, report to family [April 28, 1916], A. L. Wales Papers; Aked to Ford, March 9, 1916; Jean Smith and Arnold Toynbee, eds., *Gilbert Murray: An Unfinished Autobiography* (London: George Allen & Unwin, 1960), 110–11; Otlet, Notes on the Conference, Box 13, FPP Papers; and Lochner, *Don Quixote*, 146.

216–17 Schwimmer's involvement: Pogany to Huebsch, March 30, 1916, FPE Papers; Ragaz to Balch [May 20, 1916], Ragaz Papers; Ragaz diary, Feb. 29 and March 10, 1916.

217 Aked-Holt roles: Caesar diary, March 6, 1916; Wales report to family [April 28, 1916], and Holt to Liebold, March 11, 1916, Box 8, Acc. 572, FA.

217 "Were just running": Liebold Reminiscences, 267.

217–18 Conference business matters: Holt-Liebold correspondence, March 1916, TC 18, Acc. 79 and Box 39, Acc. 2; Estimated Monthly Budget, Box 5, Acc. 79; and Anderson to Plantiff, April 3, 1916, Box 39, Acc. 2, all in FA; Lochner, *Don Quixote*, 154; and Larsson to Ford, [April 24, 1916], Larsson Papers.

218-25 Writing and publicizing the Appeal to the Belligerents: Report of Commission B, TC 1, Acc. 79, FA; Ragaz to family, March 22 and 26, 1916; Ragaz diary, March 30, 1916; *SFB*, May 18, 1916; Holt statement, April 6, 1916, FPE Papers; Lindhagen, *På Vikingastråt*, 14–32; "To Governments, Parliaments and Peoples of the Belligerent Nations," Easter 1916, TC 1, Acc. 79, FA: Lochner, *Don Quixote*, 151; Maverick diary, March 30 and April 13, 15 and 16, 1916; Pogany to Ramondt, March 13, 1916, Schwimmer Papers; Lochner to Ford, March 13 and April 10, 1916, FPP Papers; Anderson to Plantiff, April 3, 1916 and Liebold to Plantiff, April 17, 1916, Box 39, Acc. 2, FA; and Caesar diary, April 14, 1916.

225-26 Gobat-Ragaz resignations: Gobat to Holt and Ragaz to Holt, both April 15, 1916, Ragaz Papers.

226-27 Conference reorganization: *SFB*, May 17, 1916.

228 Ragaz reaction: Ragaz to Balch [May 20, 1916]; Ragaz to family, March 18 and April 24, 1916, Ragaz Papers; and Ragaz diary, March 30, 1916.

228 "The mistake we made": Lochner, *Don Quixote*, 139–40.

228 Impact of Appeal to Belligerents: *Ibid.*, 151–53; Balch, "The Stockholm Conference," 141–42; Wales to family, May 8, 1916, Wales Papers; and *NYT*, April 20, 1916

228 "We are 'starting something' ": Lochner to H. C. Morris, May 10, 1916, CPS Papers.

229 "I am not sure": House to Charles Seymour, March 14, 1925 in Seymour, *Intimate Papers*, 2:231–32.

229 Schwimmer's mediation attempt: Maverick diary, spring and summer, 1916.

CHAPTER 12: *"The idea refuses to die"*

Subjects discussed during conference meetings are in the Minutes of the Provisional Committee (April 24–May 15, 1916), Central Committee (May 16–Aug. 18, 1916), Committee on Activities and Outlook (May 18–July 28, 1916), Committee on Constructive Peace (May 19–July 24, 1916) and Mediation Committee (May 20–July 24, 1916), Box 2, Acc. 79, FA and in "Weekly Summaries," May 30–July 27, 1916, Box 11, FPP Papers.

230 "I think the reorganization": Balch to Addams, May 11, 1916, Addams Papers.

230 Balch's arrival: *Ibid.*; Washington *Herald*, April 5, 1916; and Balch to Addams, April 7 and 21, 1916, Addams Papers.

230-31 Schwimmer-Balch meeting: Schwimmer to Lloyd, May 26, 1916, FPP Papers; Balch to Addams, April 24, 1916, Addams Papers.

231 Balch on Aked, Barry and Provisional Committee: Balch to Addams, May 11, 1916.

231 "Waste fortunately": Balch to Plantiff, in Plantiff to Liebold, May 5, 1916 and Plantiff to Ford, June 24, 1916, Box 53, Acc. 1, FA.

231-32 Peace activities: Lochner, *Don Quixote*, 152, 156–67; May 18 Resolution, TC 1, Acc. 79, FA; Detroit *News*, July 28, 1916; and Caesar diary, May 18, 1916.

232 Central Committee news releases: *Survey*, June 10, 1916, 280–81.

232-33 De Jong's declaration: de Jong to Ford, Feb. 5, 1916; "Reorganized Neutral Conference at Stockholm," May 25, 1916, TC 1, Acc. 79, FA.

233 "The direct mediative": "Interview with Mr. Lochner," typescript, n.d., Box 13, FPP Papers.

233 "Completely won over": Lochner to Ford, June 23, 1916, FPP Papers.

234 "Will so worry": Lochner and de Jong to Dear Madame, May 30, 1916, Balch Papers.

234 Neutral governments' reaction: Krag to FO, May 31, 1916, Danish FO Records, FPE file; *Papers . . . Foreign Relations, 1916, Supplement*, 28–29, 34; and Monthly Report, Swiss Group, Central Committee of Neutral Conference, Oct. 31, 1916, TC 19, Acc. 79, FA.

234 Kaiser jokes about FPE: Gerard, *My Four Years*, 343.

234 "Reserved toward foreigners": Lochner to Ford, June 23, 1916.

235 Aked visit and report: Balch to Addams, May 11, 1916; Aked, "A Better Germany," Neutral Conference Document, Box 11, FPP Papers; Clark to Jordan, July 6, 1916, Jordan Papers; and Millard, "Heterodox Preacher," Los Angeles *Times*, Dec. 5, 1937.

235–36 Jespersen-Adelswaerd biography and visit: *NYT*, May 16, 1943; Lochner to Ford, Sept. 25, 1916, FPP Papers.

236 Wilson's policy: Link, *Confusions and Crises*, 273–79; Baker, *Facing War*, 197–226; Wilson to W. H. Taft, April 14, 1916, Wilson Papers; Baker and Dodd, eds. *Public Papers of Woodrow Wilson, New Democracy*, 2:184–88; and Link, *Progressivism and Peace*, 27–31.

236 "Never has the press": "President Wilson and the Peace of Europe," Neutral Conference Document, Box 11, FPP Papers.

236–37 Neutral Conference publications: General Secretary Bulletins, Box 10, FPP Papers; "Daily Reviews," Box 1, Acc. 79, FA and Box 10, FPP Papers; "Weekly Summaries," Box 11, FPP Papers; and Shieve to German FO, July 8, 1916, RG 242, T-120, Roll 2115.

237 "Only to send": Lochner to Ford, June 23, 1916.

238 Publicity and progaganda material: Lochner to Ford, May 11, 1916; Manifesto, July 11, 1916, Box 11, FPE Papers; "Summary of Manifesto," TC 6, Acc. 79 and 12-page news release, Box 53, Acc. 1, FA.

240 Lochner reports progress: Lochner to Jones, May 24, 1916, Jones Papers; Lochner to Ford, June 23, 1916; Lochner to Tucker, June 29, 1916, Tucker Papers.

240 "We may *itinerate*": Balch to Addams, May 11, 1916.

240 Arranging Lochner home visit: Plantiff to Liebold, May 5, 1916, Box 53, Acc. 1, FA.

240–41 Plantiff returns: Plantiff to J. L. Jones, April 17, 1916, Jones Papers; Henry Ford Sundry Debtors Account, June 1916, Box 4, Acc. 286, FA.

241 Lochner's reaction to Plantiff's report: Lochner to Ford, March 30, April 10 and June 23, 1916.

241 Plantiff asks instructions: Plantiff to Ford, June 23, 1916, FPP Papers.

242 "Everybody has an idea": Plantiff to Ford, June 24, 1916, Box 53, Acc. 1, FA.

242 Problems with Aked: *Ibid.*; Ragaz to family, March 26, 1915; Lochner to Ford, June 23, 1916; Detroit *News*, July 19 and 26, 1916; and Detroit *Journal*, July 20, 1916.

242–43 Aked and Balch return: *NYT*, July 26, 1916; Detroit *News*, July 26, 1916; Aked, "What I Have Learned," 170–71; Detroit *Times*, July 21 and 26, 1916; *DFP*, July 27, 1916; and Detroit *News*, July 21, 1916.

243n Schenk detention: unsigned letter to A. Schenk, March 11, 1916, FPP Papers.

243 "Keep her there": Plantiff to Ford, June 24, 1916.

243 Balch-Wilson meeting: Addams to Wilson, Aug. 2, 1916 and Wilson to Addams, Aug. 5, 1916, Addams Papers; Balch to Polk, Aug. 22, 1916 and Polk to Balch, Sept. 30, 1916, House Papers.

244 ANCC and Wilson meeting: *NYT*, Aug. 31, 1916; Shelly to Maverick, July 11, 1916, FPE Papers; Huebsch Reminiscences, 166; and Wilson to Schiff, Aug. 31, 1916, Wilson Papers.

244 Balch's activities: Balch to Bryan, Sept. 7, 1916, Bryan Papers; Hallinan to Balch, Nov. 10, 1916, Balch Papers; and Balch, "The Stockholm Conference," 141–42.

245 "I did not wish": C. Ford to Schwimmer, Aug. 12, 1916, Evans Papers.

245–46 "Converted the peoples": Lochner, *Don Quixote*, 159–61.

246–48 Conference changes: Liebold to Neely, July 5 and 27, 1916 and Aug. 4, 1916, Acc. 2, FA; Lochner to Ford, July 25, 1916 and Sept. 15, 1916, FPP Papers; Wales to Plantiff, July 26, 1916; Plantiff to Holt, July 7, 1916; Lochner to Plantiff, Aug. 6, 10 and 19, 1916 and Plantiff to Lochner, Aug. 8 and Sept. 5, 1916, all in FPP Papers; H. Thomas to L. Kellogg, Nov. 7, 1916, Madison Branch, WPP Papers; Holt to Liebold, July 17, 1916, TC 18 and Lochner to Wigforss, Sept. 13, 1916, Box 10, both in Acc. 79, FA.

248 "Influenced by": Wales to Balch, Sept. 17, 1916, Balch Papers.

248 "Three lightning rods": Lochner to Ford, Aug. 15, 1916, FPP Papers.

248 "The future beyond": Lochner to Wigforss, Aug. 22 and 31, 1916, Box 10, Acc. 79, FA.

CHAPTER 13: *"A clean sweep of the past"*

249 Somme casualties: Esposito, *Concise History*, 514.

249 German political and military situation: Fischer, *Germany's War Aims*, 289–90; Birnbaum, *Peace Moves*, 130; and *NYT*, Nov. 27, 1916.

250 European press reaction to conference reorganization: Lochner to Plantiff, Sept. 6, 1916, FPP Papers.

250 Reorganized conference activities: Report of Mikael Lie, Sept. 8, 1916, TC 19; Scherrer-Fuellemann to Lindhagen, Nov. 3, 1916; Monthly Report, Swiss Group, Sept. 29, 1916, and Scherrer-Fuellemann to Dutch and Swiss Groups, Oct. 14, 1916, Box 10, de Jong to Wigforss, Sept. 16, 1916, TC 7; Wales manuscripts, TC 7, all in Acc. 79, FA; and Lochner to Plantiff, Dec. 6, 1916, FPP Papers.

250–51 International journal: Lochner to Ford, June 23, 1916 and Wigforss to Lochner, Dec. 29, 1916, FPP Papers; Wigforss to Balch, Dec. 14, 1916, Balch Papers.

251 Enlisting belligerent support: Wigforss to Lochner, Sept. 4, 10, 21 and 24, 1916; Wigforss to Scherrer-Fuellemann, Sept. 11, 1916; and Minutes, Swiss Group, Nov. 7, 1916, all in Box 10, Acc. 79, FA.

251 De Jong's suggestion: de Jong to M. Lie, Oct. 25, 1916; Lochner to Wigforss, Dec. 20, 1916; and Minutes, Swiss Group, Nov. 7, 1916, all in Box 10, Acc. 79, FA.

251 Lochner's activities: Lochner to Plantiff, Sept. 2, 1916 and Lochner to Ford, Sept. 18 and 27, 1916, FPP Papers; Lochner-Wigforss correspondence, Box 10, Acc. 79, FA.

251–52 Lochner's anxiety: Liebold to Plantiff, July 28, 1916, FPP Papers; Lochner, *Don Quixote*, 178.

252 Leipnik biography: Howard, *Theatre of Life*, 1:165–66; Moritzen, *Peace Movement*, 404; Drummond to S. W. Harris, Dec. 28, 1916, FO 371–2801 File No. 9113.

252 Leipnik plans: Leipnik report, Sept. 29, 1916 forwarded Oct. 18, 1916, FO 115–2053 File No. 9113; untitled report, n.d., Box 6, FPP Papers; and Lochner to Plantiff, Sept. 28, 1916, FPP Papers.

252–53 FO surveillance of expedition: F. Murchison Jones to W. L. Down, Dec. 15, 1915 and Spring Rice to FO, June 23, 1916 and Aug. 8, 1916, FO 371–2803 File No. 3207.

253 Lochner's tactics: Liebold to Lochner, Sept. 26, 1916; Lochner to Plantiff, Sept. 26 and 30, 1916, and Plantiff to Lochner, Sept. 29, 1916, all in FPP Papers.

253 Ford's political and peace activities: *NYT*, April 7, 21, 23 and May 7, July 9, Sept. 8 and 15 and Oct. 3, 1916; clipbook, unidentified article with Chicago dateline, Acc. 7, FA; and Lochner, *Don Quixote*, 184.

253–54 Lochner in America: *Ibid.*, 180–185; Lochner to Balch, Dec. 22, 1916; and to Plantiff, Oct. 21 and Dec. 6, 1916, all in FPP Papers; Lochner to Jordan, Oct. 25, 1916, Jordan Papers; Ford to Members of the Neutral Conference, Oct. 25, 1916, Box 10, Acc. 79, and Lochner to Liebold, Dec. 15, 1916, Box 8, Acc. 572, both in FA; Lochner, "Why Mr. Ford's Word is Being Doubted," [Jan. 1917], Lochner Papers; and Lochner to Plantiff, Dec. 3 and 22, FPP Papers.

254 Delegates' conflicts: see correspondence among delegates, October and November, 1916, Box 10, Acc. 79, FA.

254–55 Delegates' opposition: Lochner to Plantiff, Nov. 14, 1916, Box 8, Acc. 572 and Lochner to Wigforss, Dec. 11, 1916, Box 10, Acc. 79, FA; Wolterbeek Muller to Ford, Dec. 12, 1916 and Lochner to Plantiff, Dec. 14, 1916, FPP Papers.

255 Neutral Conference reorganized: Lochner to Plantiff, Dec. 14 and 22, 1916; Plantiff to Lochner, Dec. 16, 1916, FPP Papers; Lochner to Members of the Neutral Conference, Dec. 20, 1916, Lochner Papers; and Lochner, *Don Quixote*, 190.

255 Lochner explains new regime: Lochner to Balch, Dec. 8, 1916, Balch Papers; Lochner to Shelly, Dec. 22, 1916, FPP Papers.

256 European politics and American mediation status: Lochner, *Don Quixote*, 186; *NYT*, Sept. 26, 1916; Lloyd George, *War Memoirs*, 2:280; *Papers . . . Foreign Relations, 1916, Supplement*, 64; Fischer, *Germany's War Aims*, 290–98; Birnbaum, *Peace Moves*, 193, 218–29; Link, *Progressivism and Peace*, 195–99, 206–8, 216, 219; Memorandum of Colonel Edward M. House of a Conversation with German Ambassador (Bernstorff), Nov. 20, 1916, *Lansing Papers, Foreign Relations*, 1:153; Lansing diary, Sept. and Dec. 3, 1916, Lansing Papers; and Wilson to House, June 22, 1916 in Baker, *Facing War*, 226–27.

257 German peace note: *Papers . . . Foreign Relations, 1916, Supplement*, 94.

257 Wilson's peace move: Link, *Progressivism and Peace*, 215–19; Wilson to Lansing, Dec. 17, 1916, Baker Papers; and *Papers . . . Foreign Relations, 1916, Supplement*, 97–99.

257–58 European reaction to Wilson's note: *Ibid.*, 111–13, 117–18, 123–25; Link, *Progressivism and Peace*, 236; and Birnbaum, *Peace Moves*, 253–54.

258 Lochner and German government: Lochner to Plantiff, Dec. 6, 1916; von Stumm to Lochner, Nov. 30, 1916, FPP Papers; Ford to Emperor William II, Oct. 25, 1916 and Zimmermann to FO, Nov. 17, 1916, RG 242, T-120, Roll 2120; and Lochner to Jordan, Feb. 19, 1917, Jordan Papers.

258 First anniversary: Neely to Lochner, Dec. 6, 1916 and Clark to Neely, Jan. 9, 1917, FPP Papers; Ford and Plantiff telegram, n.d., Box 54, Acc. 62, FA; and NY *World*, Dec. 3, 1916.

258–59 Boissevain death: *NYT*, Nov. 27, 1916.

259 Lochner-Rosen interviews: Lochner to Plantiff, Dec. 8, 1916, FPP Papers; Lochner, *Don Quixote*, 175; and Lochner to Plantiff, Dec. 14, 1916, Box 8, Acc. 572, FA.

259–60 Lochner estimates Neutral Conference impact: Lochner to Shelly, Dec. 22, 1916; Lochner to Balch, Dec. 8 and 22, 1916; Lochner to Plantiff, Dec. 22 and 30, FPP Papers; NY *Tribune*, Dec. 25, 1916; *NYT*, Dec. 24 and Dec. 26, 1916.

260 "I know for certain": Lochner to Plantiff, Dec. 22, 1916.

260 Leipnik advises British: Leipnik to A. Johnstone, Dec. 9, 1916 and related memoranda, Nov. 29–Dec. 9, 1916, FO 371–2801 File No. 9113.

260 Leipnik-Rosen meeting: Fischer, *Germany's War Aims*, 297–98; Lochner to Plantiff, Dec. 30.

261 "The war can stop": Lochner to Jordan, Jan. 30, 1917, Lochner Papers.

261 "More than justify": Lochner to Plantiff, Dec. 13, 1916, Box 8, Acc. 572, FA.

261 Lochner's departure: Lochner to Wigforss, Dec. 20, 1916, Box 10, and draft letter to Neutral Guarantors and Prospective Guarantors, n.d., TC 1, Acc. 79, FA.

261 Hindenburg and Lochner news release: Scott, ed., *Official German Documents*, 2:1905–6.

261–62 Ford Company and Lochner-Leipnik plan: Lochner, Neely, Plantiff and Liebold correspondence, Dec. 26, 1916–Jan. 10, 1917. Box 8, Acc. 572; Box 55, Acc. 62; and Box 40, Acc. 2, FA.

262 Lochner-Leipnik-Wilson meeting: Wilson chronology, Box 70, Series 1, Baker Papers; Lochner, "Notes of Interview, 3 p.m., Wednesday, January 17, 1917," Lochner Papers.

263 Wilson-House correspondence: House to Wilson, Jan. 16 and 20, 1916, Wilson Papers; Wilson to House, Jan. 17, 1917, House Papers.

263 "Peace without victory" address: *Papers . . . Foreign Relations, 1917, Supplement 1*, 24–29.

263 Neutral Conference reaction: Lochner, *Don Quixote* draft MS; Clark to Wigforss, Jan. 31, 1917, FPP Papers.

263–68 Lochner's relations with Ford, Liebold and Plantiff: Lochner, *Don Quixote*, 206–24 and draft MS; Liebold-Plantiff correspondence, Jan. 23 and 24, 1917, Box 55, Acc. 62, FA; Lochner letters to Ford and to Emmy Lochner, Jan. 24–Feb. 1, 1917, Lochner Papers.

266 Germany and sub warfare: *Papers . . . Foreign Relations, 1917, Supplement 1*, 34–36; Lansing, Memorandum on the Severance of Diplomatic Relations with Germany, Feb. 4, 1917, Lansing Papers; Seymour, *Intimate Papers*, 2:439–41; and House to Wilson, Feb. 10, 1917, Wilson Papers.

266–67 Lochner-Wilson interview: Lochner, *Don Quixote*, 214–19; notes, interview with President Wilson, Feb. 1, 1917 and Lochner to Liebold, Feb. 1, 1917, Lochner Papers.

267 Ford visit to Washington: Liebold to Howard Banks, Jan. 17, 1917, Daniels Papers; Ford statement, fragment, Box 8, file 1, Acc. 572, FA; and *NYT*, Feb. 6, 1917.

268 Lochner dismissed: Liebold to Tumulty, Feb. 8, 1917, Box 8, Acc. 572, FA; Agreement, Feb. 8, 1917, signed by Liebold and Lochner, FPE Papers; Lochner to E. Lochner, Feb. 7, 1917; to J. L. Jones, Feb. 11, 1917 and to L. M. Lloyd, March 6, 1917, all in Lochner Papers; Lochner to Addams, Feb. 11, 1917, Addams Papers; and Lochner, *Don Quixote*, 222.

268–69 Closing European bureaus: Buelow to Loeken, March 20, 1917, enclosed in Loeken to Lochner, March 23, 1917, Lochner Papers; Loeken, Buelow, Plantiff and Liebold correspondence, March 21–June 12, 1917, TC 19, Acc. 79 and Box 55, Acc. 62, FA.

269 Cost of expedition and conference: Nevins and Hill, *Expansion and Challenge*, 496.

269 European delegates' reactions and activities: de Jong, Klausen et al. to Ford, Feb. 20, 1917, Box 55, Acc. 62 and Liebold to Clark, Feb. 7, 1917, Box 8, Acc. 572, FA; Lie to Lochner, Jan. 9, 1917 and Wigforss to Clark, Jan. 14 and 30,

1917, FPP Papers; *NYT*, Feb. 21, 1917, 1:1; de Jong to Carl Bonnevie, March 19, 1917, enclosed with de Jong to Larsson, March 20, 1917, Larsson Papers; Scherrer-Fuellemann to de Jong, Feb. 14, 1917 and Wolterbeek Muller to Clark, Feb. 17, 1917, Lochner Papers.

269 "To incur": Liebold to Clark, Feb. 7, 1917, Box 8, Acc. 572, FA.

269–70 Clark's problems: L. Wilson to Buelow, March 16, 1917 and May 12, 1917, TC 18 and Clark to Buelow, Feb. 28, 1916 and March 15, 1916, TC 19, Acc. 79, FA.

270 "I am filled": Clark to Jordan, Dec. 13, 1916, Jordan Papers.

270 Clark closes offices and returns: Wilson to Buelow, April 28, 1917, TC 19, Acc. 79, FA; Clark-Grose, "Candle in the Dark"; Langhorne to Secretary of State, May 26, 1917, RG 59, File No. 811.208/157.

270 Ford pledges fortune: *NYT*, Feb. 8, 1917.

270 Ford promises to defend country: *NYT*, Aug. 9, 1915.

271 "Aristocracy and capitalists": Notations of a Luncheon, Ford Motor Co., Dec. 4, 1917, enclosure, Lansing to Wilson, March 27, 1918, Wilson Papers.

271 "Old Henry": Lochner to Clark: Feb. 8, 1915, Lochner Papers.

271 Lochner at home: Feb. 1917 correspondence, Lochner Papers; Lochner to Larsson, Feb. 14, 1917, Larsson Papers.

271 "Isn't Mr. Ford's fall": Balch to Addams, n.d., Box 4, WPP Papers.

271 Wales's comments: Wales to Lochner, Dec. 29, 1917, FPP Papers; Wales to family, Feb. 17, 1917, A. L. Wales Papers.

271 Addams's comments: Addams to Lochner, Feb. 8 and 15, 1917, Lochner Papers.

271 "A splendid failure": *PPL*, Jan. 31, 1916.

272 "Three years ago": Bullitt diary, Dec. 4, 1917, House Papers.

AFTERWARDS

273 Ford cruise: G. S. Anderson to Lochner, March 7, 1917, Lochner Papers.

273 Ford yacht sold: Liebold to U.S. Navy Special Board for Patrol Vessels, May 12 and 14, 1917, Box 40, Acc. 2, FA. The *NYT*, June 9, 1917, reported Ford gave his yacht to the government.

273 Peaceworkers activities: Link, *Progressivism and Peace*, 304–14; Washington *Post*, Feb. 13, 1917; and *NYT*, April 2 and 4, 1917.

273 Bryan volunteers: Bryan to Wilson, April 6, 1917, Wilson Papers.

273–74 McClure biography: *NYT*, March 23, 1949; Lyons, *Success Story*, 371–76.

274 "If we had no more": Notes written aboard *Nieuw Amsterdam*, Box 285, Lindsey Papers.

274–75 Lindsey biography: Liebold to Lindsey, Oct. 6, 1916; Lindsey to E. W. Scripps, Nov. 3, 1917 and to H. D. Colburn, May 9, 1918, all in Lindsey Papers.

275 "The greatest mistake": Aked to Paul Fussell, in Fussell to author, May 31, 1967.

275 Aked biography: H. Harrison to Lindsey, Oct. 30, 1917 and Aked to Lindsey, Oct. 24, 1917, Lindsey Papers; "One Hundredth Anniversary Directory," San Francisco First Congregational Church; Millard, "Heterodox Preacher," Los Angeles *Times*, Dec. 5, 1937; *NYT*, Aug. 13, 1941; and Detroit *News*, Aug. 14, 1941.

275 Weatherly biography: Weatherly to Jones, Oct. 31, 1917 and Jan. 25, 1918, Jones Papers; Lincoln (Neb.) *Star*, June 24, 1944; and Dr. Charles Stephen, Jr. to author, Sept. 19, 1972.

275-76 Jones biography: Jones to Weatherly, Nov. 3, 1917 and to Fred Lynch, Aug. 19, 1916, Jones Papers; A. S. Burleson to J. Tumulty, Sept. 17, 1918, Wilson Papers; and *Unity*, Feb. 7, 1918, 357.

276 Addams biography: *Unity*, Nov. 28, 1919, 148–49; Addams, *Peace and Bread*, 109, 140–50; Addams to Lindsey, Dec. 26, 1917, Lindsey Papers; and Addams, *Second Twenty Years*, 147, 180–81, 184.

276-77 Balch biography: Fainsod, "Emily Greene Balch," 3; Notes, March 1954, Balch Papers; Randall, *Improper Bostonian*, 275, 322–23; and *NYT*, Jan. 11, 1961.

277 Lochner biography: Lochner to Loeken, June 28, 1917, Lochner Papers; Lochner, *Always the Unexpected*, 76–79; Lochner interview; and *NYT*, June 10, 1975.

277-78 Wales biography: Wales, "A Statement of My Present Position," Wales Papers; newsclip, Montreal *Star*, n.d. and Memorial Resolution, Nov. 4, 1957, A. L. Wales Papers.

278 Caesar biography: Caesar Reminiscences, 40–42; Caesar interview.

278 O'Neill career: Liebold Reminiscences, 299–300; *NYT*, April 18, 1940.

278 Plantiff-Hempel-Ford association: Plantiff to Hempel, Dec. 28, 1915 and A. Johnson to Neely, March 26, 1917, TC 18, Acc. 79; Invoice, May 23, 1917, Box 6, Acc. 286; Neely to Liebold, Nov. 8, 1916, Box 54 and Plantiff to Liebold, March 10, 1919, Box 107, Acc. 62; and Plantiff to Ford, Jan. 16, 1920, Box 8, Acc. 572, all in FA.

278 Plantiff biography: Liebold Reminiscences, 1075; Nevins and Hill, *Expansion and Challenge*, 426; Plantiff to H. Ford, Aug. 8, 1928 and to C. Ford, Jan. 9, 1933, Box 146, Acc. 1; and *NYT*, Oct. 19, 1934.

278 Marquis biography: Reed, "Why They Hate Ford," 11; Liebold Reminiscences, 1107-8; Marquis, *Henry Ford*; Nevins and Hill, *Expansion and Challenge*, 613; and *NYT*, June 22, 1948.

278-79 Ford biography and character: All information not otherwise cited is from Nevins and Hill, *Expansion and Challenge* and *Decline and Rebirth*.

279 Sixty-million-profit: Edsel Ford testimony, *Tribune* Trial Record, 5401.

279 "Parasites": Liebold Reminiscences, 177.

279n Ford war profits: Check in Henry Ford personal exhibit, Ford Museum, Dearborn, Michigan; *Pipp's Weekly*, March 25, 1922, 708; and Nevins and Hill, *Expansion and Challenge*, 82–85.

279-80 *Tribune* trial: Chicago *Tribune*, June 23, 1916; *Tribune* Trial Record, 5622-6492 ff.

280-82 Ford's anti-Semitism: Ruddiman Reminiscences, 37; Harold Troper, "Anti-Semitism in the United States, 1890–1900," unpublished Master's Thesis, University of Cincinnati, 1906.

280 Ford buys *DI*: Black Reminiscences, 7.

280 "Unbiased news": *DI*, Jan. 11, 1919, 8.

281 "The mush, the slush": *DI*, Aug. 6, 1921, 8–9.

281 "To expose an unethical": Black in Black, Donaldson and Blanchard Reminiscences, 36.

281 Sapiro settlement: *NYT*, July 8 and 17, 1927.

281 "Two very prominent": *NYT*, Dec. 5, 1921.

281-82 Bernstein suit: *NYT*, July 17, 1927; Liebold to Plantiff, July 23, 1923, Box 177, Acc. 285, FA; and *NYT*, July 8, 25 and 27, 1927.

282 Liebold biography: Black in Black, Donaldson and Blanchard Reminiscences, 36; Liebold Reminiscences, 468–69, 1518.

282 "An uneconomical thing": Liebold Reminiscences, 266.

282 Museum and Greenfield Village: Greenleaf, *From These Beginnings*, 71–85,

91–111; *NYT*, Dec. 5, 1921; William A. Birnie, "Where History Isn't Bunk," *Reader's Digest*, July 1966, 7.

282–83 Ford's behavior at plant: MacManus and Beasley, *Men, Money and Motors*, 224–43; Marquis, *Henry Ford*, 173–75; and Greenleaf, *From These Beginnings*, 25.

283 Ford's public image: Wilson, "Despot of Dearborn," 24–35; Sward, *Legend of Henry Ford*, 450–63.

283 Ford and milk and hair tonic: Detroit *Times*, July 17 and 29, 1936; Voorhees Reminiscences, 31; and Liebold Reminiscences, 3106.

283–84 Ford's postwar peace views: *NYT*, Jan. 18, Feb. 23 and July 23, 1923 and Feb. 5, 1927; jotbooks, Box 13, Acc. 62, FA; and Sward, *Legend of Henry Ford*, 460–61.

284 Ford's views before Second World War: *NYT*, Sept. 25, 1940 and Feb. 16, 1941; Ford to B. Hershey, Dec. 2, 1940, Box 81, Acc. 572, FA.

284 Ford wartime birthday statements: *NYT*, July 30, 1944, 1945 and 1946.

284–85 Schwimmer as minister: *NYT*, Nov. 26, 1918 and Feb. 2, 1919; *Times* (London), Jan. 23, 1919; Vira B. Whitehouse, *A Year as a Government Agent* (New York: Harper and Brothers, 1920), 232–66; Snowden, *Political Pilgrim*, 42–43, 48–49; Stovall to Secretary of State, Nov. 27 and 29, 1918, RG 59, File Nos. 863.00/117 and 863.00/119.

285 Schwimmer returns to Hungary: "Rosika Schwimmer: World Patriot."

285 "To cover every sin": Heubsch to Schwimmer, Nov. 28, 1919, Huebsch Papers.

285 Schwimmer returns to U.S.: Rosika Schwimmer, RG 60, File No. 38-23-147, NA; *NYT*, Sept. 5, 1927; and Catt to Schwimmer, Jan. 6, 1926, Catt Papers.

285–86 Schwimmer citizenship application and trial records: Rosika Schwimmer Citizenship file, SCPC and Schwimmer Papers.

285 "An uncompromising pacifist": Schwimmer to L. A. Stone, Sept. 19, 1925, Schwimmer Papers, cited in plaintiff brief, United States *vs.* Schwimmer, U.S. Supreme Court, Oct. term 1928, No. 484.

286 "A petitioner's rights": U.S. Circuit Court of Appeals, October term, 1927, April session, 1928, No. 3997, Rosika Schwimmer *vs.* United States of America, June 29, 1928.

286 Marvin case: NY *World*, June 30, 1928; *NYT*, June 28, 1928.

286 Supreme Court case: Rosika Schwimmer, RG 60, File No. 38-23-147; *NYT*, Sept. 30, 1928; Schwimmer, "What Price Citizenship," *No More War*, August 1929, 1; and United States *vs.* Schwimmer, Oct. term, 1928.

287 Schwimmer's fortune changes: Birmingham (Mich.) *Eccentric*, Oct. 18, 1928, newsclip, ACLU Papers; Schwimmer to Maverick, Dec. 3, 1926, Schwimmer Papers; and NY *World*, April 10, 1927.

287 "It is a little": *NYT*, May 29, 1929.

287 Schwimmer and ACLU: L. M. Lloyd to Roger Baldwin, Oct. 27, 1921; Schwimmer to Executive Committee, July 1, 1928; Baldwin to Lloyd, Oct. 22, 1929; F. Bailey to Fellowship of Reconciliation, March 9, 1929; Bailey to Lovett, Jan. 29, 1929; Lovett to Bailey, Jan. 31, 1929 and Bailey to Lovett, Feb. 28, 1929, all in ACLU cases, States Correspondence, Illinois, ACLU Papers.

287–88 Schwimmer demands Ford apology: Schwimmer to Plantiff, July 2, 1922, Box 8, Acc. 572; H. Van Venn to Ford, May 21, 1927; Liebold to Hays, St. John and Buckley, June 3, 1927; Schwimmer to Ford in *NYT*, Sept. 4, 1927 and Liebold to Schwimmer, Sept. 14, 1927 Acc. 855, FA.

288 Sinclair suit: H. Weinberger to Ford, June 9, 1933 in Weinberger to Ford,

June 22, 1936, Box 1957, Acc. 285, FA; *Upton Sinclair Presents William Fox* (Los Angeles: Upton Sinclair, 1933), 212–13; *NYT*, Oct. 12 and Nov. 22, 1933 and Feb. 18, 1934.

288–89 Schwimmer-Liebold interview: Schwimmer to Liebold, March 30, 1936, Box 1957, Acc. 285, FA: Liebold Reminiscences, 257.

289 Schwimmer peace prize: E. Sanders, K. D. Blake and K. Crane-Gartz to Ford, Boxes 1998 and 2075, Acc. 285, FA.

289 Schwimmer offers Ford second opportunity: Schwimmer to Ford, July 25, 1938 and to H. Ford II, Nov. 14, 1945, Box 2892, Acc. 285, FA.

289–90 Schwimmer's later career: *NYT*, Aug. 4, 1948; Schwimmer to Huebsch, June 1, 1936 and June 29, 1946, Huebsch Papers; "Rosika Schwimmer—World Patriot": Schwimmer to C. Macmillan, Feb. 3, 1926, Schwimmer Papers; *U.S. Reports*, 279:647; L. M. Lloyd to R. Baldwin, Oct. 14, 1929, ACLU cases, States Correspondence, Illinois, ACLU Papers; Bainbridge and Maloney, "Where Are They Now?", 29; and Huebsch Reminiscences, 173–74.

289–90 Karolyi's exile: Michael Karolyi, *Memoirs: Faith Without Illusion* (London: Jonathan Cape, 1956), 10, 168.

290 Expedition marriages: Huebsch Reminiscences, 174–75; E. R. Hixenbaugh to Ford, Jan. 8, 1941, Box 2511, Acc. 285, FA.

290–91 Peace ship drama: *DFP*, Feb. 6, 1927.

292 Expedition archives: Plantiff to F. Campsall, Sept. 26, 1919 and to Liebold, June 16, 1919, Box 106, Acc. 62, FA; Military Intelligence Division correspondence, Office of Chief of Staff, War Department, Box 14, FPP Papers.

292n Clark donates office keys: Clark-Grose, "Candle in the Dark."

292n *Oscar II* sold: Gerda Thorsen to author, Jan. 1, 1968.

292–93 Twenty-fifth anniversary: B. Hershey to Ford, Dec. 12, 1940 and Ford to Hershey, Dec. 2, 1940; H. B. Woods, Jr. to Tom Curtin, Report of Meeting, Dec. 4, 1940, all in Box 8, Acc. 572, FA; *DFP*, Dec. 6, 1940.

293 "Lust for power": NY *World Telegram*, Dec. 14, 1935.

293–94 Writers' comments: Millis, *Road to War*, 242, 245; Wells, *Shape of Things to Come*, 88; Curti, *Peace or War*, 245–46; Sullivan, *Over Here*, 169; and Baker, *Facing War*, 135.

294–95 Participants' comments: Balch, "The Stockholm Conference," 141–42; *Unity*, March 23, 1916, 55; Huebsch Reminiscences, 140–41; *The Call*, Feb. 1, 1916; Lochner, Love, Fussell, Shelly, Reeder and Tucker interviews; Lochner, *Don Quixote*, 161–62; Lochner interview, *DFP*, Nov. 26, 1950; Wales, "Further Summing Up," typescript, A. L. Wales Papers; Lamar Tooze to author, April 20, 1967; Bridgeport (Conn.) *Post*, Dec. 6, 1965; C. Bakker van Bosse to author, Nov. 7, 1967; Lindhagen, *På Vikingastråt*, 35.

296 Wilson's policy: Baker, *Neutrality*, 276–93; Curti, *Peace or War*, 243.

297 "Sentiments that will persist": Wales, "Further Summing Up."

Selected Bibliography

MANUSCRIPT COLLECTIONS

Mark M. Abbott Papers, privately owned, International Falls, Minn.

Jane Addams Papers, Swarthmore College Peace Collection.

John A. Aylward Papers, State Historical Society of Wisconsin.

Ray Stannard Baker Papers, Library of Congress.

Emily Greene Balch Papers, Swarthmore College Peace Collection.

Katherine Devereux Blake Papers, Swarthmore College Peace Collection.

William C. Bullitt Papers, House Papers, Sterling Library, Yale University.

Carrie Chapman Catt Papers, Library of Congress.

Chicago Peace Society Papers, Chicago Historical Society.

Frieda Mylecraine Cornick Papers, privately owned, Yonkers, N.Y.

Josephus Daniels Papers, Library of Congress.

Elmer Davis Papers, Library of Congress.

Sara Moore Eastman Papers, privately owned, Los Altos, Calif.

Harry Carroll Evans Papers, University of Iowa Library.

Ford Motor Company Archives, Henry Ford Museum, Dearborn, Mich.

Ford Peace Expedition Papers, Swarthmore College Peace Collection.

Ford Peace Plan Papers, Library of Congress.

Paul Fussell Papers, privately owned, Pasadena, Calif.

Ada Morse Clark Grose Papers, Hoover Institution on War, Revolution, and Peace, Stanford University.

Walter and Elinor Ryan Hixenbaugh Papers, privately owned, Cocoa Beach, Fla.

Mary Alden Hopkins Papers, Special Collections, Columbia University Library.

Edward Mandell House Papers, Sterling Library, Yale University.

Benjamin W. Huebsch Papers, Library of Congress.

Jenkin Lloyd Jones Papers, Meadville Theological School Library, Chicago and Chicago University Library.

David Starr Jordan Peace Correspondence, Hoover Institution on War, Revolution and Peace, Stanford University.

Karl Karsten Papers, Library of Congress.

Louise Phelps Kellogg Papers, State Historical Society of Wisconsin.
Paul U. Kellogg Personal Papers, Social Welfare History Archives, University of Minnesota.
Judson King, Library of Congress.
Robert Lansing Papers, Library of Congress and Princeton University Library.
Hans Larsson Papers, University of Lund Library, Sweden.
Benjamin B. Lindsey Papers, Library of Congress.
Lola Maverick Lloyd Papers, Swarthmore College Peace Collection.
Louis Paul Lochner Papers, State Historical Society of Wisconsin.
Donald M. Love, privately owned, Oberlin, Ohio.
Samuel Sidney McClure Papers, Lilly Library, Indiana University.
Lewis Maverick Papers, Hoover Institution on War, Revolution, and Peace, Stanford University.
Neutral Conference for Continuous Mediation (Sweden) Papers, Swarthmore College Peace Collection.
Allan Nevins Papers, Special Collections, Columbia University Library.
Walter Hines Page Papers, Houghton Library, Harvard University.
Alice L. Park Papers, Hoover Institution on War, Revolution, and Peace, Stanford University.
Clara Ragaz Papers, privately owned, Zurich, Switzerland.
Nell M. Reeder Papers, privately owned, Washington, D.C.
Rosika Schwimmer Papers, Hoover Institution on War, Revolution and Peace, Stanford University and Citizenship File, Swarthmore College Peace Collection.
Rosika Schwimmer–Lola Maverick Lloyd Papers, New York Public Library Manuscript Division. (In the spring of 1968 the New York Public Library Astor, Lenox and Tilden Foundations permitted me unrestricted access to the Schwimmer-Lloyd Collection, which had been previously closed to scholarly research for at least twenty years, except in a very few cases which were subject to the approval of Mme Schwimmer's former assistant, a person very like her mentor. For seven weeks Louis Kraft, who translated Schwimmer correspondence and other material written in German, and I examined the papers and then, in the fall, I was told I had been admitted to the papers in error and could not use my research material for at least a number of years. The Schwimmer-Lloyd Collection has since been opened, one trusts on a more permanent basis, but I have not found it necessary to cite it in this book for several reasons. First, there is nothing of consequence in the papers about the Ford Peace Expedition and its participants that is not in other collections. Indeed, much of the material has been copied from other repositories, often without so indicating, and, most important, Mme Schwimmer either sold or gave annotated copies of the most significant documents of her peace and later activities to the Hoover Institution on War, Revolution, and Peace, where scholars may use them without any restrictions. Second, though there is some material about Mme Schwimmer's affairs that is unique to the collection, none of it is critical to this work, and generally Mme Schwimmer wrote her associates of everything that transpired in her life and these records are in other

archives. And, finally, Mme Schwimmer's notes, diaries and accounts of events are usually so biased as to be nearly useless to the scholar.)

May Wright Sewall Papers, Indiana Division, Indiana State Library.

Rebecca Shelley Papers, University of Michigan Historical Collection.

Helen Heberling Smith Papers, privately owned, Altadena, Calif.

Christian A. Sorensen Papers, Nebraska State Historical Society.

Anna Garlin Spencer Papers, Swarthmore College Peace Collection.

William Howard Taft Papers, Library of Congress.

Lamar Tooze Papers, privately owned, Portland, Ore.

Earl Tucker Papers, privately owned, Syracuse, N.Y.

Henry Van Dyke Papers, Princeton University Library.

Oswald Villard Papers, Houghton Library, Harvard University.

Lillian Wald Papers, New York Public Library Manuscript Division.

Julia Grace Wales Papers, State Historical Society of Wisconsin and A. Letitia Wales, privately owned, St. Andrews East, Montreal, Canada.

Ora Guessford Weir Papers, privately owned, Wilton, Conn.

Francis Stirling Wilson Papers, privately owned, Mrs. F. S. Wilson, Ormond Beach, Fla.

Woodrow Wilson Papers, Library of Congress.

Wisconsin Peace Party Papers, State Historical Society of Wisconsin.

Woman's Peace Party Papers, Swarthmore College Peace Collection; Madison Branch, State Historical Society of Wisconsin.

INTERVIEWS

George Bowman, April 24, 1967, Maplewood, N.J.

Irving Caesar, May 21, 1969, New York, N.Y.

Frieda Mylecraine Cornick, January 28, 1967, Yonkers, N.Y.

Sara Bard Field Wood, July 21, 1967, Berkeley, Calif.

Paul Fussell, September 15, 1967, New York, N.Y.

Laurence Gomme, January 30, 1967, Scarsdale, N.Y.

Burnet Hershey (Jacob Hirsch), May 26, 1968, New York, N.Y.

Albert J. Hettinger, Jr., January 31, 1967, New York, N.Y.

Louis P. Lochner, February 4, 1967, Fair Haven, N.J., and several times in the spring of 1968, New York, N.Y.

Lue C. Lozier, August 13, 1967, Moberly, Mo.

Donald M. Love, February 22, 1967, Oberlin, Ohio.

Lewis Maverick, July 24, 1967, Pasadena, Calif.

Nell M. Reeder, May 3, 1967, Washington, D.C.

Rebecca Shelley, June 15 and 16, 1967, Battle Creek, Mich., and July 12 and September 4, 1967, Washington, D.C.

Earl Tucker, April 20, 1967, Syracuse, N.Y.

Van Arsdale Turner, February 25, 1967, Oxon Hill, Md.

George Wythe, December 13, 1966, Washington, D.C.

ORAL REMINISCENCES

Mark M. Abbott, taped, privately owned.

Roger Baldwin, Irving Caesar, Elmer Davis and Benjamin Huebsch, Oral History Collection, Columbia University.

Fred L. Black, Walter Blanchard, George Brown, Irving Caesar, Ben Donaldson, Joseph Galamb, Ernest Liebold, Margaret Ford Ruddiman and C. J. Smith, Accession 65, Ford Archives.

Herbert Coggins, Oral History Collection, University of California, Berkeley.

Alice L. Park, privately owned by Lockton Park.

GOVERNMENT DOCUMENTS AND RECORDS

Denmark. Danish Foreign Office Records, Ford Peace Expedition file.

Germany. *Official German Documents Relating to the World War*, ed. by James Brown Scott, 2 vols., New York, Oxford University Press, 1923.

Great Britain. *Parliamentary Debates* (Commons), 5th Series, 1915, vol. 4. Public Record Office, Records of the Foreign Office.

Norway. Norwegian Royal Ministry of Foreign Affairs, Ford Peace Expedition file.

Sweden. Swedish Foreign Office Records, Ford Peace Expedition file.

United States. Collection of Foreign Records Seized, 1941–, Records of the German Foreign Office Received by the Department of State, Record Group 242, National Archives. *Commission for Enduring Peace*, Hearings before the Committee on Foreign Affairs, H. R. 6921 and H. J. Res. 32, 64th Congress, 1st session, 1916. General Records of the Department of Justice, Record Group 60, National Archives. General Records of the Department of State, Record Group 59, National Archives. Records of the Foreign Service Posts of the Department of State, Record Group 84, National Archives.

Lansing Papers, 1914–1920. Papers Relating to the Foreign Relations of the United States, 2 vols., Washington, D.C., Government Printing Office, 1939.

Papers Relating to the Foreign Relations of the United States, 1914, Supplement, Washington, D.C., Government Printing Office, 1928.

Papers Relating to the Foreign Relations of the United States, 1915, Washington, D.C., Government Printing Office, 1924.

Papers Relating to the Foreign Relations of the United States, 1915, Supplement, Washington, D.C., Government Printing Office, 1928.

Papers Relating to the Foreign Relations of the United States, 1916, Supplement, Washington, D.C., Government Printing Office, 1929.

Papers Relating to the Foreign Relations of the United States, 1917, Supplement 1, Washington, D.C., Government Printing Office, 1931.

United States Reports, Cases Adjudged in The Supreme Court, Oct. term, 1928, vol. 279, Washington, D.C., Government Printing Office, 1929.

MEMOIRS, DIARIES, CORRESPONDENCE, PUBLISHED PAPERS

Addams, Jane, *Peace and Bread in Time of War*, New York, Macmillan, 1922.
——, *The Second Twenty Years at Hull House*, New York, Macmillan, 1930.

———, Emily Greene Balch and Alice Hamilton, *Women at The Hague; The International Congress of Women and Its Results*, New York, Macmillan, 1915.

Baker, Ray Stannard, and William Dodd, eds., *The Public Papers of Woodrow Wilson, New Democracy*, 2 vols., New York, Harper's, 1926.

Bell, Julian, ed., *We Did Not Fight, 1914–18: Experience of War Resisters*, London, Cobden, Sanderson, 1935.

Bernstorff, Johann H. von., *My Three Years in America*, New York, Scribner's, 1920.

Braley, Berton, *Pegasus Pulls a Hack: Memoirs of a Modern Minstrel*, New York, Minton, Balch, 1934.

Bryan, William Jennings and Mary Baird Bryan, *Memoirs of William Jennings Bryan*, Philadelphia, John C. Winston, 1925.

Creel, George, *Rebel at Large*, New York, Putnam's, 1947.

Eastman, Max, *Enjoyment of Living*, New York, Harper's, 1928.

Ford, Henry, in collaboration with Samuel Crowther, *My Life and Work*, Garden City, New York, Garden City Publishing, 1922.

———, *Moving Forward*, Garden City, New York, Doubleday, Doran, 1931.

———, *Today and Tomorrow*, Garden City, New York, Doubleday, Page, 1926.

Gerard, James W., *My Four Years in Germany*, New York, Doran, 1917.

Gibbs, Philip, *Realities of War*, London, Heinemann, 1920.

Graves, Robert, *Goodbye to All That*, 4th ed., London, Cassell, 1969.

Hendrick, Burton J., ed., *The Life and Letters of Walter Hines Page*, 4 vols., Garden City, New York, Doubleday, Page, 1924.

Hershey, Burnet, *The Odyssey of Henry Ford and the Great Peace Ship*, New York, Taplinger, 1967.

Howard, Esme, *Theatre of Life: Life Seen from the Stalls, 1903–1936*, 2 vols., Boston, Little, Brown, 1936.

Howe, Frederic C., *Confessions of a Reformer*, New York, Scribner's, 1925.

Jordan, David Starr, *The Days of a Man*, 2 vols., Yonkers, New York, World, 1922.

Lindhagen, Carl, *På Vikingastråt I Vasterled en Amerikaresa*, Stockholm, Wahlstrom & Widstrand, 1926.

Lloyd George, David, *War Memoirs, 1915–1916*, 2 vols., Boston, Little, Brown, 1933.

Lochner, Louis P., *Always the Unexpected: A Book of Reminiscences*, New York, Macmillan, 1956.

———, *America's Don Quixote: Henry Ford's Attempt to Save Europe*, London, Kegan Paul, Trench, Trubner, 1924. (American edition: *Henry Ford—America's Don Quixote*, New York, International Publishers, 1925.)

McClure, Samuel Sidney, *My Autobiography*, New York, Stokes, 1914.

Pethick-Lawrence, Emmeline, *My Part in a Changing World*, London, Gollancz, 1938.

Seymour, Charles, ed., *The Intimate Papers of Colonel House*, 4 vols., Boston, Houghton Mifflin, 1926.

Snowden, Ethel, *A Political Pilgrim in Europe*, New York, Doran, 1921.
Sorensen, Charles E., with Samuel T. Williamson, *My Forty Years With Ford*, New York, Norton, 1956.
Tarbell, Ida, *All in a Day's Work*, New York, Macmillan, 1939.
Villard, Oswald Garrison, *Fighting Years: Memoirs of a Liberal Editor*, New York, Harcourt, Brace, 1939.

BOOKS AND PAMPHLETS

Addams, Jane, *Newer Ideals of Peace*, New York, Macmillan, 1907.
Baker, Ray Stannard, *Woodrow Wilson, Life and Letters: Neutrality, 1914–1915* and *Facing War, 1915–1917*, Garden City, New York, Doubleday, Doran, 1935 and 1937.
Balch, Emily Greene, ed., *Approaches to the Great Settlement*, New York, Huebsch, 1918.
Baldwin, Hanson, *World War I*, New York, Harper's, 1962.
Beales, A. C. F., *The History of Peace: A Short Account of the Organised Movements for International Peace*, New York, Dial Press, 1931.
Benson, Allan L., *The New Henry Ford*, New York, Funk and Wagnalls, 1923.
Birnbaum, Karl, *Peace Moves and U-Boat Warfare: A Study of Imperial Germany's Policy Toward the United States, April 18, 1916–January 9, 1917*, Stockholm, Almqvist and Wiksell, 1958.
Bourne, Randolph S., ed., *Towards an Enduring Peace: A Symposium of Peace Proposals and Programs, 1914–1916*, New York, American Association for International Conciliation, 1916.
Bushnell, Sarah T., *The Truth About Henry Ford*, Chicago, Reilly and Lee, 1922.
Bussey, Gertrude and Margaret Times, *Women's International League for Peace and Freedom, 1916–1965: A Record of Fifty Years' Work*, London, Allen and Unwin, 1965.
Chatfield, Charles, *For Peace and Justice: Pacifism in America, 1914–1941*, Knoxville, University of Tennessee, 1971.
Churchill, Winston S., *The World Crisis*, vol. 2, New York, Scribner's, 1923.
Clancy, Louise B. and Florence Davies, *The Believer: The Life Story of Mrs. Henry Ford*, New York, Coward-McCann, 1960.
Curti, Merle, *Bryan and World Peace*, Smith College Studies, vol. 16, nos. 3–4, Northampton, Smith College, 1931.
———, *Peace or War: The American Struggle, 1636–1936*, New York, Norton, 1936.
Davis, Allen F., *American Heroine: The Life and Legend of Jane Addams*, New York, Oxford, 1973.
Degen, Marie Louise, *The History of the Woman's Peace Party*, Johns Hopkins Studies in Historical and Political Science, Ser. 57, No. 3, Baltimore, Johns Hopkins University Press, 1939.
Esposito, Vincent J., *A Concise History of World War I*, New York, Praeger, 1964.
Farrell, John C., *Beloved Lady: A History of Jane Addams' Ideas on Reform and Peace*, Baltimore, Johns Hopkins, 1967.

Fay, Sidney B., *The Origins of the World War*, 2 vols., New York, Macmillan, 1930.

Fischer, Fritz, *Germany's War Aims in the First World War*, New York, Norton, 1967.

Ford, Henry, *The Ford Plan: A Human Document; Testimony of Henry Ford before the Federal Commission on Industrial Relations, January 22, 1915*, New York, John R. Anderson, [1915].

———, Preface to *The Wisest Words Ever Written on War* by Ralph Waldo Emerson, ed. by Emilie Hapgood, New York, Hapgood, 1916.

———, in collaboration with Samuel Crowther, *Edison As I Know Him*, New York, Cosmopolitan, 1930.

George, Alexander L., and Juliette L. George, *Woodrow Wilson and Colonel House: A Personality Study*, New York, John Day, 1956, reprint, New York, Dover, 1964.

Greenleaf, William, *From These Beginnings: The Early Philanthropies of Henry and Edsel Ford, 1911–1956*, Detroit, Wayne State University, 1964.

Hamilton, J. G. de Roulhac, *Henry Ford: The Man, The Worker, The Citizen*, New York, Holt, 1927.

Henry Ford: A Personal History, Dearborn, Ford Museum, 1960.

Henry Ford's Peace Expedition Who's Who, First edition, Christiania, 1915. Second edition, Copenhagen, 1915.

Herman, Sondra R., *Eleven Against War: Studies in Internationalist Thought, 1898–1921*, Hoover Institution Press, No. 82, Stanford, Stanford University, 1969.

International Congress of Women Report, April 28–May 1, 1915, Amsterdam: International Committee of Women for Permanent Peace, 1915.

Jones, John E., *The Truth About the Henry Ford Expedition*, privately printed, 1916.

Jordan, David Starr, ed., *Ways to Lasting Peace*, Indianapolis, Bobbs-Merrill, 1916.

Larsen, Charles, *The Good Fight: The Life and Times of Ben B. Lindsey*, Chicago, Quadrangle, 1972.

Lasch, Christopher, *The New Radicalism in America, 1889–1963: The Intellectual as a Social Type*, New York, Vintage, 1967.

Leuchtenberg, William, *Perils of Prosperity, 1914–32*, Chicago, University of Chicago, 1958.

Levine, Lawrence W., *Defender of the Faith, William Jennings Bryan: The Last Decade, 1915–1925*, New York, Oxford University, 1965.

Link, Arthur S., *Wilson: The Struggle for Neutrality, 1914–1915; Confusions and Crises, 1915–1916* and *Campaigns for Progressivism and Peace, 1916–1917*, Princeton, Princeton University, 1960, 1964 and 1965.

Linn, James Weber, *Jane Addams: A Biography*, New York, Appleton-Century, 1937.

Lyon, Peter, *Success Story: The Life and Times of S. S. McClure*, Deland, Florida, Everett Edwards, 1967.

MacManus, Theodore F., and Norman Beasley, *Men, Money and Motors: The Drama of the Automobile*, New York, Harper's, 1929.

Marchand, C. Roland, *The American Peace Movement and Social Reform, 1898–1918*, Princeton, Princeton University, 1972.

Marquis, Samuel S., *Henry Ford: An Interpretation*, Boston, Little, Brown, 1923.

Martin, Lawrence W., *Peace Without Victory: Woodrow Wilson and the British Liberals*, New Haven, Yale University, 1958.

May, Henry F., *End of American Innocence: A Study of the First Years of Our Own Time, 1912–1917*, New York, Knopf, 1959.

Mayer, Arno J., *Political Origins of the New Diplomacy, 1917–1918*, New Haven, Yale University, 1959.

Merz, Charles, *And Then Came Ford*, Garden City, New York, Doubleday, Doran, 1929.

Millis, Walter, *An End to Arms*, New York, Atheneum, 1965.

——, *Road to War: America, 1914–1917*, Boston, Houghton Mifflin, 1935.

Moritzen, Julius, *The Peace Movement of America*, New York, Putnam's, 1912.

Nevins, Allan, and Frank Ernest Hill, *Ford: The Times, The Man, The Company; Expansion and Challenge, 1915–1933* and *Decline and Rebirth, 1933–1962*, New York, Scribner's, 1954, 1957 and 1963.

Olson, Sidney, *Young Henry Ford: A Picture History of the First Forty Years*, Detroit, Wayne State University, 1963.

Osgood, Robert E., *Ideals and Self-Interest in America's Foreign Relations: The Great Transformation of the Twentieth Century*, Chicago, University of Chicago, 1953.

Paxson, Frederic L., *Pre-War Years, 1913–1917*, Boston, Houghton Mifflin, 1936.

Patterson, David S., *Towards a Warless World: The Travail of the American Peace Movement, 1887–1914*, Bloomington, Indiana University, 1976.

Peterson, H. C., *Propaganda for War: The Campaign Against American Neutrality, 1914–1917*, Norman, University of Oklahoma, 1939.

—— and Gilbert C. Fite, *Opponents of War, 1917–1918*, Madison, University of Wisconsin, 1957.

Pipp, Edwin G., *Henry Ford—Both Sides of Him*, Detroit, Pipp's Magazine, 1926.

——, *The Real Henry Ford*, Detroit, Pipp's Weekly, 1922.

Randall, Mercedes M., *Improper Bostonian: Emily Greene Balch*, New York, Twayne, 1964.

Rappaport, Armin, *The British Press and Wilsonian Neutrality*, Gloucester, Mass., Peter Smith, 1965.

Richards, William C., *The Last Billionaire: Henry Ford*, New York, Scribner's, 1948.

Rosika Schwimmer: World Patriot, [New York?], International Committee for World Peace Prize Award to Rosika Schwimmer, 1937.

Simonds, William A., *Henry Ford: His Life, His Works, His Genius*, Indianapolis, Bobbs-Merrill, 1943.

Stidger, William, *Henry Ford: The Man and His Motors*, New York, Doran, 1923.

Sullivan, Mark, *Our Times, The United States, 1900: The War Begins, 1909–1914* and *Over Here, 1914–1918*, New York, Scribner's, 1932 and 1933.

Sward, Keith, *The Legend of Henry Ford*, New York, Rinehart, 1948.

Towards the Peace That Shall Last, New York, Survey Magazine, 1915.

Wales, Julia Grace, *Continuous Mediation Without Armistice*, [Chicago?], Woman's Peace Party, 1915.

——, *Mediation Without Armistice: The Wisconsin Plan*, Madison, Wisconsin Peace Society, 1915.

Wells, H. G., *Shape of Things to Come*, New York, Macmillan, 1933.

Whitney, Edson L., *The American Peace Society: A Centennial History*, Washington, D.C., American Peace Society, 1929.

Wiebe, Robert, *The Search for Order, 1877–1920*, New York, Hill and Wang, 1967.

Wik, Reynold M., *Henry Ford and Grass-roots America*, Ann Arbor, University of Michigan, 1972.

SIGNED ARTICLES

Aked, Charles F., "What I Have Learned About Peace-making: The Experience of a Member of the Ford Expedition," *Congregationalist and Christian World*, August 10, 1916, 170–71.

——, and Walter Rauschenbush, "Private Profit and the Nation's Honor," *Standard*, July 31, 1915, 1486–87.

Bainbridge, John and Russell Maloney, "Where Are They Now?", *New Yorker*, March 9, 1940, 23–29.

Balch, Emily Greene, "The Stockholm Conference," *New Republic*, September 9, 1916, 141–47.

Breuer, Elizabeth, "Henry Ford and The Believer," *Ladies Home Journal*, September 1923, 8, 122–27.

Cary, Lucian, "Henry Ford," *Collier's*, November 2, 1918, 5–6, 26–29.

Dailey, Bernard, "Henry Ford—And the Others," *Forum*, March 1916, 313–17.

Egan, Maurice Francis, "Mr. Ford's Peace Party at Copenhagen," *Collier's*, March 15, 1919, 9, 22–27.

Henry, Alice, "War and Its Fruits," *Life and Labor*, December 1914, 357–58.

Jordan, David Starr, "The Impossible War," *Independent*, February 27, 1913, 167–68.

Kellogg, Paul, "The Welcoming of Jane Addams," *Survey*, July 17, 1915, 7.

Lattimore, Florence L., "Aboard the Oscar II," *Survey*, January 15, 1916, 457–60.

——, "Jitney Diplomacy," *Survey*, February 12, 1916, 579–88.

Lindsey, Ben B., "The Beast and the Jungle," *Everybody's*, October 1909–May 1910, 433–52, 579–98, 770–84, 41–53, 231–44, 391–406, 528–40, 632–44.

Lochner, Louis P., "An Unofficial Peace Commission," *Public*, October 15, 1915, 107–9.

——, "Peace Challenging Preparedness," *Survey*, October 30, 1915, 103–4.

Lynch, Frederick, "The Leaders of the New Peace Movement in America," *Independent*, September 15, 1910, 629–38.

Malmberg, Aino, "The Protected Sex in Wartime," *Harper's Weekly*, May 8, 1915, 436–38.

Nasmyth, George, "Constructive Mediation," *Survey*, March 6, 1915, 616–20.
———, "Toward World Government," *Survey*, November 20, 1915, 183–87.
Nimmo, Harry M., "A Talk With Henry Ford," *Harper's Weekly*, May 29, 1916, 518–20.
Noble, Will F., "A Student's View of the Ford Expedition," *Mid-West Quarterly*, July 1916, 303–29.
Pound, Arthur, "The Ford Myth," *Atlantic*, January 1924, 41–49.
Reed, John, "Industry's Miracle Maker," *Metropolitan*, October 1916, 10–12, 64–68.
———, "Why They Hate Ford," *Masses*, October 1916, 11–12.
Robinson, Helen Ring, "Confessions of a Peace Pilgrim," *Independent*, February 14, 1916, 225–26.
Ruddiman, Margaret Ford, "Memories of My Brother, Henry Ford," *Michigan History*, September 1953, 225–75.
Schwimmer, Rosika, "The Humanitarianism of Henry Ford," *B'nai B'rith News*, October–November 1922, 9–10.
———, "The Women of the World Demand Peace," *Woman Voter*, October 1914, 9–10.
Steffens, Lincoln, "Ben B. Lindsey: The Just Judge," *McClure's*, October–December 1906, 563–82, 74–88, 162–76.
Sullivan, Mark, "The Last Word on Henry Ford," *Collier's*, January 1, 1916, 12–13.
Taylor, Graham, "The Chicago Peace Convention," *Advocate of Peace*, April 1915, 95–96.
Trattner, Walter I., "Julia Grace Wales and the Wisconsin Plan for Peace," *Wisconsin Magazine of History*, Spring 1961, 203–13.
Wilkins, Robert P., "North Dakota and the Ford Peace Ship," *North Dakota History*, Fall 1966, 379–98.
Wilson, Edmund, "Despot of Dearborn," *Scribner's*, July 1931, 24–35.
Wittke, Carl, "An Echo of the Ford Peace Ship," *Michigan History*, September 1948, 257–69.
Woodward, David R., "Great Britain and President Wilson's Efforts to End World War I," *Maryland Historian*, Spring 1970, 45–58.

Index